JOHN WILLIS'

SCREEN WORLD

1980

Volume 31

CROWN PUBLISHERS, INC.

ONE PARK AVENUE

NEW YORK, NEW YORK 10016

To

KATHARINE
HEPBURN

*—a radiant and vibrant personality—an actress
and star of undisputed professionalism whose
unique talent has been recognized with three
Academy Awards, as well as the love and devotion
of millions of fans.*

MERYL STREEP, DUSTIN HOFFMAN, JUSTIN HENRY
in "KRAMER VS. KRAMER"
1979 ACADEMY AWARD FOR BEST FILM

© Columbia Pictures Industrie

CONTENTS

EDITOR: JOHN WILLIS

Assistant Editor: Stanley Reeves

Staff: Joe Baltake, Marco Boyajian, Alberto Cabrera, Curt Campagna, Mark Cohen, Frances Crampon, Mark Gladstone, Maltier Hagan, Miles Kreuger, William Schelble

ACKNOWLEDGMENTS: This volume would not be possible without the cooperation of Randi Amurer, Fred Baker, Harvey Barron, Alan Benjamin, Orly Berger, Mike Berman, Roy Blanco, Bernie Block, Kerry Boyle, Steve Bratcher, Susan Brockman, Barry Cahn, Fabiano Canosa, Mike Caplan, Philip Castanza, Brandon Chase, Paul Chefrin, Diane Collins, Gary Crowdus, Lynne Dahlgren, Alberta D'Angelo, Florence Dinapoli, J. Drucker, Deanna Dvorak, Steve Fagan, Suzanne Fedak, Steve Feltes, Preston Fisher, Ray Fisher, Jane Freedman, Marvin Friedlander, Renee Furst, Peter Gastaldi, Bernie Glaser, Gordon Green, John Hanson, Bob Harris, Richard Hassanein, Bea Herman, Andy Holtzman, Marjorie Hymowitz, Barbara Javiz, Steve Johnston, Eddie Kafafian, Elenore Kane, Marcia Kesselman, Sam Kitt, Peter Krutzer, Janine Leonard, Wynn Loewenthal, Louis Marino, Leonard Marpurgo, Terri Martin, Renee Mason, Peter Meyer, Tim Meyers, Shellie Mulrad, Eileen Nad, Eric Naumann, Rashumi Paul, Frank Pergalia, Maria Peters, Vincent Petrillo, John Pierson, Ruth Pologee, Mike Rappaport, Jerry Rapport, Robert Richter, Reid Roosevelt, Dan Rosen, Tom Schwartz, Allan Shackleton, Ernie Shapiro, Eve Segal, Terri Smith, John Springer, Larry Steinfeld, Marilyn Stewart, Patricia Story, Jesse Sutherland, John Sutherland, Dan Talbot, Bill Thompson, Jerry Ticman, John Tilley, Frank Tobin, Jana Tran, Bruce Trinz, Don Velde, Joann Walker, Christopher Wood, Kathy Yarorsky, Scott Yaselow, Atew Zakim.

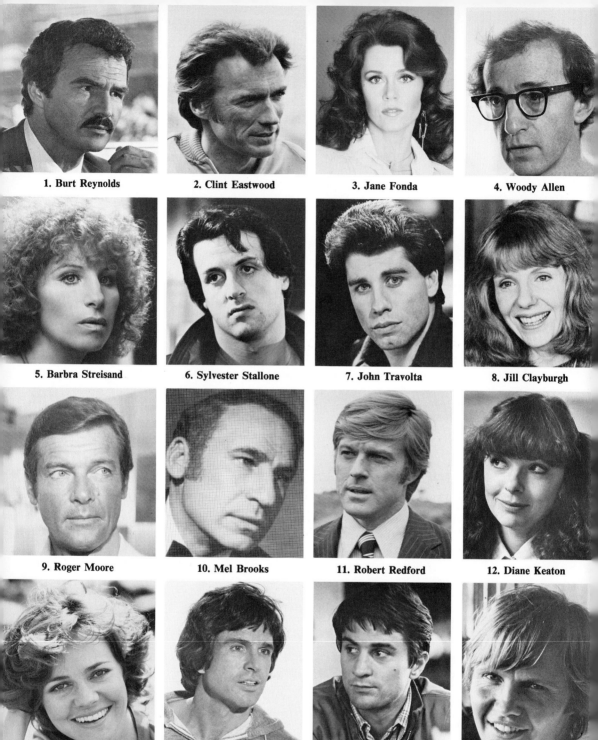

1. Burt Reynolds   2. Clint Eastwood   3. Jane Fonda   4. Woody Allen

5. Barbra Streisand   6. Sylvester Stallone   7. John Travolta   8. Jill Clayburgh

9. Roger Moore   10. Mel Brooks   11. Robert Redford   12. Diane Keaton

13. Sally Field   14. Warren Beatty   15. Robert DeNiro   16. Jon Voight

TOP 25 BOX OFFICE STARS OF 1979

17. Al Pacino **18. Richard Dreyfuss** **19. Peter Sellers** **20. Dustin Hoffman**

1979 RELEASES

January 1, 1979 through December 31, 1979

21. Jack Nicholson **22. George Hamilton** **23. Nick Nolte** **24. Paul Newman**

25. Peter Falk Sophia Loren Charles Bronson Laura Antonelli

OPENING NIGHT

(FACES) Producer, Al Ruban; Executive Producer, Sam Shaw; Direction and Screenplay, John Cassavetes; Associate Producer, Michael Lally; Assistant Director, Lisa Hallas; Art Director, Brian Ryman; Costumes, Alexandra Corwin-Hankin; Photography, Al Ruban; Music, Bo Harwood; Editor, Tom Cornwell; In color; 144 minutes; January release.

CAST

Myrtle Gordon	Gena Rowlands
Maurice Aarons	John Cassavetes
Manny Victor	Ben Gazzara
Sarah Goode	Joan Blondell
David Samuels	Paul Stewart
Dorothy Victor	Zohra Lampert
Nancy Stein	Laura Johnson
Gus Simmons	John Tuell
Jimmy	Ray Powers
Prop Man	John Finnegan
Kelly	Louise Fitch
Leo	Fred Draper
Vivian	Katherine Cassavetes
Melva Drake	Lady Rowlands
Doorman	Sharon Van Ivan
Shirley	Jimmy Christie
News Stand Operator	James Karen
Bell Boy	Jimmy Moyce
Bartender	Sherry Bain
Bar Maid	Sylvia Davis Shaw
Maître d'	Peter Lampert
Lena	Briana Carver
Charlie Spikes	Angelo Grisanti
Carla	Carol Warren
Eddie Stein	Meade Roberts
Sylvia Stein	Eleanor Zee

Top Left: Ben Gazzara, Gena Rowlands, John Cassavetes
Below: Zohra Lampert, Ben Gazzara, Gena Rowlands
Lower Left: Laura Johnson, Gena Rowlands

John Cassavetes, Ben Gazzara,
Gena Rowlands

Gena Rowlands

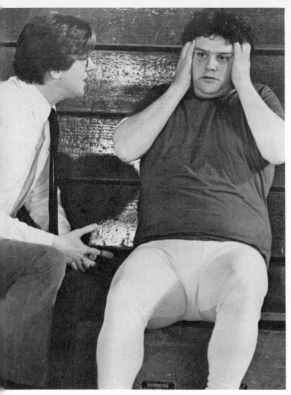

TAKE DOWN

(BUENA VISTA) Executive Producer, David B. Johnston; Producer-Director, Keith Merrill; Screenplay, Keith Merrill, Eric Hendershot; Story, Eric Hendershot; Associate Producer, Jack N. Reddish; Photography, Reed Smoot; Editor, Richard Fetterman; Music, Merrill B. Jenson; Art Director, Douglas G. Johnson; Assistant Director, Douglas Wise; Presented by American Film Consortium; In DeLuxe Color; Rated PG; 107 minutes; January release.

CAST

Ed Branish	Edward Herrmann
Jill Branish	Kathleen Lloyd
Nick Kilvitus	Lorenzo Lamas
Brooke Cooper	Maureen McCormick
Jimmy Kier	Nick Beauvy
Randy Jensen	Stephen Furst
Jasper MacGruder	Kevin Hooks
Bobby Cooper	Vincent Roberts
Ted Yacabobich	Darryl Peterson
Chauncey Washington	"T"Oney Smith
Tom Palumbo	Salvador Feliciano
Jack "No Toe" Goss	Boyd Silversmith
Robert Stankovich	Scott Burgi
Doc Talada	Lynn Baird
Warren Overpeck	Ron Bartholomew
Zeno Chicarelli	Kip Otanez
LeRoy Barron	Larry Miller
Thad Lardner	Gary Petersen
Mr. Kilvitus	Oscar Roland
Principal	Hyde Clayton
Referee	Prentiss Rowe
Mrs. Kilvitus	Elizabeth Grand
Suzette Smith	Christy Neal
Rockville Coach	Bob Kawa
Orem Coach	Fred Carl Rowland

Top: Edward Herrmann, Stephen Furst
Right: Edward Herrmann
© **American Film Consortium**

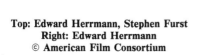

Maureen McCormick, Lorenzo Lamas

9

WHEN YOU COMIN' BACK, RED RYDER?

(COLUMBIA) Producer, Marjoe Gortner; Director, Milton Katselas; Screenplay, Mark Medoff from his play of the same title; Co-Producer, Paul Maslansky; Executive Producer, Melvin Simon; Music, Jack Nitzsche; Photography, Jules Brenner; Editor, Richard Chew; Designer, Ted Haworth; Assistant Directors, David Whorf, Victor Hsu; Costumes, Joe J. Thompkins; In Panavision and Color; Rated R; 118 minutes; February release.

CAST

Cheryl	Candy Clark
Teddy	Marjoe Gortner
Angel Childress	Stephanie Faracy
Grandma Childress	Dixie Harris
Rhea Childress	Anne Ramsey
Clarisse Ethridge	Lee Grant
Richard Ethridge	Hal Linden
Stephen Ryder	Peter Firth
Lyle Striker	Pat Hingle
Tommy Clark	Bill McKinney
Younger Mexican Man	Alex Colon
Older Mexican Man	Joe Hernandez
Radio Preacher	Leon Russell
Ceil Ryder	Audra Lindley
Bar Floozy	Sherry Unger
Bowling Alley Waitress	Elaine Story
Junior Ferguson	Riley Hill
Mexican Waitress	Carmen Ledoux
Walter	Tiny Wells
Sheriff Garcia	Ron Sobel
Customs Man	Robert Easton
Customs Doctor	Barry Cahill
Faith Healer	Mark Medoff
Mexican Father	Albert Pena

and Jamie Hilliard & the Countrymen, Hovie Lister & the Statesmen

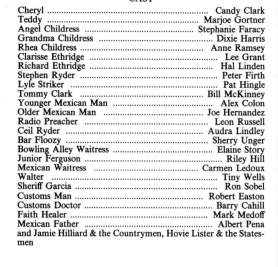

Top: Marjoe Gortner, Hal Linden, Lee Grant
Left: Candy Clark, Gortner Below: Peter Firth,
Stephanie Faracy (also Right with Gortner)
© Columbia Pictures Industries

Audra Lindley, Bill McKinney
Above: Pat Hingle

10

QUINTET

(20th CENTURY-FOX) Producer-Director, Robert Altman; Screenplay, Frank Barhydt, Robert Altman, Patricia Resnick; Story, Robert Altman, Lionel Chetwynd, Patricia Resnick; Photography, Jean Boffety; Executive Producer, Tommy Thompson; Associate Producer, Allan Nicholls; Music, Tom Pierson; Designer, Leon Ericksen; Art Director, Wolf Kroeger; Editor, Dennis M. Hill; Assistant Directors, Tommy Thompson, Charles Braive; Costumes, Scott Bushnell; In DeLuxe Color; Rated R; 100 minutes; February release.

CAST

Essex	Paul Newman
St. Christopher	Vittorio Gassman
Grigor	Fernando Rey
Ambrosia	Bibi Andersson
Vivia	Brigitte Fossey
Deuca	Nina Van Pallandt
Goldstar	David Langton
Francha	Tom Hill
Redstone's Mate	Monique Mercure
Redstone	Craig Richard Nelson
Jaspera	Maruska Stankova
Aeon	Anne Gerety
Obelus	Michael Maillot
Wood Supplier	Max Fleck
Charity House Woman	Francoise Berd

Right and Top: Paul Newman, Brigitte Fossey

Paul Newman, Fernando Rey
Above: Nina Van Pallandt, Bibi Andersson

Fernando Rey, Vittorio Gassman
Above: Bibi Andersson

HARDCORE

(COLUMBIA) Executive Producer, John Milius; Producer, Buzz Feitshans; Direction and Screenplay, Paul Schrader; Music, Jack Nitzsche; Editor, Tom Rolf; Designer, Paul Sylbert; Photography, Michael Chapman; Art Director, Ed O'Donovan; Assistant Directors, Richard Hashimoto, Kim C. Friese; An A-Team production in Metrocolor; Rated R; 105 minutes; February release.

CAST

Jake VanDorn	George C. Scott
Andy Mast	Peter Boyle
Niki	Season Hubley
Wes DeJong	Dick Sargent
Ramada	Leonard Gaines
Kurt	David Nichols
Tod	Gary Rand Graham
Detective Burrows	Larry Block
Ratan	Marc Alaimo
Felice	Leslie Ackerman
Beatrice	Charlotte McGinnis
Kristen VanDorn	Ilah Davis
Joe VanDorn	Paul Marin
Jism Jim	Will Walker
Big Dick Blaque	Hal Williams
Studs	Michael Allan Helie, Tim Dial
Jim Rucker	Roy London
Mary	Bibi Besch
Male Teller	Tracey Walter
Film Director	Bobby Kosser
Cameraman	Stephen P. Dunn
Mrs. Steensma	Jean Allison
Manager	Reb Brown
John VanDorn	James Helder
Willem	Dave Thompson
Grandfather VanDorn	John Otte

and Janet Simpson, Karen Kruer, Henry Vandenbroek, Linda Smith, Mary McFerren, Judith Ransdell, Linda Morell, Gigi Vorgan, Michael Hatch, David Hockenberry, Joseph Prus, Jean Reed Bahle, Reinder Vantil, Dee Ann Johnston, Janice Carroll, Mark Natuzzi, Al Cingolani, Cherilyn Parsons, Tracey Ratley, Antonio Esparza, Linda Cremeans, Ed Begley, Jr., Stewart Steinberg

Left: Season Hubley Above: George C. Scott, Peter Boyle Top: George C. Scott, Dick Sargent
© Columbia Pictures Industries

George C. Scott

Ilah Davis, George C. Scott

THE NORTH AVENUE IRREGULARS

(BUENA VISTA) Producer, Ron Miller; Co-Producer, Tom Leetch; Director, Bruce Bilson; Screenplay, Don Tait; Based on book by Reverend Albert Fay Hill; Associate Producer, Kevin Corcoran; Photography, Leonard J. South; Music, Robert F. Brunner; Songs, Al Kasha, Joel Hirschhorn; Editor, Gordon D. Brenner; Art Directors, John B. Mansbridge, Jack T. Collis; Assistant Directors, Christopher Seiter, Randy Carter; Costumes, Chuck Keehne, Emily Sundby; A Walt Disney production in Technicolor; Rated G; 99 minutes; February release.

CAST

Michael Hill	Edward Herrmann
Vickie	Barbara Harris
Anne	Susan Clark
Jane	Karen Valentine
Marv	Michael Constantine
Claire	Cloris Leachman
Rose	Patsy Kelly
Delaney	Douglas V. Fowley
Cleo	Virginia Capers
Tom	Steve Franken
Mrs. Carlisle	Dena Dietrich
Howard	Dick Fuchs
Dr. Fulton	Herb Voland
Harry, the Hat	Alan Hale
Carmel	Melora Hardin
Dean	Bobby Rolofson
Max	Frank Campanella
Rev. Wainwright	Ivor Francis
Mrs. Gossin	Louisa Moritz
Mother Thurber	Marjorie Bennett
Dr. Rheems	Ruth Buzzi

and Ceil Cabot, Cliff Osmond, Carl Ballantine, Damon Bradley Raskin, Linda Lee Lyons, John Kerry, Dave Morick, Darrow Igus, Dennis Robertson, Ed McCready, Dave Ketchum, John Wheeler, David Rode, Mickey Morton, Pitt Herbert, Chuck Henry, Rickie Layne, Jack Perkins, Tom Pedi, Bill McLean, Roger Creed, Walt LaRue, Jack Griffin, Len Ross, Douglas Hume, Gary Morgan, Jack Cameron White, Michael Lloyd, Kim Bullard

Top: Susan Clark, Virginia Capers, Patsy Kelly, Cloris Leachman, Karen Valentine, Barbara Harris
Right Center: Barbara Harris, Cloris Leachman
© Walt Disney Productions

Alan Hale, Edward Herrmann

Marta DuBois, Richard Yniguez

BOULEVARD NIGHTS

(WARNER BROS.) Executive Producer, Tony Bill; Producer, Bill Benenson; Director, Michael Pressman; Screenplay, Desmond Nakano; Photography, John Bailey; Editor, Richard Halsey; Music, Lalo Schifrin; Design, Jackson DeGovia; Assistant Director, Ramiro Jaloma; In color; Rated R; 102 minutes; March release.

CAST

Raymond Avila .... Richard Yniguez
Chuco Avila .... Danny De La Paz
Shady Landeros .... Marta Du Bois
Gil Moreno .... James Victor
Mrs. Avila .... Betty Carvalho
Mrs. Landeros .... Carmen Zapato
Mr. Landeros .... Victor Millan
Big Happy .... Gary Cervantes
Toby .... Roberto Covarrubias
Ernie .... Garret Pearson
Wolf .... Jerado Carmona
Casper .... Jesse Aragon

Top: Marta Dubois, Richard Yniguez
Below: Danny De La Paz, Richard Yniguez
© Warner Brothers

BUCK ROGERS IN THE 25th CENTURY

(UNIVERSAL) Executive Producer, Glen A. Larson; Producer, Richard Caffey; Director, Daniel Haller; Supervising Producer, Leslie Stevens; Screenplay, Glen A. Larson, Leslie Stevens; Photography, Frank Beascoechea; Art Director, Paul Peters; Editor, John J. Dumas; Music, Stu Phillips; Associate Producers, Andrew Mirisch, David Phinney; Assistant Directors, Phil Bowles, Jerry Sobul, Robert Villar, Judith Vogelsang; Costumes, Jean-Pierre Dorleac; Choreographer, Miriam Nelson; In Technicolor; Rated PG; 89 minutes; March release.

CAST

Buck Rogers	Gil Gerard
Princess Ardala	Pamela Hensley
Wilma Deering	Erin Gray
Kane	Henry Silva
Dr. Huer	Tim O'Connor
Draco	Joseph Wiseman
Tigerman	Duke Butler
Twiki	Felix Silla
Voice of Twiki	Mel Blanc
Young Woman	Caroline Smith
Supervisor	John Dewey-Carter
Pilot	Kevin Coates
Comtel Officer	David Cadiente
Technician	Gil Serna
Guards	Larry Duran, Kenny Endoso
Officer	Eric Lawrence
Tigerman #2	H. B. Haggerty
Wrather	Colleen Kelly
Pilots	Steve Jones, David Buchanan
Wingman	Burt Marshall

**Right: Erin Gray, Gil Gerard
Top: Gil Gerard, Pamela Hensley
© Universal City Studios**

Joseph Wiseman

Gil Gerard, Felix Silla

NORMA RAE

(20th CENTURY-FOX) Producers, Tamara Asseyev, Alex Rose; Director, Martin Ritt; Screenplay, Irving Ravetch, Harriet Frank, Jr.; Photography, John A. Alonzo; Designer, Walter Scott Herndon; Music, David Shire; Editor, Sidney Levin; Assistant Directors, James Nicholson, Glenn "Skip" Surguine; Art Director, Tracy Bousman; "It Goes Like It Goes" sung by Jennifer Warnes; In Panavision and DeLuxe Color; Rated PG; 110 minutes; March release.

CAST

Norma Rae	Sally Field
Sonny	Beau Bridges
Reuben	Ron Leibman
Vernon	Pat Hingle
Leona	Barbara Baxley
Bonnie Mae	Gail Strickland
Wayne Billings	Morgan Paull
Sam Bolen	Robert Broyles
Ellis Harper	John Calvin
Dr. Watson	Booth Colman
Lujan	Lee DeBroux
George Benson	James Luisi
Reverend Hubbard	Vernon Weddle
Al London	Gilbert Green
Lucius White	Bob Minor
Mrs. Johnson	Mary Munday
J. J. Davis	Jack Stryker
Lamar Miller	Gregory Walcott
Leroy Mason	Noble Willingham
Gardner	Lonnie Chapman
Sam Dakin	Bert Freed
Jed Buffum	Bob E. Hannah
Louise Pickens	Edith Ivey
Craig	Scott Lawton
James Brown	Frank McRae

and Gerald Okuneff (Pinkerton Man), Gina Kaye Pounders (Millie), Henry Slate (Policeman), Melissa Ann Wait (Alice), Joe A. Dorsey (Woodrow), Sherry Velvet Foster (Velma), Grace Zabriskie (Linette), Stuart Culpepper (Ray), Weona T. Brown (Vendor), Carolyn Danforth (Mavis), James W. Harris (Worker), Charlie Briggs (Warren), Billie Joyce Buck (Agnes), Fred Covington (Alston), J. Don Ferguson (Peter), Sandra Dorsey (Matron), Harold E. Finch (Agent), Clayton Landey (Teddy), William Pannell (Billy), George Robertson (Farmer), Thomas D. Samford III (J.P.), J. Roy Tatum (Woodrow Bowzer)

1979 Academy Awards for Best Actress (Sally Field) and Best Original Song ("It Goes Like It Goes")

**Left: Ron Leibman, Sally Field
Above: Pat Hingle, Sally Field Top: Beau Bridges, Gail Strickland, Sally Field
© 20th Century-Fox Film Corporation**

Sally Field, Beau Bridges

Sally Field, Ron Leibman

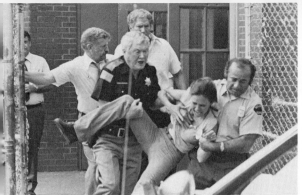

Ron Leibman, Sally Field Top Left: Henry Slate, Sally Field (also below)
Top Right: Sally Field

FAST BREAK

(COLUMBIA) Executive Producer, Jerry Frankel; Producer, Stephen Friedman; Director, Jack Smight; Screenplay, Sandor Stern; Story, Marc Kaplan; Music, David Shire, James di Pasquale; Associate Producer, Jack Grossberg; Photography, Charles Correll; Editor, Frank J. Urioste; Assistant Directors, Carl Olsen, Rafael Elortegui, William Eustace; Art Director, Norman Baron; In Metrocolor; Rated PG; 197 minutes; March release.

CAST

David Greene	Gabriel Kaplan
D.C.	Harold Sylvester
Preacher	Michael Warren
Hustler	Bernard King
Bull	Reb Brown
Swish	Mavis Washington
Bo Winnegar	Bert Remsen
Jan	Randee Heller
Alton Gutkas	John Chappell
Enid Cadwallader-Gutkas	Rhonda Bates
Ms. Tidwell	K Callan
Henry	Marty Zagon
Howard	Richard Brestoff
Lottie	Connie Sawyer
Snooty Girl	Doria Cook
Officer Wedgewood	James Jeter
Man on Bus	Steve Conte
Beaton	Larry Farmer
Hollis	Craig Impleman
Larry	Charles Penland
Krebbs	Jim Spillane
Thompson	Le Tari
Norman	Oscar Williams
Frenchie	Marty Gorowitz
Bum	Bob Levine
Hal	John McCurry
Dibber	Jack Smight
Polly	Jackie Sule
Street Kid	Laurence Fishburne III

Right: John Chappell, Rhoda Bates, Gabriel Kaplan
Above: Randee Heller, Connie Sawyer, Gabriel Kaplan
Top: Gabriel Kaplan, K. Callan
© Columbia Pictures Industries

Front: Reb Brown, Mavis Washington, Bernard King, Gabriel Kaplan, Michael Warren, Harold Sylvester

VOICES

(UNITED ARTISTS) Producer, Joe Wizan; Director, Robert Markowitz; Screenplay, John Herzfeld; Photography, Alan Metzger; Songs and Score, Jimmy Webb; Art Director, Richard Bianchi; Editor, Danford B. Greene; Associate Producer, Betty Gumm; Assistant Directors, Michael Rauch, Joan L. Feinstein; Costumes, John Boxer; Choreographer, Stuart Hodes; Songs sung by Willie Nelson, Tom Petty and the Heartbreakers, Atlanta Rhythm Section, Burton Cummings; In Metrocolor and Panavision; Presented by Metro-Goldwyn-Mayer; Rated PG; 106 minutes; March release.

CAST

Drew Rothman	Michael Ontkean
Rosemarie Lemon	Amy Irving
Frank Rothman	Alex Rocco
Raymond Rothman	Barry Miller
Nathan Rothman	Herbert Berghof
Mrs. Lemon	Viveca Lindfors
Montrose Meier	Allan Rich
Pinky	Joseph Cali
String	Rik Colitti
Snowflake	Jean Ehrlich
Patterson	Thurman Scott
Debbie	Melonie Mazman
Helen	Arva Holt
Scott Gunther	Richard Kendall
Cheryl	Mary Serrano
Paul Janssen	Thom Christopher

and Hubert Kelly (Drummer), Rory Anthony (Bass), Frank Lombardi (Organist), Dale Stroever (Guitarist), Peter Lawrence Cherone (Saxophonist), Jerry MacLauchlin (Choreographer), Tom Quinn (Fat), Tony Munafo (Ned), Pedro O'Campo (Bus Driver), Nelson Hailparn (Johnny), Franc Luz (Bobby), Heidi Bohay (Girl Friend), Jean Busada, Peggy Waller (Dancers), Bill Baldwin (Announcer), Ray Serra (Track Regular), Jose Rabelo (Cuban Customer), Thelma Lee (Secretary), Ida Beecher (Cashier), Rob DeRosa (Demetrius), Ray Suideau (Bartender)

Right: Alex Rocco, Herbert Berghof, Michael Ontkean
Above: Barry Miller, Michael Ontkean, Amy Irving
Top: Amy Irving, Viveca Lindfors
© Metro-Goldwyn-Mayer Inc.

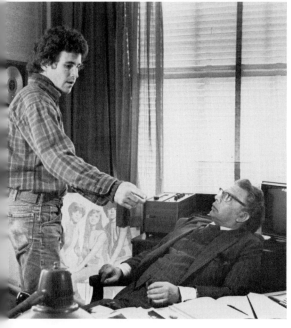

Michael Ontkean, Allan Rich

Amy Irving, Michael Ontkean

THE CHINA SYNDROME

(COLUMBIA) Producer, Michael Douglas; Director, James Bridges; Screenplay, Mike Gray, T. S. Cook, James Bridges; Executive Producer, Bruce Gilbert; Associate Producer, James Nelson; Photography, James Crabe; Designer, George Jenkins; Editor, David Rawlins; "Somewhere in Between" by Stephen Bishop; Assistant Directors, Kim Kurumada, Barrie Osborne; Costumes, Donfeld; Assistant Producers, Jack Smith, Jr., Penny McCarthy; In Metrocolor; Rated PG; 122 minutes; March release.

CAST

Kimberly Wells	Jane Fonda
Jack Godell	Jack Lemmon
Richard Adams	Michael Douglas
Herman DeYoung	Scott Brady
Bill Gibson	James Hampton
Don Jacovich	Peter Donat
Ted Spindler	Wilford Brimley
Evan McCormack	Richard Herd
Hector Salas	Daniel Valdez
Pete Martin	Stan Bohrman
Mac Churchill	James Karen
Greg Minor	Michael Alaimo
Dr. Lowell	Donald Hotton
Marge	Khalilah Ali
D. B. Royce	Paul Larson
Barney	Ron Lombard
Tommy	Tom Eure
Borden	Nick Pellegrino
Donny	Daniel Lewk
Holt	Allan Chinn
Control Guard	Martin Fiscoe
TV Director	Alan Kaul
Mort	E. Hampton Beagle
David	David Pfeiffer
Hatcher	Lewis Arquette
Robertson	Dennis McMullen
Rita Jacovich	Rita Taggart
Harmon	James Hall

and Michael Mann, David Eisenbise, Frank Cavestani, Reuben Collins, Carol Helvey, Trudy Lane, Jack Smith, Jr., David Arnsen, Betty Harford, Donald Bishop, Al Baietti, Diandra Morrell, Darrell Larson, Roger Pancake, Joe Lowry, Harry M. Williams, Dennis Barker, Joseph Garcia, James Kline, Alan Beckwith, Clay Hodges, Val Clenard

Michael Douglas, Jane Fonda

Top: Jack Lemmon, and Left with Michael Douglas, Jane Fonda Below: Peter Donat, Daniel Valdez, Michael Douglas, Jane Fonda
© Columbia Pictures Industries

Daniel Valdez, James Hampton, Jane Fonda, Michael Douglas
Above: (L) Wilford Brimley (R) Jane Fonda, Michael Douglas
Top: Jack Lemmon, Michael Douglas, Jane Fonda

OLD BOYFRIENDS

(AVCO EMBASSY) Producers, Edward R. Pressman, Michele Rappaport; Executive Producer, Paul Schrader; Director, Joan Tewkesbury; Screenplay, Paul Schrader, Leonard Schrader; Photography, William Fraker; Editor, Bill Reynolds; Art Director, Peter Jamison; Assistant Director, Tony Bishop; Costumes, Tony Faso, Suzanne Grace; Music, David Shire; In color; Rated R; 103 minutes; March release.

CAST

Diane Cruise	Talia Shire
Jeff Turrin	Richard Jordan
Wayne Van Til	Keith Carradine
Eric Katz	John Belushi
Dr. Hoffman	John Houseman
Art Kopple	Buck Henry
Kylan Turrin	Nina Jordan
Sam the Fisherman	Gerritt Graham
Sandy	P. J. Soles
Mrs. Van Til	Bethel Leslie
Pamela Shaw	John Hotchkis
David Brinks	William Bassett

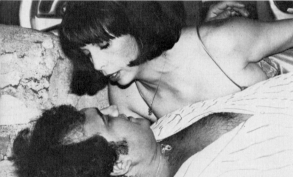

Left: Talia Shire, John Belushi (also below)
Top: John Houseman, Talia Shire
© AVCO Embassy Pictures

Buck Henry

Talia Shire, Keith Carradine
Above: Talia Shire, Richard Jordan

THE BELL JAR

(AVCO EMBASSY) Producers, Jerrold Brandt, Jr., Michael Todd, Jr.; Executive Producer, Robert A. Goldston; Director, Larry Peerce; Screenplay, Marjorie Kellogg; Photography, Gerald Hirschfeld; Assistant Directors, Steve Barnett, Frank Simpson, Dennis Murphy; Designer, John Robert Lloyd; Costumes, Donald Brooks; Editor, Marvin Wallowitz; Based on novel by Sylvia Plath; In color; Rated R; 112 minutes; March release.

CAST

Esther	Marilyn Hassett
Mrs. Greenwood	Julie Harris
Dr. Nolan	Anne Jackson
Jay Cee	Barbara Barrie
Lenny	Robert Klein
Joan	Donna Mitchell
Doreen	Mary Louise Weller
Gilling	Scott McKay
Buddy	Jameson Parker
Marco	Thaao Penghlis
Rea Ramsey	Meg Mundy
Vikki St. John	Elizabeth Hubbard
Hilda	Carol Monferdini
Betsy	Debbie McLeod
Toni LaBouchere	Karen Howard
Jane McLode	Margaret Hall

and Alana Davis, Leslie Goldstein, Shelley Rogers, Beth McDonald, Mary Ann Johnson, Brenda Currin, David Faulkner, Nicholas Guest, Ruth Antonofsky, Roxanne Hart, Christine Estabrook, Ruth Van Poons, Gil Rogers, Carolyn Hurlburt, Allan Eisennman, Dan Hamilton

Top: Barbara Barrie, Marilyn Hassett
Below: Robert Klein, Mary Louse Weller
© AVCO Embassy

Julie Harris Top: Marilyn Hassett

WALK PROUD

(UNIVERSAL) Producer, Lawrence Turman; Director, Robert Collins; Screenplay, Evan Hunter; Photography, Bobby Byrne; Art Director, William L. Campbell; Editor, Douglas Stewart; Music, Don Peake, Robby Benson; Assistant Directors, Ronald J. Martinez, Armando Huerta; Songs sung by Robby Benson, Elton John; In Panavision and Technicolor; Rated PG; 102 minutes; March release.

CAST

Emilio	Robby Benson
Sarah Lassiter	Sarah Holcomb
Mike Serrano	Henry Darrow
Cesar	Pepe Serna
Dagger	Trinidad Silva
Sergeant Gannett	Ji-Tu Cumbuka
Henry Lassiter	Lawrence Pressman
Cowboy	Domingo Ambriz
Jerry Kelsey	Brad Sullivan
Mrs. Mendez	Irene De Bari
Hugo	Eloy Phil Casados
El Tigre	Daniel Faraldo
Paco	Tony Alvarenga
Hippo	Stephen Morrell
Police Guard	Benjie Bancroft
Johnny	Lee Fraser
Carlos	Gary Cervantes
Guard	Tim Culbertson
Manuel	Panchito Gomez
Store Owner	Joe D. Jacobs
Ice Cream Vendor	Bill Lopresto
Vincente	Claudio Martinez
Policemen	Rod Masterson, Dennis O'Flaherty
Church Singer	Patricia A. Morales
Katie	Rose Portillo
El Espanol	Luis Reyes
Priest	Eduardo Ricard
Angel	Angel Salazar
Abigail Lassiter	Judith Searle
Interrogation Officer	Tony Steinhart
Prayer Maker	Felipe Turich
Stuntmen	Felipe Turich, Eddie Hice, Rafael E. Lopez, Thomas Rosales, Jr., Rick Sawaya

Right: Robby Benson, Gary Cervantes, Domingo Ambriz, Pepe Serna, Trinidad Silva Above: Ji-Tu Cumbuka, Pepe Serna Top: Pepe Serna (R)
© Universal City Studios

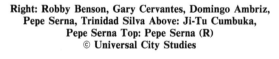

Sarah Holcomb, Robby Benson

Robby Benson, Pepe Serna

HAIR

(UNITED ARTISTS) Producers, Lester Persky, Michael Butler; Director, Milos Forman; Screenplay, Michael Weller; Choreography, Twyla Tharp; Music, Galt MacDermot; Lyrics, Gerome Ragni, James Rado; Associate Producer, Robert Greenhut; Assistant Director, Michael Hausman; Photography, Miroslav Ondricek; Costumes, Ann Roth; Designer, Stuart Wurtzel; Editor, Lynzee Klingman; A CIP Feature in Dolby Stereo and color; Rated PG; 118 minutes; March release.

CAST

Claude	John Savage
Berger	Treat Williams
Sheila	Beverly D'Angelo
Jeannie	Annie Golden
Hud	Dorsey Wright
Woof	Don Dacus
Hud's Fiancee	Cheryl Barnes
Fenton	Richard Bright
The General	Nicholas Ray
Party Guest	Charlotte Rae
Steve	Miles Chapin
Sheila's Mother	Fern Tailer
Sheila's Father	Charles Deney
Sheila's Uncle	Herman Meckler
Sheila's Aunt	Agness Breen
Berger's Mother	Antonia Rey
Berger's Father	George Manos
Vietnamese Girl	Linda Surh
Debutantes	Jane Booke, Suki Love
Claude's Father	Joe Acord
Sheldon	Michael Jeter
Prison Psychiatrist	Janet York
Lafayette, Jr.	Rahsaan Curry
The Judge	Harry Gittleson
The M.P.	Donald Alsdurf

Barracks Officers .... Steve Massicotte, Mario Nelson and Ren Woods, Toney Watkins, Carl Hall, Howard Porter, Nell Carter, Kurt Yahjian, Leata Galloway, Cyrena Lomba, Ron Young, Laurie Beechman, Debi Dye, Ellen Foley, John Maestro, Fred Ferrara, Jim Rosica, Charlaine Woodard, Trudy Perkins, Chuck Patterson, H. Douglas Berring, Russell Costen, Kenny Brawner, Lee Wells, Melba Moore, Ronnie Dyson, Rose Marie Wright, Tom Rawe, Jennifer Way, Shelley Washington, Christine Uchida, Raymond Kurshals, Richard Colton, Anthony Ferro, Sara Rudner, Pat Benoye, Cameron Burke, Richard Caceres, Tony Constantine, Ron Dunham, Leonard Feiner, Ken Gildin, Kate Glasner, Christian Holder, Chris Komar, Nancy Lefkowith, Joseph Lennon, Robert Levithan, France Mayotte, Hector Mercado, Sharon Miripolsky, Marta Renzi, Donna Ritchie, Ellen Saltonstall, Radha Sukhu, Byron Utley, Earlise Vails, Ronald Weeks, Kimmary Williams, Deborah Zalkind.

Right: Treat Williams, Charlottte Rae
Above: Twyla Tharp Top: Trudy Perkins,
Nell Carter, Charlaine Woodard
© United Artists Corp.

Don Dacus, Annie Golden, Dorsey Wright,
Treat Williams

Beverly D'Angelo, John Savage

AN ALMOST PERFECT AFFAIR

(PARAMOUNT) Producer, Terry Carr; Director, Michael Ritchie; Screenplay, Walter Bernstein, Don Petersen; Story, Michael Ritchie, Don Petersen; Photography, Henri Decae; Art Director, Willy Holt; Editor, Richard A. Harris; Music, Georges Delerue; Assistant Directors, Marc Monnet, Marius Manzone; Costumes, Tanine Autre; Miss Vitti dressed by Valentino; In color; Rated PG; 93 minutes; April release.

CAST

Hal	Keith Carradine
Maria	Monica Vitti
Freddie	Raf Vallone
Carlo	Christian De Sica
Jackson	Dick Anthony Williams
Lieutenant Montand	Henri Garcin
Amy Zon	Anna Maria Horsford

and Katya Berger, Andy Ho, Sady Rebbot, Gerard Buhr, Luong Ham Chau, Jean-Pierre Zola, Francois Viaur

Left: Keith Carradine, Monica Vitti
Below: Dick Anthony Williams, Keith Carradine
© Paramount Pictures

Keith Carradine

Raf Vallone, Monica Vitti
Above: Christian DeSica, Monica Vitti

LOVE AT FIRST BITE

(AMERICAN INTERNATIONAL) Producer, Joel Freeman; Director, Stan Dragoti; Story, Robert Kaufman, Mark Gindes; Screenplay, Robert Kaufman; Executive Producers, Robert Kaufman, George Hamilton; Music, Charles Bernstein; Photography, Edward Rosson; Designer, Serge Krizman; Editors, Mort Fallick, Allan Jacobs; Associate Producer, Harold L. Vanarnum; Choreography, Alex Romero; In CFI Color; A Melvin Simon presentation; Rated PG; 96 minutes; April release.

CAST

Count Dracula	George Hamilton
Cindy Sondheim	Susan Saint James
Dr. Jeff Rosenberg	Richard Benjamin
Lieutenant Ferguson	Dick Shawn
Renfield	Arte Johnson
Reverend Mike	Sherman Jemsley
Judge	Isabel Sanford
Flashlight Vendor	Barry Gordan
Gay in Elevator	Ronnie Schell
TV Repairman	Bob Basso
Priest	Bryan O'Byrne
Mobster	Michael Pataki
Lady in Elevator	Beverly Sanders
Desk Clerk	Basil Hoffman
Cab Driver	Stanley Brock
Billy	Danny Dayton
W. V. Man	Robert Ellenstein
Customs Inspector	David Ketchum

Top: Arte Johnson, George Hamilton Below: Hamilton, Sherman Hemsley Right: Isabel Sanford Top: Richard Benjamin, Dick Shawn
© American International Pictures

Susan Saint James, George Hamilton

Woody Allen, Diane Keaton

MANHATTAN

(UNITED ARTISTS) Producer, Charles H. Joffe; Executive Producer, Robert Greenhut; Director, Woody Allen; Screenplay, Woody Allen, Marshall Brickman; Photography, Gordon Willis; Designer, Mel Bourne; Costumes, Albert Wolsky; Editor, Susan E. Morse; Music, George Gershwin; Assistant Directors, Fredric B. Blankfein, Joan Spiegel Feinstein; In Panavision and Technicolor; Rated R; 96 minutes; April release.

CAST

Isaac Davis	Woody Allen
Mary Wilke	Diane Keaton
Yale	Michael Murphy
Tracy	Mariel Hemingway
Jill	Meryl Streep
Emily	Anne Byrne
Connie	Karen Ludwig
Dennis	Michael O'Donoghue
Party Guests	Victor Truro, Tisa Farrow, Helen Hanft
Guest of Honor	Bella Abzug
Television Director	Gary Weis
Television Producer	Kenny Vance
TV Actors	Charles Levin, Karen Allen, David Rasche
Isaac's son, Willie	Damion Sheller
Jeremiah	Wallace Shawn
Shakespearean Actors	Mark Linn Baker, Frances Conroy
Porsche Owner #1	Bill Anthony
Porsche Owner #2	John Doumanian
Pizzeria Waiter	Ray Serra

Top: Diane Keaton, Michael Murphy Below: Woody Allen, Mariel Hemingway Top Left: Meryl Streep, Woody Allen
© United Artists Corp.

**Michael Murphy, Anne Byrne Above: Diane Keaton,
Woody Allen Top: Allen, Murphy**

**Diane Keaton, Woody Allen Above: Mariel
Hemingway, Allen (also top)**

A LITTLE ROMANCE

(ORION) Director, George Roy Hill; Executive Producer, Patrick Kelley; Producers, Yves Rousset-Rouard, Robert L. Crawford; Screenplay, Allan Burns; Based on novel by Patrick Cauvin; Music, Georges Delerue; Photography, Pierre William Glenn; Editor, William Reynolds; Design, Henry Bumstead; Art Director, Francois De Lamothe; Costumes, Rosine Delamare; Assistant Directors, Carlo Lastricati, John Pepper, Bruno Cortini; In Panavision and Technicolor; Presented by Pan Arts; Rated PG; 108 minutes; April release.

CAST

Julius	Laurence Olivier
Richard King	Arthur Hill
Kay King	Sally Kellerman
Lauren	Diane Lane
Daniel	Thelonious Bernard
Brod	Broderick Crawford
George de Marco	David Dukes
Bob Duryea	Andrew Duncan
Janet Duryea	Claudette Sutherland
Londet	Graham Fletcher-Cook
Natalie	Ashby Semple
Michel Michon	Claude Brosset
Inspector Leclerc	Jacques Maury
Ms. Siegel	Anna Massey
Martin	Peter Maloney
Mme. Cormier	Dominique Lavanant
Assistant Directors	Mike Marshall, John Pepper
French Ambassador	Michel Bardinet
French Representative	Alain David Gabison
Monique	Isabelle Duby

and Jeffrey Carey, Denise Glaser, Jeanne Herviale, Carlo Lastricati, Judy Mullen, Philippe Brigaud, Lucienne Legrand

1979 Academy Award for Best Original Score

Right: Thelonious Bernard, Diane Lane, and above with Laurence Olivier
© Orion Pictures Co.

Laurence Olivier

Diane Lane, Thelonious Bernard Above: Arthur Hill, David Dukes, Sally Kellerman

HURRICANE

(PARAMOUNT) Producer, Dino De Laurentiis; Director, Jan Troell; Screenplay, Lorenzo Semple, Jr.; Based on novel "Hurricane" by Charles Nordhoff and James Norman Hall; Executive Producer, Lorenzo Semple, Jr.; Photography, Sven Nykvist; Music, Nino Rota; Editor, Sam O'Steen; Designer, Danilo Donati; Assistant Directors, Jose Lopez Rodero, Fred Viannellis, Ginette Angosse Lopez, Giovanni Soldati; Choreographer, Coco; Art Director, Giorgio Postiglione; In Dolby Stereo, Todd-AO, and Technicolor; Rated PG; 119 minutes; April release.

CAST

Captain Bruckner	Jason Robards
Charlotte Bruckner	Mia Farrow
Dr. Bascomb	Max von Sydow
Father Malone	Trevor Howard
Matangi	Dayton Ka'Ne
Jack Sanford	Timothy Bottoms
Sergeant Strang	James Keach
Lieutenant Howard	Richard Sarcione
Moana	Ariirau Tekurarere
Corporal Morrah	Willie Myers
Commander Blair	Nick Rutgers
Mrs. Blair	Nancy Hall Rutgers
Samolo	Manu Tupou
Velaga	Simplet Tefane
Running Man	Piero Bushin
Tano	Noel Teparii
Flaeiva	John Taea
Elder	Taeve Tetuamia
Siva	Bernadette Sarcione
Fire Dancer	Roo

Right: Timothy Bottoms, Mia Farrow
Top: Mia Farrow, Dayton Ka'Ne
© Paramount Pictures

Jason Robards, Dayton Ka'Ne
Above: Trevor Howard (R)

Dayton Ka'ne, Mia Farrow

THE CHAMP

(UNITED ARTISTS) Producer, Dyson Lovell; Director, Franco Zeffirelli; Screenplay, Walter Newman; Based on story by Frances Marion; Photography, Fred J. Koenekamp; Designer, Herman A. Blumenthal; Editor, Michael J. Sheridan; Assistant Directors, David Silver, Jerry Sobul, Fred Wardell; Music, Dave Grusin; Costumes, Theoni V. Aldredge; In Metrocolor; Rated PG; 121 minutes; April release.

CAST

Billy	Jon Voight
Annie	Faye Dunaway
T.J.	Ricky Schroder
Jackie	Jack Warden
Mike	Arthur Hill
Riley	Strother Martin
Dolly Kenyon	Joan Blondell
Josie	Mary Jo Catlett
Georgie	Elisha Cook
Charlie Goodman	Stefan Gierasch
Whitey	Allan Miller
Hesh	Joe Tornatore
Donna Mae	Shirlee Kong
Jeffie	Jeff Blum
Hoffmaster	Dana Elcar
Bowers	Randall Cobb
Sonny	Christoff St. John
Cuban Girl	Gina Gallego
Mrs. Riley	Jody Wilson
Groom	Reginal M. Toussaint
TV Reporter	Bob Gordon
Dolly's Trainer	Gene Picchi
Horse Owner	Anne Logan
Race Track Announcer	Bill Baldwin

and Rita Turner, Dorothy Strelsin, Lionel Dozier, Charles W. Camac, David Peden, William Fuller, Vanna Salviati, Maurice Pete Mitchell, Ernesto Morelli, Robert Ray Sutton, Philip Tuersky, Micki Varro, Geoff Marlowe, George Stidham, Willie White, Curtis Jackson, Wally Rose, Dick Young, Sonny Shields, Larry Duran, Lars Hensen, Jeff Temkin, Eddie "El Animal" Lopez, Ralph Gambina

Left: Ricky Schroder, Jon Voight, Jack Warden
Above: Faye Dunaway, Jon Voight, Ricky Schroder
Top: Joan Blondell, Faye Dunaway, Arthur Hill
© United Artists Corp.

Jon Voight, Randall Cobb

Jon Voight, Ricky Schroder

Right: Peter Bogdanovich, Ben Gazzara
© New World Pictures

SAINT JACK

(NEW WORLD) Executive Producers, Hugh M. Hefner, Edward L. Rissien; Producer, Roger Corman; Director, Peter Bogdanovich; Screenplay, Howard Sackler, Paul Theroux, Peter Bogdanovich; Based on novel by Paul Theroux; Photography, Robby Muller; Editor, William Carruth; Art Director, David Ng; A Playboy-Shoals Creek Picture in color; Rated R; 112 minutes; April release.

CAST

Jack Flowers	Ben Gazzara
William Leigh	Denholm Elliott
Frogget	James Villiers
Yardley	Joss Ackland
Smale	Rodney Bewes
Yates	Mark Kingston
Mrs. Yates	Lisa Lu
Monika	Monika Subramaniam
Judy	Judy Lim
Senator	George Lazenby
Eddie Schuman	Peter Bogdanovich
Gopi	Joseph Noel
Hing	Ong Kian Bee
Little Hing	Tan Yan Meng
Andrew	Andrew Chua
Australian Businessman	Ken Wolinski
Mike	Peter Tay
Bob	Osman Zailani
Shirley	Elizabeth Ang
Mr. Tan	S. M. Sim
Triad Gang	Peter Pang, Ronald Ng, Seow Teow Keng

Top: Ben Gazzara, Denholm Elliott
(also below and top right)

Ben Gazzara

Frances Sternhagen, Marthe Keller

FEDORA

(UNITED ARTISTS) Producer-Director, Billy Wilder; Screenplay, Billy Wilder, I.A.L. Diamond; Based on story from "Crowned Heads" by Thomas Tryon; Music, Miklos Rozsa; Photography, Gerry Fisher; Assistant Directors, Wieland Liebski, Don French; Designer, Alexandre Trauner; Art Director, Robert Andre; Costumes, Charlotte Flemming; Editor, Stefan Arnsten; In color; Rated PG; 116 minutes; April release.

CAST

Barry Detweiler	William Holden
Fedora	Marthe Keller
Dr. Vando	Jose Ferrer
Miss Balfour	Frances Sternhagen
Hotel Manager	Mario Adorf
Barry at 25	Stephen Collins
Sobryanski	Hans Jaray
Kritos	Gottfried John
Henry Fonda	Himself
Countess Sobryanski	Hildegard Knef
Michael York	Himself
Barkeeper	Panos Papadopulos
Maid	Elma Karlowa
Clerk	Christoph Kunzer

Top: William Holden, Frances Sternhagen, Hans Jaray,
Hildegard Knef, Jose Ferrer Below: Michael York,
Marthe Keller Left: Gottfried John, Holden, Ferrer
Top: Marthe Keller, William Holden
© United Artist Corp.

BATTLESTAR GALACTICA

(**UNIVERSAL**) Executive Producer, Glen A. Larson; Producer, John Dykstra; Director, Richard A. Colla; Screenplay, Glen A. Larson; Supervising Producer, Leslie Stevens; Photography, Ben Colman; Associate Producer, Winrich Kolbe; Music, Stu Phillips; Art Director, John E. Chilberg II; Editors, Robert L. Kimble, Leon Ortiz-Gil, Larry Strong; Assistant Directors, Phil Cook, Nick Marek; Costumes, Jean-Pierre Dorleac; Special Effects, Apogee Inc.; In Technicolor and Sensurround; Rated PG; 120 minutes; May release.

CAST

Captain Apollo	Richard Hatch
Lieutenant Starbuck	Dirk Benedict
Commander Adama	Lorne Greene
Uri	Ray Milland
Adar	Lew Ayres
Serina	Jane Seymour
Anton	Wilfrid Hyde-White
Count Baltar	John Colicos
Cassiopea	Laurette Spang
Dr. Paye	John Fink
Colonel Tighe	Terry Carter
Lieutenant Boomer	Herb Jefferson, Jr.
Athena	Maren Jensen
Lieutenant Jolly	Tony Swartz
Boxey	Noah Hathaway
Ensign Greenbean	Ed Begley, Jr.
Lieutenant Zac.	Rick Springfield
Young Woman	Randi Oakes
Statesman	Norman Stuart
Bridge Officer	David Greenan
Woman on duty	Sarah Rush
Operative	David Matthau
Warriors	Chip Johnson, Geoffrey Binney
Pilot	Paul Coufos
Deck Hand	Bruce Wright

**Right: Jane Seymour, Tony Swartz, Richard Hatch
Top: Dirk Benedict, Laurette Spang, Herb Jefferson,
Jr., Noah Hathaway, Jane Seymour
© Universal City Studios**

**Dirk Benedict, Maren Jensen
Above: Battlestar Galactica**

John Colicos

LAST EMBRACE

(UNITED ARTISTS) Producers, Michael Taylor, Dan Wigutow; Director, Jonathan Demme; Screenplay, David Shaber; Based on novel "13th Man" by Murray Teigh Bloom; Associate Producer, John Nicolella; Photography, Tak Fujimoto; Editor, Barry Malkin; Music, Miklos Rosza; Designer, Charles Rosen; Costumes, Jane Greenwood; Assistant Directors, Michael Rauch, Steven Felder; Art Director, James A. Taylor; In Technicolor; Rated R; 102 minutes; May release.

CAST

Harry Hannan	Roy Scheider
Ellie Fabian	Janet Margolin
Richard Peabody	John Glover
Sam Urdell	Sam Levene
Dave Quittle	Charles Napier
Eckart	Christopher Walken
Dr. Coopersmith	Jacqueline Brookes
Rabbi Drexel	David Margulies
Bernie Meckler	Andrew Duncan
Adrian	Marcia Rodd
Tour Guide	Gary Goetzman
Rabbi Jacobs	Lou Gilbert
Commuters	Mandy Patinkin, Max Wright
Dorothy Hannan	Sandy McLeod
Men in Cantina	Burt Santos, Joe Spinell, Jim McBride
Adrian's friend	Cynthia Scheider
Shopper	Sasha von Scherler
Ukelele Player	George Hillman
Newscaster	Gary Gunter

Left: Roy Scheider, Sam Levene
Top: Roy Scheider, John Glover, Janet Margolin
© United Artists Corp.

Janet Margolin, Roy Scheider

Janet Margolin, Roy Scheider

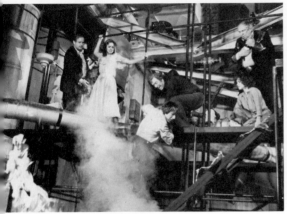

BEYOND THE POSEIDON ADVENTURE

(WARNER BROS.) Producer-Director, Irwin Allen; Screenplay, Nelson Gidding; Based on novel by Paul Gallico; Music, Jerry Fielding; Editor, Bill Brame; Designer, Preston Ames; Photography, Joseph Biroc; Associate Producer, Al Gail; Assistant Directors, Mike Salamunovich, Lindsley Parsons III; Costumes, Paul Zastupnevich; In Panavision and Technicolor; Rated PG; 122 minutes; May release.

CAST

Mike Turner	Michael Caine
Celeste Whitman	Sally Field
Captain Svevo Stefan	Telly Savalas
Frank Mazzetti	Peter Boyle
Harold Meredith	Jack Warden
Hannah Meredith	Shirley Knight
Gina Rowe	Shirley Jones
Wilbur	Karl Malden
Tex	Slim Pickens
Suzanne	Veronica Hamel
Theresa Mazzetti	Angela Cartwright
Larry Simpson	Mark Harmon
Kurt	Paul Picerni
Doyle	Patrick Culliton
Castorp	Dean Ferrandini

and Paul Stader, George Wilbur, Rick Wilson, Peter Stader, Tony Epper, Hubie Kerns, Jr., Ayn Cavellini, Gary Taraman, Peter Peterson, Sheree Kerns, Fred Shaw, Janet Brady, Bob Bralver, Joe Cirillo, Justin DeRosa, Marneen Fields, Kay Kimler, Henry Wills, Jimmy Stader, Vince Deadrick, Pamela Estrom, Fred Zendar

Top: Angela Cartwright, Jack Warden, Slim Pickens, Shirley Jones Below: Peter Boyle, Cartwright, Mark Harmon, Michael Caine, Sally Field, Pickens Top Right: Shirley Knight, and below with Jack Warden © Warner Bros.

Karl Malden, Michael Caine, Telly Savalas
Above: Michael Caine, Sally Field

37

HEAD OVER HEELS

(UNITED ARTISTS) Producers, Mark Metcalf, Amy Robinson, Griffin Dunne; Direction and Screenplay, Joan Micklin Silver; Based on novel "Chilly Scenes of Winter" by Ann Beattie; Photography, Bobby Byrne; Music, Ken Lauber; Editor, Cynthia Scheider; Designer, Peter Jamison; Assistant Directors, Lorin Salob, D. Scott Easton; Costumes, Rosanna Norton; A Triple Play production in Metrocolor; Rated PG; 109 minutes; May release.

CAST

Charles	John Heard
Laura	Mary Beth Hurt
Sam	Peter Riegert
Pete	Kenneth McMillan
Clara	Gloria Grahame
Betty	Nora Heflin
Mr. Patterson	Jerry Hardin
Susan	Tarah Nutter
Ox	Mark Metcalf
Blindman	Allen Joseph
Mrs. Delillo	Frances Bay
Dr. Mark	Griffin Dunne
Elise	Alex Johnson
Woman in Park	Beverly Booth Rowland
Waitress	Ann Beattie
Rebecca	Angela Phillips
Dancing Nurse	Margaressa Peach Taylor

Top: John Heard, Gloria Grahame, Kenneth McMillan
Below: Mark Metcalf, Heard, Peter Riegert
Top Left: Heard, Jerry Hardin Below: Heard, Nora Heflin
© United Artists

John Heard, Mary Beth Hurt
(also right center)

ALIEN

(20th CENTURY-FOX) Producers, Gordon Carroll, David Giler, Walter Hill; Director, Ridley Scott; Executive Producer, Ronald Shusett; Screenplay, Dann O'Bannon; Photography, Derek Vanlint; Editor, Terry Rawlings; Design, Michael Seymour; Art Directors, Les Dilley, Roger Christian; Special Effects, Brian Johnson, Nick Alider; Costumes, John Mollo; Assistant Director, Paul Ibbetson; Music, Jerry Goldsmith; In Panavision, Dolby Sound, and Eastmancolor; Rated R; 125 minutes; May release.

CAST

Dallas	Tom Skerritt
Ripley	Sigourney Weaver
Lambert	Veronica Cartwright
Brett	Harry Dean Stanton
Kane	John Hurt
Ash	Ian Holm
Parker	Yaphet Kotto

1979 Academy Award for Best Visual Effects

Right: Harry Dean Stanton, Ian Holm, John Hurt, Veronica Cartwright, Tom Skerritt, Sigourney Weaver, Yaphet Kotto
© 20th Century-Fox Film Corp.

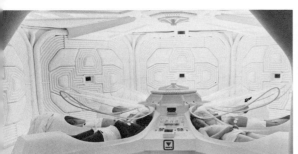

Tom Skerritt, Sigourney Weaver, Ian Holm

John Hurt, Tom Skerritt

ESCAPE FROM ALCATRAZ

(PARAMOUNT) Executive Producer, Robert Daley; Associate Producer, Fritz Manes; Producer-Director, Don Siegel; Screenplay, Richard Tuggle; Based on book by J. Campbell Bruce; Photography, Bruce Surtees; Designer, Allen Smith; Editor, Ferris Webster; Assistant Directors, Luigi Alfano, Mark Johnson, Richard Graves; In DeLuxe Color; Rated PG; 112 minutes; June release.

CAST

Frank Morris	Clint Eastwood
Warden	Patrick McGoohan
Doc	Roberts Blossom
Clarence Anglin	Jack Thibeau
John Anglin	Fred Ward
English	Paul Benjamin
Charley Butts	Larry Hankin
Wolf	Bruce M. Fischer
Litmus	Frank Ronzio
Johnson	Fred Stuthman
Wagner	David Cryer
Zimmerman	Madison Arnold
Fight Guard	Blair Burrows
Medical Assistant	Bob Balhatchet
Exam Guard	Matthew J. Locricchio
Beck	Don Michaelian
Cellblock Captain	Ray K. Goman
Bobs	Jason Ronard

and Ed Vasgersian, Ron Vernan, Stephen Bradley, Garry Goodrow, Dan Leegant, John Garabedian, Donald Siegel, Denis Berkfeldt, Jim Haynie, Tony Dario, Fritz Manes, Dana Derfus, Don Cummins, Gordon Handforth, John Scanlon, Don Watters, Lloyd Nelson, George Orrison, Gary F. Warren, Joe Whipp, Terry Wills, Robert Irvine, Joseph Knowland, James Collier, R. J. Ganzert, Robert Hirschfeld, Dale Alvarez, Sheldon Feldner, Danny Glover, Carl Lumbly, Patrick Valentino, Glenn Wright, Gilbert Thomas, Jr., Eugene W. Jackson

Left: Clint Eastwood
© Paramount Pictures

Clint Eastwood

Clint Eastwood, Larry Hankin
Above: Bruce M. Fischer, Fred Stuthman, Clint Eastwood

Clint Eastwood, Frank Ronzio
Clint Eastwood above and top

Larry Hankin, Clint Eastwood

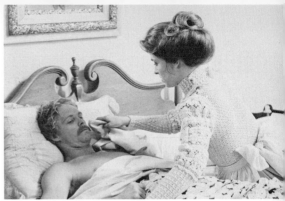

BUTCH AND SUNDANCE: THE EARLY DAYS

(20th CENTURY-FOX) Producers, Gabriel Katzka, Steven Bach; Associate Producer, Jack B. Bernstein; Director, Richard Lester; Screenplay, Allan Burns; Assistant Directors, Jack Sanders, Peter Berquist, Bob Dahlin; Designer, Brian Eatwell; Art Director, Jack DeGovia; Photography, Laszlo Kovacs; Costumes, William Theiss; In DeLuxe Color; Rated PG; 110 minutes; June release.

CAST

Sundance Kid	William Katt
Butch Cassidy	Tom Berenger
Mary	Jill Eikenberry
Bobby	Paul Plunkett
Sam	Wesley Burgess
Ray Bledsoe	Jeff Corey
Joe LeFors	Peter Weller
Captain Prewitt	Noble Willingham
Wyoming Governor	Arthur Hill
Harvey Logan	John Schuck
O. C. Hanks	Brian Dennehy
Guards	Vincent Schiavelli, Patrick Egan
Annie	Sherril Lynn Katzman
Bookkeeper	Elya Baskin
Old Robber	Peter Brocco
Banker	Liam Russell
Lily	Carol Ann Williams
Telegrapher	Charles Knapp
Daisy Mullen	Jane Austen
Skinner	Paul Price
Mike Cassidy	Michael C. Gwynne
Bill Carver	Chris Lloyd
Cyrus Antoon	Hugh Gillin
Conductor	Will Hare

Jill Eikenberry, Tom Berenger
Above: Berenger, William Katt

Top: William Katt, Jill Eikenberry Below: William Katt, Chris Lloyd, John Schuck, Tom Berenger
Left: William Katt, Tom Berenger
© 20th Century-Fox Film Corp.

THE IN-LAWS

(WARNER BROS.) Executive Producer, Alan Arkin; Producers, Arthur Hiller, William Sackheim; Director, Arthur Hiller; Screenplay, Andrew Bergman; Music, John Morris; Editor, Robert E. Swink; Designer, Pato Guzman; Photography, David M. Walsh; Associate Producer, Dorothy Wilde; Assistant Directors, Jack Roe, John Kretchmer; In Technicolor; Rated PG; 103 minutes; June release.

CAST

Vince Ricardo	Peter Falk
Sheldon Kornpett	Alan Arkin
General Garcia	Richard Libertini
Carol Kornpett	Nancy Dussault
Barbara Kornpett	Penny Peyser
Jean Ricardo	Arlene Golonka
Tommy Ricardo	Michael Lembeck
Mo	Paul Lawrence Smith
Angie	Carmine Caridi
Barry Lutz	Ed Begley, Jr.
Mr. Hirschorn	Sammy Smith
Bing Wong	James Hong
Bank Teller	Barbara Dana
Mrs. Adelman	Rozsika Halmos
Edgardo	Alvaro Carcano
Carlos	Jorge Zepeda
Alfonso	Sergio Calderon

and David Paymer, Kent Williams, John Hancock, John Finnegan, Brass Adams, Eduardo Noriega, Danny Kwan, Maurice Sneed, Rosana Soto, Jim Goodwin, Mitchell Group, Carmen Dragon, Peter Miller, Hanna King, Dick Wieand, Carlos Montalbo, Tom Degidon, Tony Di Falco, John Day, Art Evans, John Hostetter, Bill Houston

Right: Barbara Dana, Nancy Dussault
Top: Peter Falk, Alan Arkin
© Warner Bros.

Arlene Golonka, Peter Falk, Alan Arkin, Nancy Dussault Above: Falk, Arkin

Peter Falk, Alan Arkin (also above)

THE MAIN EVENT

(WARNER BROS.) Executive Producers, Howard Rosenman, Renee Missel; Producers, Jon Peters, Barbra Streisand; Director, Howard Zieff; Screenplay, Gail Parent, Andrew Smith; Editor, Edward Warschilka; Designer, Charles Rosen; Photography, Mario Tosi; Associate Producer, Jeff Werner; Assistant Directors, Gary Daigler, Pat Kehoe, Ed Milkovich; Costumes, Ruth Myers; A Barwood Film in Technicolor; Rated PG; 112 minutes; June release.

CAST

Hillary Kramer	Barbra Streisand
Eddie "Kid Natural" Scanlon	Ryan O'Neal
David	Paul Sand
Percy	Whitman Mayo
Donna	Patti D'Arbanville
Luis	Chu Chu Malave
Hector Mantilla	Richard Lawson
Gough	James Gregory
Tour Guide	Richard Altman
Stunt Double Kid	Joe Amsler
Newsman	Seth Banks
Girl in Bed	Lindsay Bloom
Nose-Kline	Earl Boen
Owner Sinthia Cosmetics	Roger Bowen
Heavyweight in Gym	Badja Medu Djola
Fighter in Kid's Camp	Rory Calhoun
Brenda	Sue Casey

and Alvin Childress, Kristine DeBell, Al Denava, Rene Dijon, Shay Duffin, Murphy Dunne, Art Evans, Ron Henriques, Anthony Renya, Maurice Sneed, Lee Harman, Vic Heutschy, Ernie Hudson, Dave Ketchum, Jimmy Lennon, Len Lesser, Eddie "Animal" Lopez, Gilda Marx, Denver Mattson, Bill Murry, Brent Musburger, Robert Nadder, Harvey Parry, John Reilly, Tim Rossovich, Jack Somack, Richard S. Steele, Karen Wookey, Darrell Zwerling

Left: Barbra Streisand
© Warner Bros.

Tim Rossovich, Harvey Parry, Barbra Streisand, Ryan O'Neal

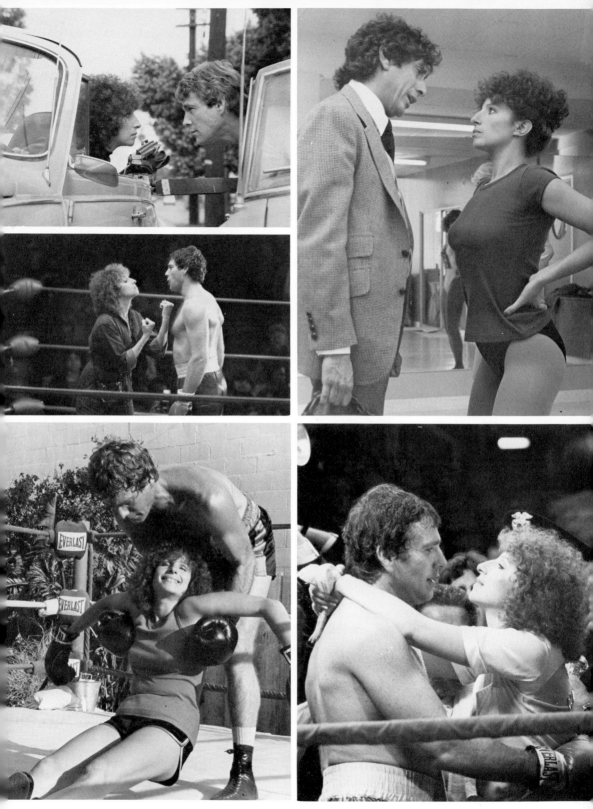

Barbra Streisand, Ryan O'Neal
(also above and top)

Ryan O'Neal, Barbra Streisand
Top: Paul Sand, Barbra Streisand

Kermit, Miss Piggy
Above: Paul Williams

THE MUPPET MOVIE

(ASSOCIATED FILM DISTRIBUTION) Executive Producer, Martin Starger; Producer, Jim Henson; Director, James Frawley; Screenplay, Jerry Juhl, Jack Burns; Co-Producer, David Lazer; Music and Lyrics, Paul Williams, Kenny Ascher; Editor, Chris Greenbury; Designer, Joel Schiller; Photography, Isidore Mankofsky; Assistant Directors, Ron Wright, Penny Flowers; Art Director, Les Gobruegge; Costumes, Gwen Capetanos; Presented by Sir Lew Grade and Martin Starger; In Dolby Stereo and color; Rated G; 98 minutes; June release. CAST: Muppet performers Jim Henson, Frank Oz, Jerry Nelson, Richard Hunt, Dave Goelz, Charles Durning, Austin Pendleton, Carroll Spinney, Steve Whitmire, Kathryn Mullen, Bob Payne, Eren Ozker, Caroly Wilcox, Olga Felgemacher, Bruce Schwartz, Michael Davis, Buz Suraci, Tony Basilicato, Adam Hunt, and Special Guest Stars: Edgar Bergen, Milton Berle, Mel Brooks, James Coburn, Dom DeLuise, Elliott Gould, Bob Hope, Madeline Kahn, Carol Kane, Cloris Leachman, Steve Martin, Richard Pryor, Telly Savalas, Orson Welles, Paul Williams

Above: Kermit, James Coburn, Fozzie Top: Kermit, Jim Henson Below: Carol Kane, Kermit, Telly Savalas, Top Left: Fozzie Below: Mel Brooks, Kermit © Associated Film Distribution

Richard Pryor Above: Milton Berle
Top: Dom DeLuise, Kermit Below: Animal

Kermit, Steve Martin, Miss Piggy

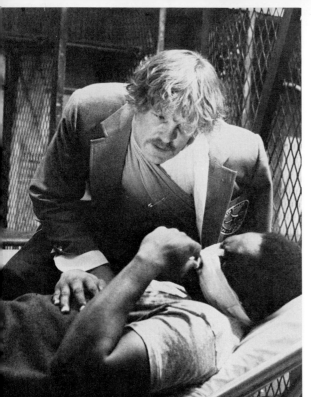

NORTH DALLAS FORTY

(PARAMOUNT) Executive Producer, Jack B. Bernstein; Producer, Frank Yablans; Director, Ted Kotcheff; Screenplay, Frank Yablans, Ted Kotcheff, Peter Gent; Based on novel by Peter Gent; Photography, Paul Lohmann; Design, Alfred Sweeney; Editor, Jay Kamen; Music, John Scott; Costumes, Dorothy Jeakins; Assistant Directors, Victor Hsu, Kalai Strode; In Panavision and Metrocolor; Rated R; 119 minutes; June release.

CAST

Phillip Elliott	Nick Nolte
Maxwell	Mac Davis
Coach Johnson	Charles Durning
Charlotte	Dayle Haddon
Jo Bob Priddy	Bo Svenson
Conrad Hunter	Steve Forrest
B. A. Strothers	G. D. Spradlin
Emmett	Dabney Coleman
Joanne	Savannah Smith
Art Hartman	Marshall Colt
Eddie Rand	Guich Koock
Mrs. Hartman	Deborah Benson
Stallings	James F. Boeke
VIP	John Bottoms
Doctor	Walter Brooke
Balford	Carlos Brown
Tony Douglas	Danny J. Bunz
Ruth	Jane Daly
Conrad, Jr.	Rad Daly
Monroe	Cliff Frazier
March	Stanley Grover

Left: Nick Nolte, Cliff Frazier
© Paramount Pictures

Nick Nolte, Mac Davis

Nick Nolte (C), Mac Davis (R) Top: (L) Nick Nolte, Dayle Haddon Below: Nick Nolte, Mac Davis, Bo Svenson Top Right: Nick Nolte, Mac Davis Below: Bo Svenson, Mac Davis, John Matuszak

Ali MacGraw, Dean-Paul Martin

PLAYERS

(PARAMOUNT) Producer, Robert Evans; Director, Anthony Harvey; Screenplay, Arnold Schulman, Executive Producer; Photography, James Crabe; Designer, Richard Sylbert; Editor, Randy Roberts; Music, Jerry Goldsmith; Associate Producer, Tommy Cook; Costumes, Richard Bruno; Assistant Directors, Jack Sanders, Scott Easton, Rimas Vainorius; In Panavision and Metrocolor; Rated PG; 120 minutes; June release.

CAST

Nicole	Ali MacGraw
Chris	Dean-Paul Martin
Marco	Maximilian Schell
Pancho	Pancho Gonzalez
Rusty	Steven Guttenberg
Ann	Melissa Prophet
Chris at 10	Drew Denny
Rusty at 10	Ian Altman
Chauffeur	David Gilruth
Themselves	Guillermo Vilas, Ion Tiriac, Dan Maskell, John McEnroe, Ilie Nastase, Tom Gullikson, John Lloyd, Denis Ralston, Vijay Amritraj, Jim McManus, John Alexander, David Pate, Jorge Mendoza

Top: Dean-Paul Martin, and below with Ali MacGraw, Pancho Gonzalez Top Left: Maximilian Schell, MacGraw Below: Ilie Nastase, Martin
© Paramount Pictures

SIDNEY SHELDON'S BLOODLINE

(PARAMOUNT) Producers, David V. Picker, Sidney Beckerman; Director, Terence Young; Screenplay, Laird Koenig; Photography, Freddie Young; Designer, Ted Haworth; Editor, Bud Molin; Music, Ennio Morricone; Associate Producer, Richard McWhorter; Costumes, Enrico Sabbatini; Assistant Directors, John Longmuir, Gianni Cozzo; In Panavision and color; Rated R; 116 minutes; June release.

CAST

Elizabeth Roffe	Audrey Hepburn
Rhys Williams	Ben Gazzara
Sir Alec Nichols	James Mason
Donatella	Claudia Mori
Simonetta Palazzi	Irene Papas
Vivian Nichols	Michelle Phillips
Charles Martin	Maurice Ronet
Helene Martin	Romy Schneider
Ivo Palazzi	Omar Sharif
Kate Erling	Beatrice Straight
Inspector Hornung	Gert Frobe
Julius Prager	Wolfgang Preiss
Man in Black	Marcel Bozzuffi
Dr. Wal	Pinkas Braun
Young Sam Roffe	Wulf Kessler
Jon Swinton	Maurice Colbourne
Tod Michaels	Guy Rolfe
Terenia	Dietlinde Turban
Krauss	Walter Kohut
Henley	Donald Symington

Top Right: Ben Gazzara, Audrey Hepburn
Below: Romy Schneider, Ben Gazzara
© Paramount Pictures

Ben Gazzara, Audrey Hepburn Above: Omar Sharif,
Irene Papas, James Mason, Hepburn, Gazzara, Romy
Schneider, Maurice Ronet

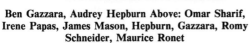

Audrey Hepburn, James Mason

51

ROCKY II

(UNITED ARTISTS) Producers, Irwin Winkler, Robert Chartoff; Direction and Screenplay, Sylvester Stallone; Photography, Bill Butler; Music, Bill Conti; Editor, Danford B. Greene; Art Director, Richard Berger; Associate Producer, Arthur Chobanian; Assistant Directors, Jerry Zeismer, Elie Cohn; In Panavision, Technicolor, and Dolby Stereo; Rated PG; 119 minutes; June release.

CAST

Rocky Balboa	Sylvester Stallone
Adrian	Talia Shire
Paulie	Burt Young
Apollo Creed	Carl Weathers
Mickey	Burgess Meredith
Apollo's Trainer	Tony Burton
Gazzo	Joe Spinell
Agent	Leonard Gaines
Mary Anne Creed	Sylvia Meals
Meat Foreman	Frank McRae
Cutman	Al Silvani
Director	John Pleshette
Announcer	Stu Nahan
Commentator	Bill Baldwin
Salesman	Jerry Ziesmer
Father Carmine	Paul J. Micale

and Earl Montgomery, Herb Nanas, Stuart Robinson, Frank Stallone, Charles Coles, Doug Flor, Robert Kondyra, James Zazzarino, Eddie Lopez, Taurean Blacque, James Casino, Samuel Davis, Ruth Ann Flynn, Linda Grey

Left: Burt Young, Sylvester Stallone, Talia Shire
Top: Sylvester Stallone, Talia Shire
© United Artists Corp.

Talia Shire, Sylvester Stallone

Sylvester Stallone, Talia Shire

Sylvester Stallone, Burgess Meredith, Stuart Robinson
Above and top: Sylvester Stallone, Talia Shire

Talia Shire, Sylvester Stallone, Butkus
Top: Tony Burton, Carl Weathers

JUST YOU AND ME, KID

(COLUMBIA) Producers, Irving Fein, Jerome M. Zeitman; Director, Leonard Stern; Screenplay, Oliver Hailey, Leonard Stern; Story, Tom Lazarus; Photography, David Walsh; Editor, John W. Holmes; Music, Jack Elliott; Design, Ron Hobbs; Art Director, Sig Tinglof; Assistant Director, Pat Kehoe; In color; Rated PG; 93 minutes; July release.

CAST

Bill	George Burns
Kate	Brooke Shields
Max	Burl Ives
Shirl	Lorraine Gary
Harris	Nicolas Coster
Dr. Device	Keye Luke
Reinhoff the Remarkable	Carl Ballantine
Manduke the Magnificent	Leon Ames
Tom	Ray Bolger
Stan	John Schuck
Sue	Andrea Howard
Roy	Christopher Knight
Demesta	William Russ
Box Boy	Robert Doran

George Burns, Brooke Shields
(also above)

Above: Burl Ives, George Burns
Top: George Burns, Keye Luke, Carl Ballantine,
Ray Bolger, Leon Ames
© Columbia Pictures Industries

54

DRACULA

(UNIVERSAL) Producer, Walter Mirisch; Director, John Badham; Screenplay, W. D. Richter; Based on play by Hamilton Deane and John L. Balderston from the novel by Bram Stoker; Music, John Williams; Executive Producer, Marvin E. Mirisch; Photography, Gilbert Taylor; Designer, Peter Murton; Costumes, Julie Harris; Associate Producer, Tom Pevsner; Assistant Director, Anthony Waye; Art Director, Brian Ackland Snow; In Technicolor, Panavision and Dolby Stereo; Rated R; 115 minutes; July release.

CAST

Dracula	Frank Langella
Van Helsing	Laurence Olivier
Seward	Donald Pleasence
Lucy	Kate Nelligan
Harker	Trevor Eve
Mina	Jan Francis
Annie	Janine Duvitski
Renfield	Tony Haygarth
Swales	Teddy Turner
Mrs. Galloway	Kristine Howarth
Tom Hindley	Joe Belcher
Scarborough Sailor	Ted Carroll
Harbourmaster	Frank Birch
Captain of Demeter	Gabor Vernon
Demeter Sailor	Frank Henson
Priest	Peter Wallis

Right: Frank Langella, and below with Kate Nelligan
© Universal City Studios

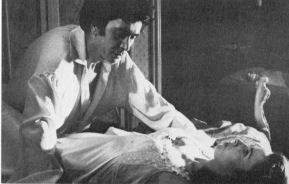

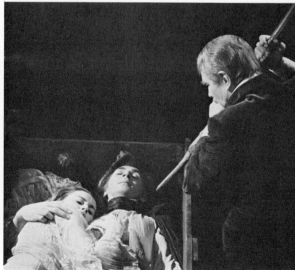

**Kate Nelligan, Laurence Olivier, Trevor Eve
Above: Donald Pleasence, Nelligan, Olivier, Eve**

Kate Nelligan, Frank Langella, Laurence Olivier

BREAKING AWAY

(20th CENTURY-FOX) Producer-Director, Peter Yates; Screenplay, Steve Tesich; Photography, Matthew F. Leonetti; Associate Producer, Art Levinson; Music, Patrick Williams; Art Director, Patrizia von Brandenstein; Editor, Cynthia Scheider; Assistant Directors, Mike Grillo, Bill Beasley; Costumes, Betsy Cox; In DeLuxe Color; Rated PG; 100 minutes; July release.

CAST

Dave Stohler	Dennis Christopher
Mike	Dennis Quaid
Cyril	Daniel Stern
Moocher	Jackie Earle Haley
Mrs. Stohler	Barbara Barrie
Mr. Stohler	Paul Dooley
Katherine	Robyn Douglass
Rod	Hart Bochner
Nancy	Amy Wright
Doctor	Peter Maloney
Mike's Brother	John Ashton
French Girl	Lisa Shure
Girl	Jennifer K. Mickel
Suzy	Pamela Jayne Soles
Race Announcer	David K. Blase
Race Officials	William S. Armstrong, Howard S. Wilcox
Mr. York	J. F. Briere
Italian Riders	Carlos Sintes, Eddy Van Guyse
Black Student Leader	Jimmy Grant
Fight Spectator	Gail L. Horton
Owner of Car Wash	Woody Hueston
Anthem Singer	Jennifer F. Nolan
Woman	Nora Owens
Sports Announcer	Douglas Rafferty
Race Starter	John W. "Bill" Ringgenberry
University President	Dr. John W. Ryan
Blond Guy	Morris Salzman
Team Captain	Tom Schwoegler
Homecoming Car Kid	Mike Silveus
Stonecutters	Alvin E. Bailey, Harold Elgar, Floyd E. Todd, Robert Woolery, Russell E. Freeman

1979 Academy Award for Best Screenplay Written for the Screen

Left: Dennis Christopher, Paul Dooley
Top: Dennis Christopher
© 20th Century-Fox Film Corp.

Dennis Quaid, Jackie Earle Haley, Dennis Christopher, Daniel Stern

Paul Dooley, Barbara Barrie Above and Top:
Robyn Douglass, Dennis Christopher

Paul Dooley, Dennis Christopher, Barbara Barrie

57

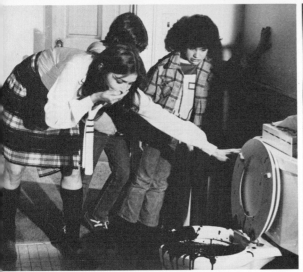

Margot Kidder, James Brolin

THE AMITYVILLE HORROR

(AMERICAN INTERNATIONAL) Producers, Ronald Saland, Elliot Geisinger; Director, Stuart Rosenberg; Executive Producer, Samuel Z. Arkoff; Screenplay, Sandor Stern; Based on book by Jay Anson; Music, Lalo Schifrin; Photography, Fred J. Koenekamp; Art Director, Jim Swados; Editor, Robert Brown; A Professional Films production in Movielab Color; A Cinema 77 film; Rated R; 126 minutes; July release.

CAST

George Lutz	James Brolin
Kathleen Lutz	Margot Kidder
Father Delaney	Rod Steiger
Father Bolen	Don Stroud
Father Ryan	Murray Hamilton
Father Nuncio	John Larch
Amy	Natasha Ryan
Greg	K. C. Martel
Matt	Meeno Peluce
Jeff	Michael Sacks
Carolyn	Helen Shaver
Jackie	Amy Wright
Sergeant Gionfriddo	Val Avery
Aunt Helena	Irene Dailey
Jimmy	Marc Vahanian
Mrs. Townsend	Elsa Raven
Bride	Ellen Saland
Agucci	Eddie Barth

Top: Amy Wright, Margot Kidder, James Brolin
Below: Michael Sacks, Helen Shaver, Brolin
Top Left: Margot Kidder, and below with
Natasha Ryan
©American International Pictures

Margot Kidder, Natasha Ryan
Top: James Brolin, Margot Kidder

Margot Kidder, James Brolin, and above
Top: Rod Steiger, Don Stroud

59

THE WANDERERS

(ORION) Executive Producer, Richard R. St. Johns; Producer, Martin Ransohoff; Director, Philip Kaufman; Screenplay, Rose Kaufman, Philip Kaufman; Based on novel by Richard Price; Photography, Michael Chapman; Editors, Ronald Roose, Stuart H. Pappe; Costumes, Robert de Mora; Art Director, Jay Moore; Associate Producer, Fred C. Caruso; Assistant Directors, Alan Hopkins, Laurie B. Eichengreen; In Technicolor; Rated R; 113 minutes; July release.

CAST

Richie	Ken Wahl
Joey	John Friedrich
Nina	Karen Allen
Despie Galasso	Toni Kalem
Turkey	Alan Rosenberg
Buddy	Jim Youngs
Perry	Tony Ganios
Peewee	Linda Manz
Emilio	William Andrews
Terror	Erland Van Lidth de Jeude
Mr. Sharp	Val Avery
Ghubby Galasso	Dolph Sweet
Clinton	Michael Wright
Marine Recruiter	Burtt Harris
Roger	Samm-Art Williams
Teddy Wong	Dion Albanese
Joey's Mom	Olympia Dukakis

and George Merolle, Terri Perri, John Califano, Richard Price, Linda Artuso, Earlie J. Butler III, Rafael Cabrera, Brian Colleary, Rosemary DeAngelis, Lorna Erickson, Ken Foree, Sally Anne Golden, Leon Grant, Jery Hewitt, Adam Kimmel, Tara King, Faith Minton, Bruce Nozick, Michael Pasternak, Sheryl Posner, Bert Samuel, Konrad Sheehan, Harry Benjamin, Alan Braunstein, Mark Lesly, Farrel R. Tannenbaum, Anthony Tirico

Right: Ken Wahl, John Friedrich, Tony Ganios, Jim Youngs Top: Karen Allen, Ken Wahl
© Polyc International B.V.

Jim Youngs, Ken Wahl, John Friedrich, Tony Ganios

LOST AND FOUND

(COLUMBIA) Executive Producer, Arnold Kopelson; Producer-Director, Melvin Frank; Screenplay, Melvin Frank, Jack Rose; Photography, Douglas Slocombe; Designer, Trevor Williams; Music, John Cameron; Editor, Bill Butler; Costumes, Julie Harris; Assistant Directors, Tony Lucibello, Max Kleven; Art Director, Ted Tester; In Panavision and Technicolor; Rated PG; 106 minutes; July release.

CAST

Adam	George Segal
Tricia	Glenda Jackson
Jemmy	Maureen Stapleton
Eden	Hollis McLaren
Lenny	John Cunningham
Reilly	Paul Sorvino
Julian	Kenneth Pogue
Zelda	Janie Sell
Ellie	Diana Barrington
Jean-Paul	Leslie Carlson
Carpentier	John Candy
Gendarme	James Morris
Ski Patrol	Bruno Engler
French Doctor	David Bolt
Attendant	Richard Adams
French Nurses	Mary Pirie, Nicole D'Amour, Denise Baillargeon
French Lawyer	Roger Periard
English Woman	Lois Maxwell
British Professor	Douglas Campbell

and John Anthony Robinow (Conductor), Robert Goodier (Mayor), Sandy Webster (Bryce), Barbara Hamilton (Mrs. Bryce), Patricia Collins (Helen), Rob Garrison (Ed), Cecil Linder (Sanders), James Hurdle (Hurley), Martin Short (Engel), John Baylis (Schuster), Dennis Strong (Porter)

Right: Glenda Jackson, George Segal, Maureen Stapleton
Top: George Segal, Glenda Jackson
© Columbia Pictures Industries

George Segal, Glenda Jackson

George Segal, Glenda Jackson

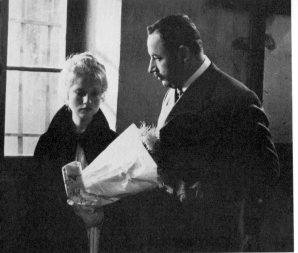

THE JUDGE AND THE ASSASSIN

(LIBRA FILMS) Producer, Raymond Danon; Director, Bertrand Tavernier; Screenplay, Jean Aurenche, Bertrand Tavernier, Pierre Bost; Editor, Armand Psenny; Music, Philippe Sarde; Photography, Pierre William Glenn; Executive Producer, Ralph Baum; Designer, Antoine Roman; Costumes, Jacqueline Moreay; Songs, Jean-Roger Caussimon, Philippe Sarde; In Eastmancolor; Not rated; 130 minutes; August release.

CAST

Judge Rousseau	Philippe Noiret
Sergeant Joseph Bouvier	Michel Galabru
Rose	Isabelle Huppert
Attorney	Jean-Claude Brialy
Mme. Rousseau	Renee Faure
Louise Lesueur	Cecile Vassort
Mme. Lesueur	Monique Chaumette
Bassompierre	Yves Robert

Left: Isabelle Huppert, Philippe Noiret
© Libra Films

Isabelle Huppert, Philippe Noiret
Above: Jean-Claude Brialy, Noiret

Michael Galabru, and above with
Isabelle Huppert, Philippe Noiret

MORE AMERICAN GRAFFITI

(UNIVERSAL) Producer, Howard Kazanjian; Direction and Screenplay, B.W.L. Norton; Based on characters created by George Lucas; Executive Producer, George Lucas; Photography, Caleb Deschanel; Art Director, Ray Storey; Editor, Tina Hirsch; Assistant Directors, Thomas Lofaro, Steven Lofaro; Costumes, Agnes Rodgers; In Dolby Stereo and color; Rated PG; 111 minutes; August release.

CAST

Debbie Dunham	Candy Clark
Little Joe	Bo Hopkins
Steve Bolander	Ron Howard
John Milner	Paul LeMat
Carol Rainbow	Mackenzie Phillips
Terry the Toad	Charles Martin Smith
Laurie Bolander	Cindy Williams
Eva	Anna Bjorn
Major Creech	Richard Bradford
Ralph	John Brent
Country Joe	Country Joe McDonald
Newt	Scott Glenn
Sinclair	James Houghton
Lance	John Lansing
Carlos	Manuel Padilla
Beckwith	Ken Place
Teensa	Mary Kay Place
Eric	Tom Ruben
Bobbie	Doug Sahm

and Will Seltzer, Monica Tenner, Ralph Wilcox, Carol-Ann Williams, Wolfman Jack, Rosanna Arquette, Tom Baker, Eric Barnes, Becky Bedoy, Buzz Borelli, Ben Bottoms, Patrick Burns, George Cantero, Chet Carter, Dion Chesse, Gil Christner, Don Coughlin

Top: Ron Howard, Cindy Williams, Candy Clark, Charles Martin Smith Below: (L)Candy Clark, John Brent (R) Paul LeMat, Jonathan Gries
© Universal City Studios

Ron Howard (L)

APOCALYPSE NOW

(UNITED ARTISTS) Producer-Director, Francis Coppola; Screenplay, John Milius, Francis Coppola; Narration, Michael Herr; Co-Producers, Fred Roos, Gray Frederickson, Ton Sternberg; Photography, Vittorio Storaro; Designer, Dean Tavoularis; Music, Carmine Coppola, Francis Coppola; Editor, Richard Marks; Associate Producer, Mona Skager; Art Director, Angelo Graham; An Omni Zoetrope production in Panavision, Dolby Stereo, and color; Rated R; 146 minutes; August release.

CAST

Colonel Kurtz	Marlon Brando
Lieutenant Colonel Kilgore	Robert Duvall
Captain Willard	Martin Sheen
Chef	Frederic Forrest
Chief	Albert Hall
Lance	Sam Bottoms
Clean	Larry Fishburne
Photo Journalist	Dennis Hopper
General	G. D. Spradlin
Colonel	Harrison Ford
Civilian	Scott Glenn
Agent	Bill Graham
Playmates	Cyndi Wood, Colleen Camp, Linda Carpenter

1979 Academy Awards for Best Cinematography, Best Sound

**Top: Robert Duvall, Albert Hall, Martin Sheen
Below: Dennis Hopper
© United Artists Corp.**

**Marlon Brando
Top: Robert Duvall**

Frederic Forrest, Martin Sheen
Above: Marlon Brando, Martin Sheen

Martin Sheen, and top with Dennis
Hopper, Frederic Forrest

65

RICH KIDS

(UNITED ARTISTS) Producers, George W. George, Michael Hausman; Executive Producer, Robert Altman; Director, Robert M. Young; Screenplay, Judith Ross; Photography, Ralf D. Bode; Art Director, David Mitchell; Costumes, Hilary M. Rosenfeld; Music, Craig Doerge; Songs, Craig Doerge, Allan Nicholls; Editor, Edward Beyer; Assistant Directors, Michael Hausman, Joel Tuber; In Panavision and Technicolor; A Lion's Gate Film; Rated PG; 96 minutes; August release.

CAST

Franny Philips	Trini Alvarado
Jamie Harris	Jeremy Levy
Madeleine Philips	Kathryn Walker
Paul Philips	John Lithgow
Ralph Harris	Terry Kiser
Steve Sloan	David Selby
Barbara Peterfreund	Roberta Maxwell
Simon Peterfreund	Paul Dooley
Stewardess	Diane Stilwell
Ralph's Secretary	Dianne Kirksey
Madeleine's Mother	Irene Worth
Lawyer	Olympia Dukakis
Juilliard Student	Jill Eikenberry
Gym Teacher	Kathryn Grody
Corine	Bea Winde
Susan	Stacy Peppell
Jamie's Grandfather	Jack Hausman
Receptionist	Lacey Neuhaus
Beverly	Patti Hansen
Boy on Bus	Michael Miller
Shag	Shag Starbird

Left: Kathryn Walker, Irene Worth
Top: Jeremy Levy, Trini Alvarado
© United Artists Corp.

Jeremy Levy, Trini Alvarado
Above: David Selby, Kathryn Walker

Paul Dooley, John Lithgow, Roberta Maxwell,
Kathryn Walker Above (L) Terry Kiser, Jeremy Levy

THE CONCORDE—AIRPORT '79

(UNIVERSAL) Producer, Jennings Lang; Director, David Lowell Rich; Screenplay, Eric Roth; Story, Jennings Lang; Inspired by the film "Airport" based on novel by Arthur Hailey; Photography, Philip Lathrop; Designer, Henry Bumstead; Editor, Dorothy Spencer; Music, Lalo Schifrin; Costumes, Burton Miller; Assistant Directors, Newton Arnold, Katy Emde; In Technicolor; Rated PG; 123 minutes; August release.

CAST

Metrand	Alain Delon
Maggie	Susan Blakely
Kevin	Robert Wagner
Isabelle	Sylvia Kristel
Patroni	George Kennedy
Eli	Eddie Albert
Francine	Bibi Andersson
Margarita	Charo
Robert Palmer	John Davidson
Alicia	Andrea Marcovicci
Loretta	Martha Raye
Elaine	Cicely Tyson
Boisie	Jimmie Walker
O'Neill	David Warner
Nelli	Mercedes McCambridge
Coach Markov	Avery Schreiber
Amy	Sybil Danning
Gretchen	Monica Lewis
Dr. Stone	Nicolas Coster
William Halpern	Robin Gammell

and Ed Begley, Jr., Jon Cedar, Sheila DeWindt, Pierre Jalbert, Kathleen Maguire, Macon McCalman, Stacy Heather Tolkin, Selma Archerd, Brian Cutler, Michele Lesser, Conrad Palmisano, Jerry M. Prell, Dick McGarvin, George Sawaya, Leonora Wolpe, David Matthau, Frank Parker, Mario Machado

Top: Alain Delon, David Warner, George Kennedy
Below: Kennedy, Bibi Andersson Right: Cicely
Tyson, Nicholas Coster Top: Susan Blakely,
Robert Wagner
©Universal City Studies Inc.

Monica Lewis, Eddie Albert, John Davidson
Above: Martha Raye, Michele Lesser

67

THE SEDUCTION OF JOE TYNAN

(UNIVERSAL) Producer, Martin Bregman; Executive Producer, Louis A. Stroller; Director, Jerry Shatzberg; Screenplay, Alan Alda; Photography, Adam Holender; Editor, Evan Lottman; Art Director, David Chapman; Music, Bill Conti; Assistant Directors, Ralph Singleton, Yudi Bennett; Costumes, Jo Ynocencio; In Technicolor; Rated R; 107 minutes; August release.

CAST

Joe Tynan	Alan Alda
Ellie	Barbara Harris
Karen Traynor	Meryl Streep
Senator Kittner	Rip Torn
Senator Birney	Melvyn Douglas
Francis	Charles Kimbrough
Aldena Kittner	Carrie Nye
Senator Pardew	Michael Higgins
Janet	Blanche Baker
Joe's Secretary	Maureen Anderman
Jerry	Chris Arnold
Reporter on TV	John Badila
Arthur Briggs	Robert Christian
Edward Anderson	Maurice Copeland
Congresswoman at Party	Lu Elrod
Golf Pro	Clarence Felder
Eric	Gus Fleming
Merv Griffin	Himself
Sheila Lerner	Marian Hailey-Moss
Alex Heller	Dan Hedaya
Barry Traynor	Bill Moor

and Ronald Hunter, Walter Klavun, Norman La Rochelle, Kaiulani Lee, Charles Levin, Christopher McHale, Ron Menchine, M. B. Miller, Novella Nelson, Stephen D. Newman, Eric Pederson, Wyman Pendleton, Don Plumley, Ben Prestbury, Frederick Rolf, Adam Ross, Peter Schroeder, William Shust, Martha Sherrill, Ben Slack, Leon B. Stevens, Frank Stoegerer, Suzanne Stone, Kay Todd, Nathan Wilansky

Top: Alan Alda (L), Melvyn Douglas (R), also left
Below: Meryl Streep, Alda, Robert Christian
Left: Barbara Harris, Alan Alda, Meryl Streep

Alan Alda
Above: Rip Torn

... AND JUSTICE FOR ALL

(COLUMBIA) Producers, Norman Jewison, Patrick Palmer; Director, Norman Jewison; Screenplay, Valerie Curtin, Barry Levinson; Executive Producer, Joe Wizan; Photography, Victor J. Kemper; Designer, Richard MacDonald; Music, Dave Grusin; Costumes, Ruth Myers; Editor, John F. Burnett; Assistant Directors, Win Phelps, Bob Dahlin; Art Director, Peter Samish; In Metrocolor; Rated R; 120 minutes; September release.

CAST

Arthur Kirkland	Al Pacino
Judge Rayford	Jack Warden
Judge Fleming	John Forsythe
Grandpa Sam	Lee Strasberg
Jay Porter	Jeffrey Tambor
Gail Packer	Christine Lahti
Arnie	Sam Levene
Ralph Agee	Robert Christian
Jeff McCullaugh	Thomas Waites
Warren Fresnell	Larry Bryggman
Frank Bowers	Craig T. Nelson
Carl Travers	Dominic Chianese
Leo Fauci	Victor Arnold
Officer Leary	Vincent Beck
Elderly Man	Michael Gorrin
Larry	Baxter Harris
Prison Doctor	Joe Morton
Deputy Sheriff	Alan North
Desk Clerk Kiley	Tom Quinn
Sherry	Beverly Sanders
Gitel	Connie Sawyer
Assistant District Attorney Keene	Charles Siebert
Judge Burns	Robert Symonds
Marvin Bates	Keith Andes
Robert Wenke	Stephen Blackmore
Avillar	Vasili Bogazianos
Prison Warden	Jack Hollander

Right: Christine Lahti, Al Pacino
Top: Lee Strasberg, Al Pacino
© Columbia Pictures Industries

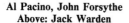

Al Pacino, John Forsythe
Above: Jack Warden

Christine Lahti, Al Pacino
(also above)

YANKS

(UNIVERSAL) Producers, Joseph Janni, Lester Persky; Director, John Schlesinger; Screenplay, Colin Welland, Walter Bernstein; Story, Colin Welland; Photography, Dick Bush; Music, Richard Rodney Bennett; Associate Producer, Teddy Joseph; Assistant Director, Simon Relph; Editor, Jim Clark; Costumes, Shirley Russell; Designer, Brian Morris; Choreographer, Eleanor Fazan; In Technicolor; Rated R; September release.

CAST

Matt	Richard Gere
Jean	Lisa Eichhorn
Helen	Vanessa Redgrave
John	William Devane
Danny	Chick Vennera
Mollie	Wendy Morgan
Mrs. Moreton	Rachel Roberts
Mr. Moreton	Tony Melody
Geoff	Martin Smith
Billy	Philip Whileman
Ken	Derek Thompson
Tim	Simon Harrison
Barmaid	Joan Hickson
Henry	Arlen Dean Snyder

and Annie Ross, Tom Nolan, John Ratzenberger, Andy Pantelidou, Francis Napier, Jeremy Newson, Harry Ditson, John Cassidy, Anthony Sher, George Harris, David Baxt, Everett McGill, Al Matthews, Eugene Lipinski, Ray Hassett, Weston Gavin, Ann Dyson, Harriet Harrison, June Ellis, Lynne Carol, Pearl Hackney

Left: Chick Vennera, Richard Gere, Arlen Dean Snyder, William Devane Top: Vennera, Gere
© **Universal City Studios**

Richard Gere, Lisa Eichhorn

Vanessa Redgrave, William Devane
Above: Lisa Eichhorn, Rachel Roberts

Kenneth Drury, Gere, Jeremy Newson, Vennera, Wendy Morgan, Ken Jones, Lizzie McKenzie, Eichhorn

**Chick Vennera, Richard Gere, Andy Pantelidou
Above: Rachel Roberts, Richard Gere**

**Richard Gere, Lisa Eichhorn Above: Vanessa
Redgrave, William Devane
Top: Gere, Chick Vennera**

**Wendy Morgan, Lisa Eichhorn (R)
Above: Richard Gere, Eichhorn**

James Woods

THE ONION FIELD

(AVCO EMBASSY) Producer, Walter Coblenz; Director, Harold Becker; Screenplay, Joseph Wambaugh from his book; Music, Eumir Deodato; Design, Brian Eatwell; Editor, John W. Wheeler; Photography, Charles Rosher; Assistant Directors, Tom Mack, D. Scott Easton; Designer, Joe Hubbard; In color; Rated R; 126 minutes; September release.

CAST

Karl Hettinger	John Savage
Greg Powell	James Woods
Jimmy Smith	Franklyn Seales
Ian Campbell	Ted Danson
Pierce Brooks	Ronny Cox
District Attorney Phil Halpin	David Huffman
Jailhouse Lawyer	Christopher Lloyd
Helen Hettinger	Diane Hull
Chrissie Campbell	Priscilla Pointer
Greg's Woman	Beege Barkett
Beat Cop	Richard Herd
Emmanuel McFadden	Le Tari
Glenn Bates	Richard Venture
Billy	Lee Weaver
District Attorney Marshall Schulman	Phillip R. Allen
Jimmy's Lawyer #2	Pat Corley
Mrs. Powell	K. Callan
Mr. Powell	Sandy McPeak
Nana	Lillian Randolph
LAPD Captain	Ned Wilson
IAD Captain	Jack Rader
Judge #2	Raleigh Bond
Greg's Lawyer #2	Stanley Grover
District Attorney Dino Fulgoni	Michael Pataki
Prison Guard #1	Steve Conte

Top: John Savage, Ted Danson, James Woods,
Franklyn Seales Below: Danson, Woods
Left: Savage, Danson Top: Woods, Seales,
Lee Weaver
© AVCO Embassy

David Huffman, Pat Corley, Franklyn Seales
Above: Woods, Seales Top: John Savage
Below: Beege Barkett, Seales

John Savage, Diane Hull Above: Franklyn
Seales, James Woods (also top)

METEOR

(AMERICAN INTERNATIONAL) Producers, Arnold Orgolini, Theodore Parvin; Director, Ronald Neame; Screenplay, Stanley Mann, Edmund H. North; Designer, Edward Carfagno; Assistant Director, Danny McCauley; Photography, Paul Lohmann; Art Director, David Constable; Editor, Carl Kress; Costumes, Albert Wolsky; In Panavision and color; Rated PG; 103 minutes; October release.

CAST

Bradley	Sean Connery
Tatiana	Natalie Wood
Dubov	Brian Keith
Sherwood	Karl Malden
Adlon	Martin Landau
Hunter	Roger Robinson
Manheim	Bo Brundin
Alan	James Richardson
Jan	Katherine DeHetre
Easton	Joe Campanella
Mason	Michael Zaslow
Watson	John McKinney
President	Henry Fonda
Secretary of Defense	Richard Dysart
Tom Easton	John Findlater
Bill Frager	Paul Tulley
Michael McKendrick	Allen Williams
Russian Premier	Gregory Gay
Hawk-Faced Party Member	Zitto Kazann
Mrs. Bradley	Bibi Besch
Sir Michael Hughes	Trevor Howard
Yamashiro	Clyde Kusatsu
Coast Guard Officer	Burke Byrnes

Left: Karl Malden Top: Natalie Wood
© **American International Pictures**

Natalie Wood

Henry Fonda

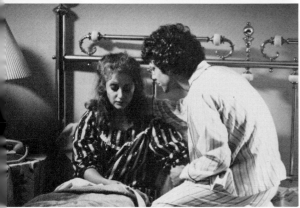

WHEN A STRANGER CALLS

(COLUMBIA) Producers, Doug Chapin, Steve Feke; Director, Fred Walton; Screenplay, Steve Feke, Fred Walton; Executive Producers, Melvin Simon, Barry Krost; Photography, Don Peterman; Music, Dana Kaproff; Designer, Elayne Barbara Ceder; Editor, Sam Vitale; Associate Producer, Larry Kostroff; Assistant Directors, Ed Ledding, Lynn Morgan; In color; Rated R; 97 minutes; October release.

CAST

Jill Johnson	Carol Kane
Mrs. Mandrakis	Rutanya Alda
Dr. Mandrakis	Carmen Argenziano
Nancy	Kirsten Larkin
Sgt. Sacker	Bill Boyett
John Clifford	Charles Durning
Lieutenant Charlie Garber	Ron O'Neal
Houseboy	Heetu
Dr. Monk	Rachel Roberts
Curt Duncan	Tony Beckley
Tracy	Colleen Dewhurst
Bill	Michael Champion
Bartender	Joe Reale
Retired Man	Ed Wright
Retired Woman	Louise Wright
Mrs. Garber	Carol O'Neal
Maintenance Man	Dennis McMullen
Cheater	Wally Taylor
Bar Customer	John Tobyansen
Bianca Lockart	Sarah Dammann
Stevie Lockart	Richard Bail
Stephen Lockart	Steven Anderson
Sharon	Lenora May
Maître d'	Randy Holland
Policemen	Trent Dolan, Frank DiElsi, Arell Blanton, DeForest Covan, Charles Boswell

Top: Carmen Argenziano, Rutanya Alda, Carol Kane
Below: Carol Kane, Steven Anderson Right: Kane
Top: Charles Durning
© Columbia Pictures Industries

Carol Kane

"10"

(ORION) Producers, Blake Edwards, Tony Adams; Direction and Screenplay, Blake Edwards; Music, Henry Mancini; Lyrics, Carol Bayer Sager, Robert Wells; Photography, Frank Stanley; Editor, Ralph E. Winters; Designer, Rodger Maus; Assistant Directors, Mickey McCardle, Nick Marck, Karen Murray; Costumes, Pat Edwards; In Panavision and Metrocolor; Rated R; 120 minutes; October release.

CAST

George	Dudley Moore
Sam	Julie Andrews
Jenny	Bo Derek
Hugh	Robert Webber
Mary Lewis	Dee Wallace
David	Sam Jones
Bartender	Brian Dennehy
Reverend	Max Showalter
Josh	Rad Daly
Mrs. Kissel	Nedra Volz
Fred Miles	James Noble
Ethel Miles	Virginia Kiser
Covington	John Hawker
Dental Assistant	Deborah Rush
Neighbor	Don Calfa
Larry	Walter George Alton
Redhead	Annette Martin
Dr. Croce	John Hancock
TV Director	Lorry Goldman
Pharmacist	Arthur Rosenberg
Waitress	Mari Gorman

and Marcy Hanson, Senilo Tanney, Kitty DeCarlo, Bill Lucking, Owen Sullivan, Debbie White, Laurence Carr, Camila Ashland, Burke Byrnes, Doug Sheehan, J. Victor Lopez, Jon Linton, John Chappell, Art Kassul

Top: Julie Andrews, Dudley Moore, Bo Derek
© Orion Pictures Co.

Dudley Moore, Julie Andrews

THE BLACK STALLION

(UNITED ARTISTS) Producers, Tom Sternberg, Fred Roos; Director, Carroll Ballard; Executive Producer, Francis Coppola; Screenplay, Melissa Mathison, Jeanne Rosenberg, William D. Wittliff; Based on novel by Walter Farley; Photography, Caleg Deschanel; Editor, Robert Dalva; Music, Carmine Coppola; Art Directors, Aurelio Crugnola, Earl Preston; Assistant Director, Doug Claybourne; In Dolby Stereo and Technicolor; Rated G; 118 minutes; October release.

CAST

Alec Ramsey	Kelly Reno
Henry Dailey	Mickey Rooney
Alec's mother	Teri Garr
Snoe	Clarence Muse
Alex's father	Hoyt Axton
Neville	Michael Higgins
Jake	Ed McNamara
Arab	Dogmi Larbi
Jockeys	John Burton, John Buchanan
Becky	Kristen Vigard
Rescue Captain	Fausto Tozzi

Left: Kelly Reno, Mickey Rooney
Below: Kelly Reno
© United Artists Corp.

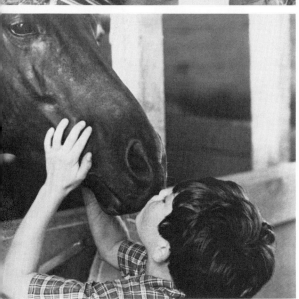

Teri Garr, Kelly Reno,
Mickey Rooney, Clarence Muse

Kelly Reno

AVALANCHE EXPRESS

(20th CENTURY-FOX) Producer-Director, Mark Robson; Screenplay, Abraham Polonsky; Based on novel by Colin Forbes; Photography, Jack Cardiff; Editor, Garth Craven; Designer, Fred Tuch; Costumes, Mickey Shirard; Associate Producer, Lynn Guthrie; Music, Allyn Ferguson; Assistant Director, Wieland Liebske; A Lorimar production in Panavision and color; Rated PG; 88 minutes; October Release.

CAST

Marenkov	Robert Shaw
Wargrave	Lee Marvin
Elsa Lang	Linda Evans
Bunin	Maximilian Schell
Haller	Mike Connors
Leroy	Joe Namath
Scholten	Horst Buchholz
Geiger	David Hess
Neckermann	Arthur Brauss
Helga Mann	Kristine Nel
Olga	Sylva Langover

Right: Linda Evans, Lee Marvin, Mike Connors
Below: Joe Namath
© 20th Century-Fox Film Corp.

Lee Marvin, Robert Shaw, Horst Buchholz
Above: Robert Shaw, Claudio Casinelli

Lee Marvin, Robert Shaw, Mike Connors

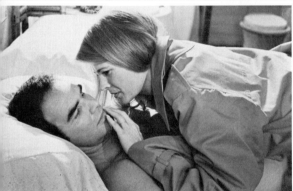

STARTING OVER

(PARAMOUNT) Producers, Alan J. Pakula, James L. Brooks; Director, Alan J. Pakula; Screenplay, James L. Brooks; Based on novel by Dan Wakefield; Photography, Sven Nykvist; Designer, George Jenkins; Editor, Marion Rothman; Costumes, John Boxer; Music, Marvin Hamlisch; Associate Producers, Isabel M. Halliburton, Douglas Z. Wick; Assistant Directors, Alex Hapsas, Herb Gains; In Movielab Color; Rated R; 106 minutes; October release.

CAST

Phil Potter	Burt Reynolds
Marilyn Homberg	Jill Clayburgh
Jessica Potter	Candice Bergen
Michael "Mickey" Potter	Charles Durning
Marva Potter	Frances Sternhagen
Paul	Austin Pendleton
Marie	Mary Kay Place
Dan Ryan	MacIntyre Dixon
Larry	Jay Sanders
Salesman	Charles Kimbrough
Everett	Richard Whiting
Workshop Members	Alvie Wise, Wallace Shawn
John Morganson	Sturgis Warner
Students	Mary C. Wright, Daniel Stern, George Hirsch
Doorman	Ian Martin
Lord & Taylor Lady	Aerin Asher
Victor	Ben Pesner
Room Service Waiter	Mort Marshall
Stephanie	Gilmer McCormick
Older Woman	Helen Stenborg

and Michael Kaufman, Marvin Lichterman, Anne De Salvo, Connie Fleming, Alison Stevens, Michael McDermott, Russell Horton, Harold Lamson, Michael Belleran, Deborah Reagan, Kevin Bacon, Tara King, A. C. Weary, Cass Self, Lisa Sloan, Gabby Glatzer, Ed Murphy, Harriet Rawlings, Simon McQueen, Stacy Holiday, Nadine Darling, Kitty Muldoon, John Murray, Eric Geiger, Sol Schwade, Trudy Clemens, Anthony Romano

Top: Candice Bergen (also left), Burt Reynolds
Left Center: Candice Bergen, Burt Reynolds
©Paramount Pictures

Jill Clayburgh, Candice Bergen

Jill Clayburgh, Burt Reynolds
Top: Burt Reynolds

Jill Clayburgh, Burt Reynolds
Top: Jill Clayburgh

THE FISH THAT SAVED PITTSBURGH

(UNITED ARTISTS) Producers, Gary Stromberg, David Dashev; Director, Gilbert Moses; Screenplay, Jaison Starkes, Edmond Stevens; Story, Gary Stromberg, David Dashev; Associate Producer, David Salven; Music, Thom Bell; Photography, Frank Stanley; Editors, Frank Mazolla, Arthur Schmidt, Bud Friedgen, Jr.; Art Director, Herbert Spencer Deverill; Choreographer, Debra Allen; Assistant Directors, Jerry Grandey, Gene Deruelle, Buddy Nadler, Beau Markes; Costumes, Patricia Norris; In Technicolor and Dolby Stereo; Rated PG; 104 minutes; November release.

CAST

Moses Guthrie	Julius Erving
H. S. and Halsey Tilson	Jonathan Winters
Rev. Grady Jackson	Meadowlark Lemon
Setshot	Jack Kehoe
Himself	Kareem Abdul-Jabbar
Toby Millman	Margaret Avery
Tyrone Millman	James Bond III
"Harry the Trainer"	Michael V. Gazzo
"Driftwood"	Peter Isacksen
George Brockington	Nicholas Pryor
Wally Cantrell	M. Emmet Walsh
Mona Mondieu	Stockard Channing
Coach "Jock" Delaney	Flip Wilson
Himself	Marvin Albert
P. A. Announcer	George Von Benko
Ola	Debra Allen
Man ordering	Damian Austin
Himself	Alfred Beard, Jr.
Brandy	Dee Dee Bridgewater
Michelle	Alix Elias

and The Spinners and The Sylvers

Top Right: James Bond III, Stockard Channing
© United Artists Corp.

Julius Erving, James Bond III
Above: Jonathan Winters

Margaret Avery, Julius Erving
Above: Dee Dee Bridgewater, Debbie Allen

THE RUNNER STUMBLES

(20th CENTURY-FOX) Producer-Director, Stanley Kramer; Screenplay, Milan Stitt, from his play of same title; Executive Producer, Melvin Simon; Photography, Laszlo Kovacs; Music, Ernest Gold; Associate Producer, Mario Iscovich; Designer, Alfred Sweeney, Jr.; Editor, Pembroke J. Herring; Assistant Directors, Craig Huston, Nick Marck; In color; 109 minutes; November release.

CAST

Father Rivard	Dick Van Dyke
Sister Rita	Kathleen Quinlan
Mrs. Shandig	Maureen Stapleton
Monsignor Nicholson	Ray Bolger
Erna	Tammy Grimes
Toby	Beau Bridges
Prosecutor	Allen Nause
Amos	John Procaccino
James	Billy J. Jacoby
Sister Immaculata	Sister Marguerite Morrissey
Sister Martha	Zoaunne LeRoy
Maurice	Don Riley
Sheriff	Ted D'Arms
Louise	Kendall Kay Munsey
Marie	Casey Kramer
Matt Webber	Jim Doyle
Sophie	Katharine Kramer
Judge	Bill Dore
Dr. McNabb	Jock Dove
Fire Chief	Larry Buck

Right: Kathleen Quinlan, Dick Van Dyke, and
Top with Maureen Stapleton
© 20th Century-Fox Film Corp.

Dick Van Dyke, Beau Bridges
Above: Kathleen Quinlan, Tammy Grimes, Van Dyke

Dick Van Dyke, Kathleen Quinlan

NATURAL ENEMIES

(CINEMA 5) Producer, John E. Quill; Associate Producers, Harry Daley, Robert Burke; Directed, Written, and Edited by Jeff Kanew; Based on novel by Julius Horwitz; Music, Don Ellia; Photography, Richard E. Brooks; Art Director, Hank Aldrich; Costumes, Peggy Farrell; Assistant Director, Sol Fol; In TVC Color; Rated R; 100 minutes; November release.

CAST

Paul Steward	Hal Holbrook
Miriam Steward	Louise Fletcher
Tony Steward	Peter Armstrong
Sheila Steward	Beth Berridge
Alex Steward	Steve Austin
Man on Train	Jim Pappas
Secretary	Ellen Barber
Astronaut	John Bartholemew
Doctor	Charles Randall
Harry Rosenthal	Jose Ferrer
The Madam	Lisa Carroll
Dr. Baker	Viveca Lindfors
Cab Driver	Frank Bongiorno
Conductor	Harry Daley
Woman on Train	Patricia Elliott
Newscaster	Robert Perry
Girls in Brothel	June Berry, Alisha Fontaine, Pat Mauceri, Michele O'Brien, Claire Reilly

**Left: Louise Fletcher
Top: Hal Holbrook
© Cinema 5**

Jose Ferrer

Viveca Lindfors

PROMISES IN THE DARK

(ORION) Producer-Director, Jerome Hellman; Executive Producer, Sheldon Schrager; Screenplay, Loring Mandel; Associate Producer, Gail Mutrux; Music, Leonard Rosenman; Photography, Adam Holender; Editor, Bob Wyman; Costumes, Ann Roth; Designer, Walter Scott Herndon; Assistant Directors, Kim Kurumada, Albert Shapiro; In Metrocolor; Rated PG; 115 minutes; November release.

CAST

Dr. Alexandra Kenda	Marsha Mason
Bud Koenig	Ned Beatty
Fran Koenig	Susan Clark
Dr. Jim Sandman	Michael Brandon
Buffy Koenig	Kathleen Beller
Gerry Hulin	Paul Clemens
Dr. Walter McInerny	Donald Moffat
Dr. Frucht	Philip Sterling
Nurse Farber	Bonnie Bartlett
Dr. Blankenship	James Noble
Emergency Room Doctor	Arthur Rosenberg
Mrs. Pritkin	Peggy McCay
Alan	Robert Doran
Sue	Lenora May
Ellie	Alexandra Johnson
Emergency Room Nurse	Fran Bennett
Woman in Restaurant	Eloise Hardt
Tony in Bud's Office	Bernie Kuby
Secretary in Bud's Office	Karen Anders
Mrs. Gans	Edith Fields
Mrs. Kepos	Alice Beardsley

and Frank Robinson, Lidia Kristen, M. E. Lorange, Lynn Farrell, Kim Fowler, Janet Taylor, Jack Anderson, Henry D. Fetter, Dayson Decourcy, Teryn Jenkins, Paul Van, Ellen Shaw

Top: Marsha Mason, Kathleen Beller
Right Center: Paul Clemens, Kathleen Beller
© Orion Pictures Co.

Ned Beatty, Kathleen Beller, Susan Clark

85

Bette Midler

THE ROSE

(20th CENTURY-FOX) Producers, Marvin Worth, Aaron Russo; Director, Mark Rydell; Screenplay, Bill Kerby, Bo Goldman; Story, Bill Kerby; Photography, Vilmos Zsigmond; Designer, Richard MacDonald; Executive Producer, Tony Ray; Music, Paul A. Rothchild; Title Song, Amanda McBroom; Costumes, Theoni V. Aldredge; Editor, Robert L. Wolfe; Assistant Directors, Larry Franco, Chris Soldo; Choreographer, Toni Basil; Art Director, Jim Schoppe; In DeLuxe Color and Dolby Stereo; Rated R; 134 minutes, November release.

CAST

Rose	Bette Midler
Rudge	Alan Bates
Dyer	Frederic Forrest
Billy Ray	Harry Dean Stanton
Dennis	Barry Primus
Mal	David Keith
Sarah	Sandra McCabe
Mr. Leonard	Will Hare
Monty	Rudy Bond
Don Frank	Don Calfa
Dealer	James Keane
Rose's Mother	Doris Roberts
Rose's Father	Sandy Ward
Emcee	Michael Greer
Female Impersonators	Claude Sacha, Michael St. Laurent, Sylvester, Pearl Heart
Waiter	Butch Ellis
Trucker	Richard Dioguardi
Milledge	John Dennis Johnston
TV Promoter	Jonathan Banks
Short Order Cook	Jack O'Leary

and Luke Andreas, Harry Northup, Cherie Latimer, Seamon Glass, Pat Corley, Dennis Erdman, Hugh Gillin, Joyce Roth, Frank Speiser, Constance Cawlfield, Annie McGuire, Hildy Brooks, Jack Starrett, David Garfield, Jack Hollander, Sandra Seacat, Chip Zien

**Top: Bette Midler, Frederic Forrest
Below: Bette Midler Top Left: Alan
Bates, Bette Midler Below, Midler**
© 20th Century-Fox Film Corp.

86

THE GREAT SANTINI

(WARNER BROS.) An Orion Picture; Producers, Charles A. Pratt, Bing Crosby Productions; Direction and Screenplay, Lewis John Carlino; Based on novel by Pat Conroy; Photography, Ralph Woolsey; Editor, Houseley Stevenson; Design, Jack Poplin; Assistant Director, Edward Markley; Music, Elmer Bernstein; In color; Rated PG; 115 minutes; November release.

CAST

Bull Meechum	Robert Duvall
Lillian Meechum	Blythe Danner
Ben Meechum	Michael O'Keefe
Mary Anne Meechum	Lisa Jane Persky
Karen Meechum	Julie Anne Haddock
Matthew Meechum	Brian Andrews
Toomer Smalls	Stan Shaw
Red Pettus	Theresa Merritt
Colonel Hedgepath	Paul Mantee

Right: Michael O'Keefe, Robert Duvall
© Orion Pictures Co.

Blythe Danner, Robert Duvall

1941

(UNIVERSAL/COLUMBIA) Producer, Buzz Feitshans; Director, Steven Spielberg; Screenplay, Robert Zemeckis, Bob Gale; Story, Robert Zemeckis, Bob Gale, John Milius; Executive Producer, John Milius; Photography, William A. Fraker; Designer, Dean Edward Mitzner; Editor, Michael Kahn; Music, John Williams; Associate Producers, Michael Kahn, Janet Healy; Assistant Directors, Jerry Ziesmer, Steve Perry, Chris Soldo; Costumes, Deborah Nadoolman; Art Director, William F. O'-Brien; Choreography, Paul DeRolf, Judy Van Wormer; An A-Team production in Panavision and Metrocolor; Rated PG; 120 minutes; December release.

CAST

Sergeant Tree	Dan Aykroyd
Ward Douglas	Ned Beatty
Wild Bell Kelso	John Belushi
Joan Douglas	Lorraine Gary
Claude	Murray Hamilton
Von Kleinschmidt	Christopher Lee
Birkhead	Tim Matheson
Commander Mitamura	Toshiro Mifune
Maddox	Warren Oates
General Stilwell	Robert Stack
Sitarski	Treat Williams
Donna	Nancy Allen
Gas Mama	Lucille Bensen
Macey	Jordan Brian
Foley	John Candy
Patron	Elisha Cook
Lydia Hedberg	Patti LuPone
Miss Fitzroy	Penny Marshall
Hollis Wood	Slim Pickens
Scioli	Lionel Stander
Malcomb	Dub Taylor

Left: Patti LuPone, Penny Marshall, Marjorie Gaines, Trish Garland, Joseph P. Flaherty, Iggie Wolfington Above: Robert Stack Top: Treat Williams, Bobby DiCicco © Universal City Studios

Dan Aykroyd (C)

Marjorie Gaines, Carol Culver, Trish Garland

BEING THERE

(UNITED ARTISTS) Producer, Andrew Braunsberg; Director, Hal Ashby; Screenplay, Jerzy Kosinski, from his novel; Photography, Caleb Deschanel; Designer, Michael Haller; Costumes, May Routh; Executive Producer, Jack Schwartzman; Associate Producer, Charles Mulvehill; Music, John Mandel; Editor, Don Zimmerman; Assistant Directors, David S. Hamburger, Toby Lovallo; Art Director, James Schoppe; In Metrocolor; A North Star International picture; Rated PG; 130 minutes; December release.

CAST

Chance	Peter Sellers
Eve Rand	Shirley MacLaine
Benjamin Rand	Melvyn Douglas
President "Bobby"	Jack Warden
Dr. Robert Allenby	Richard Dysart
Vladimir Skrapinov	Richard Basehart
Louise	Ruth Attaway
Thomas Franklin	Dave Clennon
Sally Hayes	Fran Brill
Johanna Franklin	Denise DuBarry
Lolo (boy on corner)	Oteil Burbridge
Abbaz (kid with knife)	Ravenell Keller III
Policeman by White House	Brian Corrigan
Old Woman Asked for Lunch	Alfredine Brown
David	Donald Jacob
Jeffery	Ernest M. McClure
Perkins	Kenneth Patterson
Wilson	Richard Venture
Arthur	Arthur Grundy
Lewis	W. C. "Mutt" Burton
X-ray Technician	Henry B. Dawkins
Rand's Secretary	Georgine Hall
Nurse Constance	Nell P. Leaman
Nurse Teresa	Villa Mae Barkley
First Lady	Alice Hirson
Presidential Adviser	James Noble

1979 Academy Award for Best Supporting Actor
(Melvyn Douglas)

Top: Jack Warden, Melvyn Douglas Right: Fran Brill, David Clennon, Peter Sellers Below: Shirley MacLaine, Melvyn Douglas
© United Artists Corp.

Peter Sellers

STAR TREK
The Motion Picture

(PARAMOUNT) Producer, Gene Roddenberry; Director, Robert Wise; Screenplay, Harold Livingston; Story, Alan Dean Foster; Music, Jerry Goldsmith; Based on "Star Trek," created by Gene Roddenberry; Photography, Richard H. Kline; Designer, Harold Michelson; Editor, Todd Ramsay; Associate Producer, Jon Povill; In Panavision, Dolby Stereo, and Metrocolor; Rated G; 132 minutes; December release.

CAST

Captain Kirk	William Shatner
Spock	Leonard Nimoy
Dr. McCoy	DeForest Kelley
Scotty	James Doohan
Sulu	George Takei
Dr. Chapel	Majel Barrett
Chekov	Walter Koenig
Uhura	Nichelle Nichols
Ilia	Persis Khambatta
Decker	Stephen Collins
Klingon Captain	Mark Lenard
Alien Boy	Billy Van Zandt
Janice Rand	Grace Lee Whitney
Epsilon Technician	Roger Aaron Brown
Airlock Technician	Gary Faga
Commander Branch	David Gautreaux
Assistant to Rand	John D. Gowans
Cargo Deck Ensign	Howard Itzkowitz
Lieutenant Commander Sonak	Jon Rashad Kamal
Chief DiFalco	Marcy Lafferty
Technician	Jeri McBride
Lieutenant	Michele Ameen Billy
Chief Ross	Terrence O'Connor
Lieutenant Cleary	Michael Rougas

William Shatner

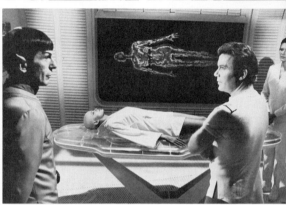

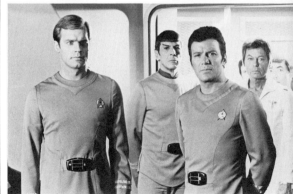

Leonard Nimoy Above: Persis Khambatta, Stephen Collins, William Shatner

Stephen Collins, Leonard Nimoy William Shatner, DeForest Kelley

91

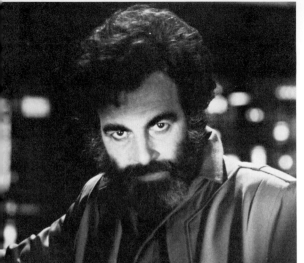

THE BLACK HOLE

(BUENA VISTA) Producer, Ron Miller; Director, Gary Nelson; Screenplay, Jeb Rosebrook, Gerry Day; Story, Jeb Rosebrook, Bob Barbash, Richard Landau; Photography, Frank Phillips; Music, John Barry; Designer, Peter Ellenshaw; Art Directors, John B. Mansbridge, Al Roelofs, Robert T. McCall; Editor, Gregg McLaughlin; Costumes, Bill Thomas; Assistant Directors, Tom McCrory, Christopher Miller, Joseph P. Moore; A Walt Disney Production in Technovision, Dolby Stereo, and Technicolor; Rated PG; 97 minutes; December release.

CAST

Dr. Hans Reinhardt	Maximilian Schell
Dr. Alex Durant	Anthony Perkins
Captain Dan Holland	Robert Forster
Lieutenant Charles Pizer	Joseph Bottoms
Dr. Kate McCrae	Yvette Mimieux
Harry Booth	Ernest Borgnine
Captain S.T.A.R.	Tommy McLoughlin

Left: Maximilian Schell
© Walt Disney Productions

Ernest Borgnine, Anthony Perkins, Yvette Mimieux, Robert Forster

Joseph Bottoms
Above: Ernest Borgnine

THE JERK

(UNIVERSAL) Producers, David V. Picker, William E. McEuen; Director, Carl Reiner; Screenplay, Steve Martin, Carl Gottlieb, Michael Elias; Story, Steve Martin, Carl Gottlieb; Photography, Victor J. Kemper; Designer, Jack T. Collis; Editor, Bud Molin; Associate Producer, Peter MacGregor-Scott; Costumes, Theadora Van Runkle; Music, Jack Elliott; Assistant Directors, Newton Arnold, Ed Milkovich; In color; Rated R; 104 minutes; December release.

CAST

Navin	Steve Martin
Marie	Bernadette Peters
Patty Bernstein	Catlin Adams
Mother	Mabel King
Father	Richard Ward
Taj	Dick Anthony Williams
Carl Reiner	Himself
Stan Fox	Bill Macy
Madman	M. Emmet Walsh
Frosty	Dick O'Neill
Hobart	Maurice Evans
Hester	Helena Carroll
Elvira	Ren Wood
Punk #1	Pepe Serna
Blues Singers	Sonny Terry, Brownie McGee
Harry Hartounian	Jackie Mason
Bank Manager	David Landsberg
Father De Cordoba	Domingo Ambriz
Con Men	Richard Foronjy, Lenny Montana
Iron Balls McGinty	Carl Gottlieb
Announcer	Clete Roberts

Top: Steve Martin (C) Below: Bernadette Peters, Steve Martin Right: Martin, Sharon Johansen, Jackie Mason Top: Catlin Adams, Martin
© Universal City Studios Inc.

Bernadette Peters, Steve Martin, and above with Jerry G. Velasco

93

Roy Scheider, Leland Palmer

ALL THAT JAZZ

(COLUMBIA/20th CENTURY-FOX) Executive Producer, Daniel Melnick; Producer, Robert Alan Aurthur; Director, Bob Fosse; Associate Producers, Kenneth Utt, Wolfgang Gattes; Photography, Giuseppe Rotunno; Editor, Alan Heim; Designer, Philip Rosenberg; Costumes, Tony Walton; Choreography, Bob Fosse; Assistant Directors, Wolfgang Gattes, Joseph Ray; In Technicolor; Rated R; 123 minutes; December release.

CAST

Joe Gideon	Roy Scheider
Angelique	Jessica Lange
Kate Jagger	Ann Reinking
Audrey Paris	Leland Palmer
Davis Newman	Cliff Gorman
O'Connor Flood	Ben Vereen
Michelle	Erzsebet Foldi
Dr. Ballinger	Michael Tolan
Joshua Penn	Max Wright
Jonesy Hecht	William LeMassena
Leslie Perry	Chris Chase
Victoria	Deborah Geffner
Kathryn	Kathryn Doby
Paul Dann	Anthony Holland
Ted Christopher	Robert Hitt
Larry Goldie	David Margulies
Stacy	Sue Paul
Young Joe	Keith Gordon
Comic	Frankie Man
Eddie	Alan Heim
Lucas Sergeant	John Lithgow
Mother	Sloane Shelton
Dr. Garry	Ben Masters

1979 Academy Awards for Best Film Editing, Best Art Direction, Best Costume Design, Best Adaptation Score

Top: Roy Scheider, Jessica Lange
Below: Erzsebet Foldi, Scheider
Top Left: Roy Scheider Below: Sandahl Bergman
© 20th Century-Fox Film Corp.

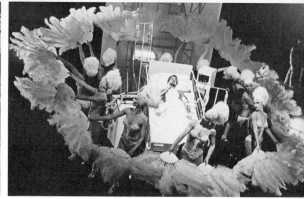

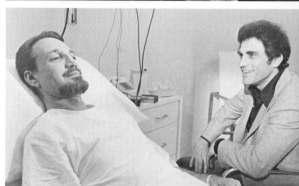

**Roy Scheider, Ann Reinking Above: Reinking,
Erzsebet Foldi Top: Ben Vereen, Scheider
Below: Scheider, Deborah Geffner**

**Roy Scheider, Jessica Lange
Above: Scheider, Cliff Gorman**

GOING IN STYLE

(WARNER BROS.) Producers, Tony Bill, Fred T. Gallo; Direction and Screenplay, Martin Brest; Executive Producer, Leonard Gaines; Story, Edward Cannon: Music, Michael Small; Costumes, Anna Hill Johnstone; Editors, Robert Swink, C. Timothy O'Meara; Designer, Stephen Hendrickson; Art Director, Gary Weist; Photography, Billy Williams; Assistant Directors, Mike Rauch, Bill Eustace; In Technicolor; Rated PG; 97 minutes; December release.

CAST

Joe	George Burns
Al	Art Carney
Willie	Lee Strasberg
Pete	Charles Hallahan
Kathy	Pamela Payton-Wright
Colleen	Siobhan Keegan
Kevin	Brian Neville
Boy in Park	Constantine Hartofolis
Teller	Mary Testa
Mrs. Fein	Jean Shevlin
Hot Dog Vendor	James Manis
Store Cashier	Margot Stevenson
Gypsy Cab Driver	Tito Goya
Bank Guard	William Pabst
Bank Manager	Christopher Wynkoop
Moon	Joseph Sullivan
Cab Driver	Bob Maroff
Bellhop	Vivian Edwards
Waitress	Barbara Ann Miller
Cashiers	Catherine Billich, Betty Bunch
FBI Agents	Anthony D. Call, William Larson, Reathal Bean, Alan Brooks

Right: George Burns, Art Carney, Lee Strasberg
(also above, and below with William Pabst)
© Warner Bros.

George Burns, Art Carney, Lee Strasberg

Art Carney, George Burns

Bo Derek
Top: Robert Webber, Dudley Moore

Dudley Moore, Bo Derek

CUBA

(UNITED ARTISTS) Producers, Arlene Sellers, Alex Winitsky; Director, Richard Lester; Executive Producer, Denis O'Dell; Screenplay, Charles Wood; Music, Patrick Williams; Photography, David Watkin; Assistant Directors, David Tringham, Roberto Parra, Steve Lanning, Javier Carrasco; Designer, Shirley Russell; Editor, John Victor Smith; Costumes, Shirley Russell; Designer, Gil Parrondo; Art Director, Denis Gordon Orr; In Technicolor; Rated R; 122 minutes; December release.

CAST

Robert Dapes	Sean Connery
Alexandra Pulido	Brooke Adams
Gutman	Jack Weston
Ramirez	Hector Elizondo
Skinner	Denholm Elliott
General Bello	Martin Balsam
Juan Pulido	Chris Sarandon
Faustino	Alejandro Rey
Therese	Lonette McKee
Julio	Danny De La Paz
Miss Wonderly	Louisa Moritz
Press Agent	Dave King
Don Pulido	Walter Gotell
Colonel Rosell Y Leyva	Earl Cameron
Dolores	Pauline Peart
Maria	Anna Nicholas
Jesus	David Rappaport
Carillo	Tony Matthews
Cecilia	Leticia Garrado
Gary	John Morton
Spencer	Anthony Pullen Shaw
Ramon	Stefan Kalipha

Right: Pauline Peart, Jack Weston, Chris
Sarandon, Brooke Adams Top: Sean Connery,
Hector Elizondo
© United Artists Corp.

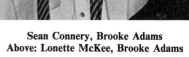

Danny De La Paz, Brooke Adams
Above: Martin Balsam, Sean Connery

Sean Connery, Brooke Adams
Above: Lonette McKee, Brooke Adams

97

Robert Redford

THE ELECTRIC HORSEMAN

(COLUMBIA/UNIVERSAL) Producer, Ray Stark; Director, Sydney Pollack; Screenplay, Robert Garland; Story, Paul Gaer, Robert Garland, Shelly Burton; Photography, Owen Roizman; Designer, Stephen Grimes; Editor, Sheldon Kahn; Music, Dave Gusin; Songs sung by Willie Nelson; Associate Producer, Ronald L. Schwary; Assistant Directors, M. Michael Moore, Bart Roe; Art Director, J. Dennis Washington; Choreography, Bernardine Kent; Costumes, Bernie Pollack; In Panavision and Technicolor; Rated PG; 121 minutes; December release.

CAST

Sonny	Robert Redford
Hallie	Jane Fonda
Charlotta	Valerie Perrine
Wendell	Willie Nelson
Hunt Sears	John Saxon
Fitzgerald	Nicolas Coster
Danny	Allan Arbus
Farmer	Wilford Brimley
Gus	Will Hare
Toland	Basil Hoffman
Leroy	Timothy Scott
Dietrich	James B. Sikking
Tommy	James Kline
Bernie	Frank Speiser
Bud Broderick	Quinn Redeker
Joanna Camden	Lois Areno
Lucinda	Sarah Harris
Louise	Tasha Zemrus
Dennis	James Novak

Top: Timothy Scott, Robert Redford Below:Scott,
Redford, Willie Nelson Left: Robert Redford
© Columbia Pictures Industries

Robert Redford, Jane Fonda
Top: Jane Fonda

Jane Fonda, Robert Redford

CHAPTER TWO

(COLUMBIA) Producer, Ray Stark; Director, Robert Moore; Screenplay, Neil Simon; Photography, David M. Walsh; Executive Producer, Roger M. Rothstein; Designer, Gene Callahan; Music, Marvin Hamlisch; Lyrics, Carole Bayer Sager; Associate Producer–Editor, Margaret Booth; Editor, Michael A. Stevenson; Assistant Directors, Jack Roe, John Kretchmer; Costumes, Vicki Sanchez; Art Director, Pete Smith; In Metrocolor; Rated PG; 124 minutes; December release.

CAST

George Schneider	James Caan
Jennie MacLaine	Marsha Mason
Leo Schneider	Joseph Bologna
Faye Medwick	Valerie Harper
Lee Michaels	Alan Fudge
Gwen Michaels	Judy Farrell
Marilyn	Debra Mooney
Customs Officer	Isabel Cooley
Elderly lady	Imogene Bliss
Maître d'	Barry Michlin
Gary	Ray Young
Martin	George Rondo
Electric Girl	Cheryl Bianchi
Waiters	Greg Zadikov, Paul Singh, Sumant
Actress	Elizabeth Farley
Tina	Sunday Brennan
Bucky	Danny Gellis
Judge	Henry Sutton
Umpire	E.D. Miller
Director	Howard Jeffrey
Barbara	Marie Reynolds

Right: Marsha Mason, Valerie Harper
© Columbia Pictures Industries

Debra Mooney, Marsha Mason, Valerie Harper, James Caan, Joseph Bologna

James Caan, Joseph Bologna
Above: Marsha Mason, James Caan

James Caan, Marsha Mason

THE YOUNG CYCLE GIRLS (Peter Perry) Executive Producer, Sue Perry; Producer-Director, Peter Perry; Screenplay, John Arnoldy; Photography, Ron Garcia; Editor, Marco Perri; In color; Rated R; 80 minutes; January release. CAST: Loraine Ferris, Daphne Lawrence, Deborah Marcus, Lonnie Pense, Kevin O'Neill, Bee Lechat, Billy Bullet

NO LONGER ALONE (World Wide) Producer, Frank R. Jacobson; Executive Producer, William F. Brown; Director, Nicholas Webster; Screenplay, Lawrence Hilben; Based on autobiography by Joan Winmill Brown; Photography, Michael Reed; Editor, J. Michael Hooser; Design, John Lageu; Costumes, Klara Kerpin; Music, Tedd Smith; Assistant Director, Ed Harper; In color; Rated PG; 99 minutes: January release. CAST: Belinda Carroll (Joan), Roland Culver (A. E. Matthews), James Fox (Alan), Wilfrid Hyde-White (Lord Hume), Simon Williams (William Douglas Home), Helen Cherry (Miss Godfrey), Samantha Gates (Joan at 12), Karen Dines (Joan at 6), Gordon Devol (Robert Kennedy), Robert Rietty (Joan's father), Vivienne Burgess (Grandmother)

THE LATE GREAT PLANET EARTH (Pacific International) Producers, Robert Amram, Alan Belkin; Executive Producer, Michael F. Leone; Associate Producer, Joy Shelton Davis; Direction and Screenplay, Robert Amram; Biblical sequences Written and Directed by Rolf Forsberg; Music, Dana Kaproff; Based on book by Hal Lindsey with C. C. Carlson; In CFI Color; Rated PG; 90 minutes; January release. CAST: Orson Welles

THE SWEET CREEK COUNTY WAR (Key International) Producers, Ken Byrnes, J. Frank James; Direction and Screenplay, J. Frank James; Executive Producers, Ray Cardi, Marie Cardi; Music, Richard Bowden; Photography, Gregory von Berblinger; Editor, Ronald Sinclair; In color; Rated PG; 99 minutes; January release. CAST: Richard Eagan (Judd), Albert Salmi (Breakworth), Nita Talbot (Alice), Slim Pickens (Jitters), Robert J. Wilke (Lucas), Joe Orton (Lyle), Ray Cardi (Rowdy), Tom Jackman (Virgil)

STAYING ALIVE (Mishkin) Producers, William Mishkin, Robert A. Endelson; Director, Robert A. Endelson; Screenplay, Straw Weisman; Photography, Lloyd Freidus; Music, Jeff Slavin; In color; 89 minutes; Rated R; January release. CAST: William Sanderson, Robert Judd, Catherine Peppers, Lela Small, Reginal Bythewood, Yvonne Ross, Daniel Faraldo, Peter Yoshida, Bonni Martin, William Cargill, Richard A. Rubin, David Dewlow, Ramon Saunders, Nick Mariano

BARRACUDA (Republic) Produced and Written by Wayne Crawford, Harry Kerwin; Director, Harry Kerwin; Presented by Manfred Menz; In color; Rated PG; January release. CAST: Wayne David Crawford, Jason Evers, Roberta Leighton, William Kerwin, Bert Freed, Cliff Emmich

SHE CAME TO THE VALLEY (R.G.V. Pictures) Producers, Albert Band, Frank Ray Perilli; Director, Albert Band; Screenplay, Frank Ray Perilli, Albert Band; Based on novel by Cleo Dawson; Music, Tommy Leonetti; Executive Producer, Robert S. Bremson; Associate Producers, W. T. Ellis, T. L. Duncan; Photography, Daniel Pearl; In color; Rated PG; January release. CAST: Ronee Blakley, Dean Stockwell, Scott Glenn, Freddy Fender

CRY TO THE WIND (Sebastian International) Produced and Written by Daiv James Nielsen; Direction and Photography, Robert W. Davison: Executive Producer, James Davis; Music, Merrill Jenson; Lyrics, Susan Evans McCloud, Jimmie Rogers; In color; Rated G; January release. CAST: Sheldon Woods (Ethan), Cameron Garnick (Wade)

BILLY IN THE LOWLANDS (Theatre Co. of Boston) Direction and Screenplay, Jan Egleson; Photography, D'Arcy Marsh; Music, The Nighthawks; Not rated; 88 minutes; January release. CAST: Henry Tomaszewski (Billy), Paul Benedict (His Father), David Morton (Joey), David Clennon (Social Worker), Ernie Lowe (Officer Duncan), Genevieve Reale (Liz), Bronia Wheeler (Mother), Robert Owczarek (Uncle)

A LOOK AT LIV (Win Kao Productions) Direction, Richard Kaplan; Screenplay, Jerry Winters, Richard Kaplan; Not rated; 67 minutes; January release. CAST: Liv Ullmann, Bibi Andersson, Ingmar Bergman, David Carradine, Peter Finch, Gene Hackman, Erland Josephson, Sven Nykvist, Janna Ullman, Linn Ullmann, Max von Sydow

Hector Troy, John Heard
in "On the Yard"

ON THE YARD (Midwest Films) Producer, Joan Micklin Silver; Director, Raphael D. Silver; Screenplay, Malcolm Braly from his novel of same title; Photography, Alan Metzer; Editor, Evan Lottman; Art Director, Leon Harris; Music, Charles Gross; Assistant Director-Associate Producer, Mike Haley: Costumes, Robert Harris; In Technicolor; Rated R; 102 minutes; January release. CAST: John Heard (Juleson), Thomas Waites (Chilly), Mike Kellin (Red), Richard Bright (Nunn), Joe Grifasi (Morris), Lane Smith (Blake), Richard Hayes (Stick), Hector Troy (Gasolino), Richard Jamieson (Carpenter), Thomas Toner (Warden), Ron Faber (Manning), David Clennon (Psychiatrist), Don Blakely (Tate), J. C. Quin (Luther), Dominic Chianese (Mendoza), Eddie Jones (Olson), Ben Slack (Clemmons), James Remar (Larson), Dave McCalley (Redmond), Ludwick Villani (Candy), John Taylor (Schulte), Ivan Yount (Inmate), Ralph Hobbs (Zeke), David Berman (Caterpillar), Joseph Mazurkiewicz, Lowell Manfall, Peg French (Parole Board), Ralph Basalla (Processor), Walter Sanders (Cool Breeze), Roland Jackson (Cadillac), Leon J. Cassady, Frank Conrad, Leroy Newsome (Bakery Workers), Robert Johnson (Mechanic), Fred Jones, James Johnson, George Gamble, John Demmitt (Therapy Session), John Kephart, Alan Gramley, Jan Chwiej (Prison Squad), John Berhosky (Bus Guard), William Carver (Night Guard), Morris Pratt (Office Guard)

CIRCLE OF IRON (AVCO Embassy) Producers, Sandy Howard, Paul Maslansky; Director, Richard Moore; Screenplay, Sterling Silliphant, Stanley Mann; Photography, Ronnie Taylor; Editor, Ernie Walter; In color; Rated R; 102 minutes; January release. CAST: David Carradine (Blind Man/Monkey Man/Rhythm Man/Death), Jeff Cooper (Cord), Roddy McDowall (White Robe), Eli Wallach (Man in Oil), Erica Creer (Tara), Christopher Lee (Zetan), Anthony De Longis (Morthand), Earl Maynard (Black Giant), Heinz Bernard (Gerryman), Zipora Peled (His Wife), Jeremy Kaplan (Monkeyboy), Kam Yuen (Red Band), Elizabeth Motzkin (Japanese Woman), Bobby Ne'eman (Thug Leader), Dov Friedman (Young Monk), Ronen Nabah (Beautiful Boy), Michal Nedivi (Boy's Mother), Nissim Zohar (Boy's Father)

Orsen Welles in "The Late
Great Planet Earth"

101

Richard Pryor
"Live in Concert"

Tom McKitterick, Marcelino Sanchez, Terry Michos,
Michael Beck, Deborah Van Valkenburgh, Brian Tyler
in "The Warriors" © Paramount Pictures

RICHARD PRYOR LIVE IN CONCERT (Special Event Entertainment) Executive Producer, Saul Barnett; Producers, Del Jack, J. Mark Travis; Director, Jeff Margolis; A Hillard Elkins-Steve Blauner production; Not rated; 78 minutes; January release. CAST: Richard Pryor

THE BERMUDA TRIANGLE (Schick Sunn Classics) Producers, Charles E. Sellier, Jr., James L. Conway; Director, Richard Friedenberg; Screenplay, Stephen Lord; Photography, Henning Schellerup; Editor, John Link; Art Director, Charles Bennett; Music, John Cameron; Assistant Directors, Jeff Richard, Sam Baldoni; In Dolby Stereo and color; Rated G; 93 minutes; January release. CAST: Donald Albee, Lin Berlitz, Howard W. Bishop, Jr., Larry Bisman, John Bohan, R. J. Bohner, Vince Davis, David C. Ellzey, Steve Farrell, Bobbie Faye Ferguson, Tony Frank, Ed Fry, John William Galt, Anne Galvan, Michael Glanfield, Albert Hall, Brian Herskowitz, Robert Hibbard, Leland Holmes, Joe Houde, Charles E. Houston, Ron Jackson, Harlan Jordan, Warren Kemmerling, Tommy Kendrick, Joel P. Kenney, Fritz Lieber, James Logan, Bob Magruder, Hedley Mattingly, Tom Matts, Harriet Medin, Paul Menzel, Richard M. Mills, Glenn Morshower, Warren A. Munson III, John Pochna, Thalmus Rasulala, Arthur Roberts, Roxie Roker, Clement St. George, Kimo Schulze, Oliver Seale, Jeremiah Todd, Vickery Turner, Michael Van Dalsem, Warren Vanders, Don Wiseman, Jim Wiggins

FIVE DAYS FROM HOME (Universal) Producer-Director, George Peppard; Executive Producer, Robert S. Bremson; Screenplay, William Moore; Photography, Harvey Genkins; Editor, Samuel E. Beetley; Music, Bill Conti; Lyrics, Norman Gimbel; In CFI Color; Rated PG; 108 minutes; January release. CAST: George Peppard (T. M. Pryor), Neville Brand (Markley), Sherry Boucher (Wanda), Victor Campos (Jose), Robert Donner (Baldwin), Ronnie Claire Edwards (Marian), Jessie Lee Fulton (Mrs. Peabody), William Larsen (J. J.), Robert Magruder (Colonel), Savannah Smith (Georgie), Don Wyse (Howie), Ralph Story (TV Newsman)

THE WARRIORS (Paramount) Producer, Lawrence Gordon; Executive Producer, Frank Marshall; Director, Walter Hill; Screenplay, David Shaber, Walter Hill; Based on novel by Sol Yurick; Photography, Andrew Laszlo; Editor, David Holden; Music, Barry De Vorzon; Art Directors, Don Swanagan, Bob Wightman; Costumes, Bobbie Mannix, Mary Ellen Winston; Associate Producer, Joel Silver; Assistant Directors, David O. Sosna, Bob Barth, Peter Gries; In Panavision and Movielab Color; Rated R; 90 minutes; February release. CAST: Michael Beck (Swan), James Remar (Ajax), Thomas Waites (Fox), Dorsey Wright (Cleon), Brian Tyler (Snow), David Harris (Cochise), Tom McKitterick (Cowboy), Marcelino Sanchez (Rembrandt), Terry Michos (Vermin), Deborah Van Valkenburgh (Mercy), Roger Hill (Cyrus), David Patrick Kelly (Luther), Lynn Thigpen (D. J.), Ginny Ortiz (Candy Store Girl); Gramercy Riffs: Edward Sewer, Ron Ferrell, Fernando Castillo, Hubert Edwards, Larry Sears, Mike James, Gregory Cleghorne, George Lee Miles, Stanley Timms, John Maurice, Jamie Perry, Winston Yarde; Rogues: Joel Weiss, Harold Miller, Dan Bonnell, Dan Battles, Tom Jarus, Michael Garfield, Chris Harley, Mark Baltzar; Turnbull A.C.'s: J. W. Smith, Cal St. John, Joe Zimmardi, Carrotte, William Williams, Marvin Foster, John Barnes, Ken Thret, Michael Jeffrey; Orphans: Paul Greco, Apache Ramos, Tony Michael Pann, Neal Gold, James Margolin, Chuck Mason, Andy Engels, Ian Cohen, Charles Serrano, Charles Doolan; Baseball Furies: Jerry Hewitt, Bob Ryder, Joseph Bergman, Richard Ciotti, Tony Latham, Eugene Bicknell, T. J. McNamara, Steven James, Lane Ruoff, Harry Madsen, Billy Anagnos, John Gibson; Lizzies: Lisa Maurer, Kate Klugman, Dee Dee Benrey, Jordan Cae Harrell, Donna Ritchie, Doran Clark, Patty Brown, Iris Alahanti, Victoria Vanderkloot, Laura DeLano, Suki Rothchild, Heidi Lynch; Punks: Craig Baxley, A. J. Bajunas, Gary Baxley, Konrad Sheehan, Eddie Earl Hatch, Tom Huff, Leon Delaney; Police: Irwin Keyes, Larry Silvestri, Sonny Landham, Frank Ferrara, Pat Flannery, Leo Ciani, Charlie McCarthy

THE ASTROLOGER (Interstar) Producer, Mark Buntzman; Director, Jim Glickenhaus; Based on novel by John Cameron; Music, Fred Fiedel; Editor, Victor Zimet; In Movielab Color; Rated R; February release. CAST: Bob Byrd, Monica Tidewell, Mark Buntzman

CHORUS CALL (Entertainment Ventures) Producers, Allen Williams, Davis Freeman; Direction, Screenplay, and Songs by Antonio Shepherd; In color; Rated R; February release. CAST: Kay Parker, Darby Lloyd Rains, Beth Anne, Susan London

JOKES MY FOLKS NEVER TOLD ME (New World) Producers, Steven A. Vail, Ted Woolery; Director, Gerry Woolery; Screenplay, Steven A. Vail, John G. Thompson; Executive Producer, Andras Maros; In color; Rated R; February release. No cast credits.

THE HITTER (Peppercorn-Wormser) Producers, Gary Herman, Christopher Leitch; Director, Christopher Leitch; Screenplay, Ben Harris; Music, Garfeel Ruff; Executive Producer, Ronald K. Goldman; In color; Rated R; February release. CAST: Ron O'Neal, Sheila Frazier, Adolph Caesar, Bill Cobbs, Dorothy Fox

"The Bermuda Triangle"
© Sunn Classic Pictures

Stephen Collins, Kathleen Quinlan
in "The Promise" © Universal City Studios

Bill Thornbury, Kathy Lester
in "Lady in Lavender"

FYRE (Compass International) Executive Producer, Robert Fenton; Associate Producer, Leonard Kramer; Photography, Hanania Baer; Editor, Marshall M. Borden; Producer, Ted Zephro; Director, Richard Grand; Screenplay, Richard Grand, Ted Zephro; In color; Not rated; 87 minutes; February release. CAST: Allen Garfield (Preacher), Lynn Theel (Fyre), Tom Baker (Nick), Cal Haynes (Seymour), Donna Wilkes (Carol), Bruce Kirby, Jack Andreozzi, Wynn Irwin, Mario Roccozzo, Cheryl Jensen, Ron Thomas, Meg Gallagher, Jon Ian Jacobs

THE PROMISE (Universal) Producers, Fred Weintraub, Paul Heller; Director, Gilbert Cates; Executive Producer, Tully Friedman; Screenplay, Garry Michael White; Based on story by Fred Weintraub, Paul Heller; Music, David Shire; Associate Producer, Eva Monley; Photography, Ralph Woolsey; Art Director, William Sandell; Editor, Peter E. Berger; Title Song (David Shire, Marilyn and Alan Bergman) sung by Melissa Manchester; Assistant Directors, Thomas Lofaro, Stephen Lofaro; In Technicolor and Panavision; Rated PG; 98 minutes; March release. CAST: Kathleen Quinlan (Nancy/Marie), Stephen Collins (Michael), Beatrice Straight (Marion), Laurence Luckinbill (Dr. Gregson), William Prince (Calloway), Michael O'Hare (Ben), Bibi Besch (Dr. Allison), Robin Gammell (Dr. Wickfield), Katherine DeHetre (Wendy), Paul Ryan (Dr. Fenton), Tom O'Neill (Painter), Kirchy Prescott (Nurse), John Allen Vick, Dan Leegant (Cab Drivers), Jerry Walter (Cal), Bob Hirschfeld (Dr. Meisner), Alan Newman (Barker), Carey Loftin, Max Balchowsky, Mickey Gilbert (Truck Drivers)

TOURIST TRAP (Compass International) Executive Producer, Charles Band; Producer, J. Larry Carroll; Director, David Schmoeller; Screenplay, David Schmoeller, J. Larry Carroll; Photography, Nicholas Von Sternberg; Music, Pino Donnagio; Art Director, Robert Burns: Assistant Directors, Ron Underwood, David Wyler; Editor, Ted Nicoloau; In Metrocolor; Rated PG; 85 minutes; March release. CAST: Chuck Connors (Slausen), Jon Van Ness (Jerry), Jocelyn Jones (Molly), Robin Sherwood (Eileen), Tanya Roberts (Becky), Keith McDermott (Woody), Dawn Jeffory (Tina)

PHANTASM (AVCO Embassy) Produced, Directed, Written, Photographed and Edited by Don Coscarelli; Design, S. Tyer; Art Director, David Gavin Brown; Music, Fred Myrow, Malcolm Seagrave; Co-Producer, Paul Pepperman; In color; Rated R; 90 minutes; March release. CAST: Michael Baldwin (Mike), Bill Thornbury (Jody), Regie Bannister (Reggie), Kathy Lester (Lavendar), Terrie Kalbus (Granddaughter), Ken Jones (Caretaker), Susan Harper (Girl Friend), Lynn Eastman (Sally), David Arntzen (Toby), Ralph Richmond (Bartender), Bill Cone (Tommy), Laura Mann (Double Lavendar), Mary Ellen Shaw (Fortune Teller), Myrtle Scotton (Maid)

REAL LIFE (Paramount) Producer, Penelope Spheeris; Director, Albert Brooks; Screenplay, Albert Brooks, Monica Johnson, Harry Shearer; Music, Mort Lindsey; Editor, David Finfer; Photography, Eric Saarinen; Executive Producers, Norman Epstein, Jonathan Kovler; Art Direction, Linda Spheeris, Linda Marder; Assistant Directors, David M. McGiffert, Rafael Elortegui; In color and Panavision; Rated PG; 99 minutes; March release. CAST: Dick Haynes (Harris), Albert Brooks (Himself), Matthew Tobin (Dr. Hill), J. A. Preston (Dr. Cleary), Mort Lindsey (Himself), Joseph Schaffler (Paul), Phyllis Quinn (Donna), James Ritz (Jack), Clifford Einstein, Harold Einstein, Mandy Einstein, Karen Einstein (Role Reversal Family), James L. Brooks (Evaluator), Zeke Manners (Driver), Charles Grodin (Warren), Frances Lee McCain (Jeanette), Lisa Urette (Lisa), Robert Stirrat (Eric), Dudley DeZonia, Barbara DeZonia, Carolyn Silas, Adam Grant (The Feltons), Belle Richter (Jeanette's Mother), Jerry Jensen (Jeanette's Father), Michele Grace (Nurse), Thelma Bernstein (Margaret), Johnny Haymer (Dr. Rennert), Nudie (Horse Owner), Charles H. Reid (Surgeon), Susan Clark (Nurse), Ward Rodgers (Minister), David Spielberg (Dr. Nolan), Julie Payne (Dr. Kramer), Jennings Lang (Martin), Leo McElroy (Jim), Carlos Jurado, S. W. Smith, Fred Wolfson (Reporters), Norman Bartold (Dr. Hayward), Harry Shearer (Pete)

"Tourist Trap"

Frances Lee McCain, Charles Grodin, Albert Brooks in "Real Life" © Paramount Pictures 103

Richard Basehart, Burgess Meredith, Ned Beatty
in "The Great Bank Hoax" © Warner Bros.

Tim Matheson, Susan Blakely, Jack Warden
in "Dreamer" © 20th Century-Fox Film Corp.

THE GREAT BANK HOAX (Warner Bros.) Direction and Screenplay, Joseph Jacoby; Photography, Walter Lassally; Editor, Ralph Rosenblum; Music, Arthur B. Rubinstein; Producers, Ralph Rosenblum, Joseph Jacoby; Rated PG; 89 minutes; March release. CAST; Richard Basehart (Manny), Ned Beatty (Julius), Charlene Dallas (Cathy), Burgess Meredith (Stutz), Michael Murphy (Rev. Manigma), Paul Sand (Smedly), Constance Forslund (Patricia), Arthur Godfrey (Major Bryer)

ALL THINGS BRIGHT AND BEAUTIFUL (World Northal) Producer, Margaret Matheson; Director, Eric Till; Screenplay, Alan Plater; Based on books by James Herriot; Photography, Arthur Ibbetson; Editor, Thom Noble; Music, Laurie Johnson; In color; Rated G; 94 minutes; March release. CAST: John Alderton (James), Colin Blakely (Siegfried), Lisa Harrow (Helen), Bill Maynard (Hinchcliffe), Richard Pearson (Granville), Paul Shelley (Carmody), John Barrett (Crump), Rosemary Martin (Mrs. Dalby)

REMEMBER MY NAME (Lagoon) Producer, Robert Altman; Direction and Screenplay, Alan Rudolph; Photography, Tak Fujimoto; Editors, Thomas Walls, William A. Sawyer; In Dolby Stereo; Music, Alberta Hunter; Rated R; 94 minutes; March release. CAST: Geraldine Chaplin (Emily), Anthony Perkins (Curry), Moses Gunn (Pike), Berry Berenson (Barbara), Jeff Goldblum (Nudd), Timothy Thomerson (Jeff), Alfre Woodard (Rita), Marilyn Coleman (Teresa), Jeffrey S. Perry (Harry), Carlos Brown (Rusty), Dennis Franz (Franks)

STARCRASH (New World) Producers, Nat and Patrick Wachsberger; Director, Lewis Coates; Screenplay, Lewis Coates, Nat Wachsberger; Photography, Paul Beeson, Roberto D'Ettorre; Music, John Barry; Designer, Aurelio Crugnolla; Editor, Sergio Montanari; Title Song sung by Cher Winz; In Metrocolor and Dolby Stereo; Rated PG; 92 minutes; March release. CAST: Marjoe Gortner (Akton), Caroline Munro (Stella), Christopher Plummer (Emperor), David Hasselhoff (Simon), Robert Tessier (Thor), Joe Spinell (Count Zarth Arn), Nadia Cassini (Queen of the Amazon), Judd Hamilton (Elle), Hamilton Camp (Voice of Elle)

DIRT (American Cinema) Executive Producers, Michael F. Elone, Roger Riddell; Producers, Alan F. Bodoh, John Patrick Graham; Directors, Eric Karson, Cal Naylor; Associate Producer, Skeeter McKitterick; Screenplay, S. S. Schweitzer, Bud Freidgen, Tom Madigan, R. R. Young; Music, Dick Halligan; A Pacific Films/Sports VIP Presentation in color; Rated PG; 95 minutes; March release. CAST features Parnelli Jones, Mickey Thompson, Malcolm Smith

COMING ATTRACTIONS (National-American) Producer, Joel Chernoff; Director, Ira Miller; Screenplay, Varley Smith, Ian Praiser, Ira Miller, Royce D. Applegate; Executive Producers, Lee D. Weisel, Byron H. Lasky; Music and Lyrics, Murphy Dunne; In color; Rated R; March release. CAST: Bill Murray, Buddy Hackett, J. P. Morgan, Dave Landsberg, Ed Lauter, Avery Schreiber, Misty Rowe, Howard Hessman

A MATTER OF LOVE (William Mishkin) Producer, Lew Mishkin; Director, Chuck Vincent; Screenplay, James Vidos, Chuck Vincent; Based on novel by Sharon Mason; In color; Rated R; 88 minutes; March release. CAST: Michelle Harris, Marc Anderson, Christy Neal, Jeff Alin

RIVALS (World Entertainment) Producer-Director, Lyman Dayton; Screenplay, Keith Merrill; Executive Producer, J. Louis Deli Gatti; In color; Rated PG; March release. CAST: Stewart Petersen, Philip Brown, Dana Kimmell

THE MELON AFFAIR (EMC) Producer-Director, Art Lieberman; In color; Rated R; March release. CAST: Frank Corsentino, Haji, Michael Finn, Marius Mazhanian, Lee McLaughlin, Charles Knatt

ELVIS (Dick Clark) Produced and Written by Tony Lawrence; Director, John Carpenter; Executive Producer, Dick Clark; In color; 180 minutes; Not rated; March release. CAST: Kurt Russell (Elvis), Season Hubley (Priscilla), Shelley Winters (Elvis' Mother), Bing Russell (Vernon Presley), Pat Hingle (Colonel Parker), Randy Gray (Elvis as a Boy), Charlie Hodge (Elvis' Valet), Charles Cyphers (Sam Phillips)

Caroline Munro, Christopher Plummer, David
Hasselhoff in "Starcrash" © New World Pictures

Season Hubley, Kurt Russell
in "Elvis!"

DREAMER (20th Century-Fox) Producer, Michael Lobell; Director, Noel Nosseck; Screenplay, James Proctor, Larry Bischof; Photography, Bruce Surtees; Art Director, Archie Sharp; Music, Bill Conti; Editor, Fred Chulack; Assistant Directors, William Hole, Peter Bergquist; Associate Producer, James Herbert; Costumes, Guy Verhille; In DeLuxe Color; Rated PG; 93 minutes; April release. CAST: Tim Matheson (Dreamer), Susan Blakely (Karen), Jack Warden (Harry), Richard B. Shull (Taylor), Barbara Stuart (Angie), Owen Bush (The Fan), Marya Small (Elaine), Matt Clark (Spider), John Crawford (Riverboat Captain), Chris Schenkel (Himself), Nelson Burton, Jr. (Color Man), Morgan Farley (Old Timer), Pedro Gonzalez Gonzalez (Too), Speedy Zapata (Juan), Jobe Cerny (Patterson), Azizi Johari (Lady), Dick Weber (Johnny), Julian Byrd (Red), Rita Ascot Boyd (Grandma), Marie E. Brady (Old Lady), Pat Mullins Brown (Nurse), Richard Cosentino (Official), Beverly Dunn Davis (Betty), Monroe Diestel (Young Dreamer), Wally Engelhardt (Bus Driver), Bert Hinchman, Scott Larson (Policemen), Ray Hoffstetter (Minicam Operator), Richard McGougan (Truck Driver), Stephen A. Bement (Jock), Felix Shuman (Used Car Salesman)

PINOCCHIO'S STORYBOOK ADVENTURES (First American) Produced, Directed and Written by Ron Merk; In Eastmancolor; Rated G; 80 minutes; April release. CAST: John Fields (Papa Gepetto), Armand MacKinnon (Maestro Eisenbeiss), Owen Edward (Cargill), Ellen Prince (Voice of Pinocchio)

BURNOUT (Crown International) Produced and Written by Martin J. Rosen; Director, Graham Meech-Burkestone; Photography, H. Paul Savage; Music, Jack Miller, Peter Dobson; Assistant Director, H. Paul Savage; In DeLuxe Color; Rated PG; 90 minutes; April release. CAST: Mark Schneider (Scott), Robert Louden, John Zenda, Crystal Ramar, Darryle Buehl, Nick Cirino, Walt Rhodes, Randy Troxel, Jerry Jones, Marvin Graham, Tony Nancy, Dale Funk, Linda Vaughn, Eloise Buford

TILT (Warner Bros.) Executive Producer, Ron Joy; Producer-Director, Rudy Durand; Screenplay, Rudy Durand, Donald Cammell; Based on story by Mr. Durand; Photography, Richard Kline; Editors, Bob Wyman, Don Guidice; Designer, Ned Parsons; Music, Lee Holdridge; Assistant Director, Pat Kehoe; In Dolby Stereo and Technicolor; Rated PG; 111 minutes; April release. CAST: Brooke Shields (Tilt), Ken Marshall (Neil), Charles Durning (Whale), John Crawford (Mickey), Harvey Lewis (Henry), Robert Brian Berger (Replay), Geoffrey Lewis (Truck Driver), Gregory Walcott (Davenport), Helen Boll (Mrs. Davenport)

GOOD LUCK, MISS WYCKOFF (Bel Air/Gradison) Producer, Raymond Stross; Associate Producer, Robert Lecky; Director, Marvin J. Chomsky; Screenplay, Polly Platt; Based on novel by William Inge; Photography, Alex Phillips, Jr.; Editor, Rita Roland; Music, Ernest Gold; Art Director, Jim Bissell; Costumes, Rom Rasmussen; In Metrocolor; Rated R; 105 minutes; April release. CAST: Anne Heywood (Evelyn), Donald Pleasence (Steiner), Robert Vaughn (Dr. Neal), Carolyn Jones (Beth), Dorothy Malone (Mildred), Ronee Blakley (Betsy), Dana Elcar (Havermeyer), Doris Roberts (Rene), John Lafayette (Rafe), Earl Holliman (Ed), Jocelyn Brando (Lisa)

BENEATH THE VALLEY OF THE ULTRAVIXENS (RM Films International) Produced, Directed, Photographed, and Edited by Russ Meyer; Screenplay, R. Hyde and B. Callum from a story by Russ Meyer; In color; Not rated; 93 minutes; April release. CAST: Francesca Natividad (Lavonia), Anne Marie (Eufaula), Ken Kerr (Lamar), June Mack (Sal), Lola Langusta (Stripper), Pat Wright (Peterbuilt), Michael Finn (Fidelis), Steve Tracy (Rhett), Sharon Hill (Flovilla), Henry Rowland (Martin), Robert E. Pearson (Dr. Lavender)

THE DARK (Film Ventures International) Producers, Dick Clark, Edward L. Montoro; Executive Producer, Derek Power; Director, John "Bud" Cardos; Screenplay, Stanford Whitmore; Music, Roger Kellaway; Photography, John Morrill; Associate Producer, Igo Kantor; Editor, Martin Dreffke; Assistant Directors, Willard Kirkham, Herbert Willis; Art Director, Rusty Rosene; In Panavision and DeLuxe Color; Rated R; 92 minutes; April release. CAST: William Devane (Roy), Cathy Lee Crosby (Zoe), Richard Jaeckel (Mooney), Keenan Wynn (Moss), Warren Kemmerling (Capt. Speer), Biff Elliott (Bresler), Jacquelyn Hyde (DeRenzey), Casey Kasem (Pathologist), Vivian Blaine (Courtney), John Bloom (Killer), William Derringer (Herman), Jay Lawrence (Jim), Russ Marin (Dr. Baranowski), Vernon Washington (Henry), Mel Anderson, John Dresden, Horton Willis (Policemen), Roberto Contreras (Bartender), Paul Crist, Joann Kirk (Stewardesses), Erik Howell (Antwine), Ron Iglesias (Rudy), William Lampley (Young Man), Sandra Walker McCulley (Carhop), Valla Rae McDade (Camille), Ken Menyard (Sportscaster), Monica Peterson (Mrs. Lydell), Penny Ann Phillips (Zelza), Jeffrey Reese (Randy), Kathie Richards (Shelly)

Michael Parks, Jessica Harper
in "The Evictors" © AIP

HOLLYWOOD KNIGHT (First American Films) Produced and Written by Michael Christian; Directed and Photographed by David Worth; Editors, David Worth, Wayne Wahrman; Music, Michael Lloyd, John D'Andrea; Associate Producers, Vito A. Sasso, Robert G. Diamond; Executive Producer, John B. Kelly; In color; Rated PG; 84 minutes; April release. CAST: Michael Christian (Guy), Josette Banzet (Cherie), Keenan Wynn (Jed), Donna Wilkes (Chrissy), John Crawford (Sheriff)

FAIRY TALES (Fairy Tales Distributors) Producer, Charles Band; Director, Harry Tampa; Screenplay, Frank Ray Perilli, Franne Schacht; Photography, Daniel Pearl; Music, Andrew Belling; Lyrics, Lee Arries; Editor, Laurence Jacobs; In color; Rated R; April release. CAST: Don Sparks, Sy Richardson, Brenda Fogarty, Martha Reeves, Linnea Quigley, Irwin Corey, Nai Bonet, Robert Staats, Angela Aames, Bob Leslie

CALIFORNIA DREAMING (American International) Executive Producer, Louis S. Arkoff; Producer Christian Whittaker; Director, John Hancock; Screenplay, Ned Wynn; Photography, Bobby Byrne; Designer, Bill Hiney; Editors, Herb Dow, Roy Peterson; Music, Fred Karlin; A Cinema 77 Film in Movielab Color; Presented by Samuel Z. Arkoff; Rated R; 92 minutes; April release. CAST: Glynnis O'Connor (Corky), Seymour Cassel (Duke), Dorothy Tristan (Fay), Dennis Christopher (T.T.), John Calvin (Rick), Tanya Roberts (Stephanie), Jimmy Van Patten (Mike), Todd Susman (Jordy), Alice Playten (Corrine), Ned Wynn (Earl), John Fain (Tenner), Marshall Efron (Ruben)

THE EVICTORS (American International) Producer-Director, Charles B. Pierce; Screenplay, Charles B. Pierce, Garry Rusoff, Paul Fisk; Music, Jaime Mendoza-Nava; Associate Producer, Steve Lyons; Editor, Shirak Khojayan; Photography, Chuck Bryant; In Panavision and Movielab Color; Presented by Samuel Z. Arkoff; Rated PG; 92 minutes; April release. CAST: Vic Morrow (Jake), Michael Parks (Ben), Jessica Harper (Ruth), Sue Anne Langdon (Olie), Dennis Fimple (Bumford), Bill Thurman (Preacher), Jimmy Clem (Buckner), Harry Thomasson (Wheeler), Twyla Taylor (Mrs. Bumford), Glen Roberts (Dwayne)

Cathy Lee Crosby, William Devane
in "The Dark" © FVI

Marta Heflin, Paul Dooley
in "A Perfect Couple" © 20th Century-Fox

Susan Kiger, Lindsay Bloom
in "H.O.T.S."

A PERFECT COUPLE (20th Century-Fox) Producer-Director, Robert Altman; Screenplay, Robert Altman, Allan Nicholls; Photography, Edmond L. Koons: Editor, Tony Lombardo; Executive Producer, Tommy Thompson; Music, Allan Nicholls; Associate Producers, Robert Eggenweiler, Scott Bushnell; Assistant Directors, Tommy Thompson, Bill Cosentino; In Dolby Stereo, Panavision and DeLuxe Color; Rated PG; 111 minutes; April release. CAST: Paul Dooley (Alex), Marta Heflin (Sheila), Titos Vandis (Panos), Belita Moreno (Eleousa), Henry Gibson (Fred), Dimitra Arliss (Athena), Allan Nicholls (Dana 115), Ann Ryerson (Skye 147), Poppy Lagos (Melpomeni), Dennis Franz (Costa), Margery Bond (Wilma), Mona Golabek (Mona), Terry Wills (Ben), Susan Blakeman (Penelope), Melanie Bishop (Star), Fred Bier, Jette Seear (Imperfect Couple), Ted Neeley (Teddy), Heather MacRae (Mary), Tomi-Lee Bradley (Sydney-Ray), Steven Sharp (Bobbi), Tony Berg, Craig Doerge, Jeff Eyrich, David Luell, Butch Sandford, Art Wood, Ren Woods, Tom Pierson

DAWN OF THE DEAD (United Film Distribution) Producer, Richard P. Rubinstein; Direction and Screenplay, George A. Romero; Photography, Michael Gornick; Assistant Producer, Donna Siegel; Assistant Director, Christine Forrest; Music, The Goblins with Dario Argento; Editor, George A. Romero; In Technicolor; A Laurel Group production in association with Alfredo Cuomo and Claudio Argento; Presented by Herbert R. Steinmann and Billy Baxter; Not rated; 125 minutes; April release. CAST: David Emge (Stephen), Ken Foree (Peter), Scott Reiniger (Roger), Gaylen Ross (Francine), and The Zombies

RAVAGERS (Columbia) Executive Producer, Saul David; Producer, John W. Hyde; Director, Richard Compton; Screenplay, Donald S. Sanford; Based on novel *Path to Savagery* by Robert Edmond Alter; Photography, Vincent Saizis; Editor, Maury Winetrobe; Designer, Ronald E. Hobbs; Costumes, Ron Talsky; Assistant Director, Pat Kehoe; Music, Fred Karlin; In Panavision and Metrocolor; Rated PG; 91 minutes; May release. CAST: Richard Harris (Falk), Ann Turkel (Faina), Art Carney (Sergeant), Ernest Borgnine (Rann), Anthony James (Leader), Woody Strode (Brown), Alana Hamilton (Miriam), Seymour Cassel (Blindman)

OVER THE EDGE (Orion) Producer, George Litto; Director, Jonathan Kaplan; Screenplay, Charlie Hass, Tim Hunter; Photography, Andrew Davis; Editor, Robert Bargere; Music, Sol Kaplan; Design, Jim Newport; Assistant Director, Ed Ledding; In color; Rated PG; 95 minutes; May release. CAST: Michael Kramer (Carl), Pamela Ludwig (Cory), Matt Dillon (Richie), Vincent Spano (Mark), Tom Fergus (Claude), Harry Northup (Doberman), Andy Romano (Fred), Ellen Geer (Sandra), Richard Jamison (Cole), Julia Pomeroy (Julia), Tiger Thompson (Johnny)

SMOKEY AND THE HOTWIRE GANG (NMD) Producer-Director, Anthony Cardoza; Screenplay, T. Gary Cardoza; In color; Rated PG; May release. CAST: James Keach, Stanley Livingston, Tony Lorea, Carla Ziegfeld

AMERICAN NITRO (Cannon) Producers, Bill Kimberlin, Jim Kimberlin, Tim Geideman; Director, Bill Kimberlin; Music, Art Twain, Denny Jaeger; In color; Rated PG; 75 minutes; May release. CAST: Don Prudhomme, Tom McEwen, T. V. Tommy Ivo, Bob Correll

H.O.T.S. (Derio) Executive Producer, W. Terry Davis; Producers, W. Terry Davis, Don Schain; Director, Gerald Sindell; Screenplay, Cheri Caffaro, Joan Buchanan; Photography, Harvey Genkins; Music, David Davis; Editor, Barbara Pokras; Art Director, Eric Butler; Assistant Directors, Gerald Olson, Michael Healy; Great American Dream Machine Movie Company production in DeLuxe Color; Songs sung by Danny Bonaduce, Pam Miller; Rated R; 95 minutes; May release. CAST: Susan Kiger (Honey), Lisa London (O'Hara), Pamela Jean Bryant (Teri), Kimberley Cameron (Sam), Mary Steelsmith (Clutz), Angela Aames (Boom-Boom), Lindsay Bloom (Melody), K. C. Winkler (Cynthia), Sandy Johnson (Stephanie), Marilyn Rubin (Jackie), Donald Petrie (Doug), Larry Gilman (Mad Dog), Dan Reed (Stormin' Norman), Danny Bonaduce (Richie), David Gibbs (Macho Man), Marvin Katzoff (Big Boy), Steve Bond (John), Talmadge Scott (Hunk), Ken Olfson (Dean), Dick Bakalyan (Charlie), Louis Guss (Bugs), Dorothy Meyer (Ezzetta), Scott Ellsworth (Professor), Bunny Summers (Singer)

"Dawn of the Dead"
© Dawn Associates

Jerry Reed, Luis Avalos, Suzanne Pleshette,
Dom DeLuise in "Hot Stuff" © Columbia Pictures

MALIBU HIGH (Crown International) Producer, Lawrence D. Foldes; Director, Irv Berwick; Photography, William De Diego; Editor, Dan Perry; Screenplay, John Buckley, Tom Singer; Story, John Buckley; Associate Producer, Tom Singer; A Star Cinema production in color; Rated R; 92 minutes; May release. CAST: Jill Lansing (Kim), Stuart Taylor (Kevin), Katie Johnson (Lucy), Tammy Taylor (Annette), Garth Howard (Lance), Phyllis Benson (Mrs. Bentley), Al Mannino (Tony), John Grant (Donaldson), John Harmon (Elmhurst), Robert Gordon (Harry), Jim Devney (Wyngate), Cambra Zweigler (Valerie), Susan Gorton (Miss Primm), William Cohen (Jeweler), Bill Burke (Mr. H), Ken Layton (Mooney), Scott Walters (Paperboy)

SUNSHINE RUN (First American) Produced, Directed, and Written by Chris Robinson; Music, Tommy Oliver; Presented by John B. Kelly; In color; Rated PG; 102 minutes; May release. CAST: Chris Robinson (Sunshine), David Legge (Levi), Phyllis Robinson (The Woman), Ted Cassidy (Striker), Robert Leslie (Bounty Hunter)

THE CLOSET CASANOVA (Belladonna) Producer-Director, Ted Roter; Screenplay, Peter Balakoff, Belinda Balakoff; Photography, Ray Icely; Art Director, Caryl Christian; Editor, Peter Balakoff; In color; Rated R; 76 minutes; May release. CAST: Genadee Cook (Caroline), Ted Roter (Paul), Diane Miller (Lisa), Margo Hanson (Belinda), William Margold (Peter), John Boland (Bill), Ann Webster (Nancy), Tomy (Millie), Jana Knox (Polly), Karla Garrett (Jan), Hillary Scott (Fran), Charles Gabriels (Lew), Jacques Girard, Richard Aaron, Robert Monday, Eileen Leese, Carol Romo, Mary Fraga, George K. Monagham, Mickle Scott, Ron LaSauce, James Rain, Kalifa, Honey West, Bruce Allan Brown.

VAN NUYS BLVD. (Crown International) Executive Producer, Newton P. Jacobs; Producer, Marilyn J. Tenser; Associate Producer, Michael D. Castle; Direction and Screenplay, William Sachs; Photography, Joseph Mangine; Editor, George Bowers; Assistant Directors, David Osterhout, Tikki Goldberg; Art Director, Kenneth H. Hergenroeder; Costumes, Diana Daniels; Music, Ron Wright, Ken Mansfield; Choreographer, Sandy Hendrick Adler; A Marimark production in DeLuxe Color; Rated R; 93 minutes; May release. CAST: Bill Adler (Bobby), Cynthia Wood (Moon), Dennis Bowen (Greg), Melissa Prophet (Camille), David Hayward (Chooch), Tara Strohmeier (Wanda), Dana Gladstone (Al), Di Ann Monaco (Motorcyclist), Don Sawyer (Jason), Jim Kester (Frankie), Minnie E. Lindsey (Nurse), Susanne Severeid (Jo), Doug Bailey, Stephen Morrell, Bella Bruck, Mary Ellen O'Neill, Mario Bellini, Rena Harmon, Matthew Tobin, Michael Castle, Cecil Reddick, Diana Daniels, Nancy McCauley, Brando Caffey, Debbie Chenoweth, Louis Rivera, Jacqueline Jacobs

FAST CHARLIE . . . THE MOONBEAM RIDER (Universal) Producers, Roger Corman, Saul Krugman; Director, Steve Carver; Screenplay, Michael Gleason; Based on story by Ed Spielman, Howard Friedlander; Photography, William Birch; Editors, Tony Redman, Eric Orner; Music, Stu Phillips; Art Directors, Bill Sandell, David Riva; Assistant Director, David McGiffert; In color; Rated PG; 99 minutes; May release. CAST: David Carradine (Charlie), Brenda Vaccaro (Grace), L. Q. Jones (Floyd), R. G. Armstrong (Al), Terry Kiser (Lester), Jesse Vint (Calvin), Noble Willingham (Pop), Whit Clay (Wesley), Ralph James (Sheriff), Bill Hartman (Young Man), Stephen Ferry (Cannonball)

HOT STUFF (Columbia) Producer, Mort Engelberg; Director, Dom DeLuise; Screenplay, Michael Kane, Donald E. Westlake; Executive Producer, Paul Maslansky; Photography, James Pergola; Music, Patrick Williams; Title Song written and sung by Jerry Reed; Editor, Neil Travis; Assistant Directors, David M. Whorf, Sonny Persons; In Panavision and Metrocolor; Rated PG; 91 minutes; May release. CAST: Dom DeLuise (Ernie), Suzanne Pleshette (Louise), Jerry Reed (Doug), Ossie Davis (Captain), Luis Avalos (Ramon), Marc Lawrence (Carmine), Dick Davalos (Charles), Alfie Wise (Nick), Bill McCutcheon (Paully), Sydney Lassick (Hymie), Barney Martin (Kiley), Pat McCormick (Cigars), Sid Gould (Sid), Carol DeLuise (Gloria), and Peter DeLuise, David DeLuise, Michael DeLuise, Mike Falco, Crispin Tyrone Jackson, Raymond George Forchion, Luke Halpin, Joe Ruggiero, Angela Bomford, Mel Pape, Steve Gladstone, Matthew Burch, Peppy Fields, Shirley Galabow, Eduardo Corbe, Jose Bahamonde, John Disanti, Sandy Mielke, Cedar Stump, Artie Lewis, Ginger Scott, Sid Raymond, Al Nessor, Pete Conrad, George Warren, Danny Bardisa, Leonard Haber, Terese Heston, Shirley Cowell, Gigi Carrier, Katy Reaves, Norma Davids, Mike Baches, Louis Silvers, Bobby Self, Diane Johnson, Laurie Stark, Tim Chitwood, Vic Hunter, Victor Helou, Jack White, Tony Coffman, William Fuller, Ed Lupinski, Jim Ridarsick, Beau Gillespie, Don Soffer, Barry Noel, Mimi Julia Keating

Recil Calhoun, T. J. Swackhammer, Gary Springer in "Hometown U.S.A." © FVI

THE GIRLS NEXT DOOR (Columbus America) Producers, John Jones, James Hong; Director, James Hong; In color; Rated R; June release. CAST: Kirsten Baker, Perry Lang, Leslie Cederquist, Richard Singer

DOLPHIN (Michael Wiese) Producer, Michael Wiese; Directors, Hardy Jones, Michael Wiese; Written by Hardy Jones; Photography, John Knoop; Editor, John V. Fanto; Music, Basil Poledouris; In color; Not rated; 75 minutes; June release. A documentary.

DRILLER KILLER (Rochelle Films) Executive Producer, Rochelle Weisberg; Director, Abel Ferrara; Screenplay, Nicholas St. John; Photography, Ken Kelsch; Music, Joseph Delia; In color; Not rated; 90 minutes; June release. CAST: Carolyn Marz, Jimmy Laine, Baybi Day, Bob DeFrank, Peter Yellen, Harry Schultz, Tony Coca Cola and the Roosters

HOMETOWN U.S.A. (Film Ventures International) Producers, Roger Camras, Jesse Vint; Director, Max Baer; Story and Screenplay, Jesse Vint; Editor, Frank Morris; Music, Marshall Leib; Art Director, Keith Michl; Costumes, Nancy Frechtling; In Panavision and CFI Color; Rated R; 93 minutes; June release. CAST: Gary Springer (Rodent), David Wilson (Recil), Brian Kerwin (T. J.), Pat Delaney (Marilyn), Julie Parsons (Andrea), Mitzi Hoag (Mrs. Duckworth), Ned Wertimer (Mr. Duckworth), Bo Kaprall (Arnold), Betty McGuire (Mrs. Smith), Michael Prince (Mr. Smith), Nancy Osborne (Rhina), Cindy Fisher (Ginger), Debi Richter (Dolly), Shirley Anne Broger (Joanie), Jim Bohan (Childres), Virginia Feingold (Edna), Betsee Finlee, Sally Julian, Sally Kirkland, Bradley Lieberman, Kathy Mulrooney, Melissa O'Bryant, Anne O'Donnell, Lorraine Adele Osborne, Sunshine Parker, Yuliis Ruval, Jesse Vint III, Steve Kavner, Evan Gordon, Larry Cooper, Gene Hartline, Harry Monty, Maida Belove, Jon Cutler, Sherry Marks, Julia Embree, Brenda Smith, Sheri Jason, Susan Kamins, Sandy Serrano

Brenda Vaccaro, David Carradine in "Fast Charlie . . ." © Universal Studios 107

Ron O'Neal, Clu Gulager
in "A Force of One"

Bruce Lee
in "Game of Death"

A FORCE OF ONE (American Cinema) Executive Producer, Michael F. Leone; Producer, Alan Belkin; Director, Paul Aaron; Screenplay, Ernest Tidyman; Story, Pat Johnson, Ernest Tidyman; Music, Dick Halligan; Photography, Roger Shearman; Editor, Bert Lovitt; Associate Producer, Jonathan Sanger; Art Director, Norman Baron; Assistant Director, Jerald Sobul; In CFI Color; Rated PG; 90 minutes; June release. CAST: Jennifer O'Neill (Mandy Rust), Chuck Norris (Matt), Clu Gulager (Dunne), Ron O'Neal (Rollins), James Whitmore, Jr. (Moskowitz), Clint Ritchie (Melrose), Pepe Serna (Orlando), Ray Vitte (Newton), Taylor Lacher (Bishop), Chu Chu Malave (Pimp), Kevin Geer (Johnson), Eugene Butler (Murphy), James Hall (Moss), Charles Cyphers (Dr. Eppis), Bill Wallace (Jerry), Eric Laneuville (Charlie)

GAME OF DEATH (Columbia) Producer, Raymond Chow; Director, Robert Clouse; Screenplay, Jan Spears; Photography, Godfrey A. Godar; Editor, Alan Pattillo; Music, John Barry; Assistant Director, Mike Gowans; In Panavision and color; Rated R; 102 minutes; June release. CAST: Bruce Lee (Billy Lo), Gig Young (Jim), Dean Jagger (Land), Hugh O'Brian (Steiner), Colleen Camp (Ann), Robert Wall (Carl), Mel Novak (Stick), Kareem Abdul-Jabbar (Hakim), Chuck Norris (Fighter), Danny Inosanto (Pasqual), Billy McGill (John), Hung Kim Po (Lo Chen), Roy Chaio (Henry)

GOLDENGIRL (AVCO Embassy) Producer, Danny O'Donovan; Executive Producer, Elliot Kastner; Director, Joseph Sargent; Screenplay, John Kohn; Based on novel by Peter Lear; Photography, Stevan Larner; Editor, George Nicholson; Music, Bill Conti; Art Director, Syd Litwack; Assistant Director, Bill Martin; A Backstage production in Eastman Color and Dolby Stereo; Rated PG; 104 minutes; June release. CAST: Susan Anton (Goldengirl), James Coburn (Dryden), Curt Jurgens (Serafin), Leslie Caron (Dr. Lee), Robert Culp (Esselton), James A. Watson, Jr. (Winters), Harry Guardino (Valenti), Ward Costello (Cobb), Michael Lerner (Sternberg), John Newcombe (Armitage), Julianna Field (Ingrid), Sheila DeWindt (Debbie), Andrea Brown (Teammate), Anette Tannander (Krull), Nicolas Coster (Dr. Dalton)

NIGHTWING (Columbia) Executive Producer, Richard St. Johns; Producer, Martin Ransohoff; Director, Arthur Hiller; Music, Henry Mancini; Screenplay, Steve Shagan, Bud Shrake, Martin Cruz Smith; Based on novel by Martin Cruz Smith; Editor, John C. Howard; Designer, James Vance; Associate Producers, Maggie Abbott, Peter V. Herald; Photography, Charles Rosher; Assistant Directors, Gary Daigler, Scott Easton; In Metrocolor; Rated PG; 105 minutes; June release. CAST: Nick Mancuso (Duran), David Warner (Philip), Kathryn Harrold (Anne), Stephen Macht (Chee), Strother Martin (Selwyn), George Clutesi (Abner), Ben Piazza (Roger), Donald Hotton (John), Charles Hallahan (Henry), Judith Novgrod (Judy), Alice Hirson (Claire), Pat Corley (Vet), Charlie Bird (Beejay), Danny Zapien (Joe), Peter Prouse (Doctor), Jose Toledo (Harold), Richard Romancito (Ben), Flavio Martinez III (Isla), Lena Carr, Virginia P. Maney, Wade Stevens, Robert Dunbar, John R. Leonard, Sr., James Arnett, Glynn Rubin, Gary Epper, Craig Baxley

NOCTURNA (Compass International) "Granddaughter of Dracula"; Executive Producer, Nai Bonet; Producer, Vernon Becker; Direction and Screenplay, Harry Tampa; Photography, Mac Ahlberg; Music and Lyrics, Reid Whitelaw, Norman Bergen; Editor, Ian Maitland; Art Directors, Jack Krueger, Steve Davita; In Metrocolor; Rated R; 85 minutes; June release. CAST: Nai Bonet (Nocturna), John Carradine (Dracula), Yvonne DeCarlo (Jugulia), Tony Hamilton (Jimmy), Brother Theodore (Theodore), Sy Richardson (RH Factor), Ivery Bell, Michael Harrison, Norris Harris, William H. Jones, Jr. (The Moment of Truth), Adam Keefe (B.S.A. President), Monica Tidwell (Brenda), Tony Sanchez (Victim), Thomas Ryan (Policeman), Ron Toler (Taxi Driver), Pierre Epstein (John), Albert M. Ottenheimer (Dr. Bernstein), John Blyth Barrymore, Toby Handman, Angelo Vignari, Shelly Wyant (B.S.A. Members), Frank Irizarry (Disc Jockey), Irwin Keyes, Marcus Anthony (Transylvania Characters), Al Sapienza, Jerry Sroka, A. C. Weary (Musicians)

WILLIE NELSON'S 4th OF JULY CELEBRATION (Alston/Zanitsch International) Presented by Werner Brandt; In color; Rated R; June release. CAST: Willie Nelson, Waylon Jennings, Leon Russell

James Coburn, Susan Anton
in "Goldengirl" © AVCO Embassy

John Carradine, Yvonne DeCarlo
in "Nocturna"

**Talia Shire, Robert Foxworth
in "Prophecy" © Paramount Pictures**

PROPHECY (Paramount) Producer, Robert L. Rosen; Director, John Frankenheimer; Screenplay, David Seltzer; Photography, Harry Stradling, Jr.; Designer, William Craig Smith; Editor, Tom Rolf; Music, Leonard Rosenman; Costumes, Ray Summers; Associate Producer, Alan Levine; Assistant Directors, Andy Stone, Robert Cohen, Paul Tucker; In Panavision, Dolby Stereo, and Movielab Color; Rated PG; 102 minutes; June release. CAST: Talia Shire (Maggie), Robert Foxworth (Rob), Armand Assante (Hawks), Richard Dysart (Isely), Victoria Racimo (Ramona), George Clutesi (M'Rai), Tom McFadden (Pilot), Evans Evans (Cellist), Burke Byrnes (Father), Mia Bendixsen (Girl), Johnny Timko (Boy), Everett L. Creach (Kelso), Charles H. Gray (Sheriff), Lyvingston Holms, Graham Jarvis, James H. Burk, Bob Terhune, Lon Katzman, Steve Shemayme, John A. Shemayme, Jaye Durkus, Renato Moore, Mel Waters, Roosevelt Smith, Eric Mansker

RACQUET (Cal-Am Productions) Executive Producers, Joseph R. Laird, Kenneth A. Yates; Associate Producer, Jack Kindberg; Producers, David Winters, Alan Roberts; Director, David Winters; Screenplay, Steve Michaels, Earle Doud; Presented in association with Harlequin Productions; In color; Rated R; June release. CAST: Bert Convy (Tommy), Lynda Day George (Monica), Phil Silvers (Arthur), Edie Adams (Leslie), Susan Tyrrell (Miss Baxter), Bjorn Borg (Himself), Bobby Riggs (Bernie), Dorothy Konrad (Mrs. Kaufman), Monti Rock III (Scotty), Tanya Roberts (Bambi), Bruce Kimmel (Arnold), Kitty Ruth (Melissa)

THE DOUBLE McGUFFIN (Mulberry Square) Produced, Directed, and Written by Joe Camp; Story, Mr. Camp, Richard Baker; Photography, Don Reddy; Editor, Leon Seith; Music, Euel Box; Designer, Harland Wright; Art Director, Ed Richardson; Associate Producer, Dan Witt; Assistant Director, Terence A. Donnelly; In color; Rated PG; 101 minutes; June release. CAST: Ernest Borgnine (Firat), George Kennedy (Chief Talasek), Elke Sommer (Prime Minister), Ed "Too Tall" Jones, Lyle Alzado (Assassins), Rod Browning (Moras), Dion Pride (Specks), Lisa Whelchel (Jody), Jeff Nicholson (Billy), Michael Gerard (Arthur), Greg Hodges (Homer), Vinnie Spano (Foster)

**Joey Travolta, Stacey Pickren
in "Sunnyside" © AIP**

SUNNYSIDE (American International) Producer, Robert L. Schaffel; Director, Timothy Galfas; Screenplay, Timothy Galfas, Jeff King; Story, Jeff King, Robert L. Schaffel; Music, Alan Douglas, Harold Wheeler; Editors, Eric Albertson, Herbert H. Dow; Assistant Director, Ramiro Jaloma; Photography, Gary Graver; Presented by Samuel Z. Arkoff and Louis S. Arkoff; In Movielab Color; Rated R; 100 minutes; June release. CAST: Joey Travolta (Nick), John Lansing (Denny), Stacey Pickren (Donna), Andrew Rubin (Eddie), Michael Tucci (Harry), Talia Balsam (Ann), Chris Mulkey (Reggie), Joan Darling (Mrs. Martin), Richard Beauchamp (Hector), Heshimu Cumbuka (Ice), Jonathan Gries (Wild Child), E. Lamont Johnson (Rage), David Byrd (Roy)

WANDA NEVADA (United Artists) Producers, Neal Dobrofsky, Dennis Hackin; Director, Peter Fonda; Screenplay, Dennis Hackin; Executive Producer, William Hayward; Associate Producers, Hilary Holden, Thomas Perry; Photography, Michael Butler; Editor, Scott Conrad; Art Director, Lynda Paradise; Music, Ken Lauber; Assistant Directors, Ric Rondell, Robin Chamberlain; In Panavision and Technicolor; Rated PG; 105 minutes; June release. CAST: Peter Fonda (Beaudray), Brooke Shields (Wanda), Fred Ashley (Barber), Jason Clark (Alonzo), Fiona Lewis (Dorothy), Luke Askew (Muldoon), Ted Markland (Strap), Severn Darden (Merlin), Paul Fix (Texas Curly), Henry Fonda (Prospector), Larry Golden (Card Hustler), John Denos (Greaser), Bert Williams (Sherman), Robert V. Walker, H. Samuel Hackin (Poker Players), Charles Lawry (Drunk), Jack Caddin (Trucker), Teri Shields (Clerk), Benny Dobrofsky, Craig Pinkard, Tiny Wells, Bert, J. D. Clark, Danny Zapein, Geno Silva, Carol Norton, Ramona Richards, Melvin Todd, Tim James, Riley Hill, Lon Carli

THE AMERICAN GAME (World Northal) Producer, Anthony Jones; Direction and Screenplay, Jay Freund, David Wolf; Photography, Robert Elfstrom, Peter Powell; Associate Producer, Grania Gurievitch; Music, Jeffrey Kaufman; Co-Producers, Peter Powell, Robby Kenner; Editors, Jay Freund, Nancy Baker; Rated PG; 89 minutes; June release. CAST: Brian Walker, Stretch Graham, Gil Ferschtman, Dave Tawil

**Bert Convy, Bjorn Borg
in "Racquet"**

**Brooke Shields, Peter Fonda
in "Wanda Nevada" © United Artists**

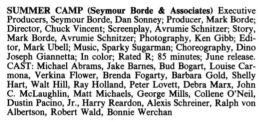

**Carl Betz, Dina Merrill
in "Deadly Encounter"**

"Nutcracker Fantasy"

SUMMER CAMP (Seymour Borde & Associates) Executive Producers, Seymour Borde, Dan Sonney; Producer, Mark Borde; Director, Chuck Vincent; Screenplay, Avrumie Schnitzer; Story, Mark Borde, Avrumie Schnitzer; Photography, Ken Gibb; Editor, Mark Ubell; Music, Sparky Sugarman; Choreography, Dino Joseph Giannetta; In color; Rated R; 85 minutes; June release. CAST: Michael Abrams, Jake Barnes, Bud Bogart, Louise Carmona, Verkina Flower, Brenda Fogarty, Barbara Gold, Shelly Hart, Walt Hill, Ray Holland, Peter Lovett, Debra Marx, John C. McLaughlin, Matt Michaels, George Mills, Collene O'Neil, Dustin Pacino, Jr., Harry Reardon, Alexis Schreiner, Ralph von Albertson, Robert Wald, Bonnie Werchan

DEADLY ENCOUNTER (First American Films) Produced, Directed, and Written by R. John Hugh; Executive Producer, L. E. Brown; Music, Stu Phillips; Photography, Robert Caramico; Editor, Robert J. Emery; Associate Producers, Thomas B. Drage, William W. Cox, J. B. Hodgskin; Presented by John B. Kelly; In color; Rated R; 90 minutes; July release. CAST: Dina Merrill (Kelley), Carl Betz (Jake), Leon Ames (Kroger), Vicki Powers (Liz), Mark Featherstone-Witty (Nigel), Susan Logan (Annie), Mark Rasmussen (Mike)

THE VILLAIN (Columbia) Producer, Mort Engelberg; Director, Hal Needham; Screenplay, Robert G. Kane; Executive Producer, Paul Maslansky; Photography, Bobby Byrne; Editor, Walter Hannemann; Art Director, Carl Anderson; Music, Bill Justis; Associate Producer, Stu Fleming; Assistant Directors, David Shamroy Hamburger, Toby Lovallo, Frank Bueno; Songs sung by Mel Tillis; In Metrocolor; Rated PG; 93 minutes; July release. CAST: Kirk Douglas (Cactus Jack), Ann-Margret (Charming Jones), Arnold Schwarzenegger (Handsome), Paul Lynde (Nervous Elk), Foster Brooks (Bank Clerk), Ruth Buzzi (Damsel in Distress), Jack Elam (Avery), Strother Martin (Parody), Robert Tessier (Mashing Finger), Mel Tillis (Telegrapher), Laura Lizer Sommers (Working Girl), Ray Bickel (Man), Jan Eddy (Sheriff), Mel Todd (Conductor), Jim Anderson (Bartender), Ed Little, Dick Dickinson, Richard Brewer, Charles Haigh, Ron Duffy, Earl W. Smith, Mike Cerre, Lee Davis, Dick Armstrong, Sheldon Rosner, Budd Stout

NUTCRACKER FANTASY (Sanrio) Producers, Walt deFaria, Mark L. Rosen, Arthur Tomioka; Executive Producer, Shintaro Tsuji; Director, Takeo Nakamura; Story, Shintaro Tsuji; Based on "The Nutcracker and the Mouseking" by E. T. A. Hoffman; Adaptation, Thomas Joachim, Eugene Fournier; Music, P.I. Tchaikovsky; Lyrics, Randy Bishop, Marty Gwinn; Choreography, Tetsutaro Shimizu; In DeLuxe Color; Rated G; 82 minutes; July release. Animation with the voices of Michele Lee, Melissa Gilbert, Lurene Tuttle, Christopher Lee, Jo Anne Worley, Dick Van Patten, Roddy McDowall, Eva Gabor, Ken Sansom, Mitchel Gardner, Jack Angel, Gene Moss, Joan Gerber, Maxine Fisher, Robin Haffner

THE DANCE OF DEATH (Paramount) Producer, John Brabourne; Director, David Giles; Written by August Strindberg; Translated by C. D. Lecock; Photography, Geoffrey Unsworth; Editor, Reginald Mills; A BHE Film; Rated G; 149 minutes; July release. CAST: Laurence Olivier (Edgar), Geraldine McEwen (Alice), Robert Lang (Kurt), Malcolm Reynolds (Allen), Janina Faye (Judith), Carolyn Jones (Jenny), Jeanne Watts (Old Woman), Peter Henry-Jones (Lieutenant), Fredrick Pyne, Barry James, David Ryall (Sentries)

SEXTETTE (Crown International) Executive Producer, Warner G. Toub; Producers, Daniel Briggs, Robert Sullivan; Director, Ken Hughes; Screenplay, Herbert Baker; Based on play "Sextette" by Mae West; Photography, James Crabe; Associate Producer, Harry Weiss; Music, Artie Butler; Choreographer, Marc Breaux; Editor, Argyle Nelson; Assistant Directors, Gene Marum, Robert Shue, Gary LaPoten; Designer, Thad Prescott; Miss West's Gowns, Edith Head; In Metrocolor; Rated PG; 91 minutes; July release. CAST: Mae West (Marlo Manners), Timothy Dalton (Sir Michael Barrington), Dom DeLuise (Dan), Tony Curtis (Alexei), Ringo Starr (Laslo), George Hamilton (Waiter), Alice Cooper (Waiter), Keith Allison (Waiter), Rona Barrett (Herself), Van McCoy (Delegate), Keith Moon (Dress Designer), Regis Philbin (Himself), Walter Pidgeon (Chairman), Harry Weiss (The Don), George Raft, Gil Stratton (Themselves)

110

**Ann-Margret, Kirk Douglas
in "The Villain" © Columbia Pictures**

**Mae West, Timothy Dalton
in "Sextette"**

Pat Delaney, Anthony Eisley
in "Half a House"

Tim Conway, Don Knotts in "The Apple
Dumpling Gang Rides Again" © Walt Disney

HALF A HOUSE (First American Films) Producer, Lenke Romanszky; Director, Brice Mack; Screenplay, Lois Hire; Story, Joe Connelly, Lois Hire; A Leno Production; A John B. Kelly Presentation; Song "A World That Never Was" by Sammy Fain, Paul Francis Webster; In color; Rated PG; 84 minutes; July release. CAST: Anthony Eisley (Jordan), Pat Delaney (Bitsy), Francine York (Jessica), Kaz Garas (Artie), Angus Duncan (Craig), Mary Grace Canfield (Thelma)

RUST NEVER SLEEPS (International Harmony) Producer, L. A. Johnson; Executive Producer, Elliott Rabinowitz; Director, Bernard Shakey; Photography, Paul Goldsmith, Jon Else, Robby Greenberg, Hiro Narita, Richard Pearce, Daniel Pearl; Editor, Bernard Shakey; In Dolby Stereo and DeLuxe Color; Rated PG; 103 minutes; July release. CAST: Neil Young, Billy Talbot, Ralph Molina, Frank "Pancho" Sampedro

THE APPLE DUMPLING GANG RIDES AGAIN (Buena Vista) Producer, Ron Miller; Co-Producer, Tom Leetch; Director, Vincent McEveety; Screenplay, Don Tait; Based on characters created by Jack M. Bickham; Photography, Frank Phillips; Music, Buddy Baker; Art Directors, John B. Mansbridge, Frank T. Smith; Editor, Gordon D. Brenner; Assistant Directors, Robert W. Webb, Alan Green; Costumes, Chuck Keehne, Mary Dye; In Technicolor; A Walt Disney Production; Rated G; 88 minutes; July release. CAST: Tim Conway (Amos), Don Knotts (Theodore), Tim Matheson (Private Jeff Reid), Kenneth Mars (Marshall), Elyssa Davalos (Millie), Jack Elam (Big Mac), Robert Pine (Lieutenant Ravencroft), Harry Morgan (Major Gaskill), Ruth Buzzi (Tough Kate), Audrey Totter (Martha), Richard X. Slattery, John Crawford, Cliff Osmond, Ted Gehring, Morgan Paull, Robert Totten, James Almanzar, Shug Fisher, Rex Holman, Roger Mobley, Ralph Manza, Stu Gilliam, A. J. Bakunas, Dave Class, Louie Elias, Jimmy Van Patten, Jay Ripley, Nick Ramus, George Chandler, Bryan O'Byrne, Jack Perkins, John Wheeler, Art Evans, Ed McCready, Ted Jordan, Pete Renaday, Bobby Rolofson, Tom Jackman, Joe Baker, Allan Studley, Mike Masters, John Arndt, Bill Erickson, Vince Deadrick, Gary McLarty, Bill Hart, Mickey Gilbert, Wally Brooks, Stacie Elias, Mike Elias

DELIRIUM (Odyssey Pictures) Executive Producer, Mark Cusumano; Producers, Sunny Vest, Peter Maris; Director, Peter Maris; Screenplay, Richard Yalem; Story, Richard Yalem, Eddie Krell, Jim Loew; Music, David Williams; Photography, John Huston, Bill Mensch; Editor, Dan Perry; In color; Rated R; 90 minutes; July release. CAST: Debi Chaney (Susan), Turk Cekovsky (Paul), Terry Ten Broeck (Larry), Barron Winchester (Eric), Nick Panouzis (Charlie), Bob Winters (Donald), Garrett Bergfeld (Mark), Harry Gorsuch (Hearn), Chris Chronopolis (Parker), Lloyd Schattyn (Simms), Jack Garvey (Devlin), Mike Kalist (Specter), Myron Kozman (Wells)

THE LADY IN RED (New World) Producer, Julie Corman; Co-Producer, Steven Kovacs; Director, Lewis Teague; Screenplay, John Sayles; Photography, Daniel Lacambre; Editors, Larry Bock, Ron Medico, Lewis Teague; Designer, Jac McAnelly; Art Director, Philip Thomas; Music, James Horner; Assistant Director, Gerald T. Olson; Costumes, Danny Morgan, Pat Tonema; In color; Rated R; 93 minutes; July release. CAST: Pamela Sue Martin (Polly), Robert Conrad (John Dillinger), Louise Fletcher (Anna), Robert Hogan (Jake), Laurie Heineman (Rose), Glen Withrow (Eddie), Rod Gist (Pinetop), Peter Hobbs (Pops), Christopher Lloyd (Frognose), Dick Miller (Patek), Nancy Anne Parsons (Tiny Alice), Alan Vint (Melvin)

KING FRAT (Mad Makers) Producer, Reuben Trane; Director, Ken Wiederhorn; In color; Rated R; July release. CAST: John DiSanti, Dan Chandler, Dan Fitzgerald, Mike Grabow, Ray Mann, Charles Pitt, Roy Sekoff, Robert Small, T. J. Tully

THE FRISCO KID (Warner Bros.) Producer, Mace Neufeld; Director, Robert Aldrich; Screenplay, Michael Elias, Frank Shaw; Photography, Robert B. Hauser; Editors, Maury Winetrobe, Irving Rosenblum, Jack Horger; Music, Frank DeVol; Rated PG; 122 minutes; July release. CAST: Gene Wilder (Avram), Harrison Ford (Tommy), Ramon Bieri, Val Bisoglio, George Ralph DiCenzo, Leo Fuchs, Penny Peyser, William Smith, Jack Somack, Beege Barkett, Shay Duffin, Walter Janowitz, Joe Kapo, Clyde Kusatsu, Cliff Pellow, Allan Rich

Laurence Olivier, Geraldine McEwen
in "Dance of Death"

Harrison Ford, Gene Wilder
in "The Frisco Kid" © Warner Bros.   **111**

Vince Van Patten, Dey Young, P. J. Soles,
Riff Ramone in "Rock 'n' Roll High School"

Farrah Fawcett, Charles Grodin
in "Sunburn" © Paramount Pictures

ROCK 'N' ROLL HIGH SCHOOL (New World) Producer, Michael Finnell; Director, Allan Arkush; Screenplay, Richard Whitley, Russ Dvonch, Joseph McBride; Story, Allan Arkush, Joe Dante; Executive Producer, Roger Corman; Photography, Dean Cundey; Editors, Larry Bock, Gail Werbin; Art Director, Marie Kordus; Assistant Directors, Gerald T. Olson, Caren Singer; Costumes, Jack Buehler; Choreographer, Siana Lee Hall; In Metrocolor; Rated PG; 93 minutes; August release. CAST: P. J. Soles (Riff), Vincent Van Patten (Tom), Clint Howard (Eaglebauer), Dey Young (Kate) Mary Woronov (Miss Togar), Dick Miller (Police Chief), Paul Bartel (McGree), Alix Elias (Coach Steroid), Don Steele (Screamin' Steve), Loren Lester (Hansel), Daniel Davies (Gretel), Lynn Farrell (Angel Dust), Herbie Braha (Manager), Grady Sutton (School Board President), Chris Somma (Shawn), Marla Rosenfield (Cheryl), Barbara Ann Walters (Cafeteria Lady), Terry Soda (Norma), Joe Van Sickle (Cop), Ann Chatterton, Debbie Evans, Jack Gill, John Hately, Kay Kimler, and The Ramones

VIETNAM: AN AMERICAN JOURNEY (Films Incorporated) Producer-Director, Robert Richter; Photography, Burleigh Wartes; Editor, Peter Kinoy; Written by Robert Richter and Peter Kinoy; In color; Not rated; 90 minutes; August release. A film on postwar Vietnam.

SOMETHING SHORT OF PARADISE (American International) Producers, James C. Gutman, Lester Berman; Director, David Helpern, Jr.; Screenplay, Fred Barron; Executive Producers, Michael Ingber, Herbert Swartz; Photography, Walter Lassally; Music, Mark Snow; Editor, Frank Bracht; Art Director, William De Seta; Assistant Director, Michael Kravitz; Presented by Samuel Z. Arkoff; In Panavision and TVC Color; Rated PG; 91 minutes; August release. CAST: Susan Sarandon (Madeleine), David Steinberg (Harris), Jean-Pierre Aumont (Jean-Fidel), Marilyn Sokol (Ruthie), Joe Grifasi, Robert Hitt (Edgar), David Rasche (David), Bob Kaliban (George), Ted Pugh (Frank), Ann Robey (Gail), William Francis (Hotel Manager), Adrienne Jalbert (Fru-Fru), Terrence O'Hara (Donny), Fred Nassif (Desk Clerk), Sonya Jennings (Beth), Ellen March (Lisa), Loretta Tupper (Alice), Martha Sherrill (Mrs. Peel)

SUNBURN (Paramount) Producers, John Daly, Gerald Green; Executive Producers, Jay Bernstein, John Quested; Director, Richard C. Sarafian; Screenplay, John Daly, Stephen Oliver, James Booth; Based on book "The Bind" by Stanley Ellin; Associate Producer, David Korda; Photography, Alex Phillips, Jr.; Assistant Directors, Steve Barnett, Mario Cisneros; Costumes, Moss Mabry; A Tuesday Films production in color; Rated PG; 101 minutes; August release. CAST: Farrah Fawcett-Majors (Ellie), Charles Grodin (Jake), Art Carney (Al), John Collins (Nera), Eleanor Parker (Mrs. Thoren), Robin Clarke (Karl), Joan Goodfellow (Joanna), Jorge Luke (Vasquez), Jack Kruschen (Gela), Alejandro Rey (Ortega), John Hillerman (Webb), Bob Orrison (Milan), Alex Sharpe (Kunz), William Daniels (Crawford), Keenan Wynn (Mark), Seymour Cassel (Dobbs), Steven Wilensky (Elmer), Joe L. Brown (Milton)

THE CLONUS HORROR (Group I) Producers, Myrl A. Schreibman, Robert S. Fiveson; Executive Producer, Walter Fiveson; Director, Robert S. Fiveson; Screenplay, Myrl A. Schreibman, Robert S. Fiveson; Photography, Max Beaufort; Editor, Robert Gordon; Music, Hod David Schudson; Art Director, Steve Nelson; Costumes, Dorinda Rice Wood; Associate Producer, Peter R. J. Deyell; Assistant Directors, Michael Lee, Paul Berkowitz; In color; Rated R; 90 minutes; August release. CAST: Tim Donnelly (Richard), Dick Sargent (Dr. Jameson), Peter Graves (Jeff), Paulette Breen (Lena), David Hooks (Richard), Keenan Wynn (Jake), James Mantell (Ricky), Zale Kessler (Nelson), Frank Ashmore (George), Lurene Tuttle (Anna), Boyd Holister (Senator)

INCOMING FRESHMEN (Cannon) Produced, Directed, and Written by Eric Lewald, Glenn Morgan; A Hi-Test Film in color; Rated R; August release. CAST: Leslie Blalock, Debralee Scott, Cheryl Gordon, Richard Harriman, Jim Overbey

KILL THE GOLDEN GOOSE (Lone Star) Producers, Patrick Strong, Stephen B. Kim; Director, Elliot Hong; Executive Producers, Jim Anthony, Barry Burton, Russell Dodson; In color; Rated R; August release. CAST: Brad Von Beltz, Ed Parker, Master Bong Soo Han

Susan Sarandon, David Steinberg
in "Something Short of Paradise" © AIP

Tranh Thi Lei in "Vietnam:
An American Journey"

Nancy Morgan, John Ritter
in "Americathon" © United Artists

Tom Hallick, Howard Platt
in "Beyond Death's Door"

AMERICATHON (United Artists) Executive Producer, Edward Rosen; Producer, Joe Roth; Director, Neil Israel; Screenplay, Neil Israel, Michael Mislove, Monica Johnson; Adaptation, Philip Proctor, Peter Bergman from their play; Photography, Gerald Hirschfeld; Designer, Stan Jolley; Editor, John C. Howard; Associate Producer, David Nichols; Designer, Mark L. Fabus; Costumes, Daniel Paredes; Choreographer, Jaime Rogers; Assistant Directors, Jack Baran, William R. Lasky, Alice West; Music, Earl Brown, Jr., David Pomeranz, Elvis Costello, Alan Parsons, Reggie Knighton, Jim Steinman; A Lorimar Production in color; Rated PG; 85 minutes; August release. CAST: Peter Riegert (Eric), Harvey Korman (Monty), Fred Willard (Vanderhoof), Zane Buzby (Mouling), Nancy Morgan (Lucy), John Ritter (Chet), Richard Schaal, Elvis Costello (Earl), Chief Dan George (Sam), Tommy Lasorda (Announcer), Jay Leno (Larry), Peter Marshall (Himself), Meat Loaf (Oklahoma Roy), Howard Hesseman (Kip), Geno Andrews (Chris), Robert Beer (David Eisenhower), Terry McGovern (Danny), Nellie Bellflower (VP Advertising), Jimmy Weldon (VP Research), David Opatoshu, Allan Arbus (Hebrabs)

IN SEARCH OF HISTORIC JESUS (Sunn Classic) Producers, Charles E. Sellier, Jr., James L. Conway; Director, Henning Schellerup; Screenplay, Malvin Wald, Jack Jacobs; Based on book by Lee Roddy, Charles E. Sellier, Jr.; Associate Producer, Bill Cornford; Music, Bob Summers; Photography, Paul Hipp; Designer, Paul Staheli; Editor, Kendall S. Rase; Costumes, Julie Staheli; In color; Rated G; 91 minutes; August release. CAST: John Rubinstein (Jesus), John Anderson (Caiaphas), Nehemiah Persoff (Herod Antipas), Brad Crandall (Narrator), Andrew Bloch (John), Morgan Brittany (Mary), Walter Brooke (Joseph), Annette Charles (Mary Magdalene), Royal Dano (Prophet), Anthony DeLongis (Peter), Lawrence Dobkin (Pilate), David Opatoshu (Herod), Richard Carlyle (Astrologer), Jeffry Druce, John Hoyt, Stanley Kamel, Al Ruscio, Harvey Solin, Richard Alfieri, Robert Bonvento, Travis DeCastro, Steve DeFrance, John Hansen, James Ingersoll, Richard Jury

BEYOND DEATH'S DOOR (Sunn Classic Pictures) Executive Producer, Charles E. Sellier, Jr.; Producer, Stan Siegel; Director, Henning Schellerup; Based on book by Maurice Rawlings; Associate Producer, Bill Cornford; Music, Bob Summers; Photography, Stephen W. Gray; Designer, Paul Staheli; Assistant Directors, Leon Dudevoir, Jim Sbardellati, Dennis White; Costumes, Julie Staheli; In Technicolor; Rated PG; 97 minutes; August release. CAST: Tom Hallick (Pete), Howard Platt (Harry), Jo Ann Harris (Lane), Melinda Naud (Susan), Taurean Blacque (Flea Bite), Bethel Leslie (Linda), Danny Goldman (Herbie), Michael Ruud (Joe), Michael McQuire (George), Peg Stewart (Jennie), John Hansen, H.E.D. Redford, Cindy Fisher, Sam Di Bello, Brenda Smith, A.J. Blake, John Aspiras, Jesse Bennett, Kirk Chambers, Craig Clyde, Elaine Daniels, Tim Eisenhart, Jessie Frazier

HOLLYWOOD OUTTAKES (Thalen Corp.) Produced and Edited by Richard Schwarz; In black and white and color; Not rated; 135 minutes; August release.

DEAD ON ARRIVAL (CalAm Artists) Executive Producers, Joseph R. Laird, Kenneth J. Fisher; Producers, Theodor Bodnar, Steve Bond; Direction and Screenplay, Charles Martin; Music, Morton Stevens; In CFI color; Rated R; August release. CAST: Jack Palance, Christopher Mitchum, Pamela Shoop, Angel Tompkins, Cara Williams, Alexandra Hay, Jeff McCracken

GAL YOUNG UN (Nunez Films) Produced, Directed, Written, Photographed, and Edited by Victor Nunez; Assistant Director, Gus Holzer; Costumes, Allen Eggleston, Susan Holzer; In color; Not rated; 105 minutes; September release. CAST: Dana Preu (Matt), David Peck (Trax), J. Smith (Elly), Gene Densmore (Storekeeper), Jennie Stringfellow (Edna), Tim McCormack (Blaine), Casey Donovan (Jeb), Mike Garlington (Eddy), Marshal New (Edgar), Bruce Cornwell (Phil), John Pieters, Gil Lazier, Tina Moore, Marc Glick, Kerry McKenney, Sarah Drylie, Randy Ser, Bernie Cook, Fred Wood, Sissy Wood, Lewis Ivey, J. D. Henry, Billie Henry, Susan Holzer, Brian Lietz, Gus Holzer, Ross Sturlin, Pat Garner

John Rubinstein, Oscar Rowland
in "Jesus" © Sunn Classic

Dana Preu, David Peck
in "Gal Young Un" © Nunez

"Swap Meet"

Barbara Jones
in "Bush Mama"

SWAP MEET (Dimension Pictures) Produced and Written by Steve Krantz; Director, Brice Mack; Music, Hemlock; In CFI Color; Rated R; 86 minutes; September release. CAST: Ruth Cox, Jonathan Gries, Debi Richter, Dan Spector, Danny Goldman, Loren Lester, Cheryl Rixon

BUSH MAMA (Tricontinental) Producer-Director-Editor, Haile Gerima; Photography, Roderick Young, Charles Burnette; Music, Onaje Kareem Kenyatta; In black and white; Not rated; 95 minutes; September release. CAST: Barbara O. Jones (Dorothy), Johnny Weathers (TC), Susan Williams (Luann), Cora Lee Day (Molly), Simmi Ella Nelson (Simmi), Bettie J. Wilson (Social Worker), Bob Ogburn, Jr. (Dahomey Man), Ben Collins (Ben), Renna Kraft (Angi), Dorian Gibbs (Street Boy), Malbertha Pickett (Welfare Recipient), Minnie Stewart (Welfare Worker), Charles Brooks (Preacher), Bertha Yates (Secretary), Chris Clay (Policeman)

SEVEN (American International) Producer-Director, Andy Sidaris; Executive Producer, Melvin Simon; Screenplay, William Driskill, Robert Baird; Story, Andy Sidaris; Associate Producer-Designer, Sal Grasso; In color; Rated R; 100 minutes; September release. CAST: William Smith (Drew), Barbara Leigh (Alexa), Guich Koock (Cowboy), Art Metrano (Kinsella), Martin Kove (Skip), Ed Parker (Himself), Richard LePore (Professor), Christopher Joy (T. K.), Susan Kiger (Jennie), Robert Relyea (Harris), Little Egypt (Kahuna), Terry Kiser (Senator), Lenny Montana, Reggie Nalder, Tadashi Yamashita, Seth Sakai, Kwam Hi Lim, Tino Tuiolosega, Henry Ayau, John-Alderman, Terry Jastrow, Russ Howell, Peter Knecht, Red Johnson, John Thorp

WASHINGTON B.C. (First American) Executive Producer, Norman W. Cohen; Producer, Roy Townshend; Director, Fred Levinson; Screenplay, Larry Spiegel, Phil Dusenberry; Presented by John B. Kelly in Metrocolor; Rated PG; 85 minutes; September release. CAST: Dan Resin (President), Richard B. Shull (Secretary of Health), Dick O'Neill (Attorney General), Joseph Sirola (Reverend Williams), Patricia Ripley (First Lady), Gary Sandy (Tom), Willard Waterman (Vice-President), K. Callan (Mr. Burd), Constance Forslund (Sara), Phil Foster (Moloney), Lee Meredith (Mrs. Meredith)

CHEERLEADERS' WILD WEEKEND (Dimension) Producer, Chuck Russell; Director, Jeff Werner; Screenplay, D. W. Gilbert, Jason Williams; Executive Producer, William Osco; Photography, Paul Ryan; Associate Producer, Jason Williams; In color; Rated R; September release. CAST: Kristine DeBell, Jason Williams, Janet Blythe, Hana Byrbo, Tracy King, Anthony Lewis, Lachelle Price, Janie Squire, Ann Wharton, Robert Huston

THE DAY IT CAME TO EARTH (Howco International) Producer, John Braden; Executive Producer-Director, Harry Z. Thomason; Screenplay, Paul Fisk; Photography, Mike Varner; Music, Joe Southerland; In Eastmancolor; Rated PG; September release. CAST: Wink Roberts, Roger Manning, Bob Ginnaven, Delight DeBruine, Rita Wilson, Ed Love, George Gobel

REDNECK COUNTY (Group I Films) Producer-Director, Richard Robinson; Screenplay, B. W. Sandefur; Photography, David Worth; In Technicolor; Rated R; 92 minutes; September release. CAST: Leslie Uggams, Shelley Winters, Michael Christian, Ted Cassidy, Dub Taylor, Slim Pickens

SAMMY STOPS THE WORLD (Special Events Entertainment) Formerly "Stop the World, I Want to Get Off"; Director, Mel Shapiro; Screenplay, Music, and Lyrics, Leslie Bricusse, Anthony Newley; Choreography, Billy Wilson; Sets and Costumes, Santo Loquasto; A Hillard Elkins production; Producers, Mark Travis, Del Jack; Photography, David Myers; Editor, William H. Yahraus; Presented by Bill Sargent; In DeLuxe Color; Not rated; 104 minutes; September release. CAST: Sammy Davis, Jr., Marian Mercer, Dennis Daniels, Donna Lowe, Debora Masterson, Joyce Nolen, Wendy Edmead, Patrick Kinser-Lau, Shelly Burch, Charles Willis, Jr., Edwetta Little

THE MAFU CAGE (Clouds) Director, Karen Arthur; Screenplay, Don Chastain from French play by Eric Wespha; Photography, John Bailey; Editor, Carol Littleton; Music, Roger Kellaway; In color; Rated R; 102 minutes; September release. CAST: Lee Grant (Ellen), Carol Kane (Cissy), Will Geer (Zom), James Olson (David)

William Smith in "Seven"
© American International Pictures

Sammy Davis, Jr. in "Stop The World, I Want to Get Off"

114

Domingo Ambriz, Linda Gillin
in "Alambrista!"

"Northern Lights"

ALAMBRISTA! (Filmhaus) "The Illegal"; Executive Producer, Barbara Schultz; Producers, Michael Hausman, Irwin W. Young; Direction, Photography, and Screenplay, Robert M. Young; Editor, Ed Beyer; Music, Michael Martin; Art Director, Lily Kilvert; In DuArt Color; Not rated; 110 minutes; September release. CAST: Domingo Ambriz (Roberto), Trinidad Silva (Joe), Linda Gillin (Sharon), Paul Berrones (Berto), George Smith (Cook), Dennis Harris (Sharon's Brother), Edward Olmos, Julius Harris (Drunks), Mark Herder (Cop), J. D. Hurt (Preacher), Ned Beatty (Anglo Coyote), Salvador Martinez (Mexican Coyote), Felix Jose Alvarez (Junkyard Cook), Lily Alvarez (Pregnant Woman)

THE SCENIC ROUTE (New Line Cinema) Produced, Directed, Written, and Edited by Mark Rappaport; Associate Producer, Elaine Sperber; Photography, Fred Murphy; Art Director, Lilly Kilvert; Not rated; 76 minutes; September release. CAST: Randy Danson (Estelle), Marilyn Jones (Lena), Kevin Wade (Paul)

SCREAMS OF A WINTER NIGHT (Dimension Pictures) Producers, Richard H. Wadsack, James L. Wilson; Executive Producer, S. Mark Lovell; Director, James L. Wilson; Screenplay, Richard H. Wadsack; Special Effects, William T. Cherry III; Score, Don Zimmers; A Full Moon Pictures production in color; Rated PG; 91 minutes; September release. CAST: Matt Borel, Gil Glascow, Mary Agen Cox, Patrick Byers, Robin Bradley, Ray Gaspard, Beverly Allen, Brandy Barrett, Jan Norton, Charles Rucker

LEGEND OF SLEEPY HOLLOW (Sunn Classics) Producers, Charles E. Sellier, Jr., James L. Conway; Director, Henning Schellerup; Screenplay, Malvin Wald, Jack Jacobs, Tom Chapman; Based on story by Washington Irving; Associate Producer, Stan Siegel; Music, Bob Summers; Photography, Paul Hipp; Designer, Paul Staheli; Editor, Michael Spence; In Technicolor; Rated PG; 97 minutes; September release. CAST: Jeff Goldblum (Ichabod), Paul Sand (Frederic), John Sylvester White (Fritz), Dick Butkus (Brom), Laura Campbell (Thelma), Meg Foster (Katrina), James Griffith, Michael Ruud, Karin Isaacson, H.E.D. Redford, "Tiger" Thompson, Michael Witt

THE BUGS BUNNY/ROAD-RUNNER MOVIE (Warner Bros.) Producer-Director, Chuck Jones; Designer, Maurice Noble; Screenplay, Mike Maltese, Chuck Jones; Editor, Treg Brown; Co-Director, Phil Monroe; Designer, Ray Aragon; Music, Dean Elliott; Editor, Horta; In color; Not rated; 92 minutes; September release. Animated cartoons.

NORTHERN LIGHTS (Cine Manifest) Produced, Directed, Written, and Edited by John Hanson, Rob Nilsson; Associate Producer, Sandra Schulberg; Photography, Judy Irola; Music, David Ozzie Ahlers; Art Directors, Marianne Astrom-DeFina, Richard Brown; Assistant Director, Richard Kletter; Not rated; 90 minutes; September release. CAST: Robert Behling (Ray), Susan Lynch (Inga), Joe Spano (John), Marianne Astrom-DeFina (Kari), Ray Ness (Henrik), Helen Ness (Jenny), Thorbjorn Rue (Thor), Nick Eldridge (Sven), Jon Ness (Howard), Gary Hanisch (Charlie), Melvin Rodvold (Ole), Adelaide Throntveit (Adelaide), Mabel Rue (Grandma), Krist Toresen, Bill Ackeridge, Gordon Smaaladen, Harold Aleshire, Don DeFina, Henry Martinson

MR. MIKE'S MONDO VIDEO (New Line Cinema) Producer-Director, Michael O'Donoghue; Executive Producer, Lorne Michaels; Written by Mitchell Glazer, Michael O'Donoghue, Emily Prager, Dirk Wittenborn; Musical Director, Paul Shaffer; Designers, Eugene Lee, Franne Lee; Associate Producer, Tricia Brock; Photography, Barry Rebo; Editors, Bob Tischler, Alan Miller; In RomaGlo Color; Rated R: 140 minutes; September release. CAST: Michael O'Donoghue, Dan Aykroyd, Edie Baskin, Robert Delford Brown, Claudette Cooper, Rhonda Coullett, Jane Curtin, Zachary Danziger, Fred Dixon, Jill Duis, Carrie Fisher, Susan Forristal, Teri Garr, Francois de la Giroday, Mitchell Glazer, Merwin Goldsmith, Michael Grando, Joan Hackett, Deborah Harry, Sarah Holcomb, Judy Jacklin, Robert Lee Jones, Teri Keane, Margot Kidder, Ellen Birney Kleinberg, Helen Lee, Stephaney Lloyd, Wendie Malick, Marii Mak, Brian McConnachie, Bill Murray, Patti Oja, Bob Perry, Emily Prager, Gilda Radner, Barry Rebo, Barry Secunda, Paul Shaffer, Sylvia Shichman, Jack Straw, Clarence Thomas, Loretta Tupper, Anna Uppstrom, Dirk Wittenborn, Frederika Zappe

"Screams of a Winter Night"

"Mr. Mike's Mondo Video"

**Swayze, Baio, McCormick, Palillo, Bradford
in "Skatetown U.S.A." © Columbia Pictures**

**Rebecca Baldin, Steve Doubet
in "Silent Scream" © Denny Harris**

HEARTLAND (Filmhaus) Producers, Michael Hausman, Beth Ferris; Director, Richard Pearce; Executive Producer, Annick Smith; Screenplay, Beth Ferris; Designer, Patrizia Von Brandenstein; Art Director, Carl Copeland; Costumes, Hilary Rosenfeld; Music, Charles Gross; Editor, Bill Yahraus; Photography, Fred Murphy; Assistant Director, Michael Hausman; In Panavision and color; Not Rated; 93 minutes; September release. CAST: Rip Torn (Clyde), Conchata Ferrell (Elinore), Barry Primus (Jack), Lilia Skala (Grandma), Megan Folsom (Jerrine), Amy Wright (Clara), Jerry Hardin (Cattlebuyer), Mary Boylan (Ma Gillis), Jeff Boschee, Robert Overholzer (Land Office Agents), Bob Sirucek (Dan), Marvin Berg (Justice of Peace), Gary Voldseth, Mike Robertson, Doug Johnson (Cowboys)

THE FALL OF THE HOUSE OF USHER (Sunn Classic) Producer, Charles E. Sellier, Jr.; Director, James L. Conway; Screenplay, Stephen Lord; Based on story by Edgar Allan Poe; In Technicolor; Rated PG; October release. CAST: Martin Landau, Charlene Tilton, Ray Walston, Dimitra Arliss, Robert Hays

THE VISITOR (International Picture Show) Producer, Ovidio Assonitis; Director, Michael J. Paradise; Screenplay, Lou Comici, Robert Bundy; Story, Michael J. Paradise, Ovidio Assonitis; In color; Rated R; October release. CAST: Mel Ferrer, Glenn Ford, Lance Henricksen, John Huston, Joanna Nail, Sam Peckinpah, Shelley Winters, Paige Conner

JESUS (Warner Bros.) Producer, John Heyman; Directors, Peter Sykes, John Kirsh; Screenplay, Barnet Fishbein; Based on Gospel of St. Luke; Associate Producer, Richard Dalton; Costumes, Rochelle Zaltzman; A Genesis Project production in color; Rated G; 117 minutes; October release. CAST: Brian Deacon (Jesus), Rivka Noiman (Mary), Yossef Shiloah (Joseph), Niko Nitai (Simon Peter), Gadi Rol (Andrew), Itzhak Ne'eman (James), Shmuel Tal (John), Kobi Assaf (Philip), Michael Varshaviak (Bartholomew), Mosko Alkalai (Matthew), Nisim Gerama (Thomas), Eli Danker (Judas Iscariot), Eli Cohen (John the Baptist), Talia Shapira (Mary Magdalene), Richard Peterson (Herod), Peter Frye (Pilate), Alexander Scourby (Narrator)

SKATETOWN U.S.A. (Columbia) Producers, William A. Levey, Lorin Dreyfuss; Director, William A. Levey; Screenplay, Nick Castle; Story, William A. Levey, Lorin Dreyfuss, Nick Castle; Executive Producer, Peter E. Strauss; Associate Producer, Nancy Youngblood; Photography, Donald M. Morgan; Editor, Gene Fowler, Jr.; Choreographer, Bob Banas; Music, Miles Goodman; Art Director, Larry Wiemer; Assistant Directors, Victor Hsu, Frank Bueno, John Syrjamaki, Michael Looney; In Metrocolor; Rated PG; 98 minutes; October release. CAST: Scott Baio (Richie), Flip Wilson (Harvey), Ron Palillo (Frankey), Ruth Buzzi (Elvira), Dave Mason (Himself), Greg Bradford (Stan), Maureen McCormick (Susan), Patrick Swayze (Ace), Billy Barty (Jimmy), David Landsberg (Irwin), Joe E. Ross (Rent-a-Cop), Lenny Bari (Alphonse), Kelly Lang (Allison), Sydney Lassick (Murray), Sandra Gould, Murray Langston, Bill Kirchenbaurer, Vic Dunlop, Denny Johnston, Gary Mule Deer, Rick Edwards, Leonard Barr, Jonna Veitch, Deborah Chenoweth, Dorothy Stratten, Brigid Devlin, Kristi Kane, Connie Downing, Lou Mulford, Steve Bourne, Stanley Mieloch, Randall Brady, Mario Licu, Richard Wygant, Ronald Kleyweg, Charles Pitt, Kenneth Wright, Garry Kluger, Sue Weicberg, Kurt Paul, Judy Landers, Gary Hudson, Harlene Winsten, Johnny Pool, Bob Minor, Maurice Cooke, April Allen, Gail Collier

THE WHOLE SHOOTIN' MATCH (Cinema Perspectives) Produced and Written by Eagle Pennell, Lin Sutherland; Direction and Photography, Eagle Pennell; Music, Chuck Pennell; Executive Producer, John Jenkins; Associate Producer, Douglas Holloway; Art Director, Jim Rexrode; In black and white; Not rated; 100 minutes; October release. CAST: Lou Perry (Loyd), Sonny Davis (Frank), Doris Hargrave (Paulette), Eric Henshaw (Olan), David Weber (T. Frank), James Harrell (Old Man)

THE WATTS MONSTER (Dimension) Producer, Charles Walker; Director, William Crain; Executive Producer, Manfred Bernhard; Screenplay, Larry LeBron; Photography, Tak Fujimoto; Music, Johnny Pate; In color; Rated R; 90 minutes; October release. CAST: Bernie Casey, Rosalind Cash, Marie O'Henry

**Brian Deacon, Eli Danker
in "Jesus" © Warner Bros.**

"Squeeze Play"

Mark Owens
in "The Orphan"

Joe Lewis in "Jaguar Lives"
© American International

DELTA FOX (Sebastian International) Produced and Directed by Beverly Sebastian, Fred Sebastian; In color; Rated R; October release. CAST: Richard Lynch, Priscilla Barnes, Stuart Whitman, John Ireland, Richard Jaeckel

SILENT SCREAM (American Cinema) Executive Producers, Joan Harris, Denny Harris; Producers, Jim Wheat, Ken Wheat; Screenplay, Ken and Jim Wheat, Wallace C. Bennett; Director, Denny Harris; Associate Producer, Leslie Zurla; In color; Rated R; 87 minutes; November release. CAST: Rebecca Balding (Scotty), Cameron Mitchell (Lieutenant McGiver), Avery Schreiber (Sergeant Rusin), Barbara Steele (Victoria), Steve Doubet (Jack), Brad Reardon (Mason), Yvonne DeCarlo (Mrs. Engels), Juli Andelman (Doris), John Widelock (Peter)

SQUEEZE PLAY (Troma Inc.) Producers, Lloyd Kaufman, Michael Herz; Director, Samuel Weil; Associate Producer, Ira Kanarick; Photography, Lloyd Kaufman; Screenplay, Haim Pekelis; Executive Producer, William Kirksey; Editor, George T. Norris; Assistant Directors, David Alexander, Charles Kaufman; In color; Rated R; 90 minutes; November release. CAST: Jim Harris (Wes), Jenni Hetrick (Samantha), Rick Gitlin (Fred), Helen Campitelli (Jamie), Rick Kahn (Tom), Diana Valentien (Maureen), Alford Corley (Buddy), Melissa Michaels (Mary Lou), Michael P. Moran (Bozo), Sonya Jennings (Max), Sharon Kyle Bramblett (Midge), Zachary (Pop), Tony Hoty (Koch), Lisa Beth Wolf (Rose), Brenda Kaplan (Brenda), Steven W. Kaman (Russ), Kenneth Raskin (Beasley), Edward D. Phillips (Chester), Rosemary Joyce (Wanda), Peter Van Norden (Beauty Parlor Manager)

ARTHUR MILLER ON HOME GROUND (CBC) Produced, Directed, and Written by Harry Rasky; Music, Lou Applebaum; Editor, Arla Saare; Photography, Hideaki Kobayashi, Kenneth Gregg, Edmund Long; Not rated; 90 minutes; November release. CAST: Lee J. Cobb, Jeri Craden, Omie Craden, Colleen Dewhurst, Faye Dunaway, Mildred Dunnock, Clark Gable, Richard Jordan, Burt Lancaster, Carol Lawrence, Cec Linder, Marilyn Monroe, Christopher Plummer, Edward G. Robinson, George C. Scott, Maureen Stapleton, Raf Vallone, Harris Yulin

JAGUAR LIVES (American International) Executive Producer, Sandy Howard; Producer, Derek Gibson; Director, Ernest Pintoff; Screenplay, Yabo Yablonsky; Music, Robert O. Ragland; Associate Producer, Quinn Donoghue; Photography, John Cabrera; Costumes, Ron Talsky; Editor, Angelo Ross; Assistant Director, Kuki Lopez Rodero; Art Director, Adolfo Cofino; Rated PG; In Movielab Color; 90 minutes; November release. CAST: Joe Lewis (Jaguar), Christopher Lee (Caine), Donald Pleasence (General Villanova), Barbara Bach (Anna), Capucine (Zina), Joseph Wiseman (Ben Ashir), Woody Strode (Sensei), John Huston (Ralph), Gabriel Melgar (Ahmed), Anthony DeLongis (Brett), Sally Faulkner (Terry), Gail Grainger (Consuela), Anthony Heaton (Coblintz), Luis Prendes (Habish), Simon Andreu (Petrie), James Smilie (Reardon), Oscar James (Collins), Ray Jewers (Jessup), Ralph Brown (Logan)

THE ORPHAN (World Northal) Direction and Screenplay, John Ballard; Art Director, Sidney Ann MacKenzie; Photography, Beda F. Batka; Theme Song, Janis Ian; Musical Score, Ted Macero; Presented by Gilman-Westergaard Enterprises and Cinema Investments Co., in association with Trimedia Southwest Associates II; In color; Rated R; 80 minutes; November release. CAST: Peggy Feury (Aunt Martha), Joanna Miles (David's Mother), Donn Whyte (David's Father), Stanley Church (Dr. Thompson), Eleanor Stewart (Mary), Afolabi Ajayi (Akin), Jane House (Jean), David Foreman (Percy), Mark Owens (David)

ONE PAGE OF LOVE (United Theatrical Amusement) Produced, Directed, and Written by Ted Roter; Assistant Director, Lynda Gibson; Photography, Roy Snowden; Art Director, Cheri Paul; Musical Director, Gordon Marron; Songs, Gordon Marron, J. R. Reilich; Performed by J. R. Reilich; In color; Rated R; 89 minutes; November release. CAST: Gena Lee (Manon), Nancy Hoffman (Suzanne), Anthony Richards (Rick), Tovia Israel (Doctor), Diane Miller (Nurse), Richard Booth (Bartender), Romona St. Leger (Mona), Jennifer West (Jeanne), Bill Margold (Swinger), Larry Frady (Man in Disco)

Arthur Miller (L) in "Arthur
Miller on Home Grounds"

"One Page of Love"

Tim Conway, Michael LaGuardia
in "The Prize Fighter" © New World

Stevie Wonder in "The Secret Life
of Plants" © Paramount Pictures

THE PRIZE FIGHTER (New World Pictures) Producer, Lang Elliott; Story, Tim Conway; Screenplay, Tim Conway, John Myers; Music, Peter Matz; Photography, Jacques Haitkin; Editor, Fabien Tordjmann; Director, Michael Preece; Co-Producer, Wanda Dell; A Tri-Star Pictures production in Panavision and DeLuxe Color; Rated PG; 99 minutes; November release. CAST: Tim Conway (Bags), Don Knotts (Shake), Davie Wayne (Pop), Robin Clark (Mike), Cisse Cameron (Polly), Mary Ellen O'Neill (Mama), Michael LaGuardia (Butcher), George Nutting (Timmy)

MOUNTAIN FAMILY ROBINSON (Pacific International Enterprises) Produced and Written by Arthur R. Dubs; Director, John Cotter; Executive Producer, Fred R. Krug; Assistant Director, Gary Maxwell; Photography, James W. Roberson; Music, Robert O. Ragland; Editors, Dan Greer, Clifford Katz; In Panavision and Color; Rated PG; November release. CAST: Robert Logan (Skip), Susan Damante Shaw (Pat), Heather Rattray (Jenny), Ham Larsen (Toby), William Bryant (Forest Ranger), George "Buck" Flower (Boomer), Calvin Bartlett (Doctor), Jim Davidson (Pilot)

ON THE AIR LIVE WITH CAPTAIN MIDNIGHT (Sebastian International) Produced, Directed, and Written by Beverly Sebastian, Ferd Sebastian; In color; Rated PG; November release. CAST: Tracy Sebastian, John Ireland, Dena Dietrich, Ted Gehring, Mia Kovacs

THE CAPTURE OF BIGFOOT (Studio Film Corp.) Producer-Director, Bill Rebane; Screenplay, Ingrid Neumayer, Bill Rebane; In color; Rated PG. CAST: Stafford Morgan, Katherine Hopkins, Richard Kennedy, George "Buck" Flower, John Goff, Otis Young, John Eimerman

ALIEN ENCOUNTER (Group I Films) Producer, Marianne Chase; Director, Edward Hunt; Screenplay, Edward Hunt, Stanton Friedman; Photography, Hanania Baer; Associate Producer, Greg McCarty; Assistant Director, Dana MacDuff; Editor, Lawrence Ross; Music, Neiman-Tillar; In DeLuxe Color and Stereophonic Sound; Presented by Brandon Chase; Rated G; 93 minutes; November release. No other credits submitted.

THE SECRET LIFE OF PLANTS (Paramount) Producer, Michael Braun; Director, Walon Green; Screenplay, Peter Tompkins, Walon Green; Based on book by Peter Tompkins and Christopher Bird; Executive Producers, Burt Kleiner, Paul Kantor; Music, Stevie Wonder; Photography, Ken Middleham; Narration, Peter Tompkins, Elizabeth Vreeland, Ruby Crystal; Editors, Christopher Lebenzon, Robert Lambert, Ian Masters; Choreography, George Faison; An Infinite Enterprises Production in Dolby Stereo, Panavision, and Metrocolor; Rated G; December release.

C.H.O.M.P.S. (American International) Executive Producer, Samuel Z. Arkoff; Producer, Joseph Barbera; Co-Producer, Burt Topper; Director, Don Chaffey; Screenplay, Dick Robbins, Duane Poole, Joseph Barbera; Based on story by Joseph Barbera; Photography, Charles F. Wheeler; Associate Producer, Joe Cavalier; Editors, Warner Leighton, Dick Darling; Music, Hoyt Curtin; Assistant Directors, Al Nicholson, Albert Shapiro; Designer, Ted Shell; In Movielab Color; Rated PG; 89 minutes; December release. CAST: Wesley Eure (Brian), Valerie Bertinelli (Casey), Conrad Bain (Ralph), Chuck McCann (Brooks), Red Buttons (Bracken), Larry Bishop (Ken), Hermione Baddeley (Mrs. Fowler), Jim Backus (Gibbs), Robert Q. Lewis (Merkle), Regis Toomey (Chief)

THE GLOVE (PRO International) Producer, Julian Roffman; Director, Ross Hagen; Music, Robert O. Ragland; Executive Producer, William B. Silberkleit; In color; Rated R; December release. CAST: John Saxon, Rosey Grier, Joanna Cassidy, Joan Blondell, Jack Carter, Aldo Ray, Keenan Wynn

THE SEARCH FOR SOLUTIONS (Playback Associates) Executive Producer, James C. Crimmins; Director, Mike Jackson; Co-Producers, Mike Jackson, Kathy Mendoza; Associate Producers, Janet Forman, Ken Werner; Music, Pat Metheny, Lyle Mays; Editors, Ken Werner, Kris Liem, Kathryn Barnier, Arnold Briedman; Writers, James C. Crimmins, Brad Darrach, L. L. Larison Cudmore, Gerald Jonas; Photography, Mike Jackson, Carl Kriegeskotte; In color; Rated G; 164 minutes; December release. A documentary in nine parts.

Heather Rattray, Robert Logan, Susan Damante
Shaw in "Mountain Family Robinson"

Red Buttons, Chuck McCann
in "C.H.O.M.P.S." © AIP

Linda Blair, Jim Bray in "Roller Boogie"
© United Artists Corp.

ROLLER BOOGIE (United Artists) Executive Producer, Irwin Yablans; Producer, Bruce Cohn Curtis; Associate Producer, Joseph Wolf; Director, Mark L. Lester; Screenplay, Barry Schneider; Story, Irwin Yablans; Assistant Directors, Dan Allingham, Richard C. Wallace; Editor, Howard Kunin; Photography, Dean Cundey; Choreography, David Winters; Art Director, Keith Michl, Music, Bob Esty; Songs, Bob Esty, Michele Aller, Michael Brooks; In Metrocolor and Dolby Stereo; A Compass International picture; Rated PG; 103 minutes; December release. CAST: Linda Blair (Terry), Jim Bray (Bobby), Beverly Garland (Mrs. Barkley), Roger Perry (Barkley), Jimmy Van Patten (Hoppy), Kimberly Beck (Lana), Rick Sciacca (Complete Control), Sean McClory (Jammer), Mark Goddard (Thatcher), Albert Insinnia (Gordo), Stoney Jackson (Phones), M. G. Kelly (J.D.), Chris Nelson (Franklin), Patrick Wright (Sergeant Danner), Dorothy Meyer (Ada), Shelley Golden (Mrs. Potter), Bill Ross (Nick), Carey Fox (Sonny), Nina Axelrod (Bobby's Friend)

SCAVENGER HUNT (20th Century-Fox) Producer, Steven A. Vail; Director, Michael Schultz; Screenplay, Steven A. Vail, Henry Harper; Co-Producer, Paul Maslansky; Executive Producer, Melvin Simon; Photography, Ken Lamkin; Music, Billy Goldenberg; Associate Producers, Craig S. Yace, Hana Cannon; Art Director, Richard Berger; Editor, Christopher Holmes; Assistant Directors, Daniel J. McCauley, Benjamin Rosenberg; In DeLuxe Color; Rated PG; 116 minutes; December release. CAST: Richard Benjamin (Stuart), James Coco (Henri), Scatman Crothers (Sam), Ruth Gordon (Arvilla), Cloris Leachman (Mildred), Cleavon Little (Jackson), Roddy McDowall (Jenkins), Robert Morley (Bernstein), Richard Mulligan (Marvin), Tony Randall (Henry), Dirk Benedict (Jeff), Willie Aames (Kenny), Stephanie Faracy (Babette), Stephen Furst (Merle), Richard Masur (Georgie), Meat Loaf (Scum), Pat McCormick (Barker), Vincent Price (Parker), Avery Schreiber (Zoo Keeper), Liz Torres (Lady Zero), Carol Wayne (Nurse), Stuart Pankin, Maureen Teefy, Missy Francis, Julie Anne Haddock, David Hollander, Shane Sinutko, Henry Polic II, Hal Landon, Jr., Emory Bass

Huntz Hall and girls
in "Gas Pump Girls"

GAS PUMP GIRLS (Cannon) Producer, David A. Davies; Director, Joel Bender; Executive Producer, David Gil; Screenplay, David A. Davies, Joel Bender, Isaac Blech; Photography, Nicholas Von Sternberg; Editor, Patrick McMahon; Songs, David and Isaac Blech; In color; Rated R; 90 minutes; December release. CAST: Kirsten Baker (June), Dennis Bowen (Roger), Huntz Hall (Uncle Joe), Steve Bond (Butch), Sandy Johnson (April), Leslie King (Jane), Linda Lawrence (Betty), Ken Lerner (Peewee), Rikki Marin (January), Demetre Phillips (Hank), Paul Tinder (Michael), Rob Kenneally (Hal), Joe E. Ross (Bruno), Mike Mazurki (Moiv), Dave Shelley (Friendly), Morris Buchanan, Kay Elliot, Norm Fields, Loutz Gage, John F. Goff, Jack Jozefson, Bill Lytle, Eileen Marek, Clifford Martin III, Peter Spitzer, Robert Sutton

BABY SNAKES (Intercontinental Absurdities) Produced, Directed, and Edited by Frank Zappa; In DeLuxe Color and Dolby Stereo; Rated R; 166 minutes; December release. CAST: Frank Zappa, Adrian Belew, Tommy Mars, Terry Bozzio, Kerry McNabe, Bruce Bickford, Rob Leacock, Ed Mann, Warren Cucurullo, Chris Martin, Klaus Hundsbichler, Roy Estrada, John Smothers, David Ditkowich, Bill Harrington, Patrick O'Hearn, Phil Parmet, Peter Wolf, Dick Pearce, Phil Kaufman, Tex Abel, Brian Rivera

THE WAR AT HOME (Catalyst) Produced and Directed by Glenn Silber, Barry Alexander Brown; Associate Producer, Writer, Elizabeth Duncan; Photography, Rick March, Bob Lerner; Editor, Chuck France; In black and white and color; Not rated; 100 minutes; December release. A documentary on student revolts during the anti-Vietnam 1960s.

PENITENTIARY (Jerry Gross) Produced, Directed, and Written by Jamaa Fanaka; Photography, Marty Ollstein; Editor, Betsy Blankett; Music, Frankie Gaye; Art Director, Adel Mazen; In color; Rated R; 99 minutes; December release. CAST: Leon Isaac Kennedy (Too Sweet), Thommy Pollard (Eugene), Hazel Spears (Linda), Badja Djola (Wilson), Gloria Delaney (Inmate), Chuck Mitchell (Lieutenant Arnsworth), Wilbur "Hi-Fi" White (Sweet Pea)

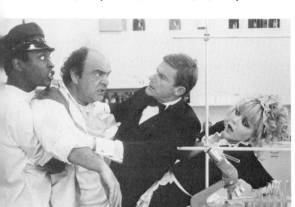

Cleavon Little, James Coco, Roddy McDowall,
Stephanie Faracy in "Scavenger Hunt" © 20th

Leon Isaac Kennedy
in "Penitentiary"

PROMISING NEW ACTORS 1979

SUSAN ANTON

DENNIS CHRISTOPHER

STEPHEN COLLINS

BO DEREK

LISA EICHHORN

MAC DAVIS

JOHN SAVAGE

JILL EIKENBERRY

AMY IRVING

RICKY SCHRODER

FRANKLYN SEALES

BETTE MIDLER

DUSTIN HOFFMAN
in "Kramer VS. Kramer"
1979 ACADEMY AWARD FOR BEST ACTOR

KRAMER VS. KRAMER

(COLUMBIA) Producer, Stanley R. Jaffe; Direction and Screenplay, Robert Benton; From novel by Avery Corman; Photography, Nestor Almendros; Designer, Paul Sylbert; Costumes, Ruth Morley; Editor, Jerry Greenberg; Associate Producer, Richard C. Fischoff; Assistant Directors, Thomas John Kane, Yudi Bennett; Music, Henry Purcell, Antonio Vivaldi; In Technicolor; Rated PG; 105 minutes; December release.

CAST

Ted Kramer	Dustin Hoffman
Joanna Kramer	Meryl Streep
Margaret Phelps	Jane Alexander
Billy Kramer	Justin Henry
John Shaunessy	Howard Duff
Jim O'Connor	George Coe
Phyllis Bernard	JoBeth Williams
Gressen	Bill Moor
Judge Atkins	Howland Chamberlain
Spencer	Jack Ramage
Ackerman	Jess Osuna
Interviewer	Nicholas Hormann
Teacher	Ellen Parker
Ted's Secretary	Shelby Brammer
Mrs. Kline	Carol Nadell
Surgeon	Donald Gantry
Receptionist	Judith Calder
Norman	Peter Lownds
Waitress	Kathleen Keller
Court Clerk	Dan Tyra
Grocer	David Golden
Petie Phelps	Petra King
Kim Phelps	Melissa Morell

and Ingeborg Sorensen, Iris Alhanti, Richard Barris, Evelyn Hope Bunn, Joann Friedman, Quentin J. Hruska, Joe Seneca, Frederic W. Hand, Scott Kuney

1979 Academy Awards for Best Picture, Best Director, Best Actor (Dustin Hoffman), Best Supporting Actress (Meryl Streep), Best Screenplay (based on material from another medium)

Left: Meryl Streep, Justin Henry
Top: Dustin Hoffman, Meryl Streep
© Columbia Pictures Industries

Justin Henry

Dustin Hoffman, Justin Henry

1979 ACADEMY AWARD FOR BEST PICTURE

Dustin Hoffman, Jane Alexander
Above: Justin Henry, Dustin Hoffman
Top: Bill Moor, Howland Chamberlain,
Jane Alexander

Dustin Hoffman, Justin Henry
Top: Meryl Streep, Howard Duff

SALLY FIELD
in "Norma Rae"
1979 ACADEMY AWARD FOR BEST ACTRESS

MERYL STREEP
in "Kramer Vs. Kramer"
1979 ACADEMY AWARD FOR BEST SUPPORTING ACTRESS

MELVYN DOUGLAS
in "Being There"
1979 ACADEMY AWARD FOR BEST SUPPORTING ACTOR

BEST BOY

(INTERNATIONAL FILM EXCHANGE) Produced, Directed, and Edited by Ira Wohl; Designed and Photographed by Tom McDonough; An Only Child Motion Pictures production in color; 111 minutes; Not rated. A documentary narrated by Ira Wohl, about his 52-year-old mentally retarded cousin Philly.

Philly (R) and family

1979 Academy Award for Best Documentary Feature

THE TIN DRUM

(NEW WORLD) Producers, Franz Seitz, Anatole Dauman; Director, Volker Schlondorff; Screenplay, Jean-Claude Carriere, Volker Schlondorff, Franz Seitz, with the collaboration of Gunter Grass, on whose novel it is based; Photography, Igor Luther; Editor, Suzanne Baron; Music, Maurice Jarre; A German-French Co-Production by Artemis Film (Germany) and Argos Films (France); In German with English subtitles; In color; 142 minutes; Rated R.

CAST

Oskar	David Bennent
Alfred Matzerath	Mario Adorf
Agnes Matzerath	Angela Winkler
Jan Bronski	Daniel Olbrychski
Maria	Katharina Tahlbach
Sigismund Markus	Charles Aznavour
Greff	Heinz Bennent
Lina Greff	Andrea Ferreol
Bebra	Fritz Hakl
Raswitha Raguna	Mariella Oliveri
Anna Kollaiczek, young	Tina Engel
Anna Kollaiczek, old	Berta Drews
Joseph Kollaiczek	Roland Beubner
Gauleiter Lobsack	Ernst Jacobi
Scheffler, the Baker	Werner Rehm
Gretchen Scheffler	Ilse Page
Mother Truczinski	Kate Jaenicke
Herbert Truczinski	Wigand Witting
Marek Walczewski	Schugger-Leo
Faingold	Wolcech Pszoniak
Meyn, the Musician	Otto Sander
Felix	Karl-Heinz Titelbach
Corporal Lankes	Bruno Thost
Miss Spollenhauer	Gerda Blisse
Father Wiehnke	Joachim Hackethal
Dr. Michon	Zygmunt Huebner
Kobyella	Mieczyslaw Czechowicz
Circus Performers	Emil Feist, Herbert Behrent

Top: David Bennent
© New World Pictures

1979 Academy Award for Best Foreign-Language Film

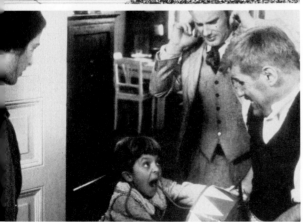

Angela Winkler, David Bennent, Daniel Olbrychski, Mario Adorf

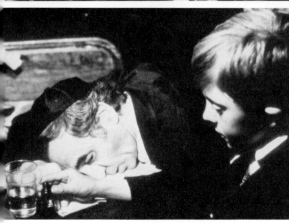

Charles Aznavour, David Bennent
Above: Aznavour, Angela Winkler

David Bennent (R)
Top: Bennent, Mario Adorf

Anne Baxter   Karl Malden   Ingrid Bergman   Ray Milland   Joan Fontaine

PREVIOUS ACADEMY AWARD WINNERS

(1) Best Picture, (2) Actor, (3) Actress, (4) Supporting Actor, (5) Supporting Actress, (6) Director,
(7) Special Award, (8) Best Foreign Language Film

1927–28: (1) "Wings," (2) Emil Jannings in "The Way of All Flesh," (3) Janet Gaynor in "Seventh Heaven," (6) Frank Borzage for "Seventh Heaven," (7) Charles Chaplin.

1928–29: (1) "Broadway Melody," (2) Warner Baxter in "Old Arizona," (3) Mary Pickford in "Coquette," (6) Frank Lloyd for "The Divine Lady."

1929–30: (1) "All Quiet on the Western Front," (2) George Arliss in "Disraeli," (3) Norma Shearer in "The Divorcee," (6) Lewis Milestone for "All Quiet on the Western Front."

1930–31: (1) "Cimarron," (2) Lionel Barrymore in "A Free Soul," (3) Marie Dressler in "Min and Bill," (6) Norman Taurog for "Skippy."

1931–32: (1) "Grand Hotel," (2) Fredric March in "Dr. Jekyll and Mr. Hyde" tied with Wallace Beery in "The Champ," (3) Helen Hayes in "The Sin of Madelon Claudet," (6) Frank Borzage for "Bad Girl."

1932–33: (1) "Cavalcade," (2) Charles Laughton in "The Private Life of Henry VIII," (3) Katharine Hepburn in "Morning Glory," (6) Frank Lloyd for "Cavalcade."

1934: (1) "It Happened One Night," (2) Clark Gable in "It Happened One Night," (3) Claudette Colbert in "It Happened One Night," (6) Frank Capra for "It Happened One Night," (7) Shirley Temple.

1935: (1) "Mutiny on the Bounty," (2) Victor McLaglen in "The Informer," (3) Bette Davis in "Dangerous," (6) John Ford for "The Informer," (7) D. W. Griffith.

1936: (1) "The Great Ziegfeld," (2) Paul Muni in "The Story of Louis Pasteur," (3) Luise Rainer in "The Great Ziegfeld," (4) Walter Brennan in "Come and Get It," (5) Gale Sondergaard in "Anthony Adverse," (6) Frank Capra for "Mr. Deeds Goes to Town."

1937: (1) "The Life of Emile Zola," (2) Spencer Tracy in "Captains Courageous," (3) Luise Rainer in "The Good Earth," (4) Joseph Schildkraut in "The Life of Emile Zola," (5) Alice Brady in "In Old Chicago," (6) Leo McCarey for "The Awful Truth," (7) Mack Sennett, Edgar Bergen.

1938: (1) "You Can't Take It with You," (2) Spencer Tracy in "Boys' Town," (3) Bette Davis in "Jezebel," (4) Walter Brennan in "Kentucky," (5) Fay Bainter in "Jezebel," (6) Frank Capra for "You Can't Take It with You," (7) Deanna Durbin, Mickey Rooney, Harry M. Warner, Walt Disney.

1939: (1) "Gone with the Wind," (2) Robert Donat in "Goodbye, Mr. Chips," (3) Vivien Leigh in "Gone with the Wind," (4) Thomas Mitchell in "Stagecoach," (5) Hattie McDaniel in "Gone with the Wind," (6) Victor Fleming for "Gone with the Wind," (7) Douglas Fairbanks, Judy Garland.

1940: (1) "Rebecca," (2) James Stewart in "The Philadelphia Story," (3) Ginger Rogers in "Kitty Foyle," (4) Walter Brennan in "The Westerner," (5) Jane Darwell in "The Grapes of Wrath," (6) John Ford for "The Grapes of Wrath," (7) Bob Hope.

1941: (1) "How Green Was My Valley," (2) Gary Cooper in "Sergeant York," (3) Joan Fontaine in "Suspicion," (4) Donald Crisp in "How Green Was My Valley," (5) Mary Astor in "The Great Lie," (6) John Ford for "How Green Was My Valley," (7) Leopold Stokowski, Walt Disney.

1942: (1) "Mrs. Miniver," (2) James Cagney in "Yankee Doodle Dandy," (3) Greer Garson in "Mrs. Miniver," (4) Van Heflin in "Johnny Eager," (5) Teresa Wright in "Mrs. Miniver," (6) William Wyler for "Mrs. Miniver," (7) Charles Boyer, Noel Coward.

1943: (1) "Casablanca," (2) Paul Lukas in "Watch on the Rhine," (3) Jennifer Jones in "The Song of Bernadette," (4) Charles Coburn in "The More the Merrier," (5) Katina Paxinou in "For Whom the Bell Tolls," (6) Michael Curtiz for "Casablanca."

1944: (1) "Going My Way," (2) Bing Crosby in "Going My Way," (3) Ingrid Bergman in "Gaslight," (4) Barry Fitzgerald in "Going My Way," (5) Ethel Barrymore in "None but the Lonely Heart," (6) Leo McCarey for "Going My Way," (7) Margaret O'Brien, Bob Hope.

1945: (1) "The Lost Weekend," (2) Ray Milland in "The Lost Weekend," (3) Joan Crawford in "Mildred Pierce," (4) James Dunn in "A Tree Grows in Brooklyn," (5) Anne Revere in "National Velvet," (6) Billy Wilder for "The Lost Weekend," (7) Walter Wanger, Peggy Ann Garner.

1946: (1) "The Best Years of Our Lives," (2) Fredric March in "The Best Years of Our Lives," (3) Olivia de Havilland in "To Each His Own," (4) Harold Russell in "The Best Years of Our Lives," (5) Anne Baxter in "The Razor's Edge," (6) William Wyler for "The Best Years of Our Lives," (7) Laurence Olivier, Harold Russell, Ernst Lubitsch, Claude Jarman, Jr.

1947: (1) "Gentleman's Agreement," (2) Ronald Colman in "A Double Life," (3) Loretta Young in "The Farmer's Daughter," (4) Edmund Gwenn in "Miracle On 34th Street," (5) Celeste Holm in "Gentleman's Agreement," (6) Elia Kazan for "Gentleman's Agreement," (7) James Baskette, (8) "Shoe Shine."

1948: (1) "Hamlet," (2) Laurence Olivier in "Hamlet," (3) Jane Wyman in "Johnny Belinda," (4) Walter Huston in "The Treasure of the Sierra Madre," (5) Claire Trevor in "Key Largo," (6) John Huston for "The Treasure of the Sierra Madre," (7) Ivan Jandl, Sid Grauman, Adolph Zukor, Walter Wanger, (8) "Monsieur Vincent."

1949: (1) "All the King's Men," (2) Broderick Crawford in "All the King's Men," (3) Olivia de Havilland in "The Heiress." (4) Dean Jagger in "Twelve O'Clock High," (5) Mercedes McCambridge in "All the King's Men," (6) Joseph L. Mankiewicz for "A Letter to Three Wives," (7) Bobby Driscoll, Fred Astaire, Cecil B. DeMille, Jean Hersholt, (8) "The Bicycle Thief."

1950: "All about Eve," (2) Jose Ferrer in "Cyrano de Bergerac," (3) Judy Holliday in "Born Yesterday," (4) George Sanders in "All about Eve," (5) Josephine Hull in "Harvey," (6) Joseph L. Mankiewicz for "All about Eve," (7) George Murphy, Louis B. Mayer, (8) "The Walls of Malapaga."

1951: (1) "An American in Paris," (2) Humphrey Bogart in "The African Queen," (3) Vivien Leigh in "A Streetcar Named Desire," (4) Karl Malden in "A Streetcar Named Desire," (5) Kim Hunter in "A Streetcar Named Desire," (6) George Stevens for "A Place in the Sun," (7) Gene Kelly, (8) "Rashomon."

1952: (1) "The Greatest Show on Earth," (2) Gary Cooper in "High Noon," (3) Shirley Booth in "Come Back, Little Sheba," (4) Anthony Quinn in "Viva Zapata," (5) Gloria Grahame in "The Bad and the Beautiful," (6) John Ford for "The Quiet Man," (7) Joseph M. Schenck, Merian C. Cooper, Harold Lloyd, Bob Hope, George Alfred Mitchell, (8) "Forbidden Games."

1953: (1) "From Here to Eternity," (2) William Holden in "Stalag 17," (3) Audrey Hepburn in "Roman Holiday," (4) Frank Sinatra in "From Here to Eternity," (5) Donna Reed in "From Here to

| **Mickey Rooney** | **Celeste Holm** | **Frank Sinatra** | **Ginger Rogers** | **James Stewart** |

Eternity," (6) Fred Zinnemann for "From Here to Eternity," (7) Pete Smith, Joseph Breen.

1954: (1) "On the Waterfront," (2) Marlon Brando in "On the Waterfront," (3) Grace Kelly in "The Country Girl," (4) Edmond O'Brien in "The Barefoot Contessa," (5) Eva Marie Saint in "On the Waterfront," (6) Elia Kazan for "On the Waterfront," (7) Greta Garbo, Danny Kaye, Jon Whitely, Vincent Winter, (8) "Gate of Hell."

1955: (1) "Marty," (2) Ernest Borgnine in "Marty," (3) Anna Magnani in "The Rose Tattoo," (4) Jack Lemmon in "Mister Roberts," (5) Jo Van Fleet in "East of Eden," (6) Delbert Mann for "Marty," (8) "Samurai."

1956: (1) "Around the World in 80 Days," (2) Yul Brynner in "The King and I," (3) Ingrid Bergman in "Anastasia," (4) Anthony Quinn in "Lust for Life," (5) Dorothy Malone in "Written on the Wind," (6) George Stevens for "Giant," (7) Eddie Cantor, (8) "La Strada."

1957: (1) "The Bridge on the River Kwai," (2) Alec Guinness in "The Bridge on the River Kwai," (3) Joanne Woodward in "The Three Faces of Eve," (4) Red Buttons in "Sayonara," (5) Miyoshi Umeki in "Sayonara," (6) David Lean for "The Bridge on the River Kwai," (7) Charles Brackett, B. B. Kahane, Gilbert M. (Bronco Billy) Anderson, (8) "The Nights of Cabiria."

1958: (1) "Gigi," (2) David Niven in "Separate Tables," (3) Susan Hayward in "I Want to Live," (4) Burl Ives in "The Big Country," (5) Wendy Hiller in "Separate Tables," (6) Vincente Minnelli for "Gigi," (7) Maurice Chevalier, (8) "My Uncle."

1959: (1) "Ben-Hur," (2) Charlton Heston in "Ben-Hur," (3) Simone Signoret in "Room at the Top," (4) Hugh Griffith in "Ben-Hur," (5) Shelley Winters in "The Diary of Anne Frank," (6) William Wyler for "Ben-Hur," (7) Lee de Forest, Buster Keaton, (8) "Black Orpheus."

1960: (1) "The Apartment," (2) Burt Lancaster in "Elmer Gantry," (3) Elizabeth Taylor in "Butterfield 8," (4) Peter Ustinov in "Spartacus," (5) Shirley Jones in "Elmer Gantry," (6) Billy Wilder for "The Apartment," (7) Gary Cooper, Stan Laurel, Hayley Mills, (8) "The Virgin Spring."

1961: (1) "West Side Story," (2) Maximilian Schell in "Judgment at Nuremberg," (3) Sophia Loren in "Two Women," (4) George Chakiris in "West Side Story," (5) Rita Moreno in "West Side Story," (6) Robert Wise for "West Side Story," (7) Jerome Robbins, Fred L. Metzler, (8) "Through a Glass Darkly."

1962: (1) "Lawrence of Arabia," (2) Gregory Peck in "To Kill a Mockingbird," (3) Anne Bancroft in "The Miracle Worker," (4) Ed Begley in "Sweet Bird of Youth," (5) Patty Duke in "The Miracle Worker," (6) David Lean for "Lawrence of Arabia," (8) "Sundays and Cybele."

1963: (1) "Tom Jones," (2) Sidney Poitier in "Lilies of the Field," (3) Patricia Neal in "Hud," (4) Melvyn Douglas in "Hud," (5) Margaret Rutherford in "The V.I.P's," (6) Tony Richardson for "Tom Jones," (8) "8½."

1964: (1) "My Fair Lady," (2) Rex Harrison in "My Fair Lady," (3) Julie Andrews in "Mary Poppins," (4) Peter Ustinov in "Topkapi," (5) Lila Kedrova in "Zorba the Greek," (6) George Cukor for "My Fair Lady," (7) William Tuttle, (8) "Yesterday, Today and Tomorrow."

1965: (1) "The Sound of Music," (2) Lee Marvin in "Cat Ballou," (3) Julie Christie in "Darling," (4) Martin Balsam in "A Thousand Clowns," (5) Shelley Winters in "A Patch of Blue," (6) Robert Wise for "The Sound of Music," (7) Bob Hope, (8) "The Shop on Main Street."

1966: (1) "A Man for All Seasons," (2) Paul Scofield in "A Man for All Seasons," (3) Elizabeth Taylor in "Who's Afraid of Virginia Woolf?," (4) Walter Matthau in "The Fortune Cookie," (5)

Sandy Dennis in "Who's Afraid of Virginia Woolf?," (6) Fred Zinnemann for "A Man for All Seasons," (8) "A Man and A Woman."

1967: (1) "In the Heat of the Night," (2) Rod Steiger in "In the Heat of the Night," (3) Katharine Hepburn in "Guess Who's Coming to Dinner," (4) George Kennedy in "Cool Hand Luke," (5) Estelle Parsons in "Bonnie and Clyde," (6) Mike Nichols for "The Graduate," (8) "Closely Watched Trains."

1968: (1) "Oliver!," (2) Cliff Robertson in "Charly," (3) Katharine Hepburn in "The Lion in Winter" tied with Barbra Streisand in "Funny Girl," (4) Jack Albertson in "The Subject Was Roses," (5) Ruth Gordon in "Rosemary's Baby," (6) Carol Reed for "Oliver!," (7) Onna White for "Oliver!" choreography, John Chambers for "Planet of the Apes" make-up, (8) "War and Peace."

1969: (1) "Midnight Cowboy," (2) John Wayne in "True Grit," (3) Maggie Smith in "The Prime of Miss Jean Brodie," (4) Gig Young in "They Shoot Horses, Don't They?," (5) Goldie Hawn in "Cactus Flower," (6) John Schlesinger for "Midnight Cowboy," (7) Cary Grant, (8) "Z."

1970: (1) "Patton," (2) George C. Scott in "Patton," (3) Glenda Jackson in "Women in Love," (4) John Mills in "Ryan's Daughter," (5) Helen Hayes in "Airport," (6) Franklin J. Schaffner for "Patton," (7) Lillian Gish, Orson Welles, (8) "Investigation of a Citizen above Suspicion."

1971: (1) "The French Connection," (2) Gene Hackman in "The French Connection," (3) Jane Fonda in "Klute," (4) Ben Johnson in "The Last Picture Show," (5) Cloris Leachman in "The Last Picture Show," (6) William Friedkin for "The French Connection," (7) Charles Chaplin, (8) "The Garden of the Finzi-Continis."

1972: (1) "The Godfather," (2) Marlon Brando in "The Godfather," (3) Liza Minnelli in "Cabaret," (4) Joel Grey in "Cabaret," (5) Eileen Heckart in "Butterflies Are Free," (6) Bob Fosse for "Cabaret," (7) Edward G. Robinson, (8) "The Discreet Charm of the Bourgeoisie."

1973: (1) "The Sting," (2) Jack Lemmon in "Save the Tiger," (3) Glenda Jackson in "A Touch of Class," (4) John Houseman in "The Paper Chase," (5) Tatum O'Neal in "Paper Moon," (6) George Roy Hill for "The Sting," (8) "Day for Night."

1974: (1) "The Godfather Part II," (2) Art Carney in "Harry and Tonto," (3) Ellen Burstyn in "Alice Doesn't Live Here Anymore," (4) Robert DeNiro in "The Godfather Part II," (5) Ingrid Bergman in "Murder on the Orient Express," (6) Francis Ford Coppola for "The Godfather Part II," (7) Howard Hawks, Jean Renoir, (8) "Amarcord."

1975: (1) "One Flew over the Cuckoo's Nest," (2) Jack Nicholson in "One Flew over the Cuckoo's Nest," (3) Louise Fletcher in "One Flew over the Cuckoo's Nest," (4) George Burns in "The Sunshine Boys," (5) Lee Grant in "Shampoo," (6) Milos Forman for "One Flew over the Cuckoo's Nest," (7) Mary Pickford, (8) "Dersu Uzala."

1976: (1) "Rocky," (2) Peter Finch in "Network," (3) Faye Dunaway in "Network," (4) Jason Robards in "All the President's Men," (5) Beatrice Straight in "Network," (6) John G. Avildsen for "Rocky," (8) "Black and White in Color."

1977: (1) "Annie Hall," (2) Richard Dreyfuss in "The Goodbye Girl," (3) Diane Keaton in "Annie Hall," (4) Jason Robards in "Julia," (5) Vanessa Redgrave in "Julia," (6) Woody Allen for "Annie Hall," (7) Maggie Booth (film editor), (8) "Madame Rosa."

1978: (1) "The Deer Hunter," (2) Jon Voight in "Coming Home," (3) Jane Fonda in "Coming Home," (4) Christopher Walken in "The Deer Hunter" (5) Maggie Smith in "California Suite," (6) Michael Cimino for "The Deer Hunter," (7) Laurence Olivier, King Vidor, (8) "Get Out Your Handkerchiefs."

FOREIGN FILMS

MURDER BY DECREE

(AVCO EMBASSY) Producers, Rene Dupont, Bob Clark; Direction and Original Story, Bob Clark; Screenplay, John Hopkins; Photography, Reg Morris; Design, Harry Pottle; Editor, Stan Cole; Costumes, Judy Moorcroft; Executive Producer, Len Herberman; In Metrocolor; Rated PG; 121 minutes; January release.

CAST

Sherlock Holmes	Christopher Plummer
Dr. Watson	James Mason
Robert Lees	Donald Sutherland
Annie Crook	Genevieve Bujold
Inspector Foxborough	David Hemmings
Mary Kelly	Susan Clark
Sir Charles Warren	Anthony Quayle
Lord Salisbury	John Gielgud
Inspector Lestrade	Frank Finlay

and Chris Wiggins, Tedde Moore, Peter Jonfield, Roy Lansford, June Brown, Hilary Sesta, Catherine Kessler

Below: Genevieve Bujold, James Mason, Christopher Plummer © Saucy Jack Inc.

Frank Finlay
Below: Donald Sutherland

John Gielgud
Below: Anthony Quayle

Christopher Plummer, Genevieve Bujold

James Mason, Christopher Plummer
Above: David Hemmings, Plummer

134

YOUR TURN, MY TURN

(NEW YORKER) Producers, Klaus Hellwig, Yves Payrot, Yves Gasser; Director, Francois Leterrier; Screenplay, Daniele Thompson, Francoise Dorin, Francois Leterrier; From novel by Francoise Dorin; Photography, Jean Penzer; Music, Georges Delerue; Editor, Marie-Josephe Yoyotte; Art Director, Jacques Saulnier; In Eastmancolor; Rated PG; 101 minutes; January release.

CAST

Agnes	Marlene Jobert
Vincent	Philippe Leotard
Serge, Agnes' husband	Daniel Duval
Jerome, Agnes' son	Vladimir Andres
Patricia, Vincent's daughter	Valerie Pascale
Marianne, Agnes' sister	Macha Meril
Stephane, Vincent's sister	Sylvie Joly
Vava	Micheline Presle
Laurence	Catherine Rich
Christine	Albina du Boisrouvray

and Annette Poivre, Marthe Villalonga, Laurence Badie, Laurence de Monaghan, Monique Melinand

Right: Vladimir Andres

Vladimir Andres, Marlene Jobert

THE CLASS OF MISS MacMICHAEL

(BRUT PICTURES) Executive Producer, George Barrie; Producer, Judd Bernard; Director, Silvio Narizzano; Screenplay, Judd Bernard, from the novel by Sandy Hutson; Associate Producer, Patricia Casey; Photography, Alex Thomson; Music, Stanley Myers; Editor, Max Benedict; Assistant Director, Jake Wright; Art Director, Hazel Peiser; A Kettledrom Film in color; 100 minutes; January release.

CAST

Conor MacMichael	Glenda Jackson
Terence Sutton	Oliver Reed
Martin	Michael Murphy
Una Ferrer	Rosalind Cash
Fairbrother	John Standing
Gaylord	Riba Akabusi
Stewart	Phil Daniels
Boysie	Patrick Murray
Marie	Sylvia O'Donnel
Belinda	Sharon Fussey
Ronnie	Herbert Norville
Timmy	Perry Benson
Adam	Tony London
Victor	Owen Whittaker
Frieda	Angela Brogan
Abel	Victor Evans
Rob	Simon Howe
John	Dayton Brown
Nick	Paul Daly
Deirdre	Deirdre Forrest
Pattie	Stephanie Patterson

and Danielle Corgan (Tina), Peta Bernard (Mabel), Judy Wiles (Miss Eccles), Mavis Pugh (Mrs. Barnett), Patsy Byrne (Mrs. Green), Ian Thompson (Mr. Bowden), Christopher Guinee (Mr. Drake), Constantin de Goguel (Major Brady), Sally Nesbitt (Mrs. Brady), Sylvia Marriott (Mrs. Wickens), Marianne Stone (Mrs. Lee), Pamela Manson (Mrs. Bellrind)

Top: Oliver Reed, Glenda Jackson
Left Center: Rosalind Cash, Glenda Jackson

Glenda Jackson, Michael Murphy

WIFEMISTRESS

(QUARTET FILMS) Executive Producer, Alberto Pugliese; Producer, Franco Cristaldi; Director, Marco Vicario; Screenplay, Rodolfo Sonego; Photography, Ennio Guarnieri; Designer, Mario Garbuglia; Costumes, Luca Sabatelli; Editor, Nino Baragli; Music, Armando Trovaioli; Associate Producer, Lucio Trentini, Franco Cuccu; In Technicolor; Rated R; 101 minutes; January release.

CAST

Antonia DeAngelis	Laura Antonelli
Luigi DeAngelis	Marcello Mastroianni
Dr. Dario Favella	Leonard Mann
Vincenzo	Gastone Moschin
Clara	Annie Belle
Count Brandini	William Berger
Miss Pagano, M.D.	Olga Karlatos
Clara's Fiance	Stefano Patrizi
Innkeeper	Helen Stoliaroff

Right: Laura Antonelli

Leonard Mann, Laura Antonelli

Marcello Mastroianni

THE INNOCENT

(ANALYSIS FILM RELEASING CORP.) Producer, Giovanni Bertolucci; Director, Luchino Visconti; Screenplay, Suso Cecchi D'Amico, Enrico Medioli, Luchino Visconti; Freely based on Gabriele d'Annunzio's novel "L'Innocente"; Costumes, Piero Tose; Art Director, Mario Garbuglai; Photography, Pasqualino De Santis; Music, Franco Mannino; In Technovision and Technicolor; 112 minutes; January release.

CAST

Tullio Hermil	Giancarlo Giannini
Guiliana	Laura Antonelli
Teresa Raffo	Jennifer O'Neill
Tullio's Mother	Rina Morelli
Count Stefano Egano	Massimo Girotti
Federico Hermil	Didier Haudepin
The Princess	Marie Dubois
Miss Elviretta	Roberta Paladini
The Prince	Claude Mann
Filippo d'Arborio, a Writer	Marc Porel

Left: Giancarlo Giannini, Laura Antonelli

Jennifer O'Neill

**Giancarlo Giannini, Jennifer O'Neill
Above: Marc Porel, Laura Antonelli**

MAX HAVELAAR

(ATLANTIC RELEASING CORP.) Producer-Director, Fons Rademakers; Executive Producer, Hiswara Darmaputera; Screenplay, Gerard Soeteman; Based on novel "Multatuli" by Eduard Douwes Dekker; Photography, Jan De Bont; Art Direction, Fred Wetik, Frank Raven; Costumes, Elly Claus; Assistant Directors, Lili Rademakers, Fred Wetik, Mochtar Soemodimedjo; Editor, Pieter Bergema; In color; 165 minutes; January release.

CAST

Max Havelaar	Peter Faber
Tina, His Wife	Sacha Bulthuis
Regent	Elang Mohamad Adenan Soesilaningrat
Demang	Maroeli Sitompul
Resident	Carl Van Der Plas
Verbrugge, Controller	Krijn Ter Braak
Slotering	Joop Admiraal
Mrs. Slotering	Rima Melati
Duclari	Rutger Hauer
Djaksa	Pitradjaja Burnama
Governor-General	Frans Vorstman
Saidjah	Henry Iantho
Adinda	Henny Zulaini
Saidjah's Father	Minih bin Misan

Top: Peter Faber (also below)
Top Right: Henry Iantho
© Atlantic Releasing Corp.

Peter Faber

THE TOY

(SHOW BIZ) Executive Producer, Pierre Grunstein; Direction, Story, and Screenplay, Francis Veber; Music, Vladimir Cosma; Assistant Directors, Jean-Michel Carbonnaux, Pierre-Alain Cremieu; Photography, Etienne Becker; Costumes, Michele Marmande-Cerf; Art Director, Bernard Evein; In French with English subtitles; Rated PG; In color; 90 minutes; February release.

CAST

Pierre Rambal-Couchet	Michel Bouquet
Francois Perin	Pierre Richard
Eric Rambal-Couchet	Fabrice Greco
Rich Man's Assistant	Jacques Francois

Pierre Richard (R)

PICNIC AT HANGING ROCK

(ATLANTIC RELEASING CORP.) Executive Producer, Patricia Lovell; Producers, James McElroy, Hal McElroy; Director, Peter Weir; Screenplay, Cliff Green; Based on novel by Joan Lindsay; Photography, Russell Boyd; Art Director, David Copping; Costumes, Judy Dorsman; Assistant Director, Mark Egerton; In Eastman color; 115 minutes; February release.

CAST

Mrs. Appleyard	Rachel Roberts
Michael Fitzhubert	Dominic Guard
Dianne De Poiters	Helen Morse
Minnie	Jacki Weaver
Miss McCraw	Vivean Gray
Dora Lumley	Kirsty Child
Miranda	Anne Lambert
Irma	Karen Robson
Marion	Jane Vallis
Edith	Christine Schuler
Sara	Margaret Nelson
Albert	John Jarratt
Rosamund	Ingrid Mason
Ben Hussey	Martin Vaughan
Doc McKenzie	Jack Fegan
Sergeant Bumpher	Wyn Roberts
Jim Jones	Garry McDonald
Edward Whitehead	Frank Gunnell

Right: Rachel Roberts
Below: Helen Morse, Margaret Nelson
© Atlantic Releasing Corp.

Vivean Gray

AGATHA

(WARNER BROS.) Producers, Jarvis Astaire, Gavrik Losey; Director, Michael Apted; Screenplay, Kathleen Tynan, Arthur Hopcraft; Based on story by Kathleen Tynan; Photography, Vittorio Storaro; Editor, Jim Clark; Music, Johnny Mandel; Design, Shirley Russell; Art Director, Sim Holland; Assistant Director, Jonathan Benson; Sweetwall production in association with Casablanca Film Works; In Technicolor; Rated PG; 98 minutes; February release.

CAST

Wally Stanton	Dustin Hoffman
Agatha Christie	Vanessa Redgrave
Archie Christie	Timothy Dalton
Evelyn	Helen Morse
Nancy Neele	Celia Gregory
William Collins	Tony Britton
Kenward	Timothy West
Lord Brackenbury	Alan Badel
John Foster	Paul Brooke
Charlotte Fisher	Carolyn Pickles
Pettelson	Robert Longden
Uncle Jones	Donald Nithsdale
Mrs. Braithwaite	Yvonne Gilan
Sergeant Jarvis	David Hargreaves
Therapist	Sandra Voe
Superintendent MacDonald	Barry Hart
Captain Rankin	Tim Seely
Nancy's Aunt	Jill Summers

Left: Vanessa Redgrave
Top: Dustin Hoffman
© Warner Bros.

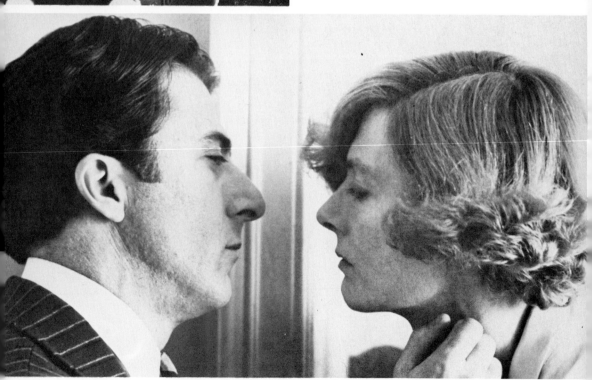

Dustin Hoffman, Vanessa Redgrave

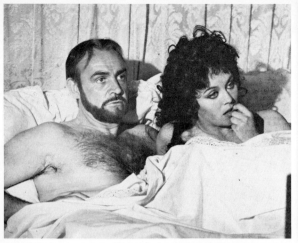

THE GREAT TRAIN ROBBERY

(UNITED ARTISTS) Producer, John Foreman; Direction and Screenplay, Michael Crichton, from his novel of same title; Music, Jerry Goldsmith; Photography, Geoffrey Unsworth; Designer, Maurice Carter; Costumes, Anthony Mendleson; Editor, David Bretherton; Assistant Directors, Anthony Waye, Gerry Gavigan, Chris Carreras; Art Director, Bert Davey; A Famous Films production in Technicolor and Dolby Sound; Presented by Dino De Laurentiis; Rated PG; 111 minutes; February release.

CAST

Edward Pierce	Sean Connery
Agar	Donald Sutherland
Miriam	Lesley-Anne Down
Edgar Trent	Alan Webb
Henry Fowler	Malcolm Terris
Inspector Sharp	Robert Lang
"Clean Willy" Williams	Wayne Sleep
Burgess	Michael Elphick
Emily Trent	Pamela Salem
Elizabeth Trent	Gabrielle Lloyd
Mr. Chubb	Clive Swift
Inspector Harranby	James Cossins
McPherson	John Bett
Dispatcher	Peter Benson
Maggie	Janine Duvitski

and Agnes Bernelle, Frank McDonald, Brian De Salvo, Joe Cahill, Michael Muldoon, Derry Power, John Dunne, George Downing, Susan Hallinan, Cecil Nash, Donald Churchill, Andre Morell, Brian Glover, Oliver Smith, Jenny Till, John Altman, Paul Kember, Geoff Ferris, Craig Stokes, Noel Johnson, Donald Hewlett, Peter Butterworth, Patrick Barr, Hubert Rees

Top: Sean Connery, Lesley-Anne Down
Below: Gabrielle Lloyd, Alan Webb, Connery,
Pamela Salem Top Right: Connery
© United Artists Corp.

Donald Sutherland, Sean Connery
(also above)

Susan Strasberg

IN PRAISE OF OLDER WOMEN

(AVCO EMBASSY) Producers, Robert Lantos, Claude Heroux; Director, George Kaczender; Executive Producers, Stephen J. Roth, Harold Greenberg; Screenplay, Paul Gottlieb; From novel by Stephen Vizinczey with same title; Photography, Mikos Lente; Art Director, Wolf Kroeger; Costumes, Olga Dimitrov; Music, Tibor Polgar; Associate Producer, Howard R. Lipson; Editors, George Kaczender, Peter Wintonick; Assistant Director, Charles Braive; An Astral Bellevue Pathe production in color; Rated R; 108 minutes; February release.

CAST

Andras Vayda	Tom Berenger
Maya	Karen Black
Bobbie	Susan Strasberg
Ann MacDonald	Helen Shaver
Klari	Marilyn Lightstone
Paula	Alexandra Stewart
Julika	Marianne McIsaac
Mitzi	Alberta Watson
Andras Vayda, Jr.	Ian Tracey
Countess	Monique LePage
Mother Vayda	Mignon Elkins
Aunt Alice	Joan Stuart
Glen MacDonald	John Bayliss
Tom Horvath	Jon Granik

and Louise Marleau, Jill Frappier, Budd Knapp, Earl Pennington, Michael Kirby, Bronwen Mantel, Wally Martin, Arden Ryshpan, Tibor Polgar, Julie Wildman, Julie Morand, Griffith Brewer, Walter Bolton, Martha Parker, Robert King, Arthur Grosser

Top: Alberta Watson, Tom Berenger Below: Marilyn Lightstone, Berenger, Karen Black
Top Left: Tom Berenger, Alexandra Stewart
Below: Helen Shaver, Berenger
© AVCO Embassy

144

THE SILENT PARTNER

(EMC FILM CORP.) Producers, Joel B. Michaels, Stephen Young; Director, Daryl Duke; Screenplay, Curtis Hanson; Based on novel "Think of a Number" by Anders Bodelson; Music, Oscar Peterson; Photography, Billy Williams; Executive Producer, Garth H. Drabinsky; Presented by Mario Kassar and Andrew Vajna; In color; Rated R; 103 minutes; March release.

CAST

Miles Cullen	Elliott Gould
Julie	Susannah York
Reikle	Christopher Plummer
Elaine	Celine Lomez
Packard	Michael Kirby
Detective	Ken Pogue
Simonson	John Candy
Louise	Gail Dahms
Berg	Michael Donaghue
Fogelman	Jack Duffy
Girl in sauna	Nancy Simmonds
Mrs. Skinner	Nuala Fitzgerald
Locksmith	Guy Sanvido
Mrs. Evanchuck	Aino Perskanen
Young woman in Bank	Michele Rosen
Newsboy	Ben Williams
Detective #2	Sandy Crawley
Boy's mother	Jan Campbell
Little boy	Jimmy Davidson
Girl at Party	Eve Norman
Detective #3	John Kerr
TV Reporter	Sue Lumaden
Bank Assistant	Candace O'Connor
Freddie	Stephen Levy

Right: Christopher Plummer
Top: Elliott Gould, Susannah York

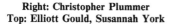

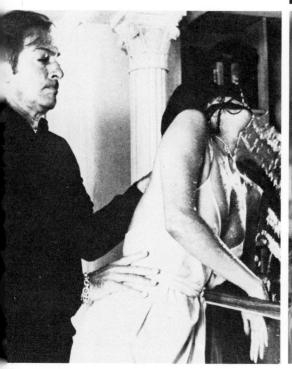

Christopher Plummer, Celine Lomez

Celine Lomez, Elliott Gould

NOSFERATU THE VAMPYRE

(20th CENTURY-FOX) Produced, Directed, and Written by Werner Herzog; Executive Producer, Walter Saxer; Photography, Jorg Schmidt-Reitwein; Designer, Henning Von Gierke; Costumes, Gisela Storch; Editor, Beate Mainka-Jellinghaus; Music, Popol Vuh/Florian Fricke, Richard Wagner, Charles Gounod; Assistant Directors, Remmelt Remmelts, Mirko Tichacek; In color; Rated PG; 106 minutes; March release.

CAST

Count Dracula	Klaus Kinski
Lucy Harker	Isabelle Adjani
Jonathan Harker	Bruno Ganz
Renfield	Roland Topor
Dr. Van Helsing	Walter Ladengast
Warden	Dan Van Husen
Harbormaster	Jan Groth
Schrader	Carsten Bodinus
Mina	Martje Grohmann
Town Official	Ryk De Gooyer
Town Employee	Clemens Scheitz
Councilman	Lo Van Hartingsveld
Coffinbearer	Tim Beekman
Captain	Jacques Dufilho

Left: Isabelle Adjani, Bruno Ganz
© 20th Century-Fox Film Corp.

Bruno Ganz, Klaus Kinski

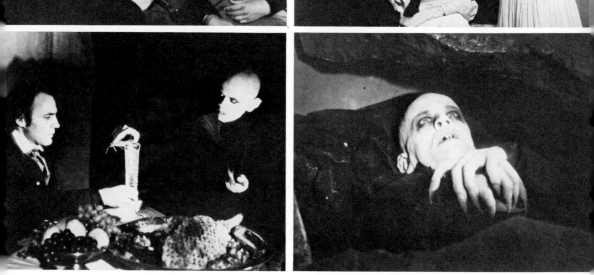

Bruno Ganz, Klaus Kinski Above: Walter Ladengast, Bruno Ganz Top: Roland Topor, Dan Van Hensen, Ladengast

Klaus Kinski Above: Bruno Ganz, Isabelle Adjani Top: Adjani, Kinski

THE FRENCH DETECTIVE

(QUARTET FILMS) Executive Producer, Georges Dancigers; Director, Pierre Granier-Deferre; Screenplay, Francis Veber; Photography, Jean Collomb; A Les Films Ariane production in color; 93 minutes; March release.

CAST

Verjeat	Lino Ventura
Lefevre	Patrick Dewaere
Lardatte	Victor Lanoux

Right: Victor Lanoux

Patrick Dewaere, Lino Ventura

THE PASSAGE

(UNITED ARTISTS) Executive Producers, John Daly, Derek Dawson; Producers, John Quested in association with Maurice Binder, Lester Goldsmith; Director, J. Lee Thompson; Screenplay, Bruce Nicolaysen from his book "Perilous Passage"; Music, Michael J. Lewis; Associate Producer, Geoffrey Helman; Assistant Directors, Kip Gowans, Arnold Schulkes; Photography, Mike Reed; Editor, Alan Strachan; In Technovision and color; Rated R; 99 minutes; March release.

CAST

The Basque	Anthony Quinn
Professor Bergson	James Mason
Von Berkow	Malcolm McDowell
Ariel Bergson	Patricia Neal
Leah Bergson	Kay Lenz
Head Gypsy	Christopher Lee
Renoudot	Michael Lonsdale
Perea	Marcel Bozzuffi
Paul Bergson	Paul Clemens
Madame	Rose Alba
Lieutenant Reincke	Neville Jason
Son of the Gypsy	Robert Rhys
German Soldier	James Broadbent
French Guide	Peter Arne
German Major	Frederick Jaeger
German Sentries	Terence York, Terence Maidment

Right: Anthony Quinn, James Mason
Below: James Mason, Patricia Neal
© United Artist Corp.

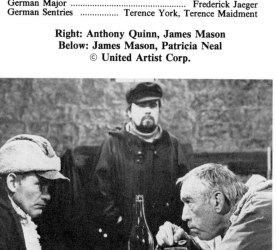

Malcolm McDowell, Kay Lenz
Above: Marcel Bozzuffi, Michael Lonsdale,
Anthony Quinn

Christopher Lee, Anthony Quinn

LOVE ON THE RUN

(NEW WORLD) Production company, Les Films du Carosse; Director, Francois Truffaut; Executive Producer, Marcel Berbert; Screenplay, Francois Truffaut, Marie-France Pisier, Jean Aurel, Suzanne Schiffman; Editor, Martine Barraqui-Curie; Photography, Nestor Almendros; Music, Georges Delerue; Title Song sung by Alain Souchon; Art Directors, Jean-Pierre Kohut-Svelko, Pierre Gompertz; Rated PG; 94 minutes; In color; April release.

CAST

Antoine Doinel	Jean-Pierre Leaud
Colette	Marie-France Pisier
Christine	Claude Jade
Liliane	Dani
Sabine	Dorothee
Colette's Mother	Rosy Varte
Divorce Judge	Marie Henriau
Xavier, Librarian	Daniel Mesguich
Monsier Lucien	Julien Bertheau
Christine's Lawyer	Jean-Pierre Ducos
Maitre Renard	Pierre Dios
Judge Aix	Alain Ollivier
Madame Ida	Monique Dury
Antoine's Friend	Emmanuel Clot
Train Wolf	Christian Lentretien
Angry Telephonist	Roland Thenot
Alphonse Doinel	Julien Dubois
Restaurant Car Child	Alexandre Janssen

Left: Jean-Pierre Leaud, Dorothee
© **New World Pictures**

Jean-Pierre Leaud, Dorothee
Above: Dani, Leaud

Dani, Leaud, Claude Jade
Above: Jade, Marie-France Pisier

150

Jean-Pierre Leaud, Julien Dubois Above: Dorothee, Leaud Top: Leaud, Pisier

Jean-Pierre Leaud

FIREPOWER

(ASSOCIATED FILM DISTRIBUTION) Producer-Director, Michael Winner; Screenplay, Gerald Wilson; Story, Bill Kerby, Michael Winner; Music, Gato Barbieri; Photography, Robert Paynter, Dick Kratina, Richard Kline; Editor, Arnold Crust; Designers, John Stoll, John Blezard, Robert Gundlach; Assistant Directors, Ted Moreley, Alex Hapsis, Francois Moullin; Miss Loren's clothes by Per Spook of Paris; A Scimitar Films production in color; Rated R; 104 minutes; April release.

CAST

Adele Tasca	Sophia Loren
Jerry Fanon/Eddie	James Coburn
Catlett	O.J. Simpson
Sal Hyman	Eli Wallach
Dr. Felix	Anthony Franciosa
Gelhorn	George Grizzard
Frank Hull	Vincent Gardenia
Halpin	Fred Stuthman
Calman	Richard Caldicot
Manley Reckford	Frank Singuineau
Stegner	George Touliatos
Cooper	Andrew Duncan
Oscar	Hank Garrett
Dominic Carbone	Billy Party
Lestor	Conrad Roberts
Nickel Sam	Jake La Motta
Trilling	Vincent Beck
Dis Orlov	Dominic Chianese
Tagua	Paul D'Amato
Vito Tasca	Paul Garcia
Dr. Ivo Tasca	Richard Roberts
Policeman	Thurman Scott
Pathologist	William Trotman
Anders	Victor Argo
Sweezy	Owen Hollander
Dunn	J.C. Quinn
Senator	Chris Gampel
Bejewelled Woman	Paula Laurence
Harold Everett	Victor Mature

Top: George Grizzard Left: Sophia Loren,
James Coburn Below: Eli Wallach
© AFD

Anthony Franciosa, O. J. Simpson

JUST LIKE AT HOME

(NEW YORKER) Director, Marta Meszaros; Screenplay, Ildiko Korody; Photography, Lajos Koltai; Music, Tamas Somlo; In Eastmancolor; Not rated; 108 minutes; April release.

CAST

Zsuzsi	Zsuzsa Czinkoczy
Andras Novak	Jan Nowicki
Anna	Anna Karina
Zsuzsi's Mother	Ildiko Pecsi
Andras' Mother	Kornelia Sallai
Andras' Father	Ferenc Bencze
Laci	Laszlo Szabo

Right: Jan Nowicki, Zsuzsa Czinkoczy

Zsuzsa Czinkoczy, Jan Nowicki

LA CAGE AUX FOLLES

(UNITED ARTISTS) Producer, Marcello Danon; Director, Edouard Molinaro; Screenplay and Adaptation, Francis Veber, Edouard Molinaro, Marcello Danon, Jean Poiret; Based on play by Jean Poiret; Art Director, Mario Garbuglia; Costumes, Piero Tosi, Ambra Danon; Editors, Robert Isnardon, Monique Isnardon; Photography, Armando Mannuzzi; Music, Ennio Morricone; In color; Rated R; 99 minutes; April release.

CAST

Renato	Ugo Tognazzi
Zaza	Michel Serrault
Charrier	Michel Galabru
Simone	Claire Maurier
Laurent	Remy Laurent
Jacob	Benny Luke
Madame Charrier	Carmen Scarpitta
Andrea	Luisa Maneri

Left: Michel Serrault, Ugo Tognazzi
© United Artists Corp.

Michel Serrault, Michel Galabru

Claire Maurier, Ugo Tognazzi

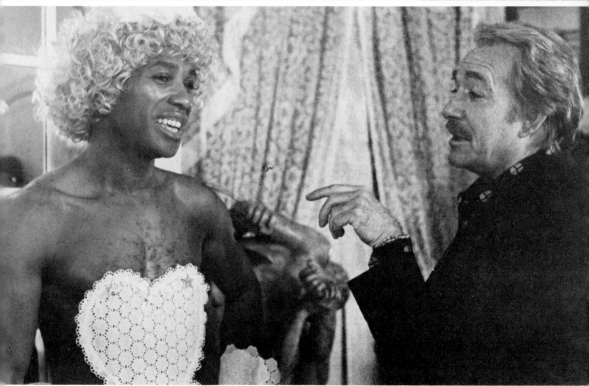

Benny Luke, Ugo Tognazzi Top: Michel Serrault, Michel Galabru

DEATH OF A BUREAUCRAT

(TRICONTINENTAL) Director, Tomas Gutierrez Alea; Screenplay, Alfredo del Cueto, Ramon F. Suarez, Tomas Gutierrez Alea; Photography, Ramon F. Suarez; Editor, Mario Gonzalez; Spanish with English subtitles; In black and white; 87 minutes; May release.

CAST

Nephew	Salvador Wood
Aunt	Silvia Planas
Bureaucrat	Manuel Estanillo
Nephew's Boss	Gaspar de Santelices
Psychiatrist	Carlos Ruiz de la Tejera
Cojimar	Omar Alfonso
Tarafa	Ricardo Suarez
El Zorro	Luis Romay
Sabor	Elsa Montero

Top: Salvador Wood, Silvia Planas
LC: Salvador Wood

THE PRISONER OF ZENDA

(UNIVERSAL) Producer, Walter Mirisch; Director, Richard Quine; Screenplay, Dick Clement, Ian La Frenais; Based on novel by Anthony Hope; Dramatized by Edward Rose; Photography, Arthur Ibbetson; Design, John J. Lloyd; Editor, Byron "Buzz" Brandt; Special Effects, Albert Whitlock; Music, Henry Mancini; Costumes, Susan Yelland; Associate Producer, Peter MacGregor-Scott; In Technicolor; Rated PG; 108 minutes; May release.

CAST

Rudolph/Syd	Peter Sellers
Princess Flavia	Lynne Frederick
General Sapt	Lionel Jeffries
The Countess	Elke Sommer
The Count	Gregory Sierra
Duke Michael	Jeremy Kemp
Antoinette	Catherine Schell
Fritz	Simon Williams
Rupert of Hentzau	Stuart Wilson
Bruno	Norman Rossington
Archbishop	John Laurie
Erik	Graham Stark
Luger	Michael Balfour
Deacon	Arthur Howard
Johann	Ian Abercrombie
Conductor	Michael Segal

and Eric Cord, Joe Dunne, Dick Geary, Mickey Gilbert, Orwin Harvey, Jaysen Hayes, Larry Holt, John Hudkins, Pete Kellet, John Moio, Victor Paul, Gil Perkins, George Robotham, Joe Yrigoyen

Elke Sommer, Peter Sellers Above: Norman Rossington, Jeremy Kemp, Peter Sellers Top Right: Sellers, Lynne Frederick

Peter Sellers (also above)

TERESA THE THIEF

(WORLD-NORTHAL) Producer, Giovanni Bertolucci; Director, Carlo Di Palma; Screenplay, Age, Scarpelli, Dacia Maraini; Based on novel "Memoirs of a Thief" by Dacia Maraini; Photography, Dario Di Palma; Editor, Ruggero Mastroianni; Costumes, Adriana Berselli; Music, Riz Ortolani; An Euro-International Film in color; Not rated; 111 minutes; Italian with English subtitles; May release.

CAST

Teresa	Monica Vitti
Hercules	Stefano Satta Flores
Dina	Isa Danieli
Bright Eyes	Carlo Delle Diane
Tonino	Michele Placido
Sisto	Valeriano Vallone

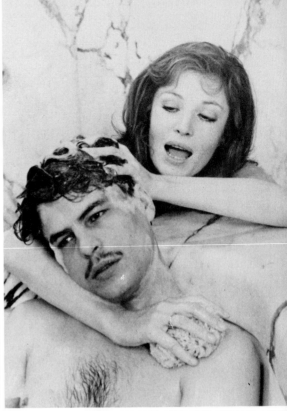

Carlo Delle Diane, Monica Vitti
(also above)

Monica Vitti, and above
with Michele Placido

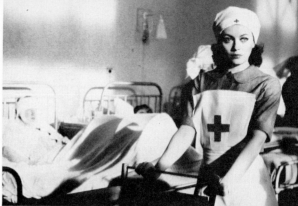

HANOVER STREET

(COLUMBIA) Producer, Paul N. Lazarus III; Direction and Screenplay, Peter Hyams; Photography, David Watkin; Designer, Philip Harrison; Music, John Barry; Editor, James Mitchell; Associate Producers, Michael Rachmil, Harry Benn; Assistant Directors, David Tringham, Andy Armstrong, Bobby Wright; Art Directors, Malcolm Middleton, Robert Cartwright; Costumes, Joan Bridge; In Panavision, Technicolor, and Dolby Sound; Rated PG; 109 minutes; May release.

CAST

David Halloran	Harrison Ford
Margaret Sellinger	Lesley-Anne Down
Paul Sellinger	Christopher Plummer
Major Trumbo	Alec McCowen
2nd Lieutenant Jerry Cimino	Richard Masur
2nd Lieutenant Martin Hyer	Michael Sacks
Sarah Sellinger	Patsy Kensit
Harry Pike	Max Wall
Colonel Ronald Bart	Shane Rimmer
Lieutenant Wells	Keith Buckley
Phyllis	Sherrie Hewson
Paula	Cindy O'Callaghan
Elizabeth	Di Trevis
French Girl	Suzanne Bertish
Soldier in Barn	Keith Alexander
Corporal Daniel Giler	Jay Benedict
Sergeant John Lucas	John Ratzenberger
Farrell	Eric Stine
Captain Harold Lester	Hugh Fraser
Beef	William Hootkins

and Kristine Howarth, Shaun Scott, Ronald Letham, Lesley Ward, Eugene Lipinski, Gary Waldhorn, John Rees, Seymour Matthews, Tony Sibbald, George Pravda, Harry Brooks, Jr., Eddie Kidd

Top: (Standing) Richard Masur, Harrison Ford, Michael Sachs Below: Christopher Plummer, Harrison Ford Top Right: Lesley-Anne Down Below: Down, Ford © Columbia Pictures

Harrison Ford, Lesley-Anne Down

MEATBALLS

(PARAMOUNT) Executive Producers, Andre Link, John Dunning; Producer, Dan Goldberg; Director, Ivan Reitman; Screenplay, Len Blum, Dan Goldberg, Janis Allen, Harold Ramis; Photography, Don Wilder; Music, Elmer Bernstein; Lyrics, Norman Gimbel; Editor, Debra Karen; Art Director, David Charles; Costumes, Judy Gellman; Associate Producer, Lawrence Nesis; Assistant Directors, Gordon Robinson, David Shepherd; In Sonolab Color; Rated PG; 92 minutes; June release.

CAST

Morty	Harvey Atkin
Crockett	Russ Banham
Lance	Ron Barry
Spaz	Jack Blum
Hardware	Matt Craven
A.L.	Kristine DeBell
Brenda	Norma Dell'Agnese
Wendy	Cindy Girling
Wheels	Todd Hoffman
Fink	Keith Knight
Roxanne	Kate Lynch
Tripper	Bill Murray
Jackie	Margot Pinvidic
Candace	Sarah Torgov
Ace	Paul Boyle
Carla	Alison Diver
Liza	Valerie Fersht
Rhino	Vince Guerriero
Andrew	Patrick Hynes
Bradley	Hadley Kay
Jeffrey	Billie Kishonti
Peter DeWitt	Allan Levson
Rudy	Chris Makepeace
Horse	James McLarty
Patti	Heather Preece
Jodi	Ruth Rennie

Top: Camp North Star's "in" group
© Haliburton Films Ltd.

Larry Solway, Bill Murray

Peter Hume, Harvey Atkin, Keith Knight, Bill Murray Above: Murray, Chris Makepeace

Bill Murray, Harvey Atkin Above: Bill Murray, Kate Lynch Top: Murray and counselors

EL SUPER

(NEW YORKER) Producers, Manuel Arce, Leon Ichaso; Directors, Leon Ichaso, Orlando Jimenez-Leal; Photography, Orlando Jimenez-Leal; Editor, Gloria Pineyro; Screenplay, Leon Ichaso, Manuel Arce; Based on play "El Super" by Ivan Acosta; Music, Enrique Ubieta; Associate Producer, Gloria Pineyro; Assistant Director, Mariano Ros; Costumes, Haydee Zambrana; In color; Not rated; 90 minutes; June release.

CAST

El Super	Raymundo Hidalgo-Gato
Aurelia	Zully Montero
Pancho	Reynaldo Medina
Aurelita	Elizabeth Pena
Cuco	Juan Granda
La China	Hilda Lee
Inspector	Phil Joint
Predicador	Leonardo Soriano
Bobby	Efrain Lopez-Neri
Ofelia	Ana Margarita Martinez-Casado

Left: Raymundo Hidalgo-Gato

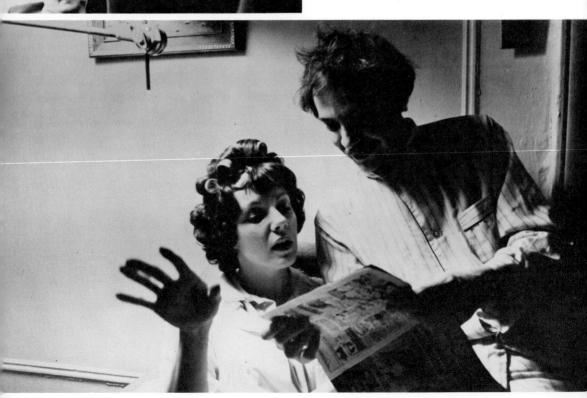

Zully Montero, Raymundo Hidalgo-Gato

DOWN AND DIRTY

(NEW LINE CINEMA) Producer, Carlo Ponti; Director, Ettore Scola; Story and Screenplay, Ruggero Maccari, Ettore Scola; Photography, Dario Di Palma; Music, Armando Trovaioli; Costumes, Dana Artona; Editor, Raimondo Crociani; Assistant Director, Giorgio Scotton; Associate Producer, Romano Dandi; In color; 95 minutes; June release.

CAST

"The Family"

Domizio	Francesco Anniballi
Gaetana	Maria Bosco
Lisetta	Giselda Castrini
Plinio	Alfredo D'Ippolito
Paride	Giancarlo Fanelli
Maria Libera	Marina Fasoli
Camillo	Ettore Garofolo
Giacinto	Nino Manfredi
Fernando	Franco Merli
Matilde	Linda Moretti
Romolo	Luciano Pagliuca
Toto	Giuseppe Paravati
Paride's Wife	Silvana Priori
Granny Antonecchia	Giovanni Rovini
Dore	Adriana Russo
Iside	Maria Luisa Santella
Adolfo	Mario Santella

and Ennio Antonelli, Marcella Battisti, Francesco Crescimone, Beryl Cunningham, Silvia Ferluga, Zoe Incrocci, Franco Marino, Marcella Michelangeli, Clarisse Monaco, Aristide Piersanti, Assunta Stacconi

MOONRAKER

(UNITED ARTISTS) Producer, Albert R. Broccoli; Director, Lewis Gilbert; Screenplay, Christopher Wood; Associate Producer, William P. Cartlidge; Executive Producer, Michael G. Wilson; Music, John Barry; Lyrics, Hal David; Title Song sung by Shirley Bassey; Designer, Ken Adam; Photography, Jean Tournier; Editor, John Glen; Assistant Directors, Ernie Day, John Glen, Michel Cheyko; Art Directors, Max Douy, Charles Bishop; Costumes, Jacques Fonteray; In Panavision, color, and Dolby Stereo; Rated PG; 126 minutes; June release.

CAST

James Bond	Roger Moore
Holly Goodhead	Lois Chiles
Drax	Michael Lonsdale
Jaws	Richard Kiel
Corinne Dufour	Corinne Clery
"M"	Bernard Lee
Frederick Gray	Geoffrey Keen
"Q"	Desmond Llewelyn
Moneypenny	Lois Maxwell
Manuela	Emily Bolton
Chang	Toshiro Suga
Dolly	Blanche Ravalec
Pilot Private Jet	Jean-Pierre Castaldi
Hostess Private Jet	Leila Shenna
General Gogol	Walter Gotell
Cavendish	Arthur Howard
Blonde Beauty	Irka Bochenko
Colonel Scott	Michael Marshall
Mission Control Director	Douglas Lambert
Consumptive Italian	Alfie Bass
Museum Guide	Anne Lonnberg
U.S. Shuttle Captain	Brian Keith
Captain Boeing 747	George Birt

and Kim Fortune, Chris Dillinger, Georges Beller, Johnny Traber, Lizzie Warville, Chichinou Kaeppler, Francoise Gayat, Catherine Serre, Christina Hui, Nicaise Jean-Louis, Beatrice Libert

Left: Roger Moore, and clockwise from left: Francoise Gayat, Chichinou Kaeppler, Irka Bochenko, Catherine Serre, Anne Lonnberg
© **Danjaq**

Michael Lonsdale

Lois Chiles, Roger Moore

Richard Kiel, Blanche Ravalec
Above: Roger Moore, Lois Chiles
(also top)

Emily Bolton, Roger Moore

THE FRAGRANCE OF WILD FLOWERS

(NEW YORKER) Director, Srdjan Karanovic; Screenplay, Rajko Grlic, Srdjan Karanovic; Art Director, Miomir Denic; Costumes, Danka Pavlovic; Music, Zoran Simujanovic; A Centar Film production in color; 92 minutes; June release.

CAST

Ivan Vasiljevic, Actor	Ljuba Tadic
Sonja, Ballet Dancer	Sonja Divac
Stinky Jeca, Boatman	Nemanja Zivic
Stana, Jeca's Girl Friend	Rastislava Gacic
Film Director	Aleksandar Bercek
Inspector	Cedomir Petrovic
Female Reporter	Gorica Popovic
Desa, Ivan's Wife	Olga Spiridonovic
Old Actor	Xica Tomic

Right: Ljuba Tadic

Rastislava Gacic, Ljuba Tadic

THE TREE OF WOODEN CLOGS

(GAUMONT/SACIS/NEW YORKER) Written, Directed, Photographed and Edited by Ermanno Olmi; Music, Johann Sebastian Bach; Art Director, Enrico Tovaglieri; Costumes, Francesca Zucchelli; In Italian with English subtitles; In Gevacolor; 185 minutes; June release.

CAST

Batisti	Luigi Ornaghi
Batistina, His Wife	Francesca Moriggi
Minek, Their Son	Omar Brignoli
Tuni	Antonio Ferrari
Widow Runk	Teresa Brescianini
Grandpa Anselmo	Giuseppe Brignoli
Peppino	Carlo Rota
Teresina	Pasqualina Brolis
Pierino	Massimo Fratus
Annetta	Francesca Villa
Bettina	Maria Grazia Caroli

and other people from the Bergamo countryside of Northern Italy

Right: Omar Brignoli

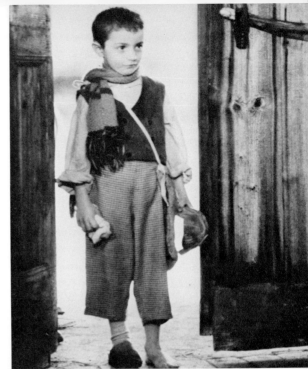

Teresa Brescianini, Carlo Rota, Francesca Moriggi, Lucia Pezzoli, Luigi Ornaghi

TILL MARRIAGE DO US PART

(FRANKLIN MEDIA) Producers, Pio Angeletti, Adriano de Micheli; Director, Luigi Comencini; Screenplay, Luigi Comencini, Ivo Perilli; Photography, Tonino delle Colli; Art Director, Dante Ferretti; Editor, Nino Baragli; Music, Feorenzo Carpi; In Italian with English subtitles; Presented by Dan Pomerantz, Kobi Jaeger; In color; Rated R; 97 minutes; July release.

CAST

Eugenia	Laura Antonelli
Raimondo, the Husband	Alberto Lionello
Pennacchini, the Chauffeur	Michele Placido
Henry, the Frenchman	Jean Rochefort
Evelyn, the Friend	Karin Schubert

Left: Laura Antonelli, Michele Placido
Below: Antonelli, Alberto Lionello

Laura Antonelli

Jean Rochefort
Above: Karin Schubert, Laura Antonelli

PEPPERMINT SODA

(GAUMONT/NEW YORKER) Direction and Screenplay, Diane Kurys; Photography, Phillippe Rousselot; Sound, Bernard Aubouy; Music, Yves Simon; Presented by Serge Laski; French with English subtitles; In color; Rated PG; 97 minutes; July release.

CAST

Anne Weber	Eleonore Klarwein
Frederique Weber	Odile Michel
Perrine Jacquet	Coralie Clement
Muriel Cazau, the Runaway	Marie Veronique Maurin
Martine Dubreuil	Valerie Stano
Sylvie Le Garrec	Anne Guillard
Pascal Carimil	Corinne Dacla
Evelyne Delcroix	Veronique Vernon
Mlle. Petitbon	Jacqueline Boyen
Mlle. Sassy	Francoise Bertin
Mme. Poliakoff	Arlette Bonnard
Mme. Clou	Dora Doll
Mlle. Colotte	Tsila Chelton
Superintendent	Jacques Rispal
Mme. Weber	Anouk Ferjac
M. Weber	Puterflam
Philippe	Yves Regnier
M. Cazau	Robert Rimbaud

**Top: Valerie Stano, Eleonore Klarwein,
Anne Guillard**

Odile Michel

POURQUOI PAS!
(Why Not!)

(NEW LINE CINEMA) Producer, Michele Dimitri; Direction and Screenplay, Coline Serreau; Photography, Jean-Francois Robin; Sound, Alain Lachassagne; Art Director, Denis Martin-Sisteron; Music, Jean-Pierre Mas; A Robert A. McNeil presentation in color; Not rated; 93 minutes; July release.

CAST

Fernand	Sami Frey
Louis	Mario Gonzalez
Alexa	Christine Murillo
Sylvie	Nicole Jamet
Inspector	Michel Aumont
Sylvie's Mother	Mathe Souverbie
Madame Picaud	Marie-Therese Saussure
Roger	Alain Solomon
Louis' Father	Jacques Rispal
Roger's Colleague	Bernard Crommbe

Top: Mario Gonzalez, Christine Murillo

Nicole Jamet, Christine Murrillo

MALIZIA

(PARAMOUNT) Producer, Silvio Clementelli; Director, Salvatore Samperi; Photography, Vittorio Storaro; Editor, Sergio Montanari; Music, Fred Bongusto; Screenplay, Ottavio Jemma, Salvatore Samperi, Alessandro Parenzo; Designer, Ezio Altieri; Assistant Director, Gianluigi Calderone; In Technicolor; Rated R; 98 minutes; Presented by Dino DeLaurentiis; July release.

CAST

Angela	Laura Antonelli
Don Ignazio	Turi Ferro
Nino	Alessandro Momo
Luciana	Tina Aumont
Nonna (Grandmother)	Lilla Brignone
Don Cirillo	Pino Caruso
Widow Corallo	Angela Luce
Antonio	Gianluigi Chirizzi
Enzino	Massimiliano Filoni
Porcello	Stefano Amato
Adelina	Grazia Di Marza

Right: Laura Antonelli, Turi Ferro
Below: Laura Antonelli, Alessandro Momo
© Paramount Pictures

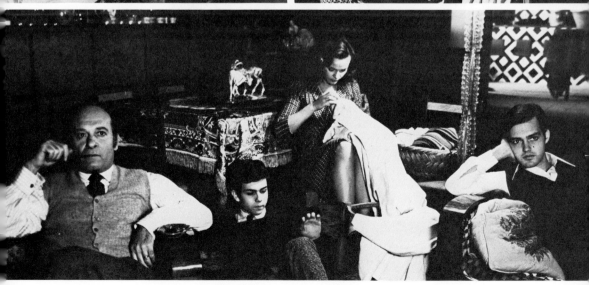

Turi Ferro, Alessandro Momo, Laura Antonelli, Gianluigi Chirizzi
Left Center: Laura Antonelli, Alessandro Momo

MONTY PYTHON'S LIFE OF BRIAN

(WARNER BROS.) Producer, John Goldstone; Director, Terry Jones; Screenplay, Graham Chapman, John Cleese, Terry Gilliam, Eric Idle, Terry Jones, Michael Palin; Executive Producers, George Harrison, Denis O'Brien; Design and Animation, Terry Gilliam; Associate Producer, Tim Hampton; Photography, Peter Biziou; Editor, Julian Doyle; Costumes, Hazel Pethig, Charles Knode; Art Director, Roger Christian; Music, Geoffrey Burgon; Assistant Director, Jonathan Benson; In color and Dolby Stereo; Rated R; 93 minutes; August release.

CAST

Mandy, Mother of Brian	Terry Jones
Jesus	Ken Colley
Brian	Graham Chapman
Wisemen	Graham Chapman, Michael Palin, John Cleese
Mr. Big Nose	Michael Palin
Mrs. Big Nose	Gwen Taylor
Mr. Cheeky	Eric Idle
Gregory	Terrence Bayler
Mrs. Gregory	Carol Cleveland
Men Further Forward	Charles McKeown, Terry Gilliam
Francis	Michael Palin
Reg	John Cleese
Stan, called Loretta	Eric Idle
Judith	Sue Jones-Davis
Harry the Haggler	Eric Idle
Woman with Sick Donkey	Gwen Taylor
Matthias	John Young
Stoner's Helpers	Bernard McKenna, Andrew MacLachlin
Weedy Samaritan	Neal Innes
Gladiator	John Case
Mr. Papadopoulis	George Harrison

Terry Jones, Terry Gilliam, Graham Chapman, Eric Idle, John Cleese, Michael Palin
Top Left: Graham Chapman, Terry Jones

John Cleese, Michael Palin Top:John
Cleese, Graham Chapman

Graham Chapman, Michael Palin
Top: Graham Chapman

DON GIOVANNI

(GAUMONT/NEW YORKER) The opera by Wolfgang Amadeus Mozart; Directed by Joseph Losey in association with Frantz Salieri; Conceived by Rolf Liebermann; Designer, Alexandre Trauner; Photography, Gerry Fisher; Editor, Reginald Beck; Italian Director, Gianni Cecchin; Screenplay, Patricia and Joseph Losey, Frantz Salieri; Opera and chorus of the Paris Opera directed by Lorin Maazel; Musical Director, Paul Myers; In Italian with English subtitles; In Panavision, Dolby Stereo, and color; Not rated; 180 minutes; August release.

CAST

Don Giovanni	Ruggero Raimondi
The Commander	John Macurdy
Donna Anna	Edda Moser
Donna Elvira	Kiri Te Kanawa
Don Ottavio	Kenneth Riegel
Leporello	Jose Van Dam
Zerlina	Teresa Berganza
Masetto	Malcolm King
Valet in Black	Eric Adjani
Harpsichordist	Janine Reiss

Ruggero Raimondi

WOYZECK

(NEW YORKER) Executive Producer, Walter Saxer; Direction and Screenplay, Werner Herzog; Based on drama by Georg Buchner; Photography, Jorg Schmidt-Reitwein; Editor, Beate Mainka-Jellinghaus; Designer, Henning von Gierke; Costumes, Gisela Storch; Music, Antonio Vivaldi, Benedetto Marcello; Assistant Director, Mirko Tichacek; In color; German with English subtitles; Not rated; 82 minutes; August release.

CAST

Woyzeck	Klaus Kinski
Marie	Eva Mattes
Captain	Wolfgang Reichmann
Doctor	Willy Semmelrogge
Drum Major	Josef Bierbichler
Andres	Paul Burian
Apprentice	Volker Prechtl
Barker	Dieter Augustin
Margaret	Irm Hermann
Jew	Wolfgang Bachler
Kathy	Rosy-Rosy Heinikel
Petty Officer	Herbert Fux
Innkeeper	Thomas Mettke
His Wife	Maria Mettke

Right: Klaus Kinski
Top: Klaus Kinski, Willy Semmelrogge

Klaus Kinski, Josef Bierbichler

Eva Mattes, Klaus Kinski

SOLDIER OF ORANGE

(INTERNATIONAL PICTURE SHOW CO.) Producer, Rob Houwer; Director, Paul Verhoeven; Based on autobiographical novel by Erik Hazelhoff; Music, Rogier Van Otterloo; Art Director, Roland De Groot; Costumes, Elly Claus; Photography, Jost Vacano; Editor, Jane Sperr; In Eastmancolor; Not rated; 150 minutes; August release.

CAST

Erik	Rutger Hauer
Guus	Jeroen Krabbe
Colonel Rafelli	Edward Fox
Susan	Susan Penhaligon
Will	Peter Faber
Esther	Belinda Meuldijk
Alex	Derek De Lint
Nico	Lex Van Delden
John	Huib Rooymans
Jacques	Dolf De Vries
Robby	Eddy Habbema
Breitner	Rijk De Gooyer
Queen Wilhelmina	Andrea Domburg
Van Der Zanden	Guus Hermus
Geisman	Rene Koldehoff
Sergeant	Del Henney

Left: Susan Penhaligon, Rutger Hauer
© International Picture Show Co.

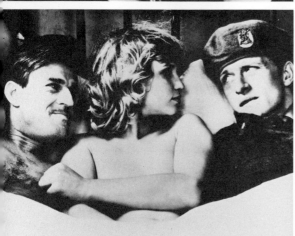

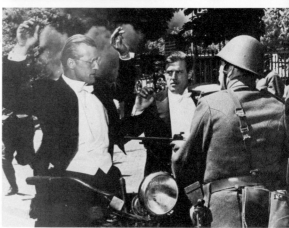

Jeroen Krabbe, Rutger Hauer Above: Krabbe, Susan Penhaligon, Hauer Top: Penhaligon, Hauer

Rutger Hauer, Jeroen Krabbe Above: Hauer, Andrea Domburg Top: Rutger Hauer

Hanna Schygulla, George Byrd

THE MARRIAGE OF MARIA BRAUN

(NEW YORKER) Director, Rainer Werner Fassbinder; Screenplay, Peter Marthesheimer, Pia Frohlich, Rainer Werner Fassbinder; Photography, Michael Ballhaus; Editor, Juliane Lorenz; Music, Peer Raben; Design, Norbert Scherer; In color; German with English subtitles; Rated R; 120 minutes, August release.

CAST

Maria Braun	Hanna Schygulla
Hermann Braun	Klaus Lowitsch
Oswald	Ivan Desny
Willi	Gottfried John
Mother	Gisela Uhlen
Hans	Gunter Lamprecht
Senkenberg	Hark Bohm
Bill	George Byrd
Betti	Elisabeth Trissenaar
Peddler	Rainer Werner Fassbinder
Vevi	Isolde Barth
Bronski	Peter Berling
Red Cross Nurse	Sonja Neudorfer
Frau Ehmcke	Lieselotte Eder
Conductor	Volker Spengler
Lawyer	Karl-Heinz von Hassel
Anwalt	Michael Ballhaus
Notary	Christine Hopf de Loup
Gentleman with Car	Dr. Horst-Dieter Klock
American G.I.'s	Gunther Kaufmann, Bruce Low
Doctor	Claus Holm
Grandpa Berger	Anton Schirsner
Justice of the Peace	Hannes Kaetner
Reporter	Martin Haussler
Wardens	Norbert Scherer, Rolf Buhrmann, Arthur Glogau

Top: Hanna Schygulla

MEETINGS WITH REMARKABLE MEN

(LIBRA) Producer, Stuart Lyons; Director, Peter Brook; Screenplay, Jeanne De Salzmann, Peter Brook; Adapted from book by G. I. Gurdjieff; Designer, George Wakhevitch; Editor, John Jympson; Music, Thomas De Hartmann, Laurence Rosenthal; Photography, Gilbert Taylor; Executive Producer, Michael Currer-Briggs; Associate Producer, Robert Watts; Assistant Director, Gus Agosti; Design, Malak Khazai; A Remar Production in Technicolor; Rated G; 108 minutes; August release.

CAST

Gurdjieff	Dragan Maksimovic
Young Gurdjieff	Mikica Dimitrijevic
Prince Lubovedsky	Terence Stamp
Professor Skridlov	Athol Fugard
Karpenko	Gerry Sundquist
Yelov	Bruce Myers
Gurdjieff's Father	Warren Mitchell
Pogossian	Donald Sumpter
Vitvitskaia	Natasha Parry
Soloviev	Fahro Konjhodzic
Father Giovanni	Tom Fleming
Dean Borsh	David Markham
Dervish	Fabijan Sovagovic
Father Maxim	Bruce Purchase
Dr. Ivanov	Martin Benson
Pavlov	Roger Lloyd Pack
Bogga Eddin	Sami Tahasuni
Teacher	Malcolm Hayes
Captain	Constantin De Goguel
Tamil	Colin Blakeley
Artillery Officer	Jeremy Wilkin

and Alan Tilvern, Tony Vogel, Ian Hogg, Ben Zimet, Ahmet Kutbay, Abbas Moayeri, Cimenli Fahrettin, Gregoire Aslan, Oscar Peck, Mitchell Horner, Nigel Greaves, Paul Henley

**Right: Warren Mitchell, Mikica Dimitrijevic
Top: Donald Sumpter, Dragan Maksimovic**

Natasha Parry

Terence Stamp

TIME AFTER TIME

(WARNER BROS.) Producer, Herb Jaffe; Direction and Screenplay, Nicholas Meyer; Story, Karl Alexander, Steve Hayes; Associate Producer, Steven-Charles Jaffe; Music Miklos Rozsa; Photography, Paul Lohmann; Designer, Edward C. Carfagno; Editor, Donn Cambern; Assistant Directors, Michael Daves, Paul Magwood; In Panavision, Dolby Stereo, and Metrocolor; Rated PG; 112 minutes; August release.

CAST

H. G. Wells	Malcolm McDowell
Stevenson	David Warner
Amy	Mary Steenburgen
Lieutenant Mitchell	Charles Cioffi
Assistant	Kent Williams
Mrs. Turner	Andonia Katsaros
Shirley	Patti D'Arbanville
Edwards	James Garrett
Harding	Keith McConnell
Richardson	Leo Lewis
McKay	Byron Webster
Jenny	Karin Mary Shea
Carol	Geraldine Baron
Inspector Gregson	Laurie Main
Adams	Joseph Maher

and Michael Evans, Ray Reinhardt, Bob Shaw, Stu Klitsner, Nicholas Shields, Gene Hartline, Clement St. George, Shirley Marchant, Larry J. Blake, Antonie Becker, Hilda Haynes, Read Morgan, Mike Gainey, Jim Haynie, Wayne Storm, John Colton, Corey Feldman, James Cranna, Earl Nicols, Bill Bradley, Clete Roberts, Rita Conde, Gail Hyatt, Shelley Hack

Left: Malcolm McDowell
© Warner Bros.

David Warner, Mary Steenburgen

Mary Steenburgen, Malcolm McDowell (above)
Top: David Warner

Mary Steenburgen, Malcolm McDowell
Top: Malcolm McDowell

181

FRENCH POSTCARDS

(PARAMOUNT) Producer, Gloria Katz; Director, Willard Huyck; Screenplay, Willard Huyck, Gloria Katz; Music, Lee Holdridge; Editor, Carol Littleton; Photography, Bruno Nuytten; Art Director, Jean-Pierre Kohut-Svelko; Assistant Director, Jean-Jacques Beineix; Costumes, Catherine Leterrier, Joan Mocine; A Geria production in color; Rated PG; 95 minutes; September release.

CAST

Joel	Miles Chapin
Laura	Blanche Baker
Alex	David Marshall Grant
Toni	Valerie Quennessen
Melanie	Debra Winger
Sayyid	Mandy Patinkin
Madame Tessier	Marie-France Pisier
Monsieur Tessier	Jean Rochefort
Mrs. Weber	Lynn Carlin
Mr. Weber	George Coe
Pascal	Christophe Bourseiller
Monsieur Levert	Francois Lalande
Christine	Anemone
Malsy	Veronique Janot
Cecile	Marie-Anne Chazelk
Madame Levert	Laurence Ligneres
Jean-Louis	Andre Penvern
Jean-Claude	Patrick Fierry
Bus Driver	Roland Neunreuther
Chief Snail	Gloria Katz

Marie-France Pisier, David Marshall Grant

Top: Jean Rochefort, Marie-France Pisier
Below: David Marshall Grant, Valerie Quennessen,
Miles Chapin Top Left: Chapin, Grant Below: Blanche
Baker (C) © Paramount Pictures Corp.

THE GREEN ROOM

(NEW WORLD) Director, Francois Truffaut; Screenplay, Francois Truffaut, Jean Gruault; Based on Henry James' writings; Music, Maurice Jaubert; Photography, Nestor Almendros; Assistant Director, Suzanne Schiffman; Art Director, Jean-Pierre Kohut-Svelko; Editor, Martine Barraque-Curie; In Eastmancolor; Rated PG; 95 minutes; September release.

CAST

Julien Davenne	Francois Truffaut
Cecilia Mandel	Nathalie Baye
Bernard Humbert	Jean Daste
Gerard Mazet	Jean-Pierre Moulin
Bishop's Secretary	Antoine Vitez
Mazet's Second Wife	Jane Lobre
Monique, Editorial Secretary	Monique Dury
Julie Davenne	Laurence Ragon
Dr. Jardine	Marcel Berbert
Orator in Cemetery	Christian Lentretien
Georges, Young Boy	Patrick Maleon

Right: Francois Truffaut

Nathalie Baye, Francois Truffaut
(also above left and right)

LOVE AND BULLETS

(ASSOCIATED FILM DISTRIBUTION) Producer, Pancho Kohner; Director, Stuart Rosenberg; Story and Screenplay, Wendell Mayes; Designer, John de Cuir; Costumes, Dorothy Jeakins; Music, Lalo Schiffrin; Editors, Michael Anderson, Lesley Walker, Tom Priestley; Photographers, Fred Koenekamp, Anthony Richmond; Assistant Directors, Jack Aldworth, Benjy Rosenberg; Art Director, Colin Grimes; In Panavision and color; Rated PG; 95 minutes; September release.

CAST

Charlie Congers	Charles Bronson
Jackie Pruitt	Jill Ireland
Joe Bamposa	Rod Steiger
Louis Monk	Strother Martin
Vittorio Farroni	Henry Silva
Brickman	Bradford Dillman
Huntz	Paul Koslo
Lobo	Michael Gazzo
Coroner	Joseph Roman
Cook	Sam Chew
Andy Minton	Albert Salmi
Caruso	Val Avery
Alibisi	John Belluci
Carlo	Rick Colliti

Left: Jill Ireland
Top: Charles Bronson
© AFD

Rod Steiger

Jill Ireland, Charles Bronson

LUNA

(20th CENTURY-FOX) Producer, Giovanni Bertolucci; Director, Bernardo Bertolucci; Photography, Vittorio Storaro; Screenplay, Giuseppe Bertolucci, Clare Peploe, Bernardo Bertolucci; English Adaptation, George Malko; Story, Franco Arcalli, Bernardo Bertolucci, Giuseppe Bertolucci; Editor, Gabriella Cristiani; Art Directors, Maria Paola Maino, Gianni Silvestri; Costumes, Lina Taviani; Assistant Directors, Gabriele Polverosi, Jirges Ristum; In Eastmancolor; Rated R; 141 minutes; September release.

CAST

Caterina Silveri	Jill Clayburgh
Joe, Her Son	Matthew Barry
Marina	Veronica Lazar
Communist	Renato Salvatori
Douglas Winter, Her Husband	Fred Gwynne
Giuseppe	Tomas Milian
Giuseppe's Mother	Alida Valli
Arianna	Elisabetta Campeti
Man in Bar	Franco Citti
Upholsterer	Roberto Benigni
Director of Caracalla	Carlo Verdone
Edward	Peter Eyre
Mustafa	Stephane Barat
Innkeeper	Pippo Campanini
Maestro Giancarlo Calo	Rodolfo Lodi
Concetta, Caterina's Maid	Shara Di Nepi
Wardrobe Mistress	Iole Silvani
Barmen	Francesco Mei, Ronaldo Bonacchi
Piano Movers	Mimmo Poli, Massimiliano Filoni
Caracalla Conductor	Alessandro Vlad

Top: Jill Clayburgh, Tomas Milian
Below: Matthew Barry, Bebetti Campeti
© 20th Century Fox Film Corp.

Matthew Barry, Jill Clayburgh
(also above and top)

185

A MAN, A WOMAN, AND A BANK

(AVCO EMBASSY) Producers, John B. Bennett, Peter Samuelson; Director, Noel Black; Screenplay, Raynold Gideon, Bruce A. Evans, Stuart Margolin; Story, Raynold Gideon, Bruce A. Evans; Photography, Jack Cardiff; Music, Bill Conti; Associate Producer, Maurice Dunster; Assistant Directors, Peter Bogart, George Margellos, Fred Frame; Designer, Anne Pritchard; Editor, Carl Kress; In color; Rated PG; 100 minutes; September release

CAST

Reese	Donald Sutherland
Stacey	Brooke Adams
Norman	Paul Mazursky
Peter	Allan Magicovsky
Marie	Leigh Hamilton
Gino	Nick Rice
Jerry	Peter Erlich
Steve	Paul Rothery
Laura	Elizabeth Barclay
Girl 2	Leanne Young
Models	Sharon Spurrell, Tibbi Landers, Annette Marie Dupuis
Guards	Jackson Davies, Walter Marsh
Junior Shipping Clerk	Alex Willows
Senior Shipping Clerk	Robert Forsythe
Vault Lady	Eunice Thompson
Elevator Repair Guard	Bob Hughes
Used Car Salesman	Alex Kliner
Citation Cop	Cam Lane
Van Cop	Howard Hughes
Duty Officer	Fred Latremouille
Locksmith	David Glyn-Jones

Top: Donald Sutherland, Brooke Adams
Right: Leigh Hamilton, Paul Mazursky
© AVCO Embassy

Paul Mazursky, Brooke Adams, Donald Sutherland
(also above)

THE LEGACY

(UNIVERSAL) Executive Producer, Arnold Kopelson; Producer, David Foster; Director, Richard Marquand; Screenplay, Jimmy Sangster, Patrick Tilley, Paul Wheeler; Story, Jimmy Sangster; Music, Michael J. Lewis; Associate Producer, Ted Lloyd; Photography, Dick Bush, Alan Hume; Designer, Disley Jones; Editor, Anne V. Coates; Costumes, Shura Cohen; Assistant Director, Michael Dryhurst; A Pethurst production in Technicolor and Dolby Stereo; Rated R; 100 minutes; September release.

CAST

Maggie Walsh	Katharine Ross
Pete Danner	Sam Elliott
Jason Mountolive	John Standing
Harry	Ian Hogg
Nurse Adams	Margaret Tyzack
Karl	Charles Gray
Jacques	Lee Montague
Barbara	Hildegard Neil
Maria	Marianne Broome
Butler	William Abney
Cook	Patsy Smart
Stable Lad	Mathias Kilroy
Gardener	Reg Harding
Clive	Roger Daltrey

Right: Sam Elliott, Katharine Ross
Below: Sam Elliott, Margaret Tyzack
© Universal City Studios

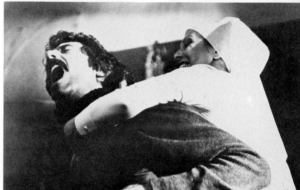

Roger Daltry, Katharine Ross Above: Ian Hogg,
Sam Elliott, Ross, John Standing

Ian Hogg, Charles Gray, Marianne Broome,
Lee Montague

THE EUROPEANS

(LEVITT-PICKMAN) Producer, Ismail Merchant; Director, James Ivory; Associate Producer, Connie Kaiserman; Screenplay, Ruth Prawer Jhabvala; From the novel by Henry James; Photography, Larry Pizer; Editor, Humphrey Dixon; Music, Richard Robbins; Art Director, Jeremiah Rusconi; Costumes; Judy Moorcroft; In color; Rated G; 90 minutes; October release.

CAST

Eugenia	Lee Remick
Robert Acton	Robin Ellis
Mr. Wentworth	Wesley Addy
Clifford Wentworth	Tim Choate
Gertrude Wentworth	Lisa Eichhorn
Charlotte Wentworth	Nancy New
Lizzie Acton	Kristin Griffith
Mrs. Acton	Helen Stenborg
Mr. Brand	Norman Snow
Felix	Tim Woodward
Augustine	Gedda Petry

Left: Lee Remick, Wesley Addy

Lee Remick

Robin Ellis, Kristin Griffith, Lee Remick
Above: Lisa Eichhorn, Nancy New

Robin Ellis, Lee Remick (also above)
Top: Ellis, Kristin Griffith

Tim Woodward, Lisa Eichhorn (also top)
Above: Tim Woodward

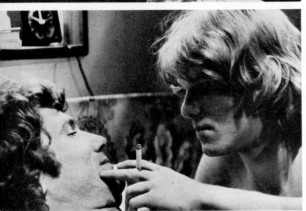

THE CONSEQUENCE

(LIBRA) Producer, Bernd Eichinger; Director, Wolfgang Petersen; Screenplay, Alexander Ziegler, Wolfgang Petersen; From book by Alexander Ziegler; Photography, Jorg-Michael Baldenius; Music, Nils Sustrate; Art Director, O. Jochen Schmidt; Editor, Gunther Witte; In black and white; Not rated; 100 minutes; October release.

CAST

Martin	Jurgen Prochnow
Thomas Manzoni	Ernst Hannawald
Overseer Manzoni	Walo Luond
Mrs. Manzoni	Edith Volkmann
Director Reichmuth	Erwin Kohlund
Prisoner Bloch	Hans Irle
Prisoner Lemmi	Alexander Ziegler
Prisoner Kunz	Erwin Parker
Housefather Diethelm	Werner Schwuchow
Warden Rusterholz	Hans-Michael Rehberg
Babette	Elisabeth Fricker
Inmate Enrico	Hans Putz
Inmate Schlumberger	Wolf Gauditz
Inmate Benny	Thomas Haerin

Top: Elisabeth Fricker, Thomas Haerin
Below: Ernst Hannawald, Werner Schwuchow, Haerin
Top Left: Ernst Hannawald, Jurgen Prochnow

Ernst Hannawald, Jurgen Prochnow
(also above)

ORCHESTRA REHEARSAL

(NEW YORKER) Produced by RAI; Direction and Screenplay, Federico Fellini; Music, Nino Rota; Photography, Giuseppe Rotunno; Editor, Ruggero Mastroianni; Assistant Director, Maurizio Mein; Designer, Dante Ferretti; Costumes, Gabriella Pescucci; Italian with English subtitles; In color; Not rated; 72 minutes; October release.

CAST

Conductor	Baldwin Baas
Harp	Clara Colosimo
Piano	Elisabeth Labi
Contrabasson	Ronaldo Bonacchi
Cello	Ferdinando Villella
Tuba	Giovanni Javarone
First Violin	David Mauhsell
Second Violin	Francesco Aluigi
Oboe	Andy Miller
Flute	Sibyl Mostert
Trumpet	Franco Mazzieri
Trombone	Daniele Pagani
Violin	Luigi Uzzo
Clarinet	Cesare Martignoni
Copyist	Umberto Zuanelli
Manager	Filippo Trincia
Union Delegate	Claudio Ciocca
Violins	Angelica Hansen, Heinz Krueger
Interviewer	Voice of Federico Fellini

Top Right: Baldwin Bass

THE LAST ROMANTIC LOVER

(NEW LINE CINEMA) Producer, Bernard Lenteric; Director, Just Jaeckin; Screenplay, Just Jaeckin, Ennio De Concini; Costumes, Zorica Lozic; Photography, Robert Fraisse; Editor, Francoise Bonnot; Music, Pierre Bachelet; Presented by Richard Winckler; In color; Rated R; 94 minutes; October release.

CAST

Elisabeth	Dayle Haddon
Pierre	Gerrard Ismael
Max	Fernando Rey
Therese	Zorica Lozic
Auguste	Albert Dray
White Clown	Roland Blanche
Juggler	Jacques Canselier
Ballon/Fakir	Eduardo Begara
Lilliputian	Jose Jaime Espinoza
Dwarf	Isabel P. Fernandez
Emperor	Georges Beller
Nantes Supreme	Yann Babilee
Pimp	Etienne Chicot
Blueblood	Francois Guetary
Greek Youth	Georges Lago
Hermit	Thierry Lhermitte
18 Carats	Tomas Pico
Scorpion	Gilles Kohler
Sapphire	J. P. Schneider
Handsome Oak	Jean Boissery
Actor	Georges Roiron

Guest Appearances by Daniel Duval, Moustache, Jean Marie Riviere, Jacqueline Staup, Dalila Di Lazaro

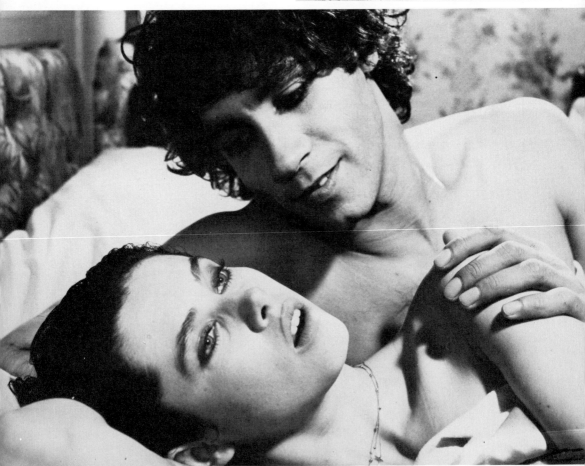

Dayle Haddon, Gerrard Ismael (also top right)

THE DIVINE NYMPH

(ANALYSIS FILM RELEASING CORP.) Executive Producers, Luigi Scattini, Mario Ferrari; Director, Giuseppe Patroni Griffi; Screenplay, G. Patroni Griffi, A. Valdarnini; Based on novel "La Divina Fanciulla" by Luciano Zuccoli; Costumes, Gabriella Pescucci; Designer, Fiorenzo Senese; Photography, Giuseppe Rotunno; Music, Ennio Morricone; Italian with English subtitles; In color; Not rated; 90 minutes; October release

CAST

Manoela Roderighi	Laura Antonelli
Dany di Bagnasco	Terence Stamp
Michele Barra	Marcello Mastroianni
Martino Ghiondelli	Michele Placido
Armellini	Duilio Del Prete
Marco Pisani	Ettore Manni
Dany's Maid	Cecilia Polizzi
Manoela's Aunt	Marina Berti
Signora Fones	Doris Duranti
Dany's Friend	Ruth League
Cameriere di Stefano	Piero Di Jorio
Majordomo Pasqualino	Carlo Tamberlani

Top: Laura Antonelli, Marcello Mastroianni
Below: Mastroianni, Antonelli, Terence Stamp
Top Right: Stamp, Antonelli

Laura Antonelli, and above
with Terence Stamp

QUADROPHENIA

(WORLD NORTHAL) Producers, Roy Baird, Bill Curbishley; Executive Producers, The Who; Director, Franc Roddam; Screenplay, Dave Humphries, Martin Stellman, Franc Roddam; Musical Directors, John Entwistle, Pete Townshend; Associate Producer, John Peverall; Assistant Directors, Ray Corbett, Mike Flynn, Kieron Phipps; Photography, Brian Tufano; Designer, Simon Holland; Editor, Mike Taylor; In color and Dolby Stereo; Rated R; 120 minutes; November release.

CAST

Jimmy	Phil Daniels
Dave	Mark Wingett
Chalky	Philip Davis
Steph	Leslie Ash
Pete	Garry Cooper
Monkey	Toyah Wilcox
Ace	"Sting"
Ferdy	Trevor Laird
Spider	Gary Shail
Jimmy's Mother	Kate Williams
Jimmy's Father	Michael Elphick
Kevin	Raymond Winstone

Top: Sting Below: Phil Daniels,
Toyah Wilcox Top Left: Daniels, Leslie
Ash Below: Michael Elphick, Daniels

Leslie Ash, Phil Daniels

RUNNING

(UNIVERSAL) Producers, Robert Cooper, Ronald Cohen; Direction and Screenplay, Steven Hilliard Stern; Co-Producer, John M. Eckert; Photography, Laszlo George; Editor, Kurt Hirschler; Designer, Roy Forge Smith; Music, Andre Gagnon; Assistant Director, Alan Simmonds; Art Director, Susan Longmire; Costumes, Lynda Kemp; Assistant Directors, Donald McCutcheon, Francois Ouimet, Ewa Zebrowski, Bruce Pustin, Bob Meneray, David Bailey; Editor, David Nicholson; In color; Rated PG; 102 minutes; November release.

CAST

Michael Andropolis	Michael Douglas
Janet Andropolis	Susan Anspach
Coach Walker	Lawrence Dane
Richard Rosenberg	Eugene Levy
Howard Grant	Charles Shamata
Chuck	Philip Akin
Pregnant Woman	Trudy Young
Mr. Finlay	Murray Westgate
Susan Andropolis	Jennifer McKinney
Andrea Andropolis	Lesleh Donaldson
Jim McKay	Himself
Boston Race Winner	Lutz Brode
Debbie Rosenberg	Deborah Templeton Burgess
Kenny	Gordon Clapp
Maloney	Marvin Goldhar
Commentator	David Laurence
Stuntman	Robert Hannah
Black Teenager	Donny Cooper
Italian Teenager	Joel Bergman
Puerto Rican Teenager	Giancarlo Esposito

**Right: Michael Douglas, and Top with
Lawrence Dane
© Universal City Studios**

Michael Douglas, Jennifer McKinney

Susan Anspach

A SIMPLE STORY

(QUARTET FILMS) Producer, Alain Sarde; Director, Claude Sautet; Screenplay, Claude Sautet, Jean-Loup Dabadie; Photography, Jean Boffety; Music, Phillipe Sarde; Editor, Jacqueline Thiedot; In French with English subtitles; Dialogue, Jean-Loup Dabadie; In color; Not rated; 110 minutes; November release.

CAST
Marie	Romy Schneider
Georges	Bruno Cremer
Serge	Claude Brasseur
Gabrielle	Arlette Bonnard
Esther	Sophie Daumier
Anna	Eva Darlan
Francine	Francine Berge
Jerome	Roger Pigaut
Marie's Mother	Madeline Robinson
Martin	Yves Knapp

Left: Romy Schneider
© Quartet Films Inc.

THE MAGICIAN OF LUBLIN

(CANNON) Executive Producer, Harry N. Blum; Producers, Menahem Golan, Yoram Globus; Director, Menahem Golan; Screenplay, Irving S. White, Menahem Golan; Music, Maurice Jarre; Photography, David Gurfinkel; Art Director, Jurgen Kiebach; Editor, Dov Hoenig; In color; Rated R; 105 minutes; November release.

CAST

Yasha	Alan Arkin
Emilla	Louise Fletcher
Zeftel	Valerie Perrine
Elzbieta	Shelley Winters
Wolsky	Lou Jacobi
Herman	Warren Berlinger
Shmul	Shai K. Ophir
Halina	Lisa Whelchel
Magda	Maia Danziger
Esther	Linda Bernstein
Bolek	Zachi Noy
Count Zaruski	Friedrich Schonfelder
Rytza	Ophelia Stral
Pan Kazarsky	Buddy Elias

Top: Lisa Welchel, Alan Arkin, Louise Fletcher
Below: Valerie Perrine Top Right: Arkin, Maia
Danziger

Alan Arkin
Above: Shelley Winters

197

BOARDWALK

(ATLANTIC RELEASING CORP.) Producer, George Willoughby; Executive Producer, Gerry Herrod; Director, Stephen Verona; Photography, Billy Williams; Screenplay, Stephen Verona, Leigh Chapman; In color; Not rated; 98 minutes; November release.

CAST

Becky Rosen	Ruth Gordon
David Rosen	Lee Strasberg
Florence	Janet Leigh
Leo	Joe Silver
Mr. Friedman	Eli Mintz
Eli	Eddie Barth
Charlie	Merwin Goldsmith
Strut	Kim Delgado
Peter	Michael Ayr
Marilyn	Forbesy Russell

and guest appearances by Lillian Roth, Sammy Cahn, Linda Manz

Top: Ruth Gordon, Janet Leigh Below: Michael Ayr, Forbesy Russel Top Left: Gordon, Lee Strasberg © Atlantic Releasing Co.

Lee Strasberg, Ruth Gordon
Above: Strasberg, Kim Delgado

ARABIAN ADVENTURE

(ASSOCIATED FILM DISTRIBUTION) Producer, John Dark; Director, Kevin Connor; Screenplay, Brian Hayles; Photography, Alan Hume; Music, Ken Thorne; Designer, Elliot Scott; Art Director, Jack Maxsted; Editor, Barry Peters; In color and Dolby Stereo; Rated G; 98 minutes; November release.

CAST

Alquazar	Christopher Lee
Khasim	Milo O'Shea
Prince Hasan	Oliver Tobias
Princess Zuleira	Emma Samms
Majeed	Puneet Sira
Bahloul	John Wyman
Achmed	John Ratzenberger
Abu	Shane Rimmer
Asaf	Hal Galili
Wazir Al Wuzara	Peter Cushing
Vahishta	Capucine
Daad El Shur	Mickey Rooney
Beggarwoman	Elizabeth Welch
Eastern Dancer	Suzanne Danielle
Mahmoud	Athar Malik
Omar, the Goldsmith	Jacob Witkin
Genie	Milton Reid

Right: Oliver Tobias Below: Mickey Rooney,
Puneet Sira
© AFD

Oliver Tobias, Milo O'Shea,
Above: also with Puneet Sira

Emma Samms

199

STAY AS YOU ARE

(NEW LINE CINEMA) Producer, Giovanni Bertolucci; Director, Alberto Lattuada; Screenplay, Alberto Lattuada, Enrico Oldoini; Story, Paolo Cavara, Enrico Oldoini; Photography, Luis Alcaine; Music, Ennio Morricone; Art Director, Luigi Scaccianoce; Costumes, Bona Nasalli Rocca; An Italo-Spanish Co-Production in color; Not rated; 95 minutes; December release.

CAST

Giulio	Marcello Mastroianni
Francesca	Nastassia Kinski
Lorenzo	Francisco Rabal
Luisa	Monica Randal
Teresa	Giuliana Calandra
Cecilia	Ann Pieroni
Ilaria	Barbara DeRossi

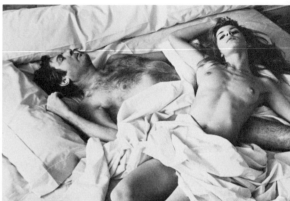

Nastassia Kinski, Marcello Mastroianni (also right center)
Top Left: Nastassia Kinski
© New Line Cinema

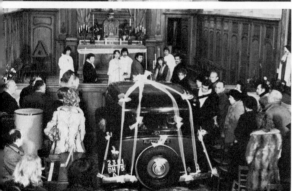

ROBERT ET ROBERT

(QUARTET FILMS) Direction and Screenplay, Claude Lelouch; Photography, Jacques LeFrancois; Music, Francis Lai, Jean-Claude Nachon; Costumes, Colette Baudot; Designer, Eric Moulard; Not rated; In color; 105 minutes; December release.

CAST

Robert Goldman	Charles Denner
Robert Villiers	Jacques Villeret
Jacques Millet	Jean-Claude Brialy
Madame Goldman	Germain Montero
Madame Villiers	Regine
Interviewer	Macha Meril
Francis Michaud	Francis Perrin
Josette Michaud	Josette Derenne
Madame Millet	Nella Bielski
Arlette	Arlette Emery
Ali	Mohamet Zinet

Top: Regine, Jacques Villeret, Charles Denner
Below: Denner, Jean-Claude Brialy

Macha Meril, Jacques Villeret
Above: Regine, Villeret

Suzanne Pleshette, Victor Buono
in "Target: Harry"

Eitaro Ozawa, Kinuyo Tanaka
in "My Love Has Been Burning"

NEVERMORE, FOREVER (French Embassy) Director, Jacqueline Doye: Screenplay, Yannick Bellon; Photography Georges Barsky; Music, Georges Delerue; Films de l'Equinoxe Production in Eastmancolor; 95 minutes; January release. CAST: Bulle Ogier (Claire), Jean-Marc Bory (Mathieu), Loleh Bellon (Agathe), Bernard Giraudeau (Denis), Marianne Epin (Sylvie), Roger Blin (Daniel)

TARGET: HARRY (ABC Pictures International) Producer, Roger Corman; Co-Producer, Gene Corman; Director, Henry Neill; Screenplay, Bob Barbash; Photography, Patrice Pouget; Associate Producer, Charles Hanawalt; Music, Les Baxter; Designer, Sharon Compton; Assistant Directors, Beech Dickerson, Alain Corneau; Editor, Monte Hellman; In DeLuxe Color; Rated R; 85 minutes; January release. CAST: Vic Morrow (Harry), Suzanne Pleshette (Diane), Victor Buono (Mosul), Cesar Romero (Duval), Stanley Holloway (Jason), Charlotte Rampling (Ruth), Michael Ansara (Segora), Katy Fraysse (Lisa), Christian Barbier (Bulley), Fikret Hakan (Inspector), Milton Reid (Kemal), Anna Capri (Francesca), Laurie Main (Simon), Victoria Hale (Michele), Jack Leonard (Valdez)

SOMEWHERE, SOMEONE (NEF/French Embassy) Produced, Directed, and Written by Yannick Bellon; Photography, Georges Barsky; Music, Georges Delerue; A Film Contact Production in Eastmancolor; 100 minutes; January release. CAST: Loleh Bellon (Raphaele), Roland Dubillard (Vincent), Hughes Quester (Boy), Christine Tsingos (Girl)

JOHN'S WIFE (French Embassy) Directed and Written by Yannick Bellon; Photography, Georges Barsky, Pierre-William Glenn; Music, Georges Delerue; A Films de l'Equinoxe Production; 105 minutes; January release. CAST: France Lambiotte (Nadine), Claude Rich (Jean), Hippolyte (Remi), James Mitchell (David), Tatiana Moukhine (Christien), Regine Mazella (Valerie)

MY LOVE HAS BEEN BURNING (New Yorker) Producers, Hisao Itoya, Kiyoshi Shimazu; Director, Kenji Mizoguchi; Screenplay, Yoshikata Yoda, Kaneto Shindo; Story, Kogo Noda; Photography, Kohei Sugiyama, Tomotaro Nashiki; Music, Senji Ito; A Shochiku production in black and white; 84 minutes; January release. CAST: Kinuyo Tanaka (Eiko), Ichiro Sugai (Shigei), Mitsuko Mito (Chiyo), Eitaro Ozawa (Ryuzo), Kuniko Miyake (Tochiko), Koreya Senda (Prime Minister), Eijiro Tono (State Counsellor), Kappei Matsumoto (Kusuo), Torahiko Hamada (Chief), Masao Shimizu (Takeshi), Makoto Kobori (Master), Sadako Sawamura (Omasa), Shinobu Araki (Eiko's Father), Ikuko Hirano (Eiko's Mother)

THE SKIP TRACER (G. G. Communications) Producer, Laara Dalen; Director, Zale Dalen; Photography, Ron Oreiux; In color; Rated PG; 93 minutes; January release. Starring David Petersen

CADDIE (Australian Films) Producer, Anthony Buckley; Director, Donald Crombie; Screenplay, Joan Long; Photography, Peter James; Art Director, Owen Williams; Costumes, Judith Dorsman; Editor, Tim Wellburn; Music, Patrick Flynn; In Panavision and color; Not rated; 107 minutes; January release. CAST: Helen Morse (Caddie), Takis Emmanuel (Peter), Jack Thompson (Ted), Jacki Weaver (Josie), Melissa Jaffer, Ron Blanchard, Drew Forsythe, Kirrili Nolan, Lynette Currin, Phillip Hinton, Mary Mackay, Lucky Grills, Robyn Nevin, Pat Evison, June Salter, Joy Hruby, Jan Adele, Johnny Garfield, Shirley Cameron, Frank Lloyd, Sid Heylan, Pat Rooney, Roy Corbett, Ray Marshall

FIONA (Rochelle Films) Producer, Brian Smedley-Aston; Director, James Kenelm Clarke; Screenplay, Michael Robson; Music, Richard Hieronymous, James Kenelm Clarke; Presented by Martin W. Greenwald, Arthur Weisberg; In color; Rated R; 82 minutes; January release. CAST: Fiona Richmond, Anthony Steele, Victor Spinetti, John Clive, Joan Benham, Heather Deely, Linda Regan, Roland Curran, Arthur Howard, Neil Cunningham, Patricia Bourdrin, Graham Stark

CHARLIE AND THE HOOKER (Group I Films) Executive Producer, Anthony Cuevas; Director, Emmanuele Summers; In Eastmancolor; Rated R; 90 minutes; January release. CAST: Francis Summers, Beatrice Balbo, Joanne Simpson, Ellen Grant

CHUQUIAGO (Tricontinental) Director, Antonio Equino; Screenplay, Oscar Soria; Photography, Antonio Equino, Julio Lemcina; Editors, Deborah Shaffer, Suzanne Fenn; Music, Alberto Villalpando; A Grupo Ukamau production; In Aymara and Spanish with English subtitles; In color; 87 minutes; February release. CAST: Nestor Yujra (Isico), Edmundo Villareel (Johnny), David Santalla (Carlos), Tatiana Aponta (Patricia), Alejandra Quispe (Candicha), Jesusa Mangudo (Frutera), Fidel Huanca (Johnny's Father), Julia de Huanca (Johnny's Mother), Raul Ruiz (Rodriguez), Pablo Davila (Lopez), Julio Cesar Paredes (Rafael), Tito Landa (Jefe), Mario Castro (Caceres), Vilma Arce (Patricia's Mother)

THE CYCLE (Icarus/Dispodex International) Director, Darius Mehrjui; Screenplay, Golam H. Saedi, Darius Mehrjui; Photography, Houshang Baharlou; Editor, Talat Mirfenderski; Based on story "Garbage Dump" by G. H. Saedi; In color; 95 minutes; Farsi with English subtitles; February release. CAST: Ezat Entezami, Fourouzan, Ali Nassirian, Said Kangarani, Bahman Forsi

"The Cycle"

Elke Sommer, Leigh Lawson
in "It's Not the Size That Counts"

"The Middleman"

THE STREETFIGHTER'S LAST REVENGE (New Line Cinema) Rated R; 85 minutes; February release. Starring Sonny Chiba and Sue Shiomi, with a special appearance by Masafumi Suzuki. No other details available.

THE PICTURE SHOW MAN (Cinema World) Produced and Written by Joan Long; Director, John Power; Music, Peter Best; A Limelight production in color; Rated PG; February release. CAST: Rod Taylor, John Meillon, Patrick Cargill, Yelena Zigon, John Ewart

WANDA, THE WICKED WARDEN (Bernie Jacon) Director, Jess Franco; In Eastmancolor; Rated R; February release. CAST: Dyanne Thorne, Lina Romay, Tanya Busselier, Eric Falk, Marianne Lederer

IT'S NOT THE SIZE THAT COUNTS (Joseph Brenner Associates) Executive Producer, Larry Gordon; Producer, Betty E. Box; Director, Ralph Thomas; Screenplay, Sid Colin; Story, Harry Corbett; Additional Dialogue, Ian LaFrenais; Photography, Tony Imi; Editor, Ray Watts; Music, Tony Macaulay; In Eastmancolor; Rated R; 90 minutes; March release. CAST: Leigh Lawson (Percy), Elke Sommer (Clarissa), Denholm Elliott (Whitebread), Judy Geeson (Dr. Fairweather), Milo O'Shea (Dr. Klein), Vincent Price (Stavos), Julie Ege (Miss Hanson), George Coulouris (Professor)

THE MIDDLEMAN (Bauer International) Producer, Subir Guha; Direction, Music, and Screenplay, Satyajit Ray; Based on story by Shankar; Photography, Soumendu Ray; Editor, Dulal Dutta; Art Director, Ashok Bose; In black and white; Bengali with English subtitles; 134 minutes; March release. CAST: Pradip Mukherjee (Somnath), Satya Banerjee (Father), Dipankar Dey (His Brother), Lily Chakravorty (Kamala), Utpal Dutt (Bishu), Rabi Ghosh (Mitter), Sudeshna Das Sharma (Kauna), Aparna Sen (Somnath's Fiancee)

EAST END HUSTLE (Troma) Producer-Director, Frank Vitale; Screenplay, Frank Vitale, Allan Bozo Moyle; Photography, Ivar Rushevic; Music, Lenny Blum, Steve Wright; Editor, Patrick Dodd; In color; 91 minutes; Rated R; March release. CAST: Andree Pelletier (Cindy), Anne-Marie Provencher (Marianne), Miguel Fernandes (Dan), Allan Bozo Moyle (Peter)

SOME LIKE IT COOL (PRO International) Formerly "Casanova & Co." Director, Francois Legrand (Franz Antel); Producer, Franz Antel, Carl Szokoll; Screenplay, Joshua Sinclair, Tom Priman; Photography, Hans Matula; Editor, Michel Lewin; Music, Riz Ortolani; In color; Rated R; 100 minutes; March release. CAST: Tony Curtis, Marisa Berenson, Hugh Griffith, Marisa Mell, Britt Ekland, Jean Lefebvre, Andrea Ferreol, Umberto Orsini, Sylva Koscina, Victor Spinetti, Lillian Mueller, Werner Pochath, Olivia Pascal

BEYOND THE DOOR #2 (Film Ventures International) Producer, Juri Vasile; Director, Mario Bava; Screenplay, Lamberto Bava, Franco Barbieri; Photography, Mario Bava, Giuseppe Maccari; Editor, Roberto Sterbini; Music, Libra; In color; Rated R; 92 minutes; March release. CAST: Daria Nicolodi (Dora), John Steiner (Bruno), David Colin, Jr. (Marco), Ivan Rassimov (Carlos)

CHALLENGE OF DEATH (Henry Tan) Producers, Henry Tan, Keung Chung Ping; In color; Rated R; March release. CAST: Wang Tao, Delung Tam, Tommy Lee

THE PSYCHIC (Group I) Director, Lucio Fulci; Presented by Brandon Chase; In Deluxe Color; Rated R; 90 minutes; March release. CAST: Jennifer O'Neill, Marc Porel, Evelyn Stewart, Jenny Tamburi, Gabriele Ferzetti

THE NIGHT THE PROWLER (International Harmony) Producer, Anthony Buckley; Director, Jim Sharman; Screenplay, Patrick White; Music, Cameron Allan; Producer, Chariot Films Pty. Ltd.; Presented by Stuart S. Shapiro and New South Wales Film Corp.; In color; Not rated; 90 minutes; March release. CAST: Ruth Cracknell, John Frawley, Kerry Walker, John Derum, Maggie Kirkpatrick, Terry Camilleri

TENT OF MIRACLES (Embrafilme) Direction and Screenplay, Nelson Pereira dos Santos; Based on novel by Jorge Amado; Photography, Helio Silva; Music, Jards Macale; Opening and closing song, Gilberto Gil; Editors, Raimundo Higino, Severino Dada; Designer, Tizuca Yamasaki; Costumes, Yurika Yamasaki; Executive Producer, Ney Sant'Anna; Produced by Regina Filmes; Not rated; 132 minutes; March release. CAST: Hugo Carvana (Fausto), Sonia Dias (Ana), Anecy Rocha (Edelweiss), Jards Macale (Young Pedro), Juarez Paraiso (Pedro), Nilda Parente (Professor), Washington Fernandes (Pedrito), Emmanoel Cavalcanti (Chief of Police), Nilda Spencer (Countess), Joffre Soares (Professor Gomes)

"Tent of Miracles"

Ursula Andress in "Slave of the
Cannibal God" © New Line Cinema

"The Glacier Fox"
© Sanrio Communications

SLAVE OF THE CANNIBAL GOD (New Line Cinema) Directed by Sergio Martino; In Eastmancolor; Rated R; 85 minutes; April release. Starring Ursula Andress, Stacy Keach. No other details available.

QUEEN OF THE GYPSIES (Sovexportfilm) Producer, Mosfilm Studio; Direction and Screenplay, Emil Lotyanu; Based on legend by Maxim Gorky; Photography, Sergei Vronsky; Music, Yevgeny Doga; Not Rated; 102 minutes; April release. CAST: Svetlana Toma, Grigory Grigoriu, Ion Shkurya

THE WRONG MOVE (Bauer International) Producer, Peter Genee; Director, Wim Wenders; Screenplay, Peter Handke; Photography, Robbie Muller; Editor, Peter Przygodda; Music, Jurgen Knieper; In color; German with English subtitles; 103 minutes; April release. CAST: Rudiger Vogler (Wilhelm Meister), Hanna Schygulla (Therese), Hans Christian Blech (Laertes), Peter Kern (Landau), Nastassia Kinski (Mignon), Ivan Desny (Industrialist), Marianne Hope (Wilhelm's Mother), Lisa Kreuzer (Janine)

A PORTRAIT OF THE ARTIST AS A YOUNG MAN (Howard Mahler) Director, Joseph Strick; Associate Producers, Richard Hallinan, Betty Botley; Screenplay, Judith Rascoe; Based on novel by James Joyce; Photography, Stuart Hetherington; Editor, Lesley Walker; Music, Stanley Myers; Costumes, Judy Nolan; A Ulysses Film production in color; Not rated; 98 minutes; April release. CAST: Bosco Hogan (Stephen), T. P. McKenna (Simon), John Gielgud (Preacher), Rosaleen Linihan (May), Maureen Potter (Dante), Cecil Sheehan (Uncle Charles), Niall Buggy (David), Brian Murray (Lynch), Terence Strick (Stephen at 3), Luke Johnston (Stephen at 10)

ASHANTI (Warner Bros.) Producer, George-Alain Vuille; Director, Richard Fleischer; Screenplay, Stephen Geller; Based on novel by Alberto Vasquez-Figueroa; In Panavision and color; Rated R; 117 minutes; April release. CAST: Michael Caine, Peter Ustinov, Beverly Johnson, Omar Sharif, Rex Harrison, William Holden

THE GLACIER FOX (Sanrio Films) Executive Producer, Shintaro Tsuji; Producer, Hiromu Tsugawa; Co-Producers, Atsushi Tomioka, Mark L. Rosen; Director, Koreyoshi Kurahara; Narration written by Walter Bloch; In color; Rated G; 90 minutes; April release. Narrated by Arthur Hill.

LEOPARD IN THE SNOW (New World) Producers, John Quested, Chris Harrop; Director, Gerry O'Hara; Screenplay, Anne Mather, Jill Hyem; Music, Kenneth V. Jones; Executive Producers, W. Lawrence Heisey; A Harlequin Films presentation; In Technicolor; Rated PG; 90 minutes; April release. CAST: Keir Dullea, Susan Penhaligon, Kenneth More, Billie Whitelaw, Gordon Thomson, Jeremy Kemp

THE SECOND AWAKENING OF CHRISTA KLAGES (New Line) Executive Producer, Eberhard Junkersdorf; Director, Margarethe von Trotta; Screenplay, Miss von Trotta, Luisa Francia; Photography, Franz Rath; Music Klaus Doldinger; Editor, Anette Dorn; In color; Not rated; 93 minutes; May release. CAST: Tina Engel (Christa), Silvia Reize (Ingrid), Katharina Thalbach (Lena), Marius Muller-Westernhagen (Werner), Peter Schneider (Hans)

DRACULA AND SON (Gaumont) Director, Edouard Molinaro; Screenplay, Molinaro, Jean-Marie Poire, Alain Godard, from book by Claude Klotz; Photography, Alan Levent; Editor, Robert Isnardon; Music, Vladimir Cosma; A Production 2000; In Eastmancolor; Not rated; 96 minutes; May release. CAST: Christopher Lee (Dracula), Bernard Menez (Son), Marie-Helene Breillat (Nicole), Catherine Breillat (Wife), Anna Gael (Woman), Jean-Claude Dauphin (Young Man)

THE BEST (Group I) Producer, Steve Harrison; Director, M. Guerin; In color; Rated R; 85 minutes; May release. CAST: Gloria Guida, Patricia Welby, Loretta Pierson, Carl Goefrey

I'LL DIE FOR MAMA (Trimurti Films) Producer, Gulshan Rai; Director, Yash Chopra; Story and Screenplay, Salim-Javed; Music, R. D. Burman; In color; May release. CAST: Amitabh Bachchan, Parveen Babi, Nirupa Roy, Shashi Kapoor

Grigory Grigoriu, Svetlana Toma
in "Queen of the Gypsies"

Rudiger Vogler, Hanna Schygulla
in "The Wrong Move"

Tina Engel, Silvia Reize in "The Second
Awakening of Christa Klages"

Heather Wright, Bill Travers
in "Free Spirit"

PLAGUE (Group I) Produced and Written by Ed Hunt, Barry
Pearson; Music, Eric Robertson; A Harmony Ridge production
in DeLuxe Color; Rated PG; May release. CAST: Daniel Pilon,
Kate Reid, Celine Lomez, Michael J. Reynolds

THE BANDITS (Lone Star) Producer, Alfredo Zacharias; Directors, Robert Conrad, Alfredo Zacharias; In color; Rated PG;
May release. CAST: Robert Conrad, Jan-Michael Vincent

THE AGE OF THE MEDICI (Audio/Brandon) Director,
Roberto Rossellini; Screenplay, Roberto Rossellini, Luciano
Scaffa, Marcella Mariani; Photography, Mario Montuori; Editor,
Jolanda Benvenuti; Music, Manuel DeSica; In color; Not rated;
252 minutes; May release. CAST: Marcello di Falco, Virginio
Gazzolo

FREE SPIRIT (Joseph Brenner) Executive Producer, Julian
Wintle; Producer, Sally Shuter; Associate Producer, Basil Ray-
burn; Direction and Screenplay, James Hill; Based on novel "Ballad of the Belstone Fox" by David Rook; Music, Laurie Johnson;
Editor, Peter Tanner; Art Director, Hazel Peiser; Presented by J.
Arthur Rank in Todd-AO 35 and Movielab Color; Rated G; 88
minutes; May release. CAST: Eric Porter (Asher), Rachel Roberts (Cathie), Jeremy Kemp (Kendrick), Bill Travers (Tod), Dennis Waterman (Stephen), Heather Wright (Jenny)

NEWSFRONT (New Yorker) Producer, David Elfick; Director,
Phillip Noyce; Associate Producer, Richard Brennan; Screenplay,
Phillip Noyce, Bob Ellis, from a concept by Phillipe Mora and
David Elfick; Photography, Vincent Monton; Music, William
Motzing; Editor, John Scott; Designer, Lissa Coote; Art Director,
Larry Eastwood; Costumes, Norma Moriceau; Assistant Direc-
tor, Errol Sullivan; In color, black and white; Rated PG; 110
minutes; May release. CAST: Bill Hunter (Len), Gerard Kennedy
(Frank), Wendy Hughes (Amy), Angela Punch (Fay), Chris Hay-
wood (Chris), John Ewart (Charlie), Don Crosby (Marwood),
John Dease (Ken), John Clayton (Cliff), Bryan Brown (Geoff),
Tony Barry (Greasy), Drew Forsythe (Bruce), Lorna Lesley (El-
lie), Mark Holden (Tim), Chad Morgan (Country Singer)

WINTER KILLS (AVCO Embassy) Executive Producers, Leon-
ard J. Goldberg, Robert Sterling; Producer, Fred Caruso; Direc-
tion and Screenplay, William Richert; Based on book by Richard
Condon; Music, Maurice Jarre; Photography, Vilmos Zsigmond;
Editor, David Bretherton; Costumes, Robert De Mora; Designer,
Robert Boyle; Associate Producer, John Stark; Assistant Direc-
tors, Pete Scoppa, Jim Arnet; Art Director, Norman Newberry;
In Panavision and color; Rated PG; 97 minutes; May release.
CAST: Jeff Bridges (Nick), John Huston (Pa Kegan), Anthony
Perkins (John Cerruti), Sterling Hayden (Z. K.), Eli Wallach
(Joe), Dorothy Malone (Emma), Tomas Milian (Frank), Belinda
Bauer (Yvette), Ralph Meeker (Baker), Toshiro Mifune (Keith),
Donald Moffat (Captain), David Spielberg (Miles), Brad Dexter
(Heller), Peter Brandon (Doctor), Michael Thoma (Ray), Ed
Madsen, Irving Selbst, Chris Soldo, Robert Courleigh, Joe Spi-
nell, Ira Rosenstein, Kyle Morris, Barbara Reid

**THE 7 BROTHERS MEET DRACULA (Dynamite Entertain-
ment)** Formerly "The Legend of the Seven Golden Vampires";
Producers, Don Houghton, Vee King Shaw; Director, Roy Ward
Baker; Screenplay, Don Houghton; Photography, John Wilcox,
Roy Ford; Music, James Bernard; In Panavision and color; Rated
R; June release. CAST: Peter Cushing, David Chiang, Julie Ege,
Robin Stewart, Shin Szu, John Forbes-Robertson, Chan Shen,
Robert Hanna

CRIMEBUSTERS (United Artists) Direction and Screenplay, E.
B. Clucher; In color; Rated PG; June release. CAST: Terrence
Hill, Bud Spencer

COLONEL DELMIRO GOUVEIA (Embrafilme) also released
as COLONEL OF THE SERTAO; Producer-Director, Geraldo
Sarno; Screenplay, Geraldo Sarno, Orlando Senna; Photography,
Lauro Escorel Filho; Music, J. Lins; Editor, Amauri Alves; De-
signer, Anisio Medeiros; In Portuguese with English subtitles; In
Eastmancolor; Not rated; 110 minutes; June release. CAST: Ru-
bens de Falco (Gouveia), Nildo Parente, Jofre Soares, Sura Berdi-
chevski, Isabel Ribeiro, Jose Dumont, Magalhaes Graca,
Conceicao Senna, Alvaro Freire, Denis Bourke, Harlido Deda.
Maria Adelia.

Bill Hunter (L)
in "Newsfront"

Rubens DeFalco
in "Colonel Delmiro Gouveia"

205

Telly Savalas in "Escape to Athena" © AFD

Susanne Reed, Charles Howerton, Sam Bottoms
in "Up from the Depths' © New World Pictures

ESCAPE TO ATHENA (Associated Film Distribution) Producers, David Niven, Jr., Jack Wiener; Director, George P. Cosmatos; Screenplay, Edward Anhalt, Richard S. Lochte; Story, Richard S. Lochte, George P. Cosmatos; Music, Lalo Schifrin; Presented by Lew Grade; Associate Producer, Colin M. Brewer; Photography, Gil Taylor; Editor, Ralph Kemplen; Design, Michael Stringer; Art Director, John Graysmark; Costumes, Yvonne Blake; Assistant Director, Derek Cracknell; Choreographer, Arlene Phillips; In Panavision and color; Rated PG; 125 minutes; June release. CAST: Roger Moore (Otto), Telly Savalas (Zeno), Elliott Gould (Charlie), David Niven (Professor Blake), Stephanie Powers (Dottie), Claudia Cardinale (Eleana), Richard Roundtree (Nat), Sonny Bono (Bruno)

MASTER KILLER (World Northal) Producers, Sir Run Run Shaw, Mona Fong; Director, Liu Chia-liang; In color; A Shaw Brothers presentation of an Oxford Films release; Rated R; 96 minutes; June release. CAST: Liu Chi-hui, Huang Yu, Lo Lieh

FILMING OTHELLO (Independent Images) Producers, Klaus and Jeurgen Hellwig; Director, Orson Welles; Photography, Gary Graver; Music, Francesco Lavagnino, Alberto Barbaris; Editor, Marty Roth; 84 minutes; Not rated; July release. CAST: members of the 1952 Mercury Films production: Orson Welles, Suzanne Cloutier, Micheal MacLiammoir, Robert Coote, Hilton Edwards, Fay Compton, Nicholas Bruce, Michael Laurence, Doris Dowling

THE BROOD (New World) Executive Producers, Pierre David, Victor Solnicki; Producer, Claude Heroux; Direction and Screenplay, David Cronenberg; Photography, Mark Irwin; Art Director, Carol Spier; Editor, Allan Collins; Assistant Directors, John Board, Libby Bowden; From Mutual Productions/Elgin International; In color; Rated R; 91 minutes; June release. CAST: Oliver Reed (Dr. Raglan), Samantha Eggar (Nola), Art Hindle (Frank), Cindy Hinds (Candice), Nuala Fitzgerald (Juliana), Henry Beckman (Barton), Susan Hogan (Ruth), Michael McGhee (Inspector), Gary McKeehan (Mike), Bob Silverman (Jan), Joseph Shaw (Dr. Desborough), Felix Silla (Child), Larry Solway (Resnikoff), Rainer Schwartz (Birkin), Nicholas Campbell (Chris)

UP FROM THE DEPTHS (New World) Producer, Cirio H. Santiago; Director, Charles B. Griffith; Executive Producer, Jack Atienza; Screenplay, Anne Dyer; Photography, Rick Remington; Editor, G. V. Bass; Music, Russell O'Malley; Assistant Directors, Jill Griffith, Manny Norman; In Metrocolor; Not rated; 75 minutes; June release. CAST: Sam Bottoms (Greg), Susanne Reed (Rachel), Virgil Frye (Earl), Kedric Wolfe (Oscar), Charles Howerton (David), Denise Hayes (Iris), Charles Doherty (Ed), Helen McNelly (Louellen)

THE KIDS ARE ALRIGHT (New World) Executive Producer, Sydney Rose; Producers, Tony Klinger, Bill Curbishley; Associate Producers, Jeff Stein, Ed Rothkowitz; Direction and Screenplay, Jeff Stein; Editor, Ed Rothkowitz; Photography, Peter Nevard, Norman Warwick, Tony Richmond; Assistant Directors, Brian Cook, Peter Butler, Richard Dobson; Music and Lyrics, Peter Townshend; A Roger Corman presentation in color and Dolby Stereo; Rated PG; 106 minutes; June release. CAST: The Who: Roger Daltrey, John Entwistle, Keith Moon, Peter Townshend, and guests Tommy Smothers, Jimmy O'Neil, Russell Harty, Melvin Bragg, Ringo Starr, Mary Ann Zabresky, Michael Leckebusch, Barry Fantoni, Jeremy Paxman, Bob Pridden, Keith Richard, Norman Gunsten, Steve Martin, Rick Danko

NICARAGUA: FREE HOMELAND OR DEATH (Tricontinental) Directors, Antonio Yglesias, Victor Vega; Spanish with English subtitles; In color; 75 minutes; July release. A documentary on the F.S.L.N. and its struggle against the Somoza dictatorship.

WINDS OF CHANGE (Sanrio) Producers, Walt DeFaria, Terry Ogisu, Hiromu Tsugawa; Executive Producer, Shintaro Tsuji; Animation Direction, Takashi; Narration written by Norman Corwin; Based on Ovid's "Metamorphoses"; Music, Alec R. Costandinos; Lyrics, Enoch Anderson; Editor, Jack Woods; In Panavision, Technicolor, and Dolby Stereo; 87 minutes; Not rated; July release. Narrated by Peter Ustinov.

Art Hindle, Oliver Reed
in "The Brood" © New World

The Who in "The Kids Are Alright"
© New World Pictures

**Ava Gardner, James Franciscus
in "City on Fire"**

UNIDENTIFIED FLYING ODDBALL (Buena Vista) a.k.a. "The Spaceman and King Arthur"; Producer, Ron Miller; Director, Russ Mayberry; Story and Screenplay, Don Tait; Based on Mark Twain's "A Connecticut Yankee in King Arthur's Court"; Associate Producer, Hugh Attwooll; Photography, Paul Beeson; Music, Ron Goodwin; Art Director, Albert Witherick; Editor, Peter Boita; Costumes, Phyllis Dalton; Assistant Director, Vincent Winter; In Technicolor; Presented by Walt Disney Productions; Rated G; 93 minutes; July release. CAST: Dennis Dugan (Tom), Jim Dale (Sir Mordred), Ron Moody (Merlin), Kenneth More (King Arthur), John LeMesurier (Sir Gawain), Rodney Bewes (Clarence), Sheila White (Alisande), Robert Beatty (Senator Milburn), Cyril Shaps (Dr. Zimmerman), Kevin Brennan (Winston), Ewen Solon (Watkins), Pat Roach (Oaf), Reg Lye (Prisoner)

ONE MAN (Billy Baxter) Producer, Michael Scott; Director, Robin Spry; Executive Producer, Roman Kroitor; Associate Producers, James de B. Domville, Tom Daly, Vladimir Valenta; Screenplay, Robin Spry, Peter Pearson, Peter Madden; Photography, Douglas Kiefer; Editor, John Kramer; Music, Ben Low; Artistic Director, Denis Boucher; Assistant Directors, Roger Frappier, Giles Walker; A National Film Board of Canada production in color; Rated PG; 87 minutes; July release. CAST: Len Cariou (Jason Brady), Jayne Eastwood (Alicia Brady), Carol Lazare (Marian), Barry Morse (Colin), August Schellenberg (Ernie), Jean Lapointe (Ben), Sean Sullivan (Rodney), Terry Haig (Dr. Gendron), Marc Legault (Leo), Danny Freedman, Gilles Renaud (Hoods), Bob Girolami (TV Announcer), Jacques Godin (Jaworski), Donovan Hare (Donovan), Kevin Hare (Kevin), Jesse Brown, Peter MacNeil, Michel Maillot, Jerome Tiberghien, Larry Kent, Jean-Pierre Bergeron, John Boylan, Dave Patrick, Richard Comar, Gary Plaxton, Joan Heeney, Miguel Fernandez, Elizabeth Suzuki, Joan Blackman, Vlasta Vrana, Elizabeth Chouvalidze, Terrence Ross, Julie Anna, Paul Loughlin, Yvon Leroux, Paul Haynes, Bronwen Mantel, Barry Lane, Janice Bryan, Helen Mullins, Laurent Poirier, Jean-Pierre Hallee, Pietro Bertolissi

BAHIA (Atlantic) Director, Marcel Camus; Presented by Stuart S. Shapiro; In color; July release.

**Len Cariou, Jayne Eastwood
in "One Man"**

CITY ON FIRE (AVCO Embassy) Executive Producers, Sandy Howard, Harold Greenberg; Producer, Claude Heroux; Director, Alvin Rakoff; Screenplay, Jack Hill, David P. Lewis, Celine LaFreniere; Associate Producers, Howard Lipson, Larry Nesis; Music, William McCauley, Matthew McCauley; Photography, René Verzier; Assistant Directors, Charles Braive, Daniel Hausmann; Designer, William McCrow; Art Director, Claude Marchand; Editors, Jean Pol Passe, Jacques Clairoux; Costumes, Yvon Duhaime; An Astral Bellevue-Pathe production in color; Rated R; 101 minutes; August release. CAST: Barry Newman (Frank Whitman), Susan Clark (Diana), Shelley Winters (Nurse), Leslie Nielsen (Mayor), James Franciscus (Jimbo), Ava Gardner (Maggie), Henry Fonda (Fire Chief), Mavor Moore (John), Jonathan Welsh (Herman), Richard Donat (Captain), Ken James (Andrew), Donald Pilon (Fox), Terry Haig (Terry), Cec Linder (Paley), Hilary LeBow (Mrs. Adams), Jeff Mappin (Beezer), Earl Pennington (Clark), Sonny Forbes (Tom), Bronwen Mantel (Sarah), Janice Chaikelson (Debbie), Steven Chaikelson (Gerald), Lee Murray (Tony), Jerome Tiberghien (Fireman)

WINSTANLEY (British Film Institute) Directors, Kevin Brownlow, Andrew Molle; Based on novel "Comrade Jacob" by David Caute; Photography, Ernest Vincze; Costumes, Carmen Mello; Art Director, Andrew Mello; Editor, Sarah Ellis; Assistant Directors, Charles Rees, Ian Sellar, Charles Ware; In black and white; Not rated; 96 minutes; August release. CAST: Miles Halliwell (Winstanley), Jerome Willis (General Lord Fairfax), Terry Higgins (Tom), Phil Oliver (Will), David Bramley (Parson), Alison Halliwell (Mrs. Platt), Dawson France (Captain Gladman), Bill Petch (Henry), Barry Shaw (Colonel Rich), Sid Rawle (Ranter), George Hawkins (Coulton), Stanley Reed (Recorder), Philip Stearns (Drake), Flora Skrine (Mrs. Drake)

SATAN'S SLAVE (Crown International) Producers, Les Young, Richard Crafter; Screenplay, David McGillivray; Music, John Scott; Director, Norman J. Warren; In color; Rated R; August release. CAST: Michael Gough, Martin Potter, Candace Glendenning, Barbara Kellermann

THE FRENCH WOMAN (Monarch) Formerly "Madame Claude"; An Orphee Arts production; Director, Just Jaeckin; Screenplay, Andre G. Brunelin from the book "Allo" by Jacques Quoirez; Photography, Robert Fraisse; Editor, Marie-Sophie Dubus; Music, Serge Gainsbourg; In Eastmancolor; Not rated; 110 minutes; August release. CAST: Francoise Fabian (Mme. Claude), Dayle Haddon (Elizabeth), Murray Head (David), Maurice Ronet (Pierre), Vibeke Knudsen (Anne- Marie), Klause Kinski (Zakis), Andre Falcon (Paul), Robert Webber (Howard), Jean Gaven (Gus), Francois Perrot (Lefevre)

THE SHAPE OF THINGS TO COME (Film Ventures) Producer, William Davidson; Executive Producer, Harry Alan Towers; Director, George McCowan; Screenplay, Martin Lager; In color; Rated PG; 95 minutes; August release. CAST: Jack Palance (Omus), Carol Lynley (Niki), John Ireland (Smedley), Barry Morse (John Caball), Nicholas Campbell (Jason), Eddie Benton (Kim), voices of Greg Swanson, Marc Parr

FAST COMPANY (Topar Films) Executive Producer, David Perlmutter; Producers, Michael Lebowitz, Peter O'Brian, Courtney Smith, David Cronenberg; From story by Alan Treen; Photography, Mark Irwin; Editor, Ron Sanders; Art Director, Carol Spier; In color; Rated PG; 90 minutes; August release. CAST: William Smith (Lucky Man), John Saxon (Phil), Claudia Jennings (Sammy), Nicholas Campbell (The Kid), Don Francks (Elder), Cedric Smith (Blacksmith), Judy Foster (Candy), George Buza (Meatball)

THE NATIONAL HEALTH or Nurse Norton's Affair (Columbia) Producers, Ned Sherrin, Terry Glinwood; Director, Jack Gold; Screenplay, Peter Nichols from his play; Photography, John Coquillon; Editor, Ralph Sheldon; A Virgin Films production; Not rated; 100 minutes; August release. CAST: Lynn Redgrave, Colin Blakely, Sheila Scott-Wilkinson, Neville Aurelius, Eleanor Bron, Jim Dale, Donald Sinden, Bob Hoskins, David Hutcheson, Mervyn Johns, Bert Palmer, Clive Swift, Gillian Barge, George Browne, Patience Collier, Jumoke Debayo, Robert Gillespie

NO SEX PLEASE—WE'RE BRITISH (Columbia) Producer, John R. Sloan; Director, Cliff Owen; Screenplay, Anthony Marriott, Johnnie Mortimer, Brian Cooke; Editor, Ralph Kemplen; Music, Eric Rogers; Not rated; 90 minutes; August release. CAST: Ronnie Corbett, Beryl Reid, Arthur Lowe, Ian Igilvy, Susan Penhaligon, Michael Bates, Cheryl Hall, David Swift, Deryck Guyler, Valerie Leon, Margaret Nolan, Gerald Sim, Michael Robbins

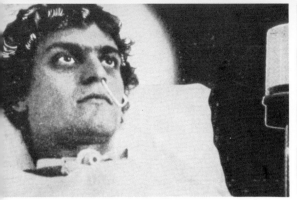

"Patrick"

Alaine Foures, Nathalie Nell
in "Rape of Love"

PATRICK (Monarch-Vanguard) Producers, Antony I. Ginnane, Richard Franklin; Screenplay, Everett De Roche; Photography, Don McAlpine; Art Director, Leslie Binns; Assistant Directors, Tom Burstall, James Parker; Editor, Edward Queen-Mason; Music, Brian May; In Agfacolor; Rated PG; 110 minutes; September release. CAST: Susan Penhaligon, Robert Helpmann, Rod Mullinar, Bruce Barry, Julia Blake, Helen Heminway, Maria Mercedes, Frank Wilson, Peter Culpan, Marilyn Rodgers, Peggy Nichols, Carole-Ann Aylett, Walter Pym

RUN AFTER ME UNTIL I CATCH YOU (Silverstein) Director, Robert Pouret; Screenplay, Nicole De Buron, Robert Pouret; Photography, Guy Durban; Editor, Armand Psenny; In Eastmancolor; Rated PG: 91 minutes; September release. CAST: Annie Girardot (Jacqueline), Jean-Pierre Marielle (Paul), Marilu Tolo (Rita), Genevieve Fontanel (Simone), Sylvain Rougerie (Patrick), Christin Laurent (Sylvie), Daniel Prevost (Champfrein)

THE SENSUOUS NURSE (Mid-Broadway) Producer, Zev Braun; Director, Nello Rossati; In color; Rated R; September release. CAST: Ursula Andress, Jack Palance, Duilio del Prete

THE COMEBACK (Lone Star) Producer-Director, Pete Walker; Screenplay, Murray Smith; Music, Stanley Myers; Photography, Peter Jessup; In color; Rated R; 100 minutes; September release. CAST: Jack Jones (Nick), Pamela Stephenson (Linda), David Doyle (Webster), Bill Owen (Mr. B), Holly Palance (Gail), Peter Turner (Harry), Richard Johnson (Macauley), Patrick Brock, June Chadwick, Penny Irving, Jeff Silk, Sheila Keith

SHAME OF THE JUNGLE (International Harmony) Producer, Boris Szulzinger; Directors, Picha, Boris Szulzinger; Executive Producers, Jenny Gerard, Michel Gast; Dialogue, Anne Beatts, Michael O'Donoghue; Presented by Stuart S. Shapiro; An SND and Valisa Films production in color; Rated R; 72 minutes; September release. Voices of Johnny Weissmuller, Jr., John Belushi, Bill Murray, Bryan-Doyle Murray, Christopher Guest

THE DEADLY ANGELS (World Northal) Producer, Runme Shaw; A Shaw Brothers presentation in color; Rated R; 80 minutes; September release. CAST: Evelyne Kraft, Dana, Shaw Yin-Yin, Chin Cheng-Lan

RAPE OF LOVE (Quartet Films) Direction and Screenplay, Yannick Bellon; French with English subtitles; Photography, Georges Barsky, Pierre William Glenn; Music, Aram; Lyrics, Miss Bellon; A CoProduction of Films de L'Equinoxe, Film du Dragon, MK2 Productions; In color; Not rated; 117 minutes; September release. CAST: Nathalie Nell (Nicole), Alain Foures (Jacques), Tatiana Moukhine (Nicole's Mother), Michele Simonnet, Pierre Arditi (Nicole's Friends), Daniel Auteuil, Bernard Granger, Alain Marcel, Gilles Tamiz, Lucienne Hamon

JUBILEE (Cinegate) Producers, Howard Malin, James Whaley; Director, Derek Jarman; Photography, Peter Middleton; Editor, Tom Priestley, Nick Barnard; Designer, Christopher Hobbs; Assistant Director, Guy Ford; Music, Suzi Pinns, Brian Eno, Adam and the Ants, Siouxsie and the Banshees, Chelsea, Wayne County, Electric Chairs, Maneaters, Amilcar; In color; Not rated; 103 minutes; September release. CAST: Jenny Runacre, Jordan, Little Nell, Linda Spurrier, Hermine Demoriane, Toyah Willcox, Richard O'Brien, Adam Ant, Ian Charleson, Karl Johnson, Neil Kennedy, Orlando, Lindsay Kemp, Gene October

THE STUD (Trans-American) Producer, Ronald S. Kass in association with Adrian Gaye; Director, Quentin Masters; Screenplay, Jackie Collins from her novel; Additional Material, Dave Humphries, Christopher Stagg; Executive Producer, Edward D. Simons; Editor, David Campling; Photography, Peter Hannan; Music, Biddu; Lyrics, Biddu, Sammy Cahn; Presented by Brent Walker; In Movielab Color; Rated R; 90 minutes; September release. CAST: Joan Collins (Fontaine), Oliver Tobias (Tony), Sue Lloyd (Vanessa), Mark Burns (Leonard), Doug Fisher (Sammy), Walter Gotell (Ben), Tony Allyn (Hal), Emma Jacobs (Alex), Peter Lukas (Ian), Natalie Ogle (Maddy), Constantin De Goguel (Lord Newton), Guy Ward (Peter), Sarah Lawson (Anne), Jeremy Child (Lawyer), Franco De Rosa (Franco), Felicity Buirski (Debbie), Minah Bird (Molly), Hilda Fenemore (Mum), Bernard Stone (Dad), Hugh Morton (Staton), Howard Nelson (Sandro), Leonard Trolley (Doctor), Shango Baku (Flowers), Tania Rogers (Janine), Michael Barrington (Vicar), Rynagh O'Grady (Meter Maid), Edmond Warwick (Tailor), Robert Tayman (Mario), Giorgio Bosso (Chef)

**Little Nell, Gene October
in "Jubilee"**

**Joan Collins, Oliver Tobias
in "The Stud"**

Ursula Andress, Beau Bridges, Ian McShane
in "The Fifth Musketeer" © Columbia Pictures

"The Devil's Playground"

THE FIFTH MUSKETEER (Columbia) Executive Producer, Heinz Lazek; Producer, Ted Richmond; Director, Ken Annakin; Screenplay, David Ambrose; Based on novel "The Man in the Iron Mask" by Alexandre Dumas and a screenplay by George Bruce; Music, Riz Ortolani; Editor, Malcolm Cooke; Designer, Elliot Scott; Photography, Jack Cardiff; Art Director, Theo Harisch; Assistant Directors, David Anderson, Robert Wright, Terry Needham; Costumes, Tony Pueo; In Eastmancolor; Rated PG; 103 minutes; September release. CAST: Sylvia Kristel (Marie-Therese), Beau Bridges (King Louis), Ursula Andress (Mme. de la Valliere), Cornel Wilde (D'Artagnan), Ian McShane (Fourquet), Lloyd Bridges (Aramis), Alan Hale, Jr. (Porthos), Helmut Dantine (Ambassador), Olivia de Havilland (Queen Anne), José Ferrer (Athos), Rex Harrison (Colbert), Roman Ariznavarreta, Bernard Bresslaw, Stephan Bastian, Victor Couzin, Karl Ferth, Fritz V. Friedl, Christine Glasner, Fritz Goblirsch, Erhart Hartmann, Bill Horrigan, Michael Janisch, Cissy Kraner, Elizabeth Neumann-Viertel, Heinz Nick, Ingrid Olofson, Stephan Paryla, Albert Rueprecht, Ute Rumm, Tony Smart, Robert Werner, Heinz Winter

NEST OF VIPERS (Paramount) Producer, Piero La Mantia; Director, Tonino Cervi; Screenplay, Tonino Cervi, Cesare Frugoni, Goffredo Parise; Based on short story "The Piano Teacher" by Roger Peyrefitte; Photography, Armando Nannuzzi; Music, Vincenzo Tempera; Editor, Nino Baragli; A Mars Film production in color; Rated R; 105 minutes; September release. CAST: Senta Berger (Carla), Ornella Muti (Elena), Christian Borromeo (Mattio), Capucine (Amalia), Giuliana Calandra, Stefano Patrizi, Giancarlo Sbragia, Paolo Bonacelli, Mattia Sbragia, Maria Monti, Eros Pagni, Antonia Cancellieri, Suzanne Creese Bates, Raffaele Di Mario, Giancarlo Marinangeli, Giovanni Caenazzo

WOMEN (New Yorker) Director, Marta Meszaros; Screenplay, Ildiko Korody, Joszef Balasz, Geza Beremenyi; Photography, Janos Kende; Music, Gyorgy Kovacs; In Eastmancolor; Not rated; 94 minutes; October release. CAST: Marina Vlady (Mari), Lili Monaort (Juli), Mikoos Tolnay (Feri), Jan Nowicki (Janos), Zsuzsa Czinocky (Szuzsi)

THE DEVIL'S PLAYGROUND (Entertainment Marketing) Produced, Directed, and Written by Fred Schepisi; Photography, Ian Baker; Music, Bruce Smeaton; Editor, Brian Kavanaugh; An IFEX presentation in color; Not rated; 107 minutes; October release. CAST: Arthur Dignam (Brother Francine), Nick Tate (Brother Victor), Simon Burke (Tom), Charles McCallum (Brother Sebastian), John Frawley (Brother Celian), Gerry Duggan (Father Hanrahan), Peter Cox (Brother James), John Diedrich (Fitz), Thomas Keneally (Father Marshall)

THE LITTLE MERMAID (G. G. Communications) Based on story by Hans Christian Andersen; Presented by N. W. Russo; In Movielab Color; Rated G; October release.

COCAINE COWBOYS (International Harmony) Producer, Christopher Francis Giercke; Director, Ulli Lommel; Screenplay, U. Lommel, S. Compton, T. Sullivan, V. Bockris; Photography, Jochen Breitenstein; Music, Elliot Goldenthal; In color; Rated R; 86 minutes; October release. CAST: Jack Palance, Andy Warhol, Tom Sullivan, Susanna Love, Esther Oldham-Farfan, Winnie Hollmann, Richard Young, Toni Manufo, Richard Bassett, The Cowboy Island Band

THE SPIDERS (Images Film) Direction and Screenplay, Fritz Lang; Photography, Emil Schonemann; David and Kimberly Shepard reconstruction of a 1919 film; Tinted; 137 minutes; November release. CAST: Carl de Vogy, Ressel Orla, Lil Dagover, Paul Morgan, Georg John, Bruno Lettinger, Edgar Pauly, Paul Biensfeldt

THE BALLAD OF ORIN (Kino International) Producers, Kiyoshi Iwashita, Seikichi Iizumi; Director, Masahiro Shinoda; Screenplay, Keiji Hasebe, Masahiro Shinoda; Japanese with English subtitles; Photography, Kazuo Miyagawa; Music, Toru Takemitsu; A Toho Ltd. presentation in color; Not rated; 100 minutes; November release. CAST: Shima Iwashita (Orin), Yoshio Harada (Heitaro), Tomoko Naraoka (Teruyo), Shoji Tonoyama (Charcoal Maker), Toshiyuki Nishida (Tsuketaro), Toru Abe (Hikosaburo)

Capucine, Ornella Muti, Christian Borromeo
in "Nest of Vipers"

"The Ballad of Orin"

Carole Laure (c)
in "Normande"

Assaf Dayan, Michal Bat-Adam, Brigitte
Catillon in "Each Other"

BLOOD AND GUNS (Movietime) Producer, Edward S. Shaw; Director, Giulio Petroni; In color; Rated R; November release. CAST: Orson Welles, Tomas Milian

NORMANDE (Fred Baker Films) Producer, Pierre Lamy; Director, Gilles Carle; Photography, Francois Protat; Screenplay, Gilles Carle, Ben Barzman; Costumes, Claudette Aubin; Editors, Gilles Carle, Avde Chiraieff; Music and Lyrics, Lewis Furey; Designer, Jocelyn Joly; Rated PG; 91 minutes; November release. CAST: Carole Laure (Normande), Reynald Bouchard (Carol), Raymond Cloutier (Bouliane), Renee Cloutier (Berthe), J. Leo Gagnon (Sculptor), Carmen Giroux (Pierette), Gaetan Guimond (Jeremy)

THE HEIST (First American Films) Producer, Ralph Baum; Direction and Screenplay, Sergio Goffi; Photography, Dan Dist; Music, George Gararentz; In color; Rated R; 85 minutes; November release. CAST: Robert Hossein, Charles Aznavour, Virna Lisi, and Europe's top stunt drivers.

L'AGE D'OR (Corinth) Producer, Le Vicomte de Noailles; Director-Editor, Luis Bunuel; Screenplay, Luis Bunuel, Salvador Dali; Photography, Albert Duverger; Music, Wagner, Mendelssohn, Beethoven, Debussy; In black and white; Not rated; 60 minutes; November release. CAST: Lya Lys (The Woman), Gaston Modot (The Man), Max Ernst (Bandit Chief), Pierre Prevert (Bandit), Caridad de Laberdesque, Lionel Salem, Madame Noizet

THE SHOUT (Films Incorporated) Producer, Jeremy Thomas; Director, Jerzy Skolimowski; Associate Producer, Michael Austin; Screenplay, Michael Austin, Jerzy Skolimowski; From story by Robert Graves; Photography, Mike Molloy; Editor, Barrie Vince; Assistant Director, Kip Gowans; Art Director, Simon Holland; In Dolby Stereo; Rated R; 97 minutes; November release. CAST: Alan Bates (Crossley), Susannah York (Rachel), John Hurt (Anthony), Robert Stephens (Chief Medical Officer), Tim Curry (Robert), Julian Hough (Vicar), Carol Drinkwater (Cobbler's Wife), Nick Stringer (Cobbler), John Rees (Inspector), Susan Woolridge (Harriet)

EACH OTHER (Franklin Media) Producer, Moshe Mizrahi; Direction, Story, and Screenplay, Michal Bat-Adam; Photographer, Yves Lafaye; Editor, Sophie Coussein; Music, Hubert Rostaing; Designer, Eytan Levi; Costumes, Sarah Wiener; In Hebrew and French with English subtitles; In color; Rated R; 92 minutes; November release. CAST: Michal Bat-Adam (Yola), Brigitte Catillon (Anne), Assaf Dayan (Avi), Avi Pnini (Ilan)

THE SIBERIAD (International Film Exchange/Satra Film Corp./Sovexportfilm) Director, Andrei Mikhalkov Kontchalovski; Screenplay, Valentjov, Andrei Mikhalkov Kontchalovski; Photography, Levan Paatashivili, Nikolai Dvigoubsky, Alexander Adabachian; Music, Edward Artemiev; Editor, Valentina Koulaguine; Costumes, Nathalia Litchmanova; A Mosfilm production in color; In 4 parts; Not rated; 210 minutes; November release. CAST: Vladimir Samailov, Micha Baboukov, Vitali Solomine, Yavaslava Khlapova, Nathalia Andreitchenko, Erqueni Petrov, Mikhail Kononov, Pavel Kadatchikov, Maxime Mounzouk, Aliocha Tiorkine, Serguei Shakourov, Volodia Levitan, Egueni Leonov Gladychev, Igor Othoupine

JACK THE RIPPER (Cineshowcase) Director, Jess Franco; A Cinemac production in Eastmancolor; Rated R; November release. CAST: Klaus Kinski, Josephine Chaplin

BETWEEN MIRACLES (Damon International Pictures) Director, Nino Manfredi; Screenplay, Nino Manfredi, Leo Benvenuti, Piero De Bernardi; Story, Nino Manfredi; Assistant Directors, Sofia Scandurra, Giorgio Scotton; Designer, Giorgio Giovannini; Music, Maurizio e Guido De Angelis; Editor, Alberto Gallitti; Photography, Armando Nannuzzi; A Rizzoli Films production in Movielab Color; Not rated; 120 minutes; November release. CAST: Nino Manfredi (Benedetto), Lionel Stander (Oreste), Delia Boccardo (Giovanna), Paola Borboni (Immacolato), Maro Scaccia (Abbot), Fausto Tozzi (Surgeon), Mariangela Melato (Camp Counsellor), Tano Cimarosa (Zio), Gastone Peschcci (Giovanna's suitor), Enrico Concutelli (Another Friar), Alfredo Bianchini (Priest), Paolo Armeni (Benedetto as a child), Antonietta Patti (Benedetto's Aunt)

John Hurt, Alan Bates, Susannah York
in "The Shout"

Delia Boccardo, Lionel Stander, Nino Manfredi
in "In Between Miracles" © Damon Intnl.

Sos Sarkisian (c)
in "Life Triumphs"

Natalia Arinbasarova, Asanali Ashimov,
Nonna Terentieva in "Trans-Siberian Express"

LIFE TRIUMPHS (International Film Exchange/Satra Film Corp./Sovexportfilm) Produced by Armenfilm Studio; Director, Genrikh Malyan; In color; 100 minutes; November release. CAST: Sos Sarkisyan (Naapet), Sophik Sargsian (Nubar), Mger Mkrtchian

THE MEN (International Film Exchange/Satra Film Corp./Sovexportfilm) Director, Edmond Keosayan; An Armenfilm Studio production in color; 80 minutes; November release. CAST: Alla Tumanyan, Armen Djigarkhanyan, Frunze Mkrtchyan, Azat Sherents

FIVE EVENINGS (International Film Exchange/Satra Film Corp./Sovexportfilm) Director, Nikita Mikhalkov; Based on play by Alexander Volodin; A Mosfilm Studio production in black and white; Not rated; 100 minutes; November release. CAST: Lyudmilla Gurchenko (Tamara), Stanislav Lyubshin (Ilyin), Igor Nefedov (Slava), Larisa Kuznetsova (Katya)

ANDREA (Group I Films) Executive Producer, Louis Morro; Producer-Director, Leopold Pomes; Photography, John Surrey; Music, Richard Mirall; In color; Rated R; 90 minutes; November release. CAST: Marina Langner, Lawrence St. Marks, Richard Massey

QUE VIVA MEXICO (International Film Exchange) Director, Sergei Eisenstein; Narrator, Grigory Aleksandrov; Selected Recitations, Sergei Bondarchuk; A Mosfilm production in black and white; 90 minutes; November release.

AUTUMN MARATHON (International Film Exchange) Director, Georgy Danelia; Screenplay, Alexander Volodin; A Mosfilm production in color; Not rated; 90 minutes; November release. CAST: Oleg Basilashvili, Natalia Gundareva, Marina Neyelova, Yevgeny Leonov

THE ORPHANS (International Film Exchange) Director, Nikolai Gubenko; A Mosfilm Studio production in color; Not rated; 100 minutes; November release. CAST: Yuozas Budraitis (Alexei), Georgy Burkov (Sergei), Alexander Kalyagin (Denis), Zhanna Bolotova (Alla/Teacher)

THE TRANS-SIBERIAN EXPRESS (International Film Exchange/Satra Film Corp./Sovexportfilm) Director, Eldar Urazbayev; A Kazakhfilm Studio production in Cinemascope and color; Not rated; 100 minutes; November release. CAST: Asanali Ashimov, Nonna Terentyeva, Oleg Tabakov, Natalia Arinbasarova

HOLIDAY HOOKERS (M & M) Formerly "Love by Appointment"; Producer, Alfred Leone; Director, Armando Nannuzzi; Music, Riz Ortolani; In Technicolor; Rated R; November release. CAST: Ernest Borgnine, Francoise Fabian, Corinne Clery, Robert Alda, Silvia Dionisio, Norma Jordan

GAYANE (Special Event Entertainment) Ballet by Aram Khachaturian; Director, Horace King; Conceived, created, and choreographed by Boris Eifman; Performed by Ballet Company of Riga, Latvia, with the Riga Symphony Orchestra conducted by Alexander Vilumanis; In Dolby Stereo; Not rated; 80 minutes; November release. CAST: Larisa Tulsova (Gayane), Alexander Rumyantsev (Giko), Genadi Gorbanyov (Armen), Maris Koristin (Machak)

DIRTY MONEY (Allied Artists) Producer, Robert Dorfmann; Direction and Screenplay, Jean-Pierre Melville; Photography, Walter Wottitz; Editor, Patricia Ranaut; Art Director, Theo Meurisse; Music, Michel Colombier; Lyrics, Charles Aznavour; Not rated; 100 minutes; November release. CAST: Alain Delon (Coleman), Catherine Deneuve (Cathy), Richard Crenna (Simon), Riccardo Cucciolla (Paul), Michael Conrad (Costa), Andre Pousse, Paul Crauchet, Simone Valere, Jean Desailly

ANNA KARENINA (Corinth) A Mosfilm production; Producers, B. Boguslavsky, B. Geller; Screenplay, Bavov-Arbhin; Based on novel by Leo Tolstoy; Music, Rodion Shchedrin; Director, Margarita Pilihina; Choreography, Maya Plisetskaya; Bolshoi Theatre Orchestra conducted by Yuri Simonov; In Cinemascope and color; 81 minutes; December release. CAST: Maya Plisetskaya (Anna Karenina), Alexander Godunov (Vronsky), Vladimir Tihonov (Karenin), Yuri Vladimirov (Station Master), and the Bolshoi Ballet.

Alyosha Cherstvov (C)
in "The Orphans"

Oleg Basilashvili, Natalia Gundareva
in "Autumn Marathon"

Karen Black, James Franciscus, Margaux Hemingway,
Lee Majors in "Killer Fish" © AFD

SPARTACUS (Corinth) A Mosfilm production; Camera Direction, Yuri Grigorovich, V. Derbenev; Choreography, Yuri Grigorovich; Music, Aram Khachaturian; In Cinemascope and color; 95 minutes; Not rated; December release. CAST: Vladimir Vasiliev (Spartacus), Natalia Bessmertnova (Friggia), Maris Liepa (Krass), Nina Timofeyeva (Eghina) and the Bolshoi Ballet.

RED, WHITE AND ZERO (Entertainment Marketing) Producer, Oscar Lewenstein; three short films; Not rated; 100 minutes; December release. "The Ride of the Valkyrie" directed and written by Peter Brook; Music by Howard Blake; Starring Zero Mostel. "The White Bus" directed by Lindsay Anderson; Story and Screenplay, Shelagh Delaney; Photography, Miroslav Ondricek; Music, Misha Donat. CAST: Patricia Healey, Arthur Lowe, John Sharp, Julie Perry, Victor Henry, Stephen Moore, Fanny Carby, Anthony Hopkins. "Red and Blue" directed by Tony Richardson; Screenplay, Tony Richardson, Julian More; Songs, Cyrus Bassiak. CAST: Vanessa Redgrave, Douglas Fairbanks, Jr., Michael York, Gary Raymond, John Bird

ACES HIGH (Cinema Shares) Producer, S. Benjamin Fisz; Director, Jack Gold; Screenplay, Howard Barker; Based on play "Journey's End" by R. C. Sheriff; Photography, Peter Allwork; Editor, Anne Coates; Music, Richard Hartley; In color; Not rated; 114 minutes; December release. CAST: Malcolm McDowell (Gresham), Christopher Plummer (Sinclair), Simon Ward (Crawford), Peter Firth (Croft), John Gielgud (Headmaster), Trevor Howard (Lieutenant Colonel Silkin), Richard Johnson (Colonel Lyle), Ray Milland (Brigadier Whale), David Wood (Thompson), David Daker (Bennett), Elliott Cooper (Wade), Pascale Christophe (Croft's Girl Friend), Jeanne Patou (Chanteuse)

IVAN THE TERRIBLE (Corinth) A Mosfilm production; Producer, Adolf Fradis; Film Director, L. Ohrimenko; Screenplay and Stage Direction, Vadim Derbenev, Yuri Grigorovich; Camera Direction, Vadim Derbenev, Victor Pischalnikov; Music, Sergei Prokofiev; Choreography, Yuri Grigorovich; Bolshoi Theatre Orchestra conducted by Algis Jouritis; In Cinemascope and color; 97 minutes; Not rated; December release. CAST: Yuri Vladimirov (Ivan the Terrible), Natalia Bessmertnova (Anastasia), Boris Akimov (Kurbsky), and members of the Bolshoi Ballet.

Penny Patterson, Koko
in "Koko—A Talking Gorilla"

TERROR (Crown International) Producers, Les Young, Richard Crafter; Director, Norman J. Warren; Screenplay, David McGillivray; Story, Les Young, Moira Young; Music, Ivor Slaney; Photography, Les Young; Associate Producer, Moira Young; Art Director, Hayden Pearce; Editor, Jim Elderton; Assistant Directors, Bryan Hirst, Nigel Goldsack, Leyland Wyler; In color; Rated R; 86 minutes; December release. CAST: John Nolan (James), Carolyn Courage (Ann), James Aubrey (Philip), Sarah Keller (Suzy), Tricia Walsh (Viv), Glynis Barber (Carol), Michael Craze (Gary), Rosie Collins (Diane), Chuck Julian, Elaine Ives-Cameron, Patti Love, Mary Maude, William Russell, Peter Craze, Peter Attard, Peter Sproule, Colin Howells, Peter Mayhew, Milton Reid, Mike O'Malley

KILLER FISH (Associated Film Distribution) Producer, Alex Ponti; Director, Anthony M. Dawson; Executive Producers, Olivier Perroy, Turi Vasile, Enzo Barone; Screenplay, Michael Rogers; Photography, Alberto Spagnoli; Music, Guido and Maurizio De Angelis; Editor, Roberto Sterbini; Art Director, Francesco Bronzi; Costumes, Adriana Berselli, Salvatore Russo; Presented by Sir Lew Grade; In color; Rated PG; 101 minutes; December release. CAST: Lee Majors (Robert), Karen Black (Kate), James Franciscus (Paul), Margaux Hemingway (Gabrielle), Marisa Berenson (Ann), Gary Collins (Gary), Roy Brocksmith (Ollie), Dan Pastorini (Hans), Frank Pesce (Warren), Charlie Guardino (Lloyd), Anthony Steffen (Max), Fabio Sabag (Quintin), George Cherques (Inspector), Chico Arago (Ben), Sonia Citicica (Nurse), Celso Faria (Airline Passenger)

TODO MODO (Nu-Image Film) Producer, Daniele Senatore; Director, Elio Petri; Screenplay, Elio Petri, Berto Pelosso; Based on novel by Leonardo Sciascia; In color; Not rated; 120 minutes; December release. CAST: Gian Maria Volonte ("M"), Marcello Mastroianni (Don Gaetano), Mariangela Melato (President's Wife), Renato Salvatori (Judge), Michel Piccoli ("Him"), Franco Citti (Chauffeur), Ciccio Ingrassia (Voitrano), Cesare Gelli (Inspector), Tino Scotti (Cook)

MY NAME IS ROCCO PAPALEO (Rumson) Producers, Pio Angeletti, Andriano De Michell; Director, Ettore Scola; Screenplay, Ruggero Maccari, Ettore Scola; Photography, Claudio Cirilo; Art Director, Luciano Ricceri; Editor, Ruggero Mastroianni; Music, Armando Trovaioli; In color; Not rated; 120 minutes; December release. CAST: Marcello Mastroianni (Rocco), Lauren Hutton (Jenny)

GOODBYE, FLICKMANIA (Nippon Herald) Producer, Hideto Isoda; Direction and Screenplay, Masato Harada; Photography, Genkichi Hasegawa; Editor, Ko Suzuki; Music, Ryudo Uzaki; Art Director, Yuji Maruyama; In color; Japanese with English subtitles; Not rated; 110 minutes; December release. CAST: Takuzo Kawatani (Dan-San), Naohiko Shigeta (Shuma), Atsuko Asano (Minami), Renji Ishibashi, Hiromitsu Suzuki, Miyako Yamaguchi, Toby Kadoguchi, Yuji Kosugi

THE CAULDRON OF DEATH (Film Ventures International) Director, Tulio Demicheli; Screenplay, Joe Maesso; Presented by Edward L. Montoro; In color; Rated R; December release. CAST: Chris Mitchum, Arthur Kennedy, Barbara Bouchet, Melisa Longo, Edward Fajardo, Angel Alvarez

THE TATTOO CONNECTION (World Northal) Producer, H. Wong; Director, Lee Tso-Nam; Screenplay, Luk Pak Sang; Music, Anders Nelsson, Perry Martin; In color; Rated R; December release. CAST: Jim Kelly, Chen Sing, Tan Tao Liang, Norman Wingrove, Bolo Yung

KOKO, A TALKING GORILLA (New Yorker) Director, Barbet Schroeder; Photography, Nestor Almendros; Editor, Dominique Auvray, Denise de Casablanca; A documentary; Not rated; 84 minutes; December release.

AUGUSTINE OF HIPPO (Entertainment Marketing Corp.) Director, Roberto Rossellini; Screenplay, Roberto Rossellini, Marcella Mariani, Luciano Scaffa, Carlo Cremona; Editor, Iolanda Benvenuti; Music, Mario Nascimbene; Producer, Francesco Orefici; Not rated; In color; 120 minutes; December release. CAST: Dary Berkani, Virgilio Gazzolo, Bruco Cataneo, Leonardo Fioravanti, Dannunzio Papini, Bepy, Mannejuolo, Livio Galassi, Fablo Carriba

LE CINEMA DE PAPA (Columbia Films) Producer, Pierre Grunstein; Direction and Screenplay, Claude Berri; Photography, Jean Penzer; Editor, Sophie Coussein; Music, Lino Leonardi; Not rated; 95 minutes; In color; December release. CAST: Yves Robert, Claude Berri, Alain Cohen, Catherine Goldman, Arlette Gilbert, Francis Lamarque, Francois Biletdoux, Prudence Harrington, Henia Ziv

Edie Adams

Eddie Albert

Ursula Andress

Lew Ayres

Elizabeth Ashley

BIOGRAPHICAL DATA

(Name, real name, place and date of birth, school attended)

ABBOTT, DIAHNNE: NYC, 1945.

ABBOTT, JOHN: London, June 5, 1905.

ABEL, WALTER: St. Paul, MN, June 6, 1898. AADA.

ABRAHAM, F. MURRAY: Pittsburgh, PA, Oct. 24, 1939. UTx.

ADAMS, BROOKE: NYC, 1949. Dalton.

ADAMS, DON: NYC, 1927.

ADAMS, EDIE (Elizabeth Edith Enke): Kingston, PA, Apr. 16, 1929. Juilliard, Columbia.

ADAMS, JULIE (Betty May): Waterloo, Iowa, Oct. 17, 1928. Little Rock Jr. College.

ADAMS, MAUD (Maud Wikstrom): Lulea, Sweden.

ADDAMS, DAWN: Felixstowe, Suffolk, Eng., Sept. 21, 1930. RADA.

ADDY, WESLEY: Omaha, NB, Aug. 4, 1913. UCLA.

ADJANI, ISABELLE: Paris, 1955.

ADLER, LUTHER: NYC, May 4, 1903.

ADRIAN, IRIS (Iris Adrian Hostetter): Los Angeles, May 29, 1913.

AGAR, JOHN: Chicago, Jan. 31, 1921.

AGUTTER, JENNY: London, 1953.

AHERNE, BRIAN: Worcestershire, Eng., May 2, 1902. Malvern College, U. of London.

AIMEE, ANOUK: Paris, Apr. 27, 1934. Bauer-Therond.

AKINS, CLAUDE: Nelson, GA, May 25, 1936. Northwestern U.

ALBERGHETTI, ANNA MARIA: Pesaro, Italy, May 15, 1936.

ALBERT, EDDIE (Eddie Albert Heimberger): Rock Island, IL, Apr. 22, 1908. U. of Minn.

ALBERT, EDWARD: Los Angeles, Feb. 20, 1951. UCLA.

ALBERTSON, JACK: Malden, MA, 1910.

ALBRIGHT, LOLA: Akron, OH, July 20, 1925.

ALDA, ALAN: NYC, Jan. 28, 1936. Fordham.

ALDA, ROBERT (Alphonso D'Abruzzo): NYC, Feb. 26, 1914. NYU.

ALEJANDRO, MIGUEL: NYC, 1958.

ALEXANDER, JANE (Quigley): Boston, MA, Oct. 28, 1939. Sarah Lawrence.

ALLEN, REX: Wilcox, AZ, Dec. 31, 1922.

ALLEN, STEVE: New York City, Dec. 26, 1921.

ALLEN, WOODY: Brooklyn, Dec. 1, 1935.

ALLENTUCK, KATHERINE: NYC, Oct. 16, 1954. Calhoun.

ALLYSON, JUNE (Ella Geisman): Westchester, NY, Oct. 7, 1917.

ALVARADO, TRINI: NYC, 1967.

AMECHE, DON (Dominic Amichi): Kenosha, WI, May 31, 1908.

AMES, ED: Boston, July 9, 1929.

AMES, LEON (Leon Wycoff): Portland, IN, Jan. 20, 1903.

AMOS, JOHN: Newark, NJ, Dec. 27, 1940. Colo. U.

ANDERSON, JUDITH: Adelaide, Australia, Feb. 10, 1898.

ANDERSON, MICHAEL, JR.: London, Eng., 1943.

ANDERSSON, BIBI: Stockholm, Nov. 11, 1935. Royal Dramatic Sch.

ANDES, KEITH: Ocean City, NJ, July 12, 1920. Temple U., Oxford.

ANDRESS, URSULA: Switz., Mar. 19, 1936.

ANDREWS, DANA: Collins, MS, Jan. 1, 1909. Sam Houston Col.

ANDREWS, EDWARD: Griffin, GA, Oct. 9, 1914. U. VA.

ANDREWS, HARRY: Tonbridge, Kent, Eng., Nov. 10, 1911.

ANDREWS, JULIE (Julia Elizabeth Wells): Surrey, Eng., Oct. 1, 1935.

ANGEL, HEATHER: Oxford, Eng., Feb. 9, 1909. Wycombe Abbey.

ANN-MARGRET (Olsson): Valsjobyn, Sweden, Apr. 28, 1941. Northwestern U.

ANSARA, MICHAEL: Lowell, MA, Apr. 15, 1922. Pasadena Playhouse.

ANTHONY, TONY: Clarksburg, WV, Oct 16, 1937. Carnegie Tech.

ANTON, SUSAN: Yucaipa, CA. San Bernardino Col.

ARCHER, JOHN (Ralph Bowman): Osceola, NB, May 8, 1915. USC.

ARDEN, EVE (Eunice Quedens): Mill Valley, CA, Apr. 30, 1912.

ARKIN, ALAN: NYC, Mar. 26, 1934. LACC.

ARNAZ, DESI: Santiago, Cuba, Mar. 2, 1915. Colegio de Dolores.

ARNAZ, DESI, JR.: Los Angeles, Jan. 19, 1953.

ARNAZ, LUCIE: Hollywood, July 17, 1951.

ARNESS, JAMES (Aurness): Minneapolis, MN, May 26, 1923. Beloit College.

ARTHUR, BEATRICE: NYC, May 13, 1926. New School.

ARTHUR, JEAN: NYC, Oct. 17, 1905.

ARTHUR, ROBERT (Robert Arthaud): Aberdeen, WA, June 18, 1925. U. Wash.

ASHLEY, ELIZABETH: Ocala, FL, Aug. 30, 1939.

ASSANTE, ARMAND: NYC, Oct. 4, 1949. AADA.

ASTAIRE, FRED (Fred Austerlitz): Omaha, NB, May 10, 1899.

ASTIN, JOHN: Baltimore, MD, Mar. 30, 1930. U. Minn.

ASTIN, PATTY DUKE (see Patty Duke)

ASTOR, MARY (Lucile V. Langhanke): Quincy, IL, May 3, 1906. Kenwood-Loring School.

ATHERTON, WILLIAM: Orange, CT, July 30, 1947. Carnegie Tech.

ATTENBOROUGH, RICHARD: Cambridge, Eng., Aug. 29, 1923. RADA.

AUBERJONOIS, RENE: NYC, June 1, 1940. Carnegie Tech.

AUDRAN, STEPHANE: Versailles, Fr., 1933.

AUGER, CLAUDINE: Paris, Apr. 26, 1942. Dramatic Cons.

AULIN, EWA: Stockholm, Sweden, Feb. 14, 1950.

AUMONT, JEAN PIERRE: Paris, Jan. 5, 1909. French Nat'l School of Drama.

AUTRY, GENE: Tioga, TX, Sept. 29, 1907.

AVALON, FRANKIE (Francis Thomas Avallone): Philadelphia, Sept. 18, 1939.

AYRES, LEW: Minneapolis, MN, Dec. 28, 1908.

AZNAVOUR, CHARLES (Varenagh Aznourian): Paris, May 22, 1924.

BACALL, LAUREN (Betty Perske): NYC, Sept. 16, 1924. AADA.

BACKUS, JIM: Cleveland, Ohio, Feb. 25, 1913. AADA.

BADDELEY, HERMIONE: Shropshire, Eng., Nov. 13, 1906. Margaret Morris School.

| Michael Beck | Marisa Berenson | Dirk Benedict | Jacqueline Bisset | David Birney |

BAILEY, PEARL: Newport News, VA, March 29, 1918.

BAIN, BARBARA: Chicago, Sept. 13, 1934. U. Ill.

BAIO, SCOTT: Brooklyn, 1961.

BAKER, CARROLL: Johnstown, PA, May 28, 1931. St. Petersburg Jr. College.

BAKER, DIANE: Hollywood, CA, Feb. 25, 1938. USC.

BAKER, LENNY: Boston, MA, Jan. 17, 1945. Boston U.

BALABAN, ROBERT: Chicago, Aug. 16, 1945. Colgate.

BALIN, INA: Brooklyn, Nov. 12, 1937. NYU.

BALL, LUCILLE: Celaron, NY, Aug. 6, 1910. Chatauqua Musical Inst.

BALSAM, MARTIN: NYC, Nov. 4, 1919. Actors Studio.

BANCROFT, ANNE (Anna Maria Italiano): Bronx, NY, Sept. 17, 1931. AADA.

BANNEN, IAN: Airdrie, Scot., June 29, 1928.

BARDOT, BRIGITTE: Paris, Sept. 28, 1934.

BARRAULT, MARIE-CHRISTINE: Paris, 1946.

BARRETT, MAJEL (Hudec): Columbus, OH, Feb. 23. Western Reserve U.

BARRON, KEITH: Mexborough, Eng., Aug. 8, 1936. Sheffield Playhouse.

BARRY, DONALD (Donald Barry de Acosta): Houston, TX, Jan.11, 1912. Texas School of Mines.

BARRY, GENE (Eugene Klass): NYC, June 14, 1921.

BARRYMORE, JOHN BLYTH: Beverly Hills, CA, June 4, 1932. St. John's Military Academy.

BARTHOLOMEW, FREDDIE: London, Mar. 28, 1924.

BARYSHNIKOV, MIKHAIL: Riga, Latvia, Jan. 27, 1948.

BASEHART, RICHARD: Zanesville, OH, Aug. 31, 1914.

BATES, ALAN: Allestree, Derbyshire, Eng., Feb. 17, 1934. RADA.

BAXTER, ANNE: Michigan City, IN, May 7, 1923. Ervine School of Drama.

BAXTER, KEITH: South Wales, Apr. 29, 1933. RADA.

BEAL, JOHN (J. Alexander Bliedung): Joplin, MO, Aug. 13, 1909. Pa. U.

BEATTY, ROBERT: Hamilton, Ont., Can., Oct. 19, 1909. U. of Toronto.

BEATTY, WARREN: Richmond, VA, March 30, 1937.

BECK, MICHAEL: Horseshoe Lake, AR, 1948.

BEDELIA, BONNIE: NYC, Mar. 25, 1948. Hunter Col.

BEDI, KABIR: India, 1945.

BEERY, NOAH, JR.: NYC, Aug. 10, 1916. Harvard.

BELAFONTE, HARRY: NYC, Mar. 1, 1927.

BELASCO, LEON: Odessa, Russia, Oct. 11, 1902.

BEL GEDDES, BARBARA: NYC, Oct. 31, 1922.

BELL, TOM: Liverpool, Eng., 1932.

BELLAMY, RALPH: Chicago, June 17, 1904.

BELLER, KATHLEEN: NYC, 1957.

BELMONDO, JEAN PAUL: Paris, Apr. 9, 1933.

BENEDICT, DIRK: Montana, 1945. Whitman Col.

BENJAMIN, RICHARD: NYC, May 22, 1938. Northwestern U.

BENNETT, BRUCE (Herman Brix): Tacoma, WA, May 19, 1909. U. Wash.

BENNETT, JILL: Penang, Malay, Dec. 24, 1931.

BENNETT, JOAN: Palisades, NJ, Feb. 27, 1910. St. Margaret's.

BENSON, ROBBY: Dallas, TX, Jan. 21, 1957.

BERENSON, MARISSA: NYC, Feb. 15, 1947.

BERGEN, CANDICE: Los Angeles, May 9, 1946. U. Pa.

BERGEN, POLLY: Knoxville, TN, July 14, 1930. Compton Jr. College.

BERGER, HELMUT: Salzburg, Aus., 1945.

BERGER, SENTA: Vienna, May 13, 1941. Vienna Sch. of Acting.

BERGER, WILLIAM: Austria, Jan. 20, 1937. Columbia.

BERGERAC, JACQUES: Biarritz, France, May 26, 1927. Paris U.

BERGMAN, INGRID: Stockholm, Sweden, Aug. 29, 1915. Royal Dramatic Theatre School.

BERLE, MILTON (Milton Berlinger): NYC, July 12, 1908. Professional Children's School.

BERLIN, JEANNIE: Los Angeles, Nov. 1, 1949.

BERLINGER, WARREN: Brooklyn, Aug. 31, 1937. Columbia.

BERNARDI, HERSCHEL: NYC, 1923.

BERRI, CLAUDE (Langmann): Paris, July 1, 1934.

BERTO, JULIET: Grenoble, France, Jan. 1947.

BEST, JAMES: Corydon, IN, July 26, 1926.

BETTGER, LYLE: Philadelphia, Feb. 13, 1915. AADA.

BEYMER, RICHARD: Avoca, IA, Feb. 21, 1939.

BIKEL, THEODORE: Vienna, May 2, 1924. RADA.

BIRNEY, DAVID: Washington, DC, Apr. 23, 1939. Dartmouth, UCLA.

BISHOP, JOEY (Joseph Abraham Gottlieb): Bronx, NY, Feb. 3, 1918.

BISHOP, JULIE (formerly Jacqueline Wells): Denver, CO, Aug. 30, 1917. Westlake School.

BISSET, JACQUELINE: Waybridge, Eng., Sept. 13, 1944.

BIXBY, BILL: San Francisco, Jan. 22, 1934. U. Cal.

BLACK, KAREN (Ziegler): Park Ridge, IL, July 1, 1942. Northwestern.

BLAINE, VIVIAN (Vivian Stapleton): Newark, NJ, Nov. 21, 1923.

BLAIR, BETSY (Betsy Boger): NYC, Dec. 11, 1923.

BLAIR, JANET (Martha Jane Lafferty): Blair, PA, Apr. 23, 1921.

BLAIR, LINDA: Westport, CT, 1959.

BLAKE, AMANDA (Beverly Louise Neill): Buffalo, NY, Feb. 20, 1921.

BLAKE, ROBERT (Michael Gubitosi): Nutley, NJ, Sept. 18, 1933.

BLAKELY, SUSAN: Frankfurt, Germany 1950. U. Tex.

BLAKLEY, RONEE: Stanley, ID, 1946. Stanford U.

BLOOM, CLAIRE: London, Feb. 15, 1931. Badminton School.

BLYTH, ANN: Mt. Kisco, NY, Aug. 16, 1928. New Wayburn Dramatic School.

BOCHNER, HART: CA, 1957. U. Cal.

BOGARDE, DIRK: London, Mar. 28, 1918. Glasgow & Univ. College.

BOLGER, RAY: Dorchester, MA, Jan. 10, 1903.

BOLKAN, FLORINDA (Florinda Soares Bulcao): Ceara, Brazil, Feb. 15, 1941.

BOND, DEREK: Glasgow, Scot., Jan. 26, 1920. Askes School.

BONDI, BEULAH: Chicago, May 3, 1892.

BOONE, PAT: Jacksonville, FL, June 1, 1934. Columbia U.

BOONE, RICHARD: Los Angeles, June 18, 1916. Stanford U.

BOOTH, SHIRLEY (Thelma Ford): NYC, Aug. 30, 1907.

Coral Browne   Peter Boyle   Dyan Cannon   Beau Bridges   Diahann Carroll

BORGNINE, ERNEST (Borgnino): Hamden, CT, Jan. 24, 1918. Randall School.

BOTTOMS, JOSEPH: Santa Barbara, CA, 1954.

BOTTOMS, TIMOTHY: Santa Barbara, CA, Aug. 30, 1951.

BOULTING, INGRID: Transvaal, So. Africa, 1947.

BOVEE, LESLIE: Bend, OR, 1952.

BOWKER, JUDI: Shawford, Eng., Apr. 6, 1954.

BOYLE, PETER: Philadelphia, PA, 1937. LaSalle Col.

BRACKEN, EDDIE: NYC, Feb. 7, 1920. Professional Children's School.

BRADY, SCOTT (Jerry Tierney): Brooklyn, Sept. 13, 1924. Bliss-Hayden Dramatic School.

BRAND, NEVILLE: Kewanee, IL, Aug. 13, 1920.

BRANDO, JOCELYN: San Francisco, Nov. 18, 1919. Lake Forest College, AADA.

BRANDO, MARLON: Omaha, NB, Apr. 3, 1924. New School.

BRASSELLE, KEEFE: Elyria, OH, Feb. 7, 1923.

BRAZZI, ROSSANO: Bologna, Italy, Sept. 18, 1916. U. Florence.

BRIAN, DAVID: NYC, Aug. 5, 1914. CCNY.

BRIDGES, BEAU: Los Angeles, Dec. 9, 1941. UCLA.

BRIDGES, JEFF: Los Angeles, Dec. 4, 1949.

BRIDGES, LLOYD: San Leandro, CA, Jan. 15, 1913.

BRISEBOIS, DANIELLE: Brooklyn, June 28, 1969.

BRITT, MAY (Maybritt Wilkins): Sweden, March 22, 1936.

BRODIE, STEVE (Johnny Stevens): Eldorado, KS, Nov. 25, 1919.

BROLIN, JAMES: Los Angeles, July 18, 1940. UCLA.

BROMFIELD, JOHN (Farron Bromfield): South Bend, IN, June 11, 1922. St. Mary's College.

BRONSON, CHARLES (Buchinsky): Ehrenfield, PA, Nov. 3, 1920.

BROWN, GEORG STANFORD: Havana, Cuba, June 24, 1943. AMDA.

BROWN, JAMES: Desdemona, TX, Mar. 22, 1920. Baylor U.

BROWN, JIM: St. Simons Island, NY, Feb. 17, 1935. Syracuse U.

BROWN, TOM: NYC, Jan. 6, 1913. Professional Children's School.

BROWNE, CORAL: Melbourne, Aust., July 23, 1913.

BROWNE, LESLIE: NYC, 1958.

BRUCE, VIRGINIA: Minneapolis, Sept. 29, 1910.

BRYNNER, YUL: Sakhalin Island, Japan, July 11, 1915.

BUCHHOLZ, HORST: Berlin, Ger., Dec. 4, 1933. Ludwig Dramatic School.

BUETEL, JACK: Dallas, TX, Sept. 5, 1917.

BUJOLD, GENEVIEVE: Montreal, Can., July 1, 1942.

BUONO, VICTOR: San Diego, CA, 1939. Villanova.

BURKE, PAUL: New Orleans, July 21, 1926. Pasadena Playhouse.

BURNETT, CAROL: San Antonio, TX, Apr. 26, 1933. UCLA.

BURNS, CATHERINE: NYC, Sept. 25, 1945. AADA.

BURNS, GEORGE (Nathan Birnbaum): NYC, Jan. 20, 1896.

BURR, RAYMOND: New Westminster, B.C., Can., May 21, 1917. Stanford, U. Cal., Columbia.

BURSTYN, ELLEN (Edna Rae Gillooly): Detroit, MI, Dec. 7, 1932.

BURTON, RICHARD (Richard Jenkins): Pontrhydyfen, S. Wales, Nov. 10, 1925. Oxford.

BUSEY, GARY: Tulsa, OK, 1944.

BUTTONS, RED (Aaron Chwatt): NYC, Feb. 5, 1919.

BUZZI, RUTH: Wequetequock, RI, July 24, 1936. Pasadena Playhouse.

BYGRAVES, MAX: London, Oct. 16, 1922. St. Joseph's School.

BYRNES, EDD: NYC, July 30, 1933. Haaren High.

CAAN, JAMES: Bronx, NY, Mar. 26, 1939.

CABOT, SUSAN: Boston, July 6, 1927.

CAESAR, SID: Yonkers, NY, Sept. 8, 1922.

CAGNEY, JAMES: NYC, July 17, 1899. Columbia.

CAGNEY, JEANNE: NYC, Mar. 25, 1919. Hunter.

CAINE, MICHAEL (Maurice Michelwhite): London, Mar. 14, 1933.

CAINE, SHAKIRA (Baksh): Guyana, Feb. 23, 1947. Indian Trust Col.

CALHOUN, RORY (Francis Timothy Durgin): Los Angeles, Aug. 8, 1922.

CALLAN, MICHAEL (Martin Calinieff): Philadelphia, Nov. 22, 1935.

CALVERT, PHYLLIS: London, Feb. 18, 1917. Margaret Morris School.

CALVET, CORRINE (Corrine Dibos): Paris, Apr. 30, 1929. U. Paris.

CAMERON, ROD (Rod Cox): Calgary, Alberta, Can., Dec. 7, 1912.

CAMP, COLLEEN: San Francisco, 1953.

CAMPBELL, GLEN: Delight, AR, Apr. 22, 1935.

CANALE, GIANNA MARIA: Reggio Calabria, Italy, Sept. 12.

CANNON, DYAN (Samille Diane Friesen): Tacoma, WA, Jan. 4, 1929.

CANOVA, JUDY: Jacksonville, FL, Nov. 20, 1916.

CAPERS, VIRGINIA: Sumter, SC, 1925. Juilliard.

CAPUCINE (Germaine Lefebvre): Toulon, France, Jan. 6, 1935.

CARA, IRENE: NYC, Mar. 18, 1958.

CARDINALE, CLAUDIA: Tunis, N. Africa, Apr. 15, 1939. College Paul Cambon.

CAREY, HARRY, JR.: Saugus, CA, May 16, 1921. Black Fox Military Academy.

CAREY, MACDONALD: Sioux City, IA, Mar. 15, 1913. U. of Wisc., U. Iowa.

CAREY, PHILIP: Hackensack, NJ, July 15, 1925. U. Miami.

CARMICHAEL, HOAGY: Bloomington, IN, Nov. 22, 1899. Ind. U.

CARMICHAEL, IAN: Hull, Eng., June 18, 1920. Scarborough Col.

CARNE, JUDY (Joyce Botterill): Northampton, Eng., 1939. Bush-Davis Theatre School.

CARNEY, ART: Mt. Vernon, NY, Nov. 4, 1918.

CARON, LESLIE: Paris, July 1, 1931. Nat'l Conservatory, Paris.

CARPENTER, CARLETON: Bennington, VT, July 10, 1926. Northwestern.

CARR, VIKKI (Florence Cardona): July 19, 1942. San Fernando Col.

CARRADINE, DAVID: Hollywood, Dec. 8, 1936. San Francisco State.

CARRADINE, JOHN: NYC, Feb. 5, 1906.

CARRADINE, KEITH: San Mateo, CA, Aug. 8, 1951. Colo. State U.

CARRADINE, ROBERT: San Mateo, CA, 1954.

CARREL, DANY: Tourane, Indochina, Sept. 20, 1936. Marseilles Cons.

CARROLL, DIAHANN (Johnson): NYC, July 17, 1935. NYU.

CARROLL, MADELEINE: West Bromwich, Eng., Feb. 26, 1902. Birmingham U.

CARROLL, PAT: Shreveport, LA, May 5, 1927. Catholic U.

CARSON, JOHN DAVID: 1951, Calif. Valley Col.

| Julie Christie | Chevy Chase | Corinne Clery | Bert Convy | Claudette Colbert |

CARSON, JOHNNY: Corning, IA, Oct. 23, 1925. U. of Neb.

CARSTEN, PETER (Ransenthaler): Weissenberg, Bavaria, Apr. 30, 1929. Munich Akademie.

CASH, ROSALIND: Atlantic City, NJ, Dec. 31, 1938. CCNY.

CASON, BARBARA: Memphis, TN, Nov. 15, 1933. U. Iowa.

CASS, PEGGY (Mary Margaret): Boston, May 21, 1925.

CASSAVETES, JOHN: NYC, Dec. 9, 1929. Colgate College, AADA.

CASSEL, JEAN-PIERRE: Paris, Oct. 27, 1932.

CASSIDY, DAVID: NYC, Apr. 12, 1950.

CASSIDY, JOANNA: Camden, NJ, 1944. Syracuse U.

CASTELLANO, RICHARD: Bronx, NY, Sept. 3, 1934.

CAULFIELD, JOAN: Orange, NJ, June 1, 1922. Columbia U.

CAVANI, LILIANA: Bologna, Italy, Jan. 12, 1937. U. Bologna.

CELI, ADOLFO: Sicily, July 27, 1922. Rome Academy.

CHAKIRIS, GEORGE: Norwood, OH, Sept. 16, 1933.

CHAMBERLAIN, RICHARD: Beverly Hills, CA, March 31, 1935. Pomona.

CHAMPION, GOWER: Geneva, IL, June 22, 1921.

CHAMPION, MARGE: Los Angeles, Sept. 2, 1925.

CHANNING, CAROL: Seattle, Jan. 31, 1921. Bennington.

CHANNING, STOCKARD (Susan Stockard): NYC, 1944. Radcliffe.

CHAPIN, MILES: NYC, Dec. 6, 1954. HB Studio.

CHAPLIN, GERALDINE: Santa Monica, CA, July 31, 1944. Royal Ballet.

CHAPLIN, SYDNEY: Los Angeles, Mar. 31, 1926. Lawrenceville.

CHARISSE, CYD (Tula Ellice Finklea): Amarillo, TX, Mar. 3, 1922. Hollywood Professional School.

CHASE, CHEVY: NYC, 1943.

CHER (Cherlin Sarkesian): May 20, 1946.

CHIARI, WALTER: Verona, Italy, 1930.

CHRISTIAN, LINDA (Blanca Rosa Welter): Tampico, Mex., Nov. 13, 1923.

CHRISTIAN, ROBERT: Los Angeles, Dec. 27, 1939. UCLA.

CHRISTIE, JULIE: Chukua, Assam, India, Apr. 14, 1941.

CHRISTOPHER, DENNIS (Carrelli): Philadelphia, PA, 1955. Temple U.

CHRISTOPHER, JORDAN: Youngstown, OH, Oct. 23, 1940. Kent State.

CHURCHILL, SARAH: London, Oct. 7, 1916.

CILENTO, DIANE: Queensland, Australia, Oct. 5, 1933. AADA.

CLAPTON, ERIC: London, Mar. 30, 1945.

CLARK, DANE: NYC, Feb. 18, 1915. Cornell, Johns Hopkins U.

CLARK, DICK: Mt. Vernon, NY, Nov. 30, 1929. Syracuse U.

CLARK, MAE: Philadelphia, Aug. 16, 1910.

CLARK, PETULA: Epsom, England, Nov. 15, 1932.

CLARK, SUSAN: Sarnid, Ont., Can., Mar. 8. RADA

CLAYBURGH, JILL: NYC, Apr. 30, 1944. Sarah Lawrence.

CLEMENTS, STANLEY: Long Island, NY, July 16, 1926.

CLERY, CORINNE: Italy, 1950.

CLOONEY, ROSEMARY: Maysville KY, May 23, 1928.

COBURN, JAMES: Laurel, NB, Aug. 31, 1928. LACC.

COCA, IMOGENE: Philadelphia, Nov. 18, 1908.

COCO, JAMES: NYC, Mar. 21, 1929.

CODY, KATHLEEN: Bronx, NY, Oct. 30, 1953.

COLBERT, CLAUDETTE (Lily Chauchoin): Paris, Sept. 13, 1905. Art Students League.

COLE, GEORGE: London, Apr. 22, 1925.

COLLINS, JOAN: London, May 23, 1933. Francis Holland School.

COLLINS, STEPHEN: Des Moines, IA, Oct. 1, 1947. Amherst.

COMER, ANJANETTE: Dawson, TX, Aug. 7, 1942. Baylor, Tex. U.

CONANT, OLIVER: NYC, Nov. 15, 1955. Dalton.

CONAWAY, JEFF: NYC, Oct. 5, 1950. NYC.

CONNERY, SEAN: Edinburgh, Scot., Aug. 25, 1930.

CONNORS, CHUCK (Kevin Joseph Connors): Brooklyn, Apr. 10, 1921. Seton Hall College.

CONNORS, MIKE (Krekor Ohanian): Fresno, CA, Aug. 15, 1925. UCLA.

CONRAD, WILLIAM: Louisville, KY, Sept. 27, 1920.

CONVERSE, FRANK: St. Louis, MO, May 22, 1938. Carnegie Tech.

CONVY, BERT: St. Louis, MO, July 23, 1935. UCLA.

CONWAY, KEVIN: NYC, May 29, 1942.

CONWAY, TIM (Thomas Daniel): Willoughby, OH, Dec. 15, 1933. Bowling Green State.

COOGAN, JACKIE: Los Angeles, Oct. 25, 1914. Villanova College.

COOK, ELISHA, JR.: San Francisco, Dec. 26, 1907. St. Albans.

COOPER, BEN: Hartford, CT, Sept. 30, 1932. Columbia U.

COOPER, JACKIE: Los Angeles, Sept. 15, 1921.

COOTE, ROBERT: London, Feb. 4, 1909. Hurstpierpont College.

CORBETT, GRETCHEN: Portland, OR, Aug. 13, 1947. Carnegie Tech.

CORBY, ELLEN (Hansen): Racine, WI, June 13, 1913.

CORCORAN, DONNA: Quincy, MA, Sept. 29, 1942.

CORD, ALEX (Viespi): Floral Park, NY, Aug. 3, 1931. NYU, Actors Studio.

CORDAY, MARA (Marilyn Watts): Santa Monica, CA, Jan. 3, 1932.

COREY, JEFF: NYC, Aug. 10, 1914. Fagin School.

CORLAN, ANTHONY: Cork City, Ire., May 9, 1947. Birmingham School of Dramatic Arts.

CORNTHWAITE, ROBERT: Apr. 28, 1917. USC.

CORRI, ADRIENNE: Glasgow, Scot., Nov. 13, 1933. RADA.

CORTESA, VALENTINA: Milan, Italy, Jan. 1, 1925.

COSBY, BILL: Philadelphia, July 12, 1937. Temple U.

COSTER, NICOLAS: London, Dec. 3, 1934. Neighborhood Playhouse.

COTTEN, JOSEPH: Petersburg, VA, May 13, 1905.

COURTENAY, TOM: Hull, Eng., Feb. 25, 1937. RADA.

COURTLAND, JEROME: Knoxville, TN, Dec. 27, 1926.

CRABBE, BUSTER (LARRY) (Clarence Linden): Oakland, CA, Feb. 7, 1908. USC.

CRAIG, JAMES (James H. Meador): Nashville, TN, Feb. 4, 1912. Rice Inst.

CRAIG, MICHAEL: India, Jan. 27, 1929.

CRAIN, JEANNE: Barstow, CA, May 25, 1925.

CRAWFORD, BRODERICK: Philadelphia, Dec. 9, 1911.

CRENNA, RICHARD: Los Angeles, Nov. 30, 1926. USC.

CRISTAL, LINDA (Victoria Moya): Buenos Aires, Feb. 25, 1934.

CROSBY, KATHRYN GRANT: (see Kathryn Grant)

Robert Culp   Arlene Dahl   Ossie Davis   Colleen Dewhurst   Brad Dourif

CROUSE, LINDSAY ANN: NYC, May 12, 1948. Radcliffe.

CROWLEY, PAT: Olyphant, PA, Sept. 17, 1932.

CRYSTAL, BILLY: NYC, 1948.

CULLUM, JOHN: Knoxville, TN, Mar. 2, 1930. U. Tenn.

CULP, ROBERT: Oakland, CA., Aug. 16, 1930. U. Wash.

CULVER, CALVIN: Canandaigua, NY, 1943.

CUMMINGS, CONSTANCE: Seattle, WA, May 15, 1910.

CUMMINGS, QUINN: Hollywood, Aug. 13, 1967.

CUMMINGS, ROBERT: Joplin, MO, June 9, 1910. Carnegie Tech.

CUMMINS, PEGGY: Prestatyn, N. Wales, Dec. 18, 1926. Alexandra School.

CURTIS, KEENE: Salt Lake City, UT, Feb. 15, 1925. U. Utah.

CURTIS, TONY (Bernard Schwartz): NYC, June 3, 1924.

CUSACK, CYRIL: Durban, S. Africa, Nov. 26, 1910. Univ. Col.

CUSHING, PETER: Kenley, Surrey, Eng., May 26, 1913.

DAHL, ARLENE: Minneapolis, Aug. 11, 1924. U. Minn.

DALLESANDRO, JOE: Pensacola, FL, Dec. 31, 1948.

DALTON, TIMOTHY: Wales, 1945. RADA.

DALTREY, ROGER: London, Mar. 1, 1945.

DALY, TYNE: NYC, 1947. AMDA.

DAMONE, VIC (Vito Farinola): Brooklyn, June 12, 1928.

DANIELS, WILLIAM: Bklyn, Mar. 31, 1927. Northwestern.

DANNER, BLYTHE: Philadelphia, PA. Bard Col.

DANO, ROYAL: NYC, Nov. 16, 1922. NYU.

DANTE, MICHAEL (Ralph Vitti): Stamford, CT, 1935. U. Miami.

DANTINE, HELMUT: Vienna, Oct. 7, 1918. U. Calif.

DANTON, RAY: NYC, Sept. 19, 1931. Carnegie Tech.

DARBY, KIM: (Deborah Zerby): North Hollywood, CA, July 8, 1948.

DARCEL, DENISE (Denise Billecard): Paris, Sept. 8, 1925. U. Dijon.

DARREN, JAMES: Philadelphia, June 8, 1936. Stella Adler School.

DARRIEUX, DANIELLE: Bordeaux, France, May 1, 1917. Lycee LaTour.

DA SILVA, HOWARD: Cleveland, OH, May 4, 1909. Carnegie Tech.

DAVIDSON, JOHN: Pittsburgh, Dec. 13, 1941. Denison U.

DAVIES, RUPERT: Liverpool, Eng., 1916.

DAVIS, BETTE: Lowell, MA, Apr. 5, 1908. John Murray Anderson Dramatic School.

DAVIS, MAC: Lubbock, TX, 1942.

DAVIS, OSSIE: Cogdell, GA, Dec. 18, 1917. Howard U.

DAVIS, SAMMY, JR.: NYC, Dec. 8, 1925.

DAY, DENNIS (Eugene Dennis McNulty): NYC, May 21, 1917. Manhattan College.

DAY, DORIS (Doris Kappelhoff): Cincinnati, Apr. 3, 1924.

DAY, LARAINE (Johnson): Roosevelt, UT, Oct. 13, 1917.

DAYAN, ASSEF: Israel, 1945. U. Jerusalem.

DEAN, JIMMY: Plainview, TX, Aug. 10, 1928.

DeCARLO, YVONNE (Peggy Yvonne Middleton): Vancouver, B.C., Can., Sept. 1, 1922. Vancouver School of Drama.

DEE, FRANCES: Los Angeles, Nov. 26, 1907. Chicago U.

DEE, JOEY (Joseph Di Nicola): Passaic, NJ, June 11, 1940. Patterson State College.

DEE, RUBY: Cleveland, OH, Oct. 27, 1924. Hunter Col.

DEE, SANDRA (Alexandra Zuck): Bayonne, NJ, Apr. 23, 1942.

DeFORE, DON: Cedar Rapids, IA, Aug. 25, 1917. U. Iowa.

DeHAVEN, GLORIA: Los Angeles, July 23, 1923.

DeHAVILLAND, OLIVIA: Tokyo, Japan, July 1, 1916. Notre Dame Convent School.

DELL, GABRIEL: Barbados, BWI, Oct. 7, 1930.

DELON, ALAIN: Sceaux, Fr., Nov. 8, 1935.

DELORME, DANIELE: Paris, Oct. 9, 1927. Sorbonne.

DEL RIO, DOLORES: (Dolores Ansunsolo): Durango, Mex., Aug. 3, 1905. St. Joseph's Convent.

DeLUISE, DOM: Brooklyn, Aug. 1, 1933. Tufts Col.

DEMAREST, WILLIAM: St. Paul, MN, Feb. 27, 1892.

DEMONGEOT, MYLENE: Nice, France, Sept. 29, 1938.

DENEUVE, CATHERINE: Paris, Oct. 22, 1943.

DeNIRO, ROBERT: NYC, Aug. 17, 1943. Stella Adler.

DENISON, MICHAEL: Doncaster, York, Eng., Nov. 1, 1915. Oxford.

DENNER, CHARLES: Tarnow, Poland, May 29, 1926.

DENNIS, SANDY: Hastings, NB, Apr. 27, 1937. Actors Studio.

DEREK, BO (Mary Cathleen Collins): Long Beach, CA, 1957.

DEREK, JOHN: Hollywood, Aug. 12, 1926.

DERN, BRUCE: Chicago, June 4, 1936. U Pa.

DEWHURST, COLLEEN: Montreal, June 3, 1926. Lawrence U.

DEXTER, ANTHONY (Walter Reinhold Alfred Fleischmann): Talmadge, NB, Jan. 19, 1919. U. Iowa.

DeYOUNG, CLIFF: Los Angeles, CA, Feb. 12, 1945. Cal State.

DHIEGH, KHIGH: New Jersey, 1910.

DICKINSON, ANGIE: Kulm, ND, Sept. 30, 1932. Glendale College.

DIETRICH, MARLENE (Maria Magdalene von Losch): Berlin, Ger., Dec. 27, 1901. Berlin Music Academy.

DILLER, PHYLLIS: Lima, OH, July 17, 1917. Bluffton College.

DILLMAN, BRADFORD: San Francisco, Apr. 14, 1930. Yale.

DILLON, MELINDA: Hope, AR, Oct. 13, 1939. Goodman Theatre School.

DOBSON, TAMARA: Baltimore, MD, 1947. Md. Inst. of Art.

DOMERGUE, FAITH: New Orleans, June 16, 1925.

DONAHUE, TROY (Merle Johnson): NYC, Jan. 27, 1937. Columbia U.

DONAT, PETER: Nova Scotia, Jan. 20, 1928. Yale.

DONNELL, JEFF (Jean Donnell): South Windham, ME, July 10, 1921. Yale Drama School.

DONNELLY, RUTH: Trenton, NJ, May 17, 1896.

DOOHAN, JAMES: Vancouver, BC, Mar. 3. Neighborhood Playhouse.

DOOLEY, PAUL: Parkersburg, WV, Feb. 22, 1928. U WV.

DORS, DIANA (Fluck): Swindon, Wilshire, Eng., Oct. 23, 1931. London Academy of Music.

D'ORSAY, FIFI: Montreal, Can., Apr. 16, 1904.

DOUGLAS, KIRK (Issur Danielovitch): Amsterdam, NY, Dec. 9, 1916. St. Lawrence U.

DOUGLAS, MELVYN (Melvyn Hesselberg): Macon, GA, Apr. 5, 1901.

DOUGLAS, MICHAEL: Hollywood, Sept. 25, 1944. U. Cal.

DOURIF, BRAD: Huntington, WV, Mar. 18, 1950. Marshall U.

DOVE, BILLIE: NYC, May 14, 1904.

Sandy Duncan   Sam Elliott   Samantha Eggar   Peter Fonda   Farrah Fawcett

DOWN, LESLEY-ANN: London, Mar. 17, 1954.

DRAKE, BETSY: Paris, Sept. 11, 1923.

DRAKE, CHARLES (Charles Rupert): NYC, Oct. 2, 1914. Nichols College.

DREW, ELLEN (formerly Terry Ray): Kansas City, MO, Nov. 23, 1915.

DREYFUSS, RICHARD: Brooklyn, NY, 1948.

DRIVAS, ROBERT: Chicago, Oct. 7, 1938. U. Chi.

DRU, JOANNE (Joanne LaCock): Logan, WV, Jan. 31, 1923. John Robert Powers School.

DUBBINS, DON: Brooklyn, NY, June 28.

DUFF, HOWARD: Bremerton, WA, Nov. 24, 1917.

DUFFY, PATRICK: Montana, 1949. U Wash.

DUKE, PATTY: NYC, Dec. 14, 1946.

DULLEA, KEIR: Cleveland, NJ, May 30, 1936. Neighborhood Playhouse, SF State Col.

DUNAWAY, FAYE: Bascom, FL, Jan, 14, 1941. Fla. U.

DUNCAN, SANDY: Henderson, TX, Feb. 20, 1946. Len Morris Col.

DUNNE, IRENE: Louisville, KY, Dec. 20, 1898. Chicago College of Music.

DUNNOCK, MILDRED: Baltimore, Jan. 25, 1900. Johns Hopkins and Columbia U.

DUPEREY, ANNY: Paris, 1947.

DURBIN, DEANNA (Edna): Winnipeg, Can., Dec. 4, 1921.

DURNING, CHARLES: Highland Falls, NY, Feb. 28, 1933. NYU.

DUSSOLLIER, ANDRE: Annecy, France, Feb. 17, 1946.

DUVALL, ROBERT: San Diego, CA, 1930. Principia Col.

DUVALL, SHELLEY: Houston, TX, 1950.

EASTON, ROBERT: Milwaukee, Nov. 23, 1930. U. Texas.

EASTWOOD, CLINT: San Francisco, May 31, 1930. LACC.

EATON, SHIRLEY: London, 1937. Aida Foster School.

EBSEN, BUDDY (Christian, Jr.): Belleville, IL, Apr. 2, 1910. U. Fla.

ECKEMYR, AGNETA: Karlsborg, Swed., July 2. Actors Studio.

EDEN, BARBARA (Moorhead): Tucson, AZ, 1934.

EDWARDS, VINCE: NYC, July 9, 1928. AADA.

EGAN, RICHARD: San Francisco, July 29, 1923. Stanford U.

EGGAR, SAMANTHA: London, Mar. 5, 1939.

EICHHORN, LISA: Reading, PA, 1952. Queens Ont. U. RADA.

EKBERG, ANITA: Malmo, Sweden, Sept. 29, 1931.

EKLAND, BRITT: Stockholm, Swed., 1942.

ELIZONDO, HECTOR: NYC, Dec. 22, 1936.

ELLIOTT, DENHOLM: London, May 31, 1922. Malvern College.

ELLIOTT, SAM: Sacramento, CA, 1944. U. Ore.

ELSOM, ISOBEL: Cambridge, Eng., Mar. 15, 1894.

ELY, RON (Ronald Pierce): Hereford, TX, June 21, 1938.

EMERSON, FAYE: Elizabeth, LA, July 8, 1917. San Diego State Col.

ENSERRO, MICHAEL: Soldier, PA, Oct. 5, 1918. Allegheny Col.

ERDMAN, RICHARD: Enid, OK, June 1, 1925.

ERICKSON, LEIF: Alameda, CA, Oct. 27, 1911. U. Calif.

ERICSON, JOHN: Dusseldorf, Ger., Sept. 25, 1926. AADA.

ESMOND, CARL: Vienna, June 14, 1906. U. Vienna.

EVANS, DALE (Francis Smith): Uvalde, TX, Oct. 31, 1912.

EVANS, GENE: Holbrook, AZ, July 11, 1922.

EVANS, MAURICE: Dorchester, Eng., June 3, 1901.

EVERETT, CHAD (Ray Cramton): South Bend, IN, June 11, 1936.

EWELL, TOM (Yewell Tompkins): Owensboro, KY, Apr. 29, 1909. U. Wisc.

FABARES, SHELLEY: Los Angeles, Jan. 19, 1944.

FABIAN (Fabian Forte): Philadelphia, Feb. 6, 1940.

FABRAY, NANETTE (Ruby Nanette Fabares): San Diego, Oct. 27, 1920.

FAIRBANKS, DOUGLAS JR.: NYC, Dec. 9, 1907. Collegiate School.

FALK, PETER: NYC, Sept. 16, 1927. New School.

FARENTINO, JAMES: Brooklyn, Feb. 24, 1938. AADA.

FARINA, SANDY (Sandra Feldman): Newark, NJ, 1955.

FARR, DEREK: London, Feb. 7, 1912.

FARR, FELICIA: Westchester, NY, Oct. 4, 1932. Penn State Col.

FARRELL, CHARLES: Onset Bay, MA, Aug. 9, 1901. Boston U.

FARROW, MIA: Los Angeles, Feb. 9, 1945.

FAULKNER, GRAHAM: London, Sept. 26, 1947. Webber-Douglas.

FAWCETT, FARRAH: Texas, Feb. 2, 1947.

FAYE, ALICE (Ann Leppert): NYC, May 5, 1912.

FEINSTEIN, ALAN: NYC, Sept. 8, 1941.

FELDON, BARBARA (Hall): Pittsburgh, Mar. 12, 1941. Carnegie Tech.

FELLOWS, EDITH: Boston, May 20, 1923.

FERRELL, CONCHATA: Charleston, WV, Mar. 28, 1943. Marshall U.

FERRER, JOSE: Santurce, P.R., Jan. 8, 1909. Princeton U.

FERRER, MEL: Elberon, NJ, Aug. 25, 1917. Princeton U.

FERRIS, BARBARA: London, 1943.

FERZETTI, GABRIELE: Italy, 1927. Rome Acad. of Drama.

FIELD, SALLY: Pasadena, CA, Nov. 6, 1946.

FIGUEROA, RUBEN: NYC 1958.

FINNEY, ALBERT: Salford, Lancashire, Eng., May 9, 1936. RADA.

FISHER, CARRIE: Los Angeles, CA, 1957. London Central School of Drama.

FISHER, EDDIE: Philadelphia, Aug. 10, 1928.

FITZGERALD, GERALDINE: Dublin, Ire., Nov. 24, 1914. Dublin Art School.

FLANNERY, SUSAN: Jersey City, NJ, July 31, 1943.

FLAVIN, JAMES: Portland, ME, May 14, 1906. West Point.

FLEMING, RHONDA (Marilyn Louis): Los Angeles, Aug. 10, 1922.

FLEMYNG, ROBERT: Liverpool, Eng., Jan. 3, 1912. Haileybury Col.

FLETCHER, LOUISE: Birmingham, AL, July 1934.

FOCH, NINA: Leyden, Holland, Apr. 20, 1924.

FOLDI, ERZSEBET: Queens, NY, 1967.

FONDA, HENRY: Grand Island, NB, May 16, 1905. Minn. U.

FONDA, JANE: NYC, Dec. 21, 1937. Vassar.

FONDA, PETER: NYC, Feb. 23, 1939. U. Omaha.

FONTAINE, JOAN: Tokyo, Japan, Oct. 22, 1917.

FORD, GLENN (Gwyllyn Samuel Newton Ford): Quebec, Can., May 1, 1916.

FORD, HARRISON: Chicago, IL, July 13, 1942. Ripon Col.

FOREST, MARK (Lou Degni): Brooklyn, Jan. 1933.

| Anthony Franciosa | Beverly Garland | James Franciscus | Teri Garr | Robert Goulet |

FORREST, STEVE: Huntsville, TX, Sept. 29, 1924. UCLA.

FORSTER, ROBERT (Foster, Jr.): Rochester, NY, July 13, 1941. Rochester U.

FORSYTHE, JOHN: Penn's Grove, NJ, Jan. 29, 1918.

FOSTER, JODIE: Bronx, NY, 1963.

FOX, EDWARD: London, 1937, RADA.

FOX, JAMES: London, 1939.

FOXWORTH, ROBERT: Houston, TX, Nov. 1, 1941. Carnegie Tech.

FOXX, REDD: St. Louis, MO, Dec. 9, 1922.

FRANCIOSA, ANTHONY: NYC, Oct. 25, 1928.

FRANCIS, ANNE: Ossining, NY, Sept. 16, 1932.

FRANCIS, ARLENE (Arlene Kazanjian): Boston, Oct. 20, 1908. Finch School.

FRANCIS, CONNIE (Constance Franconero): Newark, NJ, Dec. 12, 1938.

FRANCISCUS, JAMES: Clayton, MO, Jan. 31, 1934. Yale.

FRANCKS, DON: Vancouver, Can., Feb. 28, 1932.

FRANKLIN, PAMELA: Tokyo, Feb. 4, 1950.

FRANZ, ARTHUR: Perth Amboy, NJ, Feb. 29, 1920. Blue Ridge College.

FRANZ, EDUARD: Milwaukee, WI, Oct. 31, 1902.

FRAZIER, SHEILA: NYC, 1949.

FREEMAN, AL, JR.: San Antonio, TX, 1934. CCLA.

FREEMAN, MONA: Baltimore, MD, June 9, 1926.

FREY, LEONARD: Brooklyn, Sept. 4, 1938, Neighborhood Playhouse.

FULLER, PENNY: Durham, NC, 1940. Northwestern U.

FURNEAUX, YVONNE: Lille, France, 1928. Oxford U.

GABEL, MARTIN: Philadelphia, June 19, 1912. AADA.

GABOR, EVA: Budapest, Hungary, Feb. 11, 1920.

GABOR, ZSA ZSA (Sari Gabor): Budapest, Hungary, Feb. 6, 1918.

GAM, RITA: Pittsburgh, PA, Apr. 2, 1928.

GARBER, VICTOR: Montreal, Can., Mar. 16, 1949.

GARBO, GRETA (Greta Gustafson): Stockholm, Sweden, Sept. 18, 1905.

GARDENIA, VINCENT: Naples, Italy, Jan. 7, 1922.

GARDINER, REGINALD: Wimbledon, Eng., Feb. 27, 1903. RADA.

GARDNER, AVA: Smithfield, NC, Dec. 24, 1922. Atlantic Christian College.

GARFIELD, ALLEN: Newark, NJ, Nov. 22, 1939. Actors Studio.

GARLAND, BEVERLY: Santa Cruz, CA, Oct. 17, 1930. Glendale Col.

GARNER, JAMES (James Baumgarner): Norman, OK, Apr. 7, 1928. Okla. U.

GARNER, PEGGY ANN: Canton, OH, Feb. 3, 1932.

GARR, TERI: Lakewood, OH, 1952.

GARRETT, BETTY: St. Joseph, MO, May 23, 1919. Annie Wright Seminary.

GARRISON, SEAN: NYC, Oct. 19, 1937.

GARSON, GREER: Ireland, Sept. 29, 1906.

GASSMAN, VITTORIO: Genoa, Italy, Sept. 1, 1922. Rome Academy of Dramatic Art.

GAVIN, JOHN: Los Angeles, Apr. 8, 1935. Stanford U.

GAYNOR, JANET: Philadelphia, Oct. 6, 1906.

GAYNOR, MITZI (Francesca Marlene Von Gerber): Chicago, Sept. 4, 1930.

GAZZARA, BEN: NYC, Aug. 28, 1930. Actors Studio.

GEESON, JUDY: Arundel, Eng., Sept. 10, 1948. Corona.

GEORGE, CHIEF DAN (Geswanouth Slaholt): North Vancouver, Can., June 24, 1899.

GERARD, GIL: Little Rock, AR, 1940.

GERE, RICHARD: Philadelphia, PA, Aug. 29, 1949. U. Mass.

GHOLSON, JULIE: Birmingham, AL, June 4, 1958.

GHOSTLEY, ALICE: Eve, MO, Aug. 14, 1926. Okla U.

GIANNINI, GIANCARLO: Spezia, Italy, Aug. 1, 1942. Rome Acad. of Drama.

GIELGUD, JOHN: London, Apr. 14, 1904. RADA.

GILFORD, JACK: NYC, July 25.

GILLIS, ANNE (Alma O'Connor): Little Rock, AR, Feb. 12, 1927.

GILLMORE, MARGALO: London, May 31, 1897. AADA.

GILMORE, VIRGINIA (Sherman Poole): Del Monte, CA, July 26, 1919. U. Calif.

GINGOLD, HERMIONE: London, Dec. 9, 1897.

GISH, LILLIAN: Springfield, OH, Oct. 14, 1896.

GLASER, PAUL MICHAEL: Boston, MA, 1943. Boston U.

GLASS, RON: Evansville, IN, 1946.

GLEASON, JACKIE: Brooklyn, Feb. 26, 1916.

GODDARD, PAULETTE (Levy): Great Neck, NY, June 3, 1911.

GOLDBLUM, JEFF: Pittsburgh, PA, Oct. 22, 1952. Neighborhood Playhouse.

GOLDEN, ANNIE: NYC, 1952.

GONZALES-GONZALEZ, PEDRO: Aguilares, TX, Dec. 21, 1926.

GOODMAN, DODY: Columbus, OH, Oct. 28, 1915.

GORDON, GALE (Aldrich): NYC, Feb. 2, 1906.

GORDON, RUTH (Jones): Wollaston, MA, Oct. 30, 1896. AADA.

GORING, MARIUS: Newport, Isle of Wight, 1912. Cambridge, Old Vic.

GORMAN, CLIFF: Jamaica, NY, Oct. 13, 1936. NYU.

GORTNER, MARJOE: Long Beach, CA, 1944.

GOSSETT, LOUIS: Brooklyn, May 27, 1936. NYU.

GOULD, ELLIOTT (Goldstein): Brooklyn, Aug. 29, 1938. Columbia U.

GOULD, HAROLD: Schenectady, NY, Dec. 10, 1923. Cornell.

GOULET, ROBERT: Lawrence, MA, Nov. 26, 1933. Edmonton.

GRAHAME, GLORIA (Gloria Grahame Hallward): Los Angeles, Nov. 28, 1925.

GRANGER, FARLEY: San Jose, CA, July 1, 1925.

GRANGER, STEWART (James Stewart): London, May 6, 1913. Webber-Douglas School of Acting.

GRANT, CARY (Archibald Alexander Leach): Bristol, Eng., Jan. 18, 1904.

GRANT, DAVID MARSHALL: Westport, CT, 1955. Yale.

GRANT, KATHRYN (Olive Grandstaff): Houston, TX, Nov. 25, 1933. UCLA.

GRANT, LEE: NYC, Oct. 31, 1930. Juilliard.

GRANVILLE, BONITA: NYC, Feb. 2, 1923.

GRAVES, PETER (Aurness): Minneapolis, Mar. 18, 1926. U. Minn.

GRAY, COLEEN (Doris Jensen): Staplehurst, NB, Oct. 23, 1922. Hamline U.

GRAYSON, KATHRYN (Zelma Hedrick): Winston-Salem, NC, Feb. 9, 1922.

GREENE, ELLEN: NYC, Feb. 22. Ryder Col.

GREENE, LORNE: Ottawa, Can., Feb. 12, 1915. Queens U.

Harry Guardino   Joan Hackett   Rex Harrison   Goldie Hawn   Hal Holbrook

GREENE, RICHARD: Plymouth, Eng., Aug. 25, 1914. Cardinal Vaughn School.

GREENWOOD, JOAN: London, Mar. 4, 1919. RADA.

GREER, JANE: Washington, DC, Sept. 9, 1924.

GREER, MICHAEL: Galesburg, IL, Apr. 20, 1943.

GREY, JOEL (Katz): Cleveland, OH, Apr. 11, 1932.

GREY, VIRGINIA: Los Angeles, Mar. 22, 1917.

GRIEM, HELMUT: Hamburg, Ger. U. Hamburg.

GRIFFITH, ANDY: Mt. Airy, NC, June 1, 1926. UNC.

GRIFFITH, HUGH: Marian Glas, Anglesey, N. Wales, May 30, 1912.

GRIFFITH, MELANIE: NYC, Aug. 9, 1957. Pierce Col.

GRIMES, GARY: San Francisco, June 2, 1955.

GRIMES, TAMMY: Lynn, MA, Jan. 30, 1934. Stephens Col.

GRIZZARD, GEORGE: Roanoke Rapids, NC, Apr. 1, 1928. UNC.

GRODIN, CHARLES: Pittsburgh, PA, Apr. 21, 1935.

GROH, DAVID: NYC, May 21, 1939. Brown U., LAMDA.

GUARDINO, HARRY: Brooklyn, Dec. 23, 1925. Haaren High.

GUINNESS, ALEC: London, Apr. 2, 1914. Pembroke Lodge School.

GUNN, MOSES: St. Louis, MO, Oct. 2, 1929. Tenn. State U.

GUTTENBERG, STEVEN: Brooklyn, NY, 1958. UCLA.

GWILLIM, DAVID: Plymouth, Eng., Dec. 15, 1948. RADA.

HACKETT, BUDDY (Leonard Hacker): Brooklyn, Aug. 31, 1924.

HACKETT, JOAN: NYC, May 1, 1939. Actors Studio.

HACKMAN, GENE: San Bernardino, CA, Jan. 30, 1931.

HADDON, DALE: Montreal, Can., May 26, 1949. Neighborhood Playhouse.

HAGMAN, LARRY (Hageman): Texas, 1939. Bard Col.

HALE, BARBARA: DeKalb, IL, Apr. 18, 1922. Chicago Academy of Fine Arts.

HALL, ALBERT: Boothton, AL, Nov. 10, 1937. Columbia.

HAMILL, MARK: Oakland, CA, Sept. 25, 1952. LACC.

HAMILTON, GEORGE: Memphis, TN, Aug. 12, 1939. Hackley.

HAMILTON, MARGARET: Cleveland, OH, Dec. 9, 1902. Hathaway-Brown School.

HAMILTON, NEIL: Lynn, MA, Sept. 9, 1899.

HAMLIN, HARRY: Pasadena, CA, 1952. Yale.

HAMPSHIRE, SUSAN: London, May 12, 1941.

HARDIN, TY (Orison Whipple Hungerford II): NYC, June 1, 1930.

HARDING, ANN (Dorothy Walton Gatley): Fort Sam Houston, TX, Aug. 17, 1901.

HAREWOOD, DORIAN: Dayton, OH, Aug. 6. U. Cinn.

HARPER, VALERIE: Suffern, NY, Aug. 22, 1940.

HARRINGTON, PAT: NYC, Aug. 13, 1929. Fordham U.

HARRIS, BARBARA (Sandra Markowitz): Evanston, IL, 1937.

HARRIS, JULIE: Grosse Pointe, MI, Dec. 2, 1925. Yale Drama School.

HARRIS, RICHARD: Limerick, Ire., Oct. 1, 1930. London Acad.

HARRIS, ROSEMARY: Ashby, Eng., Sept. 19, 1930. RADA.

HARRISON, NOEL: London, Jan. 29, 1936.

HARRISON, REX: Huyton, Cheshire, Eng., Mar. 5, 1908.

HARTMAN, DAVID: Pawtucket, RI, May 19, 1942. Duke U.

HARTMAN, ELIZABETH: Youngstown, OH, Dec. 23, 1941. Carnegie Tech.

HASSETT, MARILYN: Los Angeles, CA, 1949.

HAVER, JUNE: Rock Island, IL, June 10, 1926.

HAVOC, JUNE (June Hovick): Seattle, WA, Nov. 8, 1916.

HAWN, GOLDIE: Washington, DC, Nov. 21, 1945.

HAYDEN, LINDA: Stanmore, Eng. Aida Foster School.

HAYDEN, STERLING (John Hamilton): Montclair, NJ, March 26, 1916.

HAYES, HELEN (Helen Brown): Washington, DC, Oct. 10, 1900. Sacred Heart Convent.

HAYWORTH, RITA (Margarita Cansino): NYC, Oct. 17, 1918.

HEARD, JOHN: Washington, DC, Mar. 7, 1946. Clark U.

HEATHERTON, JOEY: NYC, Sept. 14, 1944.

HECKART, EILEEN: Columbus, OH, Mar. 29, 1919. Ohio State U.

HEDISON, DAVID: Providence, RI, May 20, 1929. Brown U.

HEGYES, ROBERT: NJ, May 7, 1951.

HEMMINGS, DAVID: Guilford, Eng. Nov. 18, 1938.

HENDERSON, MARCIA: Andover, MA, July 22, 1932. AADA.

HENDRIX, WANDA: Jacksonville, FL, Nov. 3, 1928.

HENDRY, GLORIA: Jacksonville, FL, 1949.

HENNER, MARILU: NYC, Apr. 4, 1953.

HENREID, PAUL: Trieste, Jan. 10, 1908.

HENRY, BUCK (Zuckerman): NYC, 1931. Dartmouth.

HENRY, JUSTIN: Rye, NY, 1971.

HEPBURN, AUDREY: Brussels, Belgium, May 4, 1929.

HEPBURN, KATHARINE: Hartford, CT, Nov. 8, 1907. Bryn Mawr.

HERRMANN, EDWARD: Washington, DC, July 21, 1943. Bucknell, LAMDA.

HESTON, CHARLTON: Evanston, IL, Oct. 4, 1922. Northwestern U.

HEYWOOD, ANNE (Violet Pretty): Birmingham, Eng., Dec. 11, 1932.

HICKMAN, DARRYL: Hollywood, CA, July 28, 1930. Loyola U.

HICKMAN, DWAYNE: Los Angeles, May 18, 1934. Loyola U.

HILL, ARTHUR: Saskatchewan, Can., Aug. 1, 1922. U. Brit. Col.

HILL, STEVEN: Seattle, WA, Feb. 24, 1922. U. Wash.

HILL, TERENCE (Mario Girotti): Venice, Italy, Mar. 29, 1941. U. Rome.

HILLER, WENDY: Bramhall, Cheshire, Eng., Aug. 15, 1912. Winceby House School.

HILLIARD, HARRIET: (see Harriet Hilliard Nelson).

HINGLE, PAT: Denver, CO, July 19, 1923. Tex. U.

HIRSCH, JUDD: NYC, Mar. 15, 1935. AADA.

HOFFMAN, DUSTIN: Los Angeles, Aug. 8, 1937. Pasadena Playhouse.

HOLBROOK, HAL (Harold): Cleveland, OH, Feb. 17, 1925. Denison.

HOLDEN, WILLIAM: O'Fallon, IL, Apr. 17, 1918. Pasadena Jr. Coll.

HOLLIMAN, EARL: Tennesas Swamp, Delhi, LA, Sept. 11, 1928. UCLA.

HOLLOWAY, STANLEY: London, Oct. 1, 1890.

HOLM, CELESTE: NYC, Apr. 29, 1919.

HOMEIER, SKIP (George Vincent Homeier): Chicago, Oct. 5, 1930. UCLA.

| Robert Hooks | Gayle Hunnicutt | Richard Jaeckel | Madeline Kahn | Page Johnson |

HOOKS, ROBERT: Washington, DC, Apr. 18, 1937. Temple.

HOPE, BOB: London, May 26, 1903.

HOPPER, DENNIS: Dodge City, KS, May 17, 1936.

HORNE, LENA: Brooklyn, June 30, 1917.

HORTON, ROBERT: Los Angeles, July 29, 1924. UCLA.

HOUGHTON, KATHARINE: Hartford, CT, Mar. 10, 1945. Sarah Lawrence.

HOUSEMAN, JOHN: Bucharest, Sept. 22, 1902.

HOUSER, JERRY: Los Angeles, July 14, 1952. Valley Jr. Col.

HOUSTON, DONALD: Tonypandy, Wales, 1924.

HOVEY, TIM: Los Angeles, June 19, 1945.

HOWARD, KEN: El Centro, CA, Mar. 28, 1944. Yale.

HOWARD, RON: Duncan, OK, Mar. 1, 1954. USC.

HOWARD, RONALD: Norwood, Eng., Apr. 7, 1918. Jesus College.

HOWARD, TREVOR: Kent, Eng., Sept. 29, 1916. RADA.

HOWELLS, URSULA: London, Sept. 17, 1922.

HOWES, SALLY ANN: London, July 20, 1930.

HUDSON, ROCK (Roy Scherer Fitzgerald): Winnetka, IL, Nov. 17, 1924.

HUFFMAN, DAVID: Berwin, IL, May 10, 1945.

HUGHES, BARNARD: Bedford Hills, NY, July 16, 1915. Manhattan Col.

HUGHES, KATHLEEN (Betty von Gerkan): Hollywood, CA, Nov. 14, 1928. UCLA.

HULCE, THOMAS: Plymouth, MI, Dec. 6, 1953. N.C.Sch. of Arts.

HUNNICUTT, GAYLE: Ft. Worth, TX, Feb. 6, 1943. UCLA.

HUNT, MARSHA: Chicago, Oct. 17, 1917.

HUNTER, KIM (Janet Cole): Detroit, Nov. 12, 1922.

HUNTER, TAB (Arthur Galien): NYC, July 11, 1931.

HUPPERT, ISABELLE: Paris, Fr., Mar. 16, 1955.

HURT, WILLIAM: Washington, D.C., Mar. 20, 1950. Tufts, Juilliard.

HUSSEY, RUTH: Providence , RI, Oct. 30, 1917. U. Mich.

HUSTON, JOHN: Nevada, MO, Aug. 5, 1906.

HUTTON, BETTY (Betty Thornberg): Battle Creek, MI, Feb. 26, 1921.

HUTTON, LAUREN (Mary): Charleston, SC, Nov. 17, 1943. Newcomb Col.

HUTTON, ROBERT (Winne): Kingston, NY, June 11, 1920. Blair Academy.

HYDE-WHITE, WILFRID: Gloucestershire, Eng., May 13, 1903. RADA.

HYER, MARTHA: Fort Worth, TX, Aug. 10, 1924. Northwestern U.

INGELS, MARTY: Brooklyn, NY, Mar. 9, 1936.

IRELAND, JOHN: Vancouver, B.C., Can., Jan. 30, 1914.

IVES, BURL: Hunt Township, IL, June 14, 1909. Charleston Ill. Teachers College.

JACKSON, ANNE: Alleghany, PA, Sept. 3, 1926. Neighborhood Playhouse.

JACKSON, GLENDA: Hoylake, Cheshire, Eng., May 9, 1936. RADA.

JACOBI, LOU: Toronto, Can., Dec. 28, 1913.

JACOBS, LAWRENCE-HILTON: Virgin Islands, 1954.

JACOBY, SCOTT: Chicago, Nov. 19, 1956.

JAECKEL, RICHARD: Long Beach, NY, Oct. 10, 1926.

JAFFE, SAM: NYC, Mar. 8, 1892.

JAGGER, DEAN: Lima, OH, Nov. 7, 1903. Wabash College.

JAMES, CLIFTON: NYC, May 29, 1921. Ore. U.

JARMAN, CLAUDE, JR.: Nashville, TN, Sept. 27, 1934.

JASON, RICK: NYC, May 21, 1926. AADA.

JEAN, GLORIA (Gloria Jean Schoonover): Buffalo, NY, Apr. 14, 1927.

JEFFREYS, ANNE (Carmichael): Goldsboro, NC, Jan. 26, 1923. Anderson College.

JEFFRIES, LIONEL: London, 1927, RADA.

JERGENS, ADELE: Brooklyn, Nov. 26, 1922.

JESSEL, GEORGE: NYC, Apr. 3, 1898.

JOHNS, GLYNIS: Durban, S. Africa, Oct. 5, 1923.

JOHNSON, CELIA: Richmond, Surrey, Eng., Dec. 18, 1908. RADA.

JOHNSON, PAGE: Welch, WV, Aug. 25, 1930. Ithaca.

JOHNSON, RAFER: Hillsboro, TX, Aug. 18, 1935. UCLA.

JOHNSON, RICHARD: Essex, Eng., 1927. RADA.

JOHNSON, VAN: Newport, RI, Aug. 28, 1916.

JONES, CAROLYN: Amarillo, TX, Apr. 28, 1933.

JONES, CHRISTOPHER: Jackson, TN, Aug. 18, 1941. Actors Studio.

JONES, DEAN: Morgan County, AL, Jan. 25, 1936. Ashburn College.

JONES, JACK: Bel-Air, CA, Jan. 14, 1938.

JONES, JAMES EARL: Arkabutla, MS, Jan 17, 1931. U. Mich.

JONES, JENNIFER (Phyllis Isley): Tulsa, OK, Mar. 2, 1919. AADA.

JONES, SHIRLEY: Smithton, PA, March 31, 1934.

JONES, TOM (Thomas Jones Woodward): Pontypridd, Wales, June 7, 1940.

JONES, TOMMY LEE: San Saba, TX, Sept. 15, 1946. Harvard.

JORDAN, RICHARD: NYC, July 19, 1938. Harvard.

JORY, VICTOR: Dawson City, Can., Nov. 28, 1901. Cal. U.

JOURDAN, LOUIS: Marseilles, France, June 18, 1920.

JULIA, RAUL: San Juan, PR, Mar. 9, 1940. U PR.

JURADO, KATY (Maria Christina Jurado Garcia): Guadalajara, Mex., 1927.

KAHN, MADELINE: Boston, MA, Sept. 29, 1942. Hofstra U.

KANE, CAROL: Cleveland, OH, 1952.

KAPLAN, JONATHAN: Paris, Nov. 25, 1947. NYU.

KATT, WILLIAM: Los Angeles, CA, 1955.

KAUFMANN, CHRISTINE: Lansdorf, Graz, Austria, Jan. 11, 1945.

KAYE, DANNY (David Daniel Kominski): Brooklyn, Jan. 18, 1913.

KAYE, STUBBY: NYC, Nov. 11, 1918.

KEACH, STACY: Savannah, GA, June 2, 1941. U. Cal., Yale.

KEATON, DIANE (Hall): Los Angeles, CA, Jan. 5, 1946. Neighborhood Playhouse.

Aron Kincaid   Lila Kedrova   Harvey Korman   Kay Lenz   Sheldon Leonard

KEATS, STEVEN: Bronx, NY, 1945.

KEDROVA, LILA: Greece, 1918.

KEEL, HOWARD (Harold Keel): Gillespie, IL, Apr. 13, 1919.

KEELER, RUBY (Ethel): Halifax, N.S., Aug. 25, 1909.

KEITH, BRIAN: Bayonne, NJ, Nov. 14, 1921.

KELLER, MARTHE: Basel, Switz., 1945. Munich Stanislavsky Sch.

KELLERMAN, SALLY: Long Beach, CA, June 2, 1938. Actors Studio West.

KELLEY, DeFOREST: Atlanta, GA, Jan. 20, 1920.

KELLY, GENE: Pittsburgh, Aug. 23, 1912. U. Pittsburgh.

KELLY, GRACE: Philadelphia, Nov. 12, 1929. AADA.

KELLY, JACK: Astoria, NY, Sept. 16, 1927. UCLA.

KELLY, NANCY: Lowell, MA, Mar. 25, 1921. Bentley School.

KELLY, PATSY: Brooklyn, Jan. 12, 1910.

KEMP, JEREMY: Chesterfield, Eng., 1935, Central Sch.

KENNEDY, ARTHUR: Worcester, MA, Feb. 17, 1914. Carnegie Tech.

KENNEDY, GEORGE: NYC, Feb. 18, 1925.

KERR, DEBORAH: Helensburg, Scot., Sept. 30, 1921. Smale Ballet School.

KERR, JOHN: NYC, Nov. 15, 1931. Harvard, Columbia.

KHAMBATTA, PERSIS: Bombay, Oct. 2, 1950.

KIDDER, MARGOT: Yellow Knife, Can., Oct. 17, 1948. UBC.

KIER, UDO: Germany, Oct. 14, 1944.

KILEY, RICHARD: Chicago, Mar. 31, 1922. Loyola.

KINCAID, ARON (Norman Neale Williams III): Los Angeles, June 15, 1943. UCLA.

KING, ALAN: (Irwin Kniberg): Brooklyn, Dec. 26, 1927.

KING, PERRY: Alliance, OH, Apr. 30. Yale.

KITT, EARTHA: North, SC, Jan. 26, 1928.

KLEMPERER, WERNER: Cologne, Mar. 22, 1920.

KLUGMAN, JACK: Philadelphia, PA, Apr. 27, 1925. Carnegie Tech.

KNIGHT, ESMOND: East Sheen, Eng., May 4, 1906.

KNIGHT, SHIRLEY: Goessel, KS, July 5, 1937. Wichita U.

KNOWLES, PATRIC (Reginald Lawrence Knowles): Horsforth, Eng., Nov. 11, 1911.

KNOX, ALEXANDER: Strathroy, Ont., Can., Jan. 16, 1907.

KNOX, ELYSE: Hartford, CT, Dec. 14, 1917. Traphagen School.

KOENIG, WALTER: Chicago, IL, Sept. 14. UCLA.

KOHNER, SUSAN: Los Angeles, Nov. 11, 1936. U. Calif.

KORMAN, HARVEY: Chicago, IL, Feb. 15, 1927. Goodman.

KORVIN, CHARLES (Geza Korvin Karpathi): Czechoslovakia, Nov. 21. Sorbonne.

KOSLECK, MARTIN: Barkotzen, Ger., Mar. 24, 1907. Max Reinhardt School.

KOTTO, YAPHET: NYC, Nov. 15, 1937.

KREUGER, KURT: St. Moritz, Switz., July 23, 1917. U. London.

KRISTOFFERSON, KRIS: Brownsville, TX, 1936, Pomona Col.

KRUGER, HARDY: Berlin, Ger., April. 12, 1928.

KULP, NANCY: Harrisburg, PA, 1921.

KUNTSMANN, DORIS: Hamburg, 1944.

KWAN, NANCY: Hong Kong, May 19, 1939. Royal Ballet.

LACY, JERRY: Sioux City, IA, Mar. 27, 1936. LACC.

LADD, CHERYL (Stoppelmoor): Huron, SD, 1951.

LADD, DIANE (Ladnier): Meridian, MS, Nov. 29, 1932. Tulane U.

LAMARR, HEDY (Hedwig Kiesler): Vienna, Sept. 11, 1913.

LAMAS, FERNANDO: Buenos Aires, Jan. 9, 1920.

LAMAS, LORENZO: Los Angeles, Jan. 1958.

LAMB, GIL: Minneapolis, June 14, 1906. U. Minn.

LAMOUR, DOROTHY: Dec. 10, 1914. Spence School.

LANCASTER, BURT: NYC, Nov. 2, 1913. NYU.

LANCHESTER, ELSA (Elsa Sullivan): London, Oct. 28, 1902.

LANDAU, MARTIN: Brooklyn, NY, 1931. Actors Studio.

LANDON, MICHAEL (Eugene Orowitz): Collingswood, NJ, Oct. 31, 1936. USC.

LANE, ABBE: Brooklyn, Dec. 14, 1935.

LANE, DIANE: NYC, 1965.

LANGAN, GLENN: Denver, CO, July 8, 1917.

LANGE, HOPE: Redding Ridge, CT, Nov. 28, 1933. Reed Col.

LANGE, JESSICA: Minnesota, 1950. U. Minn.

LANGTON, PAUL: Salt Lake City, Apr. 17, 1913. Travers School of Theatre.

LANSBURY, ANGELA: London, Oct. 16, 1925. London Academy of Music.

LANSING, ROBERT (Brown): San Diego, CA, June 5, 1929.

LAURE, CAROLE: Montreal, Can., 1951.

LAURIE, PIPER (Rosetta Jacobs): Detroit, Jan. 22, 1932.

LAW, JOHN PHILLIP: Hollywood, Sept. 7, 1937. Neighborhood Playhouse, U. Hawaii.

LAWFORD, PETER: London, Sept. 7, 1923.

LAWRENCE, BARBARA: Carnegie, OK, Feb. 24, 1930. UCLA.

LAWRENCE, CAROL (Laraia): Melrose Park, IL, Sept. 5, 1935.

LAWRENCE, VICKI: Inglewood, CA, 1949.

LAWSON, LEIGH: Atherston, Eng., July 21, 1945. RADA.

LEACHMAN, CLORIS: Des Moines, IA, Apr. 30, 1930. Northwestern U.

LEAUD, JEAN-PIERRE: Paris, 1944.

LEDERER, FRANCIS: Karlin, Prague, Czech., Nov. 6, 1906.

LEE, CHRISTOPHER: London, May 27, 1922. Wellington College.

LEE, MICHELE (Dusiak): Los Angeles, June 24, 1942. LACC.

LEIBMAN, RON: NYC, Oct. 11, 1937. Ohio Wesleyan.

LEIGH, JANET (Jeanette Helen Morrison): Merced, CA, July 6, 1926. College of Pacific.

LEMBECK, HARVEY: Brooklyn, Apr. 15, 1923. U. Ala.

LEMMON, JACK: Boston, Feb. 8, 1925. Harvard.

LENZ, RICK: Springfield, IL, Nov. 21, 1939. U. Mich.

LEONARD, SHELDON (Bershad): NYC, Feb. 22, 1907. Syracuse U.

LEROY, PHILIPPE: Paris, Oct. 15, 1930. U. Paris.

LESLIE, BETHEL: NYC, Aug. 3, 1929. Brearley School.

LESLIE, JOAN (Joan Brodell): Detroit, Jan. 26, 1925. St. Benedict's.

LESTER, MARK: Oxford, Eng., July 11, 1958.

LEVENE, SAM: NYC, Aug. 28, 1905.

LEWIS, JERRY: Newark, NJ, Mar. 16, 1926.

LIGON, TOM: New Orleans, LA, Sept. 10, 1945.

Viveca Lindfors   Cleavon Little   Carol Lynley   Doug McClure   Walter Matthau

LILLIE, BEATRICE: Toronto, Can., May 29, 1898.

LINCOLN, ABBEY (Anna Marie Woolridge): Chicago, Aug. 6, 1930.

LINDFORS, VIVECA: Uppsala, Sweden, Dec. 29, 1920. Stockholm Royal Dramatic School.

LISI, VIRNA: Rome, 1938.

LITHGOW, JOHN: Rochester, NY, Oct. 19, 1945. Harvard.

LITTLE, CLEAVON: Chickasha, OK, June 1, 1939. San Diego State.

LOCKE, SONDRA: Shelbyville, TN, 1947.

LOCKHART, JUNE: NYC, June 25, 1925. Westlake School.

LOCKWOOD, GARY: Van Nuys, CA, Feb. 21, 1937.

LOCKWOOD, MARGARET: Karachi, Pakistan, Sept. 15, 1916. RADA.

LOLLOBRIGIDA, GINA: Subiaco, Italy, July 4, 1927. Rome Academy of Fine Arts.

LOM, HERBERT: Prague, Czechoslovakia, 1917. Prague U.

LOMEZ, CELINE: Montreal, Can., 1953.

LONDON, JULIE (Julie Peck): Santa Rosa, CA, Sept. 26, 1926.

LONOW, MARK: Brooklyn, N.Y.

LOPEZ, PERRY: NYC, July 22, 1931. NYU.

LORD, JACK (John Joseph Ryan): NYC, Dec. 30, 1928. NYU.

LOREN, SOPHIA: (Sofia Scicolone): Rome, Italy, Sept. 20, 1934.

LOUISE, TINA (Blacker): NYC, Feb. 11, 1934. Miami U.

LOVELACE, LINDA: Bryan, TX, 1952.

LOWITSCH, KLAUS: Berlin, Apr. 8, 1936. Vienna Academy.

LOY, MYRNA (Myrna Williams): Helena, MT, Aug. 2, 1905. Westlake School.

LUCAS, LISA: Arizona, 1961.

LULU: Glasglow, Scot., 1948.

LUND, JOHN: Rochester, NY, Feb. 6, 1913.

LUPINO, IDA: London, Feb. 4, 1916. RADA.

LYDON, JAMES: Harrington Park, NJ, May 30, 1923.

LYNDE, PAUL: Mt. Vernon, OH, June 13, 1926. Northwestern U.

LYNLEY, CAROL (Jones): NYC, Feb. 13, 1942.

LYNN, JEFFREY: Auburn, MA, 1909. Bates College.

LYON, SUE: Davenport, IA, July 10, 1946.

LYONS, ROBERT F.: Albany, NY. AADA.

MacARTHUR, JAMES: Los Angeles, Dec. 8, 1937. Harvard.

MacGINNIS, NIALL: Dublin, Ire., Mar. 29, 1913. Dublin U.

MacGRAW, ALI: NYC, Apr. 1, 1938. Wellesley.

MacLAINE, SHIRLEY (Beatty): Richmond, VA, Apr. 24, 1934.

MacMAHON, ALINE: McKeesport, PA, May 3, 1899. Barnard College.

MacMURRAY, FRED: Kankakee, IL, Aug. 30, 1908. Carroll Col.

MACNEE, PATRICK: London, Feb. 1922.

MacRAE, GORDON: East Orange, NJ, Mar. 12, 1921.

MADISON, GUY (Robert Moseley): Bakersfield, CA, Jan. 19, 1922. Bakersfield Jr. College.

MAHARIS, GEORGE: Astoria, NY, Sept. 1, 1928. Actors Studio.

MAHONEY, JOCK (Jacques O'-Mahoney): Chicago, Feb. 7, 1919. U. of Iowa.

MAJORS, LEE: Wyandotte, MI, Apr. 23, 1940. E. Ky. State Col.

MALDEN, KARL (Mladen Sekulovich): Gary, IN, Mar. 22, 1914.

MALONE, DOROTHY: Chicago, Jan. 30, 1925. S. Methodist U.

MANN, KURT: Roslyn, NY, July 18, 1947.

MANZ, LINDA: NYC, 1961.

MARAIS, JEAN: Cherbourg, France, Dec. 11, 1913. St. Germain.

MARGO (Maria Marguerita Guadalupe Boldoay Castilla): Mexico City, May 10, 1917.

MARGOLIN, JANET: NYC, July 25, 1943. Walden School.

MARIN, JACQUES: Paris, Sept. 9, 1919. Conservatoire National.

MARLOWE, HUGH (Hugh Hipple): Philadelphia, Jan. 30, 1914.

MARSHALL, BRENDA (Ardis Anderson Gaines): Isle of Negros, P.I., Sept. 29, 1915. Texas State College.

MARSHALL, E. G.: Owatonna, MN, June 18, 1910. U. Minn.

MARSHALL, PENNY: Bronx, NY, Oct. 15, 1942. U. N. Mex.

MARSHALL, WILLIAM: Gary, IN, Aug. 19, 1924. NYU.

MARTIN, DEAN (Dino Crocetti): Steubenville, OH, June 17, 1917.

MARTIN, DEAN PAUL: Los Angeles, CA, 1952. UCLA.

MARTIN, MARY: Weatherford, TX, Dec. 1, 1914. Ward-Belmont School.

MARTIN, STROTHER: Kokomo, IN, 1919. U. Mich.

MARTIN, TONY (Alfred Norris): Oakland, CA, Dec. 25, 1913. St. Mary's College.

MARVIN, LEE: NYC, Feb. 19, 1924.

MASON, JAMES: Huddersfield, Yorkshire, Eng., May 15, 1909. Cambridge.

MASON, MARSHA: St. Louis, MO, Apr. 3, 1942. Webster Col.

MASON, PAMELA (Pamela Kellino): Westgate, Eng., Mar. 10, 1918.

MASSEN, OSA: Copenhagen, Den., Jan. 13, 1916.

MASSEY, DANIEL: London, Oct. 10, 1933. Eton and King's Col.

MASSEY, RAYMOND: Toronto, Can., Aug. 30, 1896. Oxford.

MASTERSON, PETER: Angleton, TX, June 1, 1934. Rice U.

MASTROIANNI, MARCELLO: Fontana Liri, Italy, Sept. 28, 1924.

MATTHAU, WALTER (Matuschanskayasky): NYC, Oct. 1, 1920.

MATURE, VICTOR: Louisville, KY, Jan. 29, 1915.

MAY, ELAINE (Berlin): Philadelphia, Apr. 21, 1932.

MAYEHOFF, EDDIE: Baltimore, July 7. Yale.

McCALLUM, DAVID: Scotland, Sept. 19, 1933. Chapman Coll.

McCAMBRIDGE, MERCEDES: Jolliet, IL, March 17, 1918. Mundelein College.

McCARTHY, KEVIN: Seattle, WA, Feb. 15, 1914. Minn. U.

McCLORY, SEAN: Dublin, Ire., March 8, 1924. U. Galway.

McCLURE, DOUG: Glendale, CA, May 11, 1935. UCLA.

McCOWEN, ALEC: Tunbridge Wells, Eng., May 26, 1925. RADA.

McCREA, JOEL: Los Angeles, Nov. 5, 1905. Pomona College.

McDERMOTT, HUGH: Edinburgh, Scot., Mar. 20, 1908.

McDOWALL, RODDY: London, Sept. 17, 1928. St. Joseph's.

McDOWELL, MALCOLM (Taylor): Leeds, Eng., June 15, 1943. LAMDA.

McENERY, PETER: Walsall, Eng., Feb. 21, 1940.

McFARLAND, SPANKY: Dallas, TX, 1936.

Barbara McNair

Yvette Mimieux

Robert Morley

Liza Minnelli

Tony Musante

McGAVIN, DARREN: Spokane, WA, May 7, 1922. College of Pacific.

McGUIRE, BIFF: New Haven, CT, Oct. 25, 1926. Mass. State Col.

McGUIRE, DOROTHY: Omaha, NB, June 14, 1918.

McKAY, GARDNER: NYC, June 10, 1932. Cornell.

McKEE, LONETTE: Detroit, MI, 1954.

McKENNA, VIRGINIA: London, June 7, 1931.

McKUEN, ROD: Oakland, CA, Apr. 29, 1933.

McLERIE, ALLYN ANN: Grand Mere, Can., Dec. 1, 1926.

McNAIR, BARBARA: Chicago, March 4, 1939. UCLA.

McNALLY, STEPHEN (Horace McNally): NYC, July 29, 1913. Fordham U.

McNICHOLS, KRISTIE: Los Angeles, CA, Sept. 11, 1962.

McQUEEN, BUTTERFLY: Tampa, FL, Jan. 8, 1911. UCLA.

McQUEEN, STEVE: Slater, MO, Mar. 24, 1930.

MEADOWS, AUDREY Wuchang, China, 1919. St. Margaret's.

MEADOWS, JAYNE (formerly, Jayne Cotter): Wuchang, China, Sept. 27, 1920. St. Margaret's.

MEDWIN, MICHAEL: London, 1925. Instut Fischer.

MEEKER, RALPH (Ralph Rathgeber): Minneapolis, Nov. 21, 1920. Northwestern U.

MEKKA, EDDIE: Worcester, MA, 1932. Boston Cons.

MELATO, MARIANGELA: Milan, Italy, 1941. Milan Theatre Acad.

MELL, MARISA: Vienna, Austria, Feb. 25, 1939.

MERCADO, HECTOR JAIME: NYC, 1949. HB Studio.

MERCOURI, MELINA: Athens, Greece, Oct. 18, 1915.

MEREDITH, BURGESS: Cleveland, OH, Nov. 16, 1908. Amherst.

MEREDITH, LEE (Judi Lee Sauls): Oct., 1947. AADA.

MERKEL, UNA: Covington, KY, Dec. 10, 1903.

MERMAN, ETHEL (Ethel Zimmerman): Astoria, NY, Jan. 16, 1908.

MERRILL, DINA (Nedinia Hutton): NYC, Dec. 9, 1925. AADA.

MERRILL, GARY: Hartford, CT, Aug. 2, 1915. Bowdoin, Trinity.

MICHELL, KEITH: Adelaide, Aus., Dec. 1, 1926.

MIFUNE, TOSHIRO: Tsingtao, China, Apr. 1, 1920.

MILES, SARAH: Ingatestone, Eng., Dec. 31, 1941. RADA.

MILES, SYLVIA: NYC, Sept. 9, 1932.

MILES, VERA (Ralston): Boise City, OK, Aug. 23, 1929. UCLA.

MILFORD, PENELOPE: Winnetka, IL.

MILLAND, RAY (Reginald Truscott-Jones): Neath, Wales, Jan. 3, 1908. King's College.

MILLER, ANN (Lucille Ann Collier): Chireno, TX, Apr. 12, 1919. Lawler Professional School.

MILLER, JASON: Long Island City, NY, Apr. 22, 1939. Catholic U.

MILLER, LINDA: NYC, Sept. 16, 1942. Catholic U.

MILLER, MARVIN: St. Louis, July 18, 1913. Washington U.

MILLS, HAYLEY: London, Apr. 18, 1946. Elmhurst School.

MILLS, JOHN: Suffolk, Eng., Feb. 22, 1908.

MILNER, MARTIN: Detroit, MI, Dec. 28, 1931.

MIMIEUX, YVETTE: Los Angeles, Jan. 8, 1941. Hollywood High.

MINNELLI, LIZA: Los Angeles, Mar. 12, 1946.

MIRANDA, ISA (Isabella Sampietro): Milan, Italy, July 5, 1909.

MITCHELL, CAMERON: Dallastown, PA, Nov. 4, 1918. N.Y. Theatre School.

MITCHELL, JAMES: Sacramento, CA, Feb. 29, 1920. LACC.

MITCHUM, JAMES: Los Angeles, CA, May 8, 1941.

MITCHUM, ROBERT: Bridgeport, CT, Aug. 6, 1917.

MONTALBAN, RICARDO: Mexico City, Nov. 25, 1920.

MONTAND, YVES (Yves Montand Livi): Mansummano, Tuscany, Oct. 13, 1921.

MONTGOMERY, BELINDA: Winnipeg, Can., July 23, 1950.

MONTGOMERY, ELIZABETH: Los Angeles, Apr. 15, 1933. AADA.

MONTGOMERY, GEORGE (George Letz): Brady, MT, Aug. 29, 1916. U. Mont.

MONTGOMERY, ROBERT (Henry, Jr.): Beacon, NY, May 21, 1904.

MOON, KEITH: London, Aug. 23, 1947.

MOOR, BILL: Toledo, OH, July 13, 1931. Northwestern.

MOORE, CONSTANCE: Sioux City, IA, Jan. 18, 1919.

MOORE, DICK: Los Angeles, Sept. 12, 1925.

MOORE, FRANK: Bay-de-Verde, Newfoundland, 1946.

MOORE, KIERON: County Cork, Ire., 1925. St. Mary's College.

MOORE, MARY TYLER: Brooklyn, Dec. 29, 1936.

MOORE, ROGER: London, Oct. 14, 1927. RADA.

MOORE, TERRY (Helen Koford): Los Angeles, Jan. 7, 1929.

MORE, KENNETH: Gerrards Cross, Eng., Sept. 20, 1914.

MOREAU, JEANNE: Paris, Jan. 3, 1928.

MORENO, RITA (Rosita Alverio): Humacao, P.R., Dec. 11, 1931.

MORGAN, DENNIS (Stanley Morner): Prentice, WI, Dec. 10, 1910. Carroll College.

MORGAN, HARRY (HENRY) (Harry Bratsburg): Detroit, Apr. 10, 1915. U. Chicago.

MORGAN, MICHELE (Simone Roussel): Paris, Feb. 29, 1920. Paris Dramatic School.

MORIARTY, MICHAEL: Detroit, MI, Apr. 5, 1941. Dartmouth.

MORISON, PATRICIA: NYC, 1915.

MORLEY, ROBERT: Wiltshire, Eng., May 26, 1908. RADA.

MORRIS, GREG: Cleveland, OH, 1934. Ohio State.

MORRIS, HOWARD: NYC, Sept. 4, 1919. NYU.

MORROW, VIC: Bronx, NY, Feb. 14, 1932. Fla. Southern College.

MORSE, ROBERT: Newton, MA, May 18, 1931.

MOSS, ARNOLD: NYC, Jan. 28, 1910. CCNY.

MULLIGAN, RICHARD: NYC, Nov. 13, 1932.

MURPHY, GEORGE: New Haven, CT, July 4, 1902. Yale.

MURPHY, MICHAEL: Los Angeles, CA, 1949.

MURRAY, DON: Hollywood, July 31, 1929. AADA.

MURRAY, KEN (Don Court): NYC, July 14, 1903.

MUSANTE, TONY: Bridgeport, CT, June 30, 1936. Oberlin Col.

NADER, GEORGE: Pasadena, CA, Oct. 19, 1921. Occidental College.

NAPIER, ALAN: Birmingham, Eng., Jan. 7, 1903. Birmingham University.

NATWICK, MILDRED: Baltimore, June 19, 1908. Bryn Mawr.

NAUGHTON, JAMES: Middletown, CT, Dec. 6, 1945. Yale.

NEAL, PATRICIA: Packard, KY, Jan. 20, 1926. Northwestern U.

NEFF, HILDEGARDE (Hildegard Knef): Ulm, Ger., Dec. 28, 1925. Berlin Art Academy.

NELSON, BARRY (Robert Nielsen): Oakland, CA, 1920.

 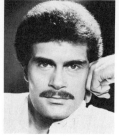   

| Olivia Newton-John | Don Nute | Glynnis O'Connor | Michael Ontkean | Estelle Parsons |

NELSON, DAVID: NYC, Oct. 24, 1936. USC.

NELSON, GENE (Gene Berg): Seattle, WA, Mar. 24, 1920.

NELSON, HARRIET HILLIARD (Peggy Lou Snyder): Des Moines, IA, July 18.

NELSON, LORI (Dixie Kay Nelson): Santa Fe, NM, Aug. 15, 1933.

NELSON, RICK (Eric Hilliard Nelson): Teaneck, NJ, May 8, 1940.

NESBITT, CATHLEEN: Cheshire, Eng., Nov. 24, 1889. Victoria College.

NEWHART, BOB: Chicago, IL, Sept. 5, 1929. Loyola U.

NEWLEY, ANTHONY: Hackney, London, Sept. 21, 1931.

NEWMAN, BARRY: Boston, MA, Mar. 26, 1938. Brandeis U.

NEWMAN, PAUL: Cleveland, OH, Jan. 26, 1925. Yale.

NEWMAR, JULIE (Newmeyer): Los Angeles, Aug. 16, 1935.

NEWTON-JOHN, OLIVIA: Cambridge, Eng., 1949.

NICHOLAS, PAUL: London, 1945.

NICHOLS, MIKE (Michael Igor Peschkowsky): Berlin, Nov. 6, 1931. U. Chicago.

NICHOLSON, JACK: Neptune, NJ, Apr. 22, 1937.

NICKERSON, DENISE: NYC, 1959.

NICOL, ALEX: Ossining, NY, Jan. 20, 1919. Actors Studio.

NIELSEN, LESLIE: Regina, Saskatchewan, Can., Feb. 11, 1926. Neighborhood Playhouse

NIMOY, LEONARD: Boston, MA, Mar. 26, 1931. Boston Col., Antioch Col.

NIVEN, DAVID: Kirriemuir, Scot., Mar. 1, 1909. Sandhurst College.

NOLAN, LLOYD: San Francisco, Aug. 11, 1902. Stanford U.

NOLTE, NICK: Omaha, NB, 1941.

NORRIS, CHRISTOPHER: NYC, Oct. 7, 1943. Lincoln Square Acad.

NORTH, HEATHER: Pasadena, CA, Dec. 13, 1950. Actors Workshop.

NORTH, SHEREE (Dawn Bethel): Los Angeles, Jan. 17, 1933. Hollywood High.

NORTON, KEN: Aug. 9, 1945.

NOVAK, KIM (Marilyn Novak): Chicago, Feb. 18, 1933. LACC.

NUGENT, ELLIOTT: Dover, OH, Sept. 20, 1900. Ohio State U.

NUREYEV, RUDOLF: Russia, Mar. 17, 1938.

NUTE, DON: Connellsville, PA, Mar. 13. Denver U.

NUYEN, FRANCE (Vannga): Marseilles, France, July 31, 1939. Beaux Arts School.

OATES, WARREN: Depoy, KY, July 5, 1928.

O'BRIAN, HUGH (Hugh J. Krampe): Rochester, NY, Apr. 19, 1928. Cincinnati U.

O'BRIEN, CLAY: Ray, AZ, May 6, 1961.

O'BRIEN, EDMOND: NYC, Sept. 10, 1915. Fordham, Neighborhood Playhouse.

O'BRIEN, MARGARET (Angela Maxine O'Brien): Los Angeles, Jan. 15, 1937.

O'BRIEN, PAT: Milwaukee, Nov. 11, 1899. Marquette U.

O'CONNELL, ARTHUR: NYC, Mar. 29, 1908. St. John's.

O'CONNOR, CARROLL: Bronx, NY, Aug. 2, 1925. Dublin National Univ.

O'CONNOR, DONALD: Chicago, Aug. 28, 1925.

O'CONNOR, GLYNNIS: NYC, Nov. 19, 1956. NYSU.

O'CONNOR, KEVIN: Honolulu, HI, May 7. U. Hi.

O'HANLON, GEORGE: Brooklyn, NY, Nov. 23, 1917.

O'HARA, MAUREEN (Maureen FitzSimons): Dublin, Ire., Aug. 17, 1920. Abbey School.

O'HERLIHY, DAN: Wexford, Ire., May 1, 1919. National U.

OLIVIER, LAURENCE: Dorking, Eng., May 22, 1907. Oxford.

O'LOUGHLIN, GERALD S.: NYC, Dec. 23, 1921. U. Rochester.

OLSON, NANCY: Milwaukee, WI, July 14. UCLA.

O'NEAL, PATRICK: Ocala, FL, Sept. 26, 1927. U. Fla.

O'NEAL, RON: Utica, NY, Sept. 1, 1937. Ohio State.

O'NEAL, RYAN: Los Angeles, Apr. 20, 1941.

O'NEAL, TATUM: Los Angeles, Nov. 5, 1963.

O'NEIL, TRICIA: Shreveport, LA, Mar. 11, 1945. Baylor U.

O'NEILL, JENNIFER: Rio de Janeiro, Feb. 20, 1949. Neighborhood Playhouse.

O'SULLIVAN, MAUREEN: Byle, Ire., May 17, 1911. Sacred Heart Convent.

O'TOOLE, ANNETTE: Houston, TX, 1953. UCLA.

O'TOOLE, PETER: Connemara, Ireland, Aug. 2, 1932. RADA.

PACINO, AL: NYC, Apr. 25, 1940.

PAGE, GERALDINE: Kirksville, MO, Nov. 22, 1924. Goodman School.

PAGET, DEBRA (Debralee Griffin): Denver, Aug. 19, 1933.

PAIGE, JANIS (Donna Mae Jaden): Tacoma, WA, Sept. 16, 1922.

PALANCE, JACK (Walter Palanuik): Lattimer, PA, Feb. 18, 1920. UNC.

PALMER, BETSY: East Chicago, IN, Nov. 1, 1929. DePaul U.

PALMER, GREGG (Palmer Lee): San Francisco, Jan. 25, 1927. U. Utah.

PALMER, LILLI: Posen, Austria, May 24, 1914. Ilka Gruning School.

PALMER, MARIA: Vienna, Sept. 5, 1924. College de Bouffement.

PAMPANINI, SILVANA: Rome, Sept. 25, 1925.

PAPAS, IRENE: Chiliomodion, Greece, Mar. 9, 1929.

PARKER, ELEANOR: Cedarville, OH, June 26, 1922. Pasadena Playhouse.

PARKER, FESS: Fort Worth, TX, Aug. 16, 1927. USC.

PARKER, JEAN (Mae Green): Deer Lodge, MT, Aug. 11, 1912.

PARKER, SUZY (Cecelia Parker): San Antonio, TX, Oct. 28, 1933.

PARKER, WILLARD (Worster Van Eps): NYC, Feb. 5, 1912.

PARKINS, BARBARA: Vancouver, Can., May 22, 1943.

PARSONS, ESTELLE: Lynn, MA, Nov. 20, 1927. Boston U.

PATRICK, DENNIS: Philadelphia, Mar. 14, 1918.

PATRICK, NIGEL: London, May 2, 1913.

PATTERSON, LEE: Vancouver, Can., Mar. 31, 1929. Ontario Col.

PAVAN, MARISA (Marisa Pierangeli): Cagliari, Sardinia, June 19, 1932. Torquado Tasso College.

PEACH, MARY: Durban, S. Africa, 1934.

PEARSON, BEATRICE: Denison, TX, July 27, 1920.

PECK, GREGORY: La Jolla, CA, Apr. 5, 1916. U. Calif.

PEPPARD, GEORGE: Detroit, Oct. 1, 1928. Carnegie Tech.

PERKINS, ANTHONY: NYC, Apr. 14, 1932. Rollins College.

PERREAU, GIGI (Ghislaine): Los Angeles, Feb. 6, 1941.

PERRINE, VALERIE: Galveston, TX, Sept. 3, 1944. U. Ariz.

PESCOW, DONNA: Brooklyn, NY, 1954.

PETERS, BERNADETTE: Jamaica, NY, Feb. 28, 1948.

Michelle Phillips

William Prince

Martha Raye

Christopher Reeve

Barbara Rhoades

PETERS, BROCK: NYC, July 2, 1927. CCNY.

PETERS, JEAN (Elizabeth): Canton, OH, Oct. 15, 1926. Ohio State U.

PETTET, JOANNA: London, Nov. 16, 1944. Neighborhood Playhouse.

PHILLIPS, MacKENZIE: Hollywood, CA, 1960.

PHILLIPS, MICHELLE (Holly Gilliam): NJ, June 4, 1944.

PICERNI, PAUL: NYC, Dec. 1, 1922. Loyola U.

PICKENS, SLIM (Louis Bert Lindley, Jr.): Kingsberg, CA, June 29, 1919.

PIDGEON, WALTER: East St. John, N.B., Can., Sept. 23, 1897.

PINE, PHILLIP: Hanford, CA, July 16, 1925. Actors' Lab.

PISIER, MARIE-FRANCE: Vietnam, May 10, 1944. U. Paris.

PLACE, MARY KAY: Port Arthur, TX, Sept., 1947. U. Tulsa.

PLAYTEN, ALICE: NYC, Aug. 28, 1947. NYU.

PLEASENCE, DONALD: Workshop, Eng, Oct. 5, 1919. Sheffield School.

PLESHETTE, SUZANNE: NYC, Jan. 31, 1937. Syracuse U.

PLUMMER, CHRISTOPHER: Toronto, Can., Dec. 13, 1927.

PODESTA, ROSSANA: Tripoli, June 20, 1934.

POITIER, SIDNEY: Miami, FL, Feb. 27, 1924.

POLITO, LINA: Naples, Italy, Aug. 11, 1954.

POLLARD, MICHAEL J. Pacific, NJ, May 30, 1939.

PORTER, ERIC: London, Apr. 8, 1928. Wimbledon Col.

POWELL, ELEANOR: Springfield, MA, Nov. 21, 1912.

POWELL, JANE (Suzanne Burce): Portland, OR, Apr. 1, 1928.

POWELL, ROBERT: London, June 1, 1944.

POWELL, WILLIAM: Pittsburgh, July 29, 1892. AADA.

POWER, TARYN: Los Angeles, CA, 1954.

POWERS, MALA (Mary Ellen): San Francisco, Dec. 29, 1921. UCLA.

PRENTISS, PAULA (Paula Ragusa): San Antonio, TX, Mar. 4, 1939. Northwestern U.

PRESLE, MICHELINE (Micheline Chassagne): Paris, Aug. 22, 1922. Rouleau Drama School.

PRESNELL, HARVE: Modesto, CA, Sept. 14, 1933. USC.

PRESTON, ROBERT (Robert Preston Meservey): Newton Highlands, MA, June 8, 1913. Pasadena Playhouse.

PRICE, VINCENT: St. Louis, May 27, 1911. Yale.

PRIMUS, BARRY: NYC, Feb. 16, 1938. CCNY.

PRINCE, WILLIAM: Nicholas, NY, Jan. 26, 1913. Cornell U.

PRINCIPAL, VICTORIA: Tokyo, Jan. 3, 1945. Dade Jr. Col.

PROVAL, DAVID: Brooklyn, NY, 1943.

PROVINE, DOROTHY: Deadwood, SD, Jan. 20, 1937. U. Wash.

PROWSE, JULIET: Bombay, India, Sept. 25, 1936.

PRYOR, RICHARD: Peoria, IL, Dec. 1, 1940.

PURCELL, LEE: Cherry Point, NC, June 15, 1947. Stephens.

PURCELL, NOEL: Dublin, Ire., Dec. 23, 1900. Irish Christian Brothers.

PURDOM, EDMUND: Welwyn Garden City, Eng., Dec. 19, 1924. St. Ignatius College.

PYLE, DENVER: Bethune, CO, 1920.

QUAYLE, ANTHONY: Lancashire, Eng., Sept. 7, 1913. Old Vic School.

QUINE, RICHARD: Detroit, MI, Nov. 12, 1920.

QUINLAN, KATHLEEN: Mill Valley, CA, Nov. 19, 1954.

QUINN, ANTHONY: Chihuahua, Mex., Apr. 21, 1915.

RAFFERTY, FRANCES: Sioux City, IA, June 16, 1922. UCLA.

RAFFIN, DEBORAH: Los Angeles, Mar. 13, 1953. Valley Col.

RAFT, GEORGE: NYC, Sept. 27, 1895.

RAINES, ELLA (Ella Wallace): Snoqualmie Falls, WA, Aug. 6, 1921. U. Wash.

RAMPLING, CHARLOTTE: Surmer, Eng., Feb. 5, 1946. U. Madrid.

RAMSEY, LOGAN: Long Beach, CA, Mar. 21, 1921. St. Joseph.

RANDALL, TONY: Tulsa, OK, Feb. 26, 1920. Northwestern U.

RANDELL, RON: Sydney, Australia, Oct. 8, 1920. St. Mary's Col.

RASULALA, THALMUS (Jack Crowder): Miami, FL, Nov. 15, 1939. U. Redlands.

RAY, ALDO (Aldo DeRe): Pen Argyl, PA, Sept. 25, 1926. UCLA.

RAYE, MARTHA (Margie Yvonne Reed): Butte, MT, Aug. 27, 1916.

RAYMOND, GENE (Raymond Guion): NYC, Aug. 13, 1908.

REAGAN, RONALD: Tampico, IL, Feb. 6, 1911. Eureka College.

REASON, REX: Berlin, Ger., Nov. 30, 1928. Pasadena Playhouse.

REDDY, HELEN: Australia, Oct. 25, 1942.

REDFORD, ROBERT: Santa Monica, CA, Aug. 18, 1937. AADA.

REDGRAVE, CORIN: London, July 16, 1939.

REDGRAVE, LYNN: London, Mar. 8, 1943.

REDGRAVE, MICHAEL: Bristol, Eng., Mar. 20, 1908. Cambridge.

REDGRAVE, VANESSA: London, Jan. 30, 1937.

REDMAN, JOYCE: County Mayo, Ire., 1919. RADA.

REED, DONNA (Donna Mullenger): Denison, IA, Jan. 27, 1921. LACC.

REED, OLIVER: Wimbledon, Eng., Feb. 13, 1938.

REED, REX: Ft. Worth, TX, Oct. 2, 1939. LSU.

REEMS, HARRY (Herbert Streicher): Bronx, NY, 1947. U. Pittsburgh.

REEVE, CHRISTOPHER: NJ, Sept. 25, 1952. Cornell, Juilliard.

REEVES, STEVE: Glasgow, MT, Jan. 21, 1926.

REID, ELLIOTT: NYC, Jan. 16, 1920.

REINER, CARL: NYC, Mar. 20, 1922. Georgetown.

REINER, ROBERT: NYC, 1945. UCLA.

REMICK, LEE: Quincy, MA, Dec. 14, 1935. Barnard College.

RETTIG, TOMMY: Jackson Heights, NY, Dec. 10, 1941.

REVILL, CLIVE: Wellington, NZ, Apr. 18, 1930.

REY, FERNANDO: La Coruna, Spain, 1917.

REYNOLDS, BURT: West Palm Beach, FL, Feb. 11, 1935. Fla. State U.

REYNOLDS, DEBBIE (Mary Frances Reynolds): El Paso, TX, Apr. 1, 1932.

REYNOLDS, MARJORIE: Buhl, ID, Aug. 12, 1921.

RHOADES, BARBARA: Poughkeepsie, NY, 1947.

RICH, IRENE: Buffalo, NY, Oct. 13, 1891. St. Margaret's School.

RICHARDS, JEFF (Richard Mansfield Taylor): Portland, OR, Nov. 1. USC.

RICHARDSON, RALPH: Cheltenham, Eng., Dec. 19, 1902.

RICKLES, DON: NYC, May 8, 1926. AADA.

| Eric Roberts | Diana Ross | Cliff Robertson | Susan Sarandon | Arnold Schwartzenegger |

RIGG, DIANA: Doncaster, Eng., July 20, 1938. RADA.

RITTER, JOHN: Burbank, CA, 1949. U. S. Cal.

ROBARDS, JASON: Chicago, July 26, 1922. AADA.

ROBBINS, GALE: Chicago, IL, May 7, 1932.

ROBERTS, ERIC: Biloxi, MS, 1956. RADA.

ROBERTS, RACHEL: Llanelly, Wales, Sept. 20, 1927. RADA.

ROBERTS, RALPH: Salisbury, NC, Aug. 17, 1922. UNC.

ROBERTS, TONY: NYC, Oct. 22, 1939. Northwestern U.

ROBERTSON, CLIFF: La Jolla, CA, Sept. 9, 1925. Antioch Col.

ROBERTSON, DALE: Oklahoma City, July 14, 1923.

ROBINSON, CHRIS: Nov. 5, 1938, West Palm Beach, FL. LACC.

ROBINSON, JAY: NYC, Apr. 14, 1930.

ROBINSON, ROGER: Seattle, WA, May 2, 1941. USC.

ROBSON, FLORA: South Shields, Eng., Mar. 28, 1902. RADA.

ROCHESTER (Eddie Anderson): Oakland, CA, Sept. 18, 1905.

ROGERS, CHARLES "BUDDY": Olathe, KS, Aug. 13, 1904. U. Kan.

ROGERS, GINGER (Virginia Katherine McMath): Independence, MO, July 16, 1911.

ROGERS, ROY (Leonard Slye): Cincinnati, Nov. 5, 1912.

ROGERS, WAYNE: Birmingham, AL, Apr. 7, 1933. Princeton.

ROLAND, GILBERT (Luis Antonio Damaso De Alonso): Juarez, Mex., Dec. 11, 1905.

ROMAN, RUTH: Boston, Dec. 23, 1922. Bishop Lee Dramatic School.

ROMERO, CESAR: NYC, Feb. 15, 1907. Collegiate School.

ROONEY, MICKEY (Joe Yule, Jr.): Brooklyn, Sept. 23, 1920.

ROSS, DIANA: Detroit, MI, Mar. 26, 1945.

ROSS, KATHARINE: Hollywood, Jan. 29, 1943. Santa Rosa Col.

ROSSITER, LEONARD: Liverpool, Eng., Oct. 21, 1926.

ROUNDS, DAVID: Bronxville, NY, Oct. 9, 1938. Denison U.

ROUNDTREE, RICHARD: New Rochelle, NY, Sept. 7, 1942. Southern Ill.

ROWLANDS, GENA: Cambria, WI, June 19, 1936.

RUBIN, ANDREW: New Bedford, MA, June 22, 1946. AADA.

RUDD, PAUL: Boston, MA, May 15, 1940.

RULE, JANICE: Cincinnati, OH, Aug. 15, 1931.

RUPERT, MICHAEL: Denver, CO, Oct. 23, 1951. Pasadena Playhouse.

RUSH, BARBARA: Denver, CO, Jan. 4. 1929. U. Calif.

RUSSELL, JANE: Bemidji, MI, June 21, 1921. Max Reinhardt School.

RUSSELL, JOHN: Los Angeles, Jan. 3, 1921. U. Calif.

RUSSELL, KURT: Springfield, MA, March 17, 1951.

RUTHERFORD, ANN: Toronto, Can., Nov. 2, 1917.

RUYMEN, AYN: Brooklyn, July 18, 1947. HB Studio.

SAINT, EVA MARIE: Newark, NJ, July 4, 1924. Bowling Green State U.

ST. JACQUES, RAYMOND (James Arthur Johnson): CT.

ST. JAMES, SUSAN: Los Angeles, Aug. 14. Conn. Col.

ST. JOHN, BETTA: Hawthorne, CA, Nov. 26, 1929.

ST. JOHN, JILL (Jill Oppenheim): Los Angeles, Aug. 19, 1940.

SALMI, ALBERT: Coney Island, NY, 1925. Actors Studio.

SALT, JENNIFER: Los Angeles, Sept. 4, 1944. Sarah Lawrence Col.

SANDS, TOMMY: Chicago, Aug. 27, 1937.

SAN JUAN, OLGA: NYC, Mar. 16, 1927.

SARANDON, CHRIS: Beckley, WV, July 24, 1942. U. WVa., Catholic U.

SARANDON, SUSAN (Tomaling): NYC, Oct. 4, 1946. Catholic U.

SARGENT, RICHARD (Richard Cox): Carmel, CA, 1933. Stanford.

SARRAZIN, MICHAEL: Quebec City, Can., May 22, 1940.

SAVAGE, JOHN (Youngs): Long Island, NY, Aug. 25, 1949. AADA.

SAVALAS, TELLY (Aristotle): Garden City, NY, Jan. 21, 1925. Columbia.

SAVOY, TERESA ANN: London, July 18, 1955.

SAXON, JOHN (Carmen Orrico): Brooklyn, Aug. 5, 1935.

SCHEIDER, ROY: Orange, NJ, Nov. 10, 1935. Franklin-Marshall.

SCHELL, MARIA: Vienna, Jan. 15, 1926.

SCHELL, MAXIMILIAN: Vienna, Dec. 8, 1930.

SCHNEIDER, MARIA: Paris, Mar. 27, 1952.

SCHNEIDER, ROMY: Vienna, Sept. 23, 1938.

SCHRODER, RICKY: Staten Island, NY, Apr. 13, 1970.

SCHWARZENEGGER, ARNOLD: Austria, 1947.

SCOFIELD, PAUL: Hurstpierpoint, Eng., Jan. 21, 1922. London Mask Theatre School.

SCOTT, GEORGE C.: Wise, VA, Oct. 18, 1927. U. Mo.

SCOTT, GORDON (Gordon M. Werschkul): Portland, OR, Aug. 3, 1927. Oregon U.

SCOTT, MARTHA: Jamesport, MO, Sept. 22, 1914. U. Mich.

SCOTT, RANDOLPH: Orange County, VA, Jan. 23, 1903. UNC.

SCOTT-TAYLOR, JONATHAN: Brazil, 1962.

SEAGULL, BARBARA HERSHEY (Herzstein): Hollywood, Feb. 5, 1948.

SEARS, HEATHER: London, 1935.

SECOMBE, HARRY: Swansea, Wales, Sept. 8, 1921.

SEGAL, GEORGE: NYC, Feb. 13, 1934. Columbia.

SELLARS, ELIZABETH: Glasgow, Scot., May 6, 1923.

SELLERS, PETER: Southsea, Eng., Sept. 8, 1925. Aloysius College.

SELWART, TONIO: Watenberg, Ger., June 9, 1906. Munich U.

SERNAS, JACQUES: Lithuania, July 30, 1925.

SEYLER, ATHENE (Athene Hannen): London, May 31, 1889.

SEYMOUR, ANNE: NYC, Sept. 11, 1909. American Laboratory Theatre.

SEYMOUR, JANE: Hillingdon, Eng., Feb. 15, 1951.

SHARIF, OMAR (Michel Shalboub): Alexandria, Egypt, Apr. 10, 1932. Victoria Col.

SHATNER, WILLIAM: Montreal, Can., Mar. 22, 1931. McGill U.

SHAW, SEBASTIAN: Holt, Eng., May 29, 1905. Gresham School.

SHAW, STAN: Chicago, IL, 1952.

SHAWLEE, JOAN: Forest Hills, NY, Mar. 5, 1929.

SHAWN, DICK (Richard Shulefand): Buffalo, NY, Dec. 1, 1929. U. Miami.

SHEARER, MOIRA: Dunfermline, Scot., Jan. 17, 1926. London Theatre School.

SHEARER, NORMA: Montreal, Can., Aug. 10, 1900.

SHEEN, MARTIN (Ramon Estevez): Dayton, OH, Aug. 3, 1940.

SHEFFIELD, JOHN: Pasadena, CA, Apr. 11, 1931. UCLA.

227

| **Maggie Smith** | **Sam Shepard** | **Sissy Spacek** | **O. J. Simpson** | **Beatrice Straight** |

SHEPARD, SAM (Rogers): Ft. Sheridan, IL, Nov. 5, 1943.

SHEPHERD, CYBIL: Memphis, TN, Feb. 18, 1950. Hunter, NYU.

SHIELDS, BROOKE: NYC, May 31, 1965.

SHIRE, TALIA: Lake Success, NY. Yale.

SHORE, DINAH (Frances Rose Shore): Winchester, TN, Mar. 1, 1917. Vanderbilt U.

SHOWALTER, MAX (formerly Casey Adams): Caldwell, KS, June 2, 1917. Pasadena Playhouse.

SIDNEY, SYLVIA: NYC, Aug. 8, 1910. Theatre Guild School.

SIGNORET, SIMONE (Simone Kaminker): Wiesbaden, Ger., Mar. 25, 1921. Solange Sicard School.

SILVERS, PHIL (Philip Silversmith): Brooklyn, May 11, 1911.

SIMMONS, JEAN: London, Jan. 31, 1929. Aida Foster School.

SIMON, SIMONE: Marseilles, France, Apr. 23, 1910.

SIMPSON, O. J. (Orenthal James): San Francisco, CA, July 9, 1947. UCLA.

SINATRA, FRANK: Hoboken, NJ, Dec. 12, 1915.

SINDEN, DONALD: Plymouth, Eng., Oct. 9, 1923. Webber-Douglas.

SKALA, LILIA: Vienna; U. Dresden.

SKELTON, RED (Richard): Vincennes, IN, July 18, 1910.

SKERRITT, TOM: Detroit, MI, 1935. Wayne State U.

SLEZAK, WALTER: Vienna, Austria, May 3, 1902.

SMITH, ALEXIS: Penticton, Can., June 8, 1921. LACC.

SMITH, CHARLES MARTIN: Los Angeles, CA, 1954. CalState U.

SMITH, JOHN (Robert E. Van Orden): Los Angeles, Mar. 6, 1931. UCLA.

SMITH, KATE (Kathryn Elizabeth): Greenville, VA, May 1, 1909.

SMITH, KENT: NYC, Mar. 19, 1907. Harvard U.

SMITH, LOIS: Topeka, KS, Nov. 3, 1930. U. Wash.

SMITH, MAGGIE: Ilford, Eng., Dec. 28, 1934.

SMITH, ROGER: South Gate, CA, Dec. 18, 1932. U. Ariz.

SMITHERS, WILLIAM: Richmond, VA, July 10, 1927. Catholic U.

SNODGRESS, CARRIE: Chicago, Oct. 27, 1946. UNI.

SNOWDEN, LEIGH: Memphis, TN, June 28, 1932. Lambeth Col.

SOLOMON, BRUCE: NYC, 1944. U. Miami, Wayne State U.

SOMERS, SUZANNE (Mahoney): San Bruno, CA, Oct. 16, 1946. Lone Mt. Col.

SOMMER, ELKE: Berlin, Nov. 5, 1940.

SONNY (Salvatore Bono): 1935.

SORDI, ALBERTO: Rome, Italy, 1919.

SORVINO, PAUL: NYC, 1939. AMDA.

SOTHERN, ANN (Harriet Lake): Valley City, ND, Jan. 22, 1907. Washington U.

SPACEK, SISSY: Quitman, TX, Dec. 25, 1949. Actors Studio.

SPENSER, JEREMY: Ceylon, 1937.

SPRINGER, GARY: NYC, July 29, 1954. Hunter Col.

STACK, ROBERT: Los Angeles, Jan. 13, 1919. USC.

STADLEN, LEWIS J.: Brooklyn, Mar. 7, 1947. Neighborhood Playhouse.

STALLONE, SYLVESTER: NYC, 1946. U. Miami.

STAMP, TERENCE: London, 1940.

STANDER, LIONEL: NYC, Jan. 11, 1908. UNC.

STANG, ARNOLD: Chelsea, MA, Sept. 28, 1925.

STANLEY, KIM (Patricia Reid): Tularosa, NM, Feb. 11, 1925. U. Tex.

STANWYCK, BARBARA (Ruby Stevens): Brooklyn, July 16, 1907.

STAPLETON, JEAN: NYC, Jan. 19, 1923.

STAPLETON, MAUREEN: Troy, NY, June 21, 1925.

STEEL, ANTHONY: London, May 21, 1920. Cambridge.

STEELE, TOMMY: London, Dec. 17, 1936.

STEENBURGEN, MARY: Newport, AR, 1953. Neighborhood Playhouse.

STEIGER, ROD: Westhampton, NY, Apr. 14, 1925.

STERLING, JAN (Jane Sterling Adriance): NYC, Apr. 3, 1923. Fay Compton School.

STERLING, ROBERT (William Sterling Hart): Newcastle, PA, Nov. 13, 1917. U. Pittsburgh.

STERN, DANIEL: Bethesda, MD, 1957.

STEVENS, ANDREW: Memphis, TN, June, 1955.

STEVENS, CONNIE (Concetta Ann Ingolia): Brooklyn, Aug. 8, 1938. Hollywood Professional School.

STEVENS, KAYE (Catherine): Pittsburgh, July 21, 1933.

STEVENS, MARK (Richard): Cleveland, OH, Dec. 13, 1920.

STEVENS, STELLA (Estelle Eggleston): Hot Coffee, MI, Oct. 1, 1936.

STEVENSON, PARKER: CT, 1953.

STEWART, ALEXANDRA: Montreal, Can., June 10, 1939. Louvre.

STEWART, ELAINE: Montclair, NJ, May 31, 1929.

STEWART, JAMES: Indiana, PA, May 20, 1908. Princeton.

STEWART, MARTHA (Martha Haworth): Bardwell, KY, Oct. 7, 1922.

STIMSON, SARA: Helotes, TX, 1973.

STOCKWELL, DEAN: Hollywood, March 5, 1936.

STORM, GALE (Josephine Cottle): Bloomington, TX, Apr. 5, 1922.

STRAIGHT, BEATRICE: Old Westbury, NY, Aug. 2, 1916. Dartington Hall.

STRASBERG, SUSAN: NYC, May 22, 1938.

STRAUD, DON: Hawaii, 1943.

STRAUSS, PETER: NY, 1947.

STREEP, MERYL (Mary Louise): Basking Ridge, NJ, Sept. 22, 1950. Vassar, Yale.

STREISAND, BARBRA: Brooklyn, Apr. 24, 1942.

STRITCH, ELAINE: Detroit, MI, Feb. 2, 1925. Drama Workshop.

STRODE, WOODY: Los Angeles, 1914.

STRUDWICK, SHEPPERD: Hillsboro, NC, Sept. 22, 1907. UNC.

STRUTHERS, SALLY: Portland, OR, July 28, 1948. Pasadena Playhouse.

SULLIVAN, BARRY (Patrick Barry): NYC, Aug. 29, 1912. NYU.

SULLY, FRANK (Frank Sullivan): St. Louis, 1910. St. Teresa's Col.

SUTHERLAND, DONALD: St. John, New Brunswick, Can., July 17, 1934. U. Toronto.

SVENSON, BO: Goteborg, Swed., Feb. 13, 1941. UCLA.

SWANSON, GLORIA (Josephine May Swenson): Chicago, Mar. 27, 1897. Chicago Art Inst.

SWEET, BLANCHE: Chicago, 1896.

SWINBURNE, NORA: Bath, Eng., July 24, 1902. RADA.

SWIT, LORETTA: Passaic, NJ, Nov. 4, AADA.

SYLVESTER, WILLIAM: Oakland, CA, Jan. 31, 1922. RADA.

Richard Thomas

Cicely Tyson

Joey Travolta

Joyce Van Patten

Chick Vennera

SYMS, SYLVIA: London, June 1, 1934. Convent School.

TABORI, KRISTOFFER: Los Angeles, Aug. 4, 1952.

TAKEI, GEORGE: Los Angeles, CA, Apr. 20. UCLA.

TALBOT, LYLE (Lysle Hollywood): Pittsburgh, Feb. 8, 1904.

TALBOT, NITA: NYC, Aug. 8, 1930. Irvine Studio School.

TAMBLYN, RUSS: Los Angeles, Dec. 30, 1934.

TANDY, JESSICA: London, June 7, 1909. Dame Owens' School.

TAYLOR, DON: Freeport, PA, Dec. 13, 1920. Penn State U.

TAYLOR, ELIZABETH: London, Feb. 27, 1932. Byron House School.

TAYLOR, KENT (Louis Weiss): Nashua, IA, May 11, 1906.

TAYLOR, ROD (Robert): Sydney, Aust., Jan. 11, 1929.

TAYLOR-YOUNG, LEIGH: Wash., DC, Jan. 25, 1945. Northwestern.

TEAGUE, ANTHONY SKOOTER: Jacksboro, TX, Jan. 4, 1940.

TEMPLE, SHIRLEY: Santa Monica, CA, Apr. 23, 1927.

TERRY-THOMAS (Thomas Terry Hoar Stevens): Finchley, London, July 14, 1911. Ardingly College.

TERZIEFF, LAURENT: Paris, June 25, 1935.

THACKER, RUSS: Washington, DC, June 23, 1946. Montgomery Col.

THATCHER, TORIN: Bombay, India, Jan. 15, 1905. RADA.

THAXTER, PHYLLIS: Portland, ME, Nov. 20, 1921. St. Genevieve.

THOMAS, DANNY (Amos Jacobs): Deerfield, MI, Jan. 6, 1914.

THOMAS, MARLO (Margaret): Detroit, Nov. 21, 1938. USC.

THOMAS, PHILIP: Columbus, OH, May 26, 1949. Oakwood Col.

THOMAS, RICHARD: NYC, June 13, 1951. Columbia.

THOMPSON, JACK (John Payne): Sydney, Aus., 1940. U. Brisbane.

THOMPSON, MARSHALL: Peoria, IL, Nov. 27, 1925. Occidental.

THOMPSON, REX: NYC, Dec. 14, 1942.

THOMPSON, SADA: Des Moines, IA, Sept. 27, 1929. Carnegie Tech.

THULIN, INGRID: Solleftea, Sweden, Jan. 27, 1929. Royal Drama Theatre.

TIERNEY, GENE: Brooklyn, Nov. 20, 1920. Miss Farmer's School.

TIERNEY, LAWRENCE: Brooklyn, Mar. 15, 1919. Manhattan College.

TIFFIN, PAMELA (Wonso): Oklahoma City, Oct. 13, 1942.

TODD, RICHARD: Dublin, Ire., June 11, 1919. Shrewsbury School.

TOLO, MARILU: Rome, Italy, 1944.

TOMLIN, LILY: Detroit, MI, Sept. 1, 1939. Wayne State U.

TOPOL (Chaim Topol): Tel-Aviv, Israel, Sept. 9, 1935.

TORN, RIP: Temple, TX, Feb. 6, 1931. U. Tex.

TORRES, LIZ: NYC, 1947. NYU.

TOTTER, AUDREY: Joliet, IL, Dec. 20, 1918.

TRAVERS, BILL: Newcastle-on-Tyne, Eng., Jan. 3, 1922.

TRAVIS, RICHARD (William Justice): Carlsbad, NM, Apr. 17, 1913.

TRAVOLTA, JOEY: Englewood, NJ, 1952.

TRAVOLTA, JOHN: Englewood, NJ, Feb. 18, 1954.

TREMAYNE, LES: London, Apr. 16, 1913. Northwestern, Columbia. UCLA.

TRINTIGNANT, JEAN-LOUIS: Pont-St. Esprit, France, Dec. 11, 1930. Dullin-Balachova Drama School.

TRYON, TOM: Hartford, CT, Jan. 14, 1926. Yale.

TSOPEI, CORINNA: Athens, Greece, June 21, 1944.

TUCKER, FORREST: Plainfield, IN, Feb. 12, 1919. George Washington U.

TURNER, LANA (Julia Jean Mildred Frances Turner): Wallace, ID, Feb. 8, 1921.

TUSHINGHAM, RITA: Liverpool, Eng., 1940.

TUTIN, DOROTHY: London, Apr. 8, 1930.

TUTTLE, LURENE: Pleasant Lake, IN, Aug. 20, 1906. USC.

TWIGGY (Lesley Hornby): London, Sept. 19, 1949.

TYLER, BEVERLY (Beverly Jean Saul): Scranton, PA, July 5, 1928.

TYRRELL, SUSAN: San Francisco, 1946.

TYSON, CICELY: NYC, Dec. 19.

UGGAMS, LESLIE: NYC, May 25, 1943.

ULLMANN, LIV: Tokyo, Dec. 10, 1938. Webber-Douglas Acad.

USTINOV, PETER: London, Apr. 16, 1921. Westminster School.

VACCARO, BRENDA: Brooklyn, Nov. 18, 1939. Neighborhood Playhouse.

VALLEE, RUDY (Hubert): Island Pond, VT, July 28, 1901. Yale.

VALLI, ALIDA: Pola, Italy, May 31, 1921. Rome Academy of Drama.

VALLONE, RAF: Riogio, Italy, Feb. 17, 1916. Turin U.

VAN, BOBBY (Stein): NYC, Dec. 6, 1930.

VAN CLEEF, LEE: Somerville, NJ, Jan. 9, 1925.

VAN DE VEN, MONIQUE: Holland, 1957.

VAN DEVERE, TRISH (Patricia Dressel): Englewood Cliffs, NJ, Mar. 9, 1945. Ohio Wesleyan.

VAN DOREN, MAMIE (Joan Lucile Olander): Rowena, SD, Feb. 6, 1933.

VAN DYKE, DICK: West Plains, MO, Dec. 13, 1925.

VAN FLEET, JO: Oakland, CA, 1922.

VAN PATTEN, DICK: NYC, Dec. 9, 1928.

VAN PATTEN, JOYCE: NYC, Mar. 9, 1934.

VAUGHN, ROBERT: NYC, Nov. 22, 1932. USC.

VEGA, ISELA: Mexico, 1940.

VENNERA, CHICK: Herkimer, NY, Mar. 27, 1952. Pasadena Playhouse.

VENTURA, LINO: Parma, Italy, July 14, 1919.

VENUTA, BENAY: San Francisco, Jan. 27, 1911.

VERA-ELLEN (Rohe): Cincinnati, Feb. 16, 1926.

VERDON, GWEN: Culver City, CA, Jan. 13, 1925.

VEREEN, BEN: Miami, FL, Oct. 10, 1946.

VILLECHAIZE, HERVE: Paris, Apr. 23, 1943.

VINCENT, JAN-MICHAEL: Denver, CO, July 15, 1944. Ventura Col.

VIOLET, ULTRA (Isabelle Collin-Dufresne): Grenoble, France.

VITALE, MILLY: Rome, Italy, July 16, 1938. Lycee Chateaubriand.

VOHS, JOAN: St. Albans, NY, July 30, 1931.

VOIGHT, JON: Yonkers, NY, Dec. 29, 1938. Catholic U.

VOLONTE, GIAN MARIA: Milan, Italy, Apr. 9, 1933.

VON SYDOW, MAX: Lund, Swed., July 10, 1929. Royal Drama Theatre.

WAGNER, LINDSAY: Los Angeles, 1949.

WAGNER, ROBERT: Detroit, Feb. 10, 1930.

WAITE, GENEVIEVE: South Africa, 1949.

Christopher Walken

Tuesday Weld

Henry Winkler

WALKEN, CHRISTOPHER: Astoria, NY, Mar. 31, 1943. Hofstra.

WALKER, CLINT: Hartfold, IL, May 30, 1927. USC.

WALKER, NANCY (Ann Myrtle Swoyer): Philadelphia, May 10, 1921.

WALLACH, ELI: Brooklyn, Dec. 7, 1915. CCNY, U. Tex.

WALLACH, ROBERTA: NYC, Aug. 2, 1955.

WALLIS, SHANI: London, Apr. 5, 1941.

WALSTON, RAY: New Orleans, Nov. 22, 1917. Cleveland Playhouse.

WALTER, JESSICA: Brooklyn, NY, Jan. 31, 1940. Neighborhood Playhouse.

WANAMAKER, SAM: Chicago, June 14, 1919. Drake.

WARD, BURT (Gervis): Los Angeles, July 6, 1945.

WARD, SIMON: London, 1941.

WARDEN, JACK: Newark, NJ, Sept. 18, 1920.

WARNER, DAVID: Manchester, Eng., 1941. RADA.

WARREN, JENNIFER: NYC, Aug. 12, 1941. U. Wisc.

WARREN, LESLEY ANN: NYC, Aug. 16, 1946.

WARRICK, RUTH: St. Joseph, MO, June 29, 1915. U. Mo.

WASHBOURNE, MONA: Birmingham, Eng., Nov. 27, 1903.

WATERSTON, SAM: Cambridge, MA, Nov. 15, 1940. Yale.

WATLING, JACK: London, Jan. 13, 1923. Italia Conti School.

WATSON, DOUGLASS: Jackson, GA, Feb. 24, 1921. UNC.

WAYNE, DAVID (Wayne McKeehan): Travers City, MI, Jan. 30, 1914. Western Michigan State U.

WAYNE, PATRICK: Los Angeles, July 15, 1939. Loyola.

WEAVER, DENNIS: Joplin, MO, June 4, 1924. U. Okla.

WEAVER, MARJORIE: Crossville, TN, Mar. 2, 1913. Indiana U.

WEAVER, SIGOURNEY: NYC, 1949. Stanford, Yale.

WEBB, ALAN: York, Eng., July 2, 1906. Dartmouth.

WEBB, JACK: Santa Monica, CA, Apr. 2, 1920.

WEBBER, ROBERT: Santa Ana, CA, Sept. 14, 1925. Compton Jr. Col.

WEDGEWORTH, ANN: Abilene, TX, Jan. 21. U. Tex.

WEISSMULLER, JOHNNY: Chicago, June 2, 1904. Chicago U.

WELCH, RAQUEL (Tejada): Chicago, Sept. 5, 1940.

WELD, TUESDAY (Susan): NYC, Aug. 27, 1943. Hollywood Professional School.

WELDON, JOAN: San Francisco, Aug. 5, 1933. San Francisco Conservatory.

WELLES, GWEN: NYC, Mar. 4.

WELLES, ORSON: Kenosha, WI, May 6, 1915. Todd School.

WERNER, OSKAR: Vienna, Nov. 13, 1922.

WEST, MAE: Brooklyn, Aug. 17, 1892.

WESTON, JACK (Morris Weinstein): Cleveland, OH, Aug. 21, 1915.

WHITAKER, JOHNNY: Van Nuys, CA, Dec. 13. 1959.

WHITE, CAROL: London, Apr. 1, 1944.

WHITE, CHARLES: Perth Amboy, NJ, Aug. 29, 1920. Rutgers U.

WHITE, JESSE: Buffalo, NY, Jan. 3, 1919.

WHITMAN, STUART: San Francisco, Feb. 1, 1929. CCLA.

WHITMORE, JAMES: White Plains, NY, Oct. 1, 1921. Yale.

WHITNEY, GRACE LEE: Detroit, MI, Apr. 1, 1930.

WIDDOES, KATHLEEN: Wilmington, DE, Mar. 21, 1939.

WIDMARK, RICHARD: Sunrise, MN, Dec. 26, 1914. Lake Forest.

WILCOX-HORNE, COLIN: Highlands NC, Feb. 4, 1937. U. Tenn.

WILCOXON, HENRY: British West Indies, Sept. 8, 1905.

WILDE, CORNEL: NYC, Oct. 13, 1915. CCNY, Columbia.

WILDER, GENE (Jerome Silberman): Milwaukee, WI, June 11, 1935. U. Iowa.

WILLIAMS, BILLY DEE: NYC, Apr. 6, 1937.

WILLIAMS, CINDY: Van Nuys, CA, Aug. 22, 1947. LACC.

WILLIAMS, DICK A.: Chicago, IL, Aug. 9, 1938.

WILLIAMS, EMLYN: Mostyn, Wales, Nov. 26, 1905. Oxford.

WILLIAMS, ESTHER: Los Angeles, Aug. 8, 1921.

WILLIAMS, GRANT: NYC, Aug. 18, 1930. Queens College.

WILLIAMS, JOHN: Chalfont, Eng., Apr. 15, 1903. Lancing College.

WILLIAMS, TREAT (Richard): Rowayton, CT. 1952.

WILLIAMSON, FRED: Gary, IN, Mar. 5, 1938. Northwestern.

WILSON, DEMOND: NYC, Oct. 13, 1946. Hunter Col.

WILSON, FLIP (Clerow Wilson): Jersey City, NJ, Dec. 8, 1933.

WILSON, NANCY: Chillicothe, OH, Feb. 20, 1937.

WILSON, SCOTT: Atlanta, GA, 1942.

WINDE, BEATRICE: Chicago, Jan. 6.

WINDOM, WILLIAM: NYC, Sept. 28, 1923. Williams Col.

WINDSOR, MARIE (Emily Marie Bertelson): Marysvale, UT, Dec. 11, 1924. Brigham Young U.

WINFIELD, PAUL: Los Angeles, 1940. UCLA.

WINKLER, HENRY: NYC, Oct. 30, 1945. Yale.

WINN, KITTY: Wash., D.C., 1944. Boston U.

WINTERS, JONATHAN: Dayton, OH, Nov. 11, 1925. Kenyon Col.

WINTERS, ROLAND: Boston, Nov. 22, 1904.

WINTERS, SHELLEY (Shirley Schrift): St. Louis, Aug. 18, 1922. Wayne U.

WINWOOD, ESTELLE: Kent, Eng., Jan. 24, 1883. Lyric Stage Academy.

WITHERS, GOOGIE: Karachi, India, Mar. 12, 1917. Italia Conti.

WITHERS, JANE: Atlanta, GA, 1926.

WOOD, NATALIE (Natasha Gurdin): San Francisco, July 20, 1938.

WOODLAWN, HOLLY (Harold Ajzenberg): Juana Diaz, PR, 1947.

WOODS, JAMES: Vernal, UT, Apr. 18, 1947. MIT.

WOODWARD, JOANNE: Thomasville, GA, Feb. 27, 1930. Neighborhood Playhouse.

WOOLAND, NORMAN: Dusseldorf, Ger., Mar. 16, 1910. Edward VI School.

WOPAT, TOM: Lodi, WI, 1951.

WORONOV, MARY: Brooklyn, Dec. 8, 1946. Cornell.

WRAY, FAY: Alberta, Can., Sept. 15, 1907.

WRIGHT, TERESA: NYC, Oct. 27, 1918.

WYATT, JANE: Campgaw, NJ, Aug. 10, 1911. Barnard College.

WYMAN, JANE (Sarah Jane Fulks): St. Joseph, MO, Jan. 4, 1914.

WYMORE, PATRICE: Miltonvale, KS, Dec. 17, 1926.

WYNN, KEENAN: NYC, July 27, 1916. St. John's.

WYNN, MAY (Donna Lee Hickey): NYC, Jan. 8, 1930.

WYNTER, DANA (Dagmar): London, June 8, 1927. Rhodes U.

YORK, DICK: Fort Wayne, IN, Sept. 4, 1928. De Paul U.

YORK, MICHAEL: Fulmer, Eng., Mar. 27, 1942. Oxford.

YORK, SUSANNAH: London, Jan. 9, 1941. RADA.

YOUNG, ALAN (Angus): North Shield, Eng., Nov. 19, 1919.

YOUNG, LORETTA (Gretchen): Salt Lake City, Jan. 6, 1912. Immaculate Heart College.

YOUNG, ROBERT: Chicago, Feb. 22, 1907.

ZACHARIAS, ANN: Stockholm, Sw., 1956.

ZETTERLING, MAI: Sweden, May 27, 1925. Ordtuery Theatre School.

ZIMBALIST, EFREM, JR.: NYC, Nov. 30, 1918. Yale.

OBITUARIES

RONALD ADAM, 82, actor, playwright, producer, and theatrical manager, died March 27, 1979, in his home outside London. His many screen appearances include "Drums," "Hell's Cargo," "Take My Life," "All over the Town," "Under Capricorn," "The Hidden Room," "Operation X," "Seven Days to Noon," "Lavender Hill Mob," "Laughter in Paradise," "Bonnie Prince Charlie," "Angels One Five," "Malta Story," "The Black Knight," "Lust for Life," "Reach for the Sky," "The Ship Was Loaded," "Cleopatra," "The Surgeon's Knife," "Three on a Spree," "Tomb of Ligeia," and "Man in a Cocked Hat." His second wife survives.

LOUISE ALLBRITTON, 59, Oklahoma-born actress, died of cancer Feb. 16, 1979, in Puerto Vallarta, Mexico. She was seen in such films as "Parachute Nurse," "Who Done It," "It Comes Up Love," "Pittsburgh," "Fired Wife," "Son of Dracula," "Her Primitive Man," "This Is the Life," "San Diego, I Love You," "Bowery to Broadway," "Men in Her Diary," "That Night with You," "Tangier," "The Egg and I," "Sitting Pretty," "An Innocent Affair," "Walk a Crooked Mile." She is survived by her husband, CBS correspondent Charles Collingwood.

JAN ARVAN, 66, character actor, died of a heart attack May 24, 1979, in Los Angeles, CA. He appeared in over 40 films, including "The Other Woman," "The Cobweb," "Istanbul," "A Million Miles to Earth," "Curse of the Faceless Man," "Three Came to Kill," "Sign of Zorro," "Gunfighters of Abilene," "A Noose for a Gunman," "Frontier Uprising," "The Brass Bottle," "The Spy with My Face," "The Poseidon Adventure," and "The Other Side of Midnight." His widow, a daughter, and a son survive.

DOROTHY ARZNER, 82, San Francisco-born director, died Oct. 1, 1979, in La Quinta, CA. She made her directing debut in 1927 with "Fashions for Women," and followed with "10 Modern Commandments," "Get Your Man," "Manhattan Cocktail," "The Wild Party," "Sarah and Son," "Anybody's Woman," "Honor among Lovers," "Merrily We Go to Hell," "Christopher Strong," "Nana," "Craig's Wife," "The Bride Wore Red," "Dance, Girl, Dance," and her last, in 1943, "First Comes Courage," after which she retired. She leaves no known survivors.

FELIX AYLMER, 90, English stage, screen, and TV character actor, died Sept. 2, 1979, in Sussex, Eng. He seldom had top billing but he was memorable in many supporting roles. His credits include "The Wandering Jew," "The Iron Duke," "Nine Days a Queen," "As You Like It," "Victoria the Great," "The Citadel," "Mill on the Floss," "Night Train," "Frightened Lady," "She Shall Have Music," "Young Mr. Pitt," "A Young Man's Fancy," "The Life and Death of Colonel Blimp," "Henry V," "The Years Between," "Hamlet," "Quartet," "Edward My Son," "Prince of Foxes," "Quo Vadis," "Ivanhoe," "Paris Express," "Knights of the Round Table," "Anastasia," "St. Joan," "Separate Tables," "Exodus," "Becket," and "The Chalk Garden." A daughter survives.

JOHN BARRY, 43, designer, died of infectious meningitis June 1, 1979, in London while working on "The Empire Strikes Back," the sequel to "Star Wars," for which he received an Academy Award. His other credits include "The Dream Maker," "The Clockwork Orange," and "Superman." No reported survivors.

JOAN BLONDELL, 73, NYC-born screen, stage, and TV actress, died of leukemia Dec. 25, 1979, in Santa Monica, CA. Her career began in 1930 and ended with the 1979 remake of "The Champ." She usually played a wisecracking blonde character in her over 80 films, including "Sinner's Holiday," "Public Enemy," "Blonde Crazy," "The Crowd Roars," "Miss Pinkerton," "Three on a Match," "Gold Diggers of 1933," "Footlight Parade," "He Was Her Man," "We're in the Money," "Sons o' Guns," "Bullets or Ballots," "Stage Struck," "Three Men on a Horse," "Gold Diggers of 1937," "Stand-In," "Kid from Kokomo," "Good Girls Go to Paris," "Topper Returns," "Cry Havoc," "A Tree Grows in Brooklyn," "The Corpse Came C.O.D.," "Nightmare Alley," "The Blue Veil," for which she received an Academy Award nomination, "Desk Set," "Will Success Spoil Rock Hunter?," "Cincinnati Kid," and "Grease." She was divorced from cameraman George Barnes, actor Dick Powell, and producer Mike Todd. Surviving are a son and a daughter, Norman and Ellen Powell, and her sister Gloria, an actress.

Louise Allbritton

Felix Aylmer

Joan Blondell

| Philip Bourneuf | Lee Bowman | George Brent | Edgar Buchanan | John Carroll | Dolores Costello |

PHILIP BOURNEUF, 71, versatile stage, screen, and TV actor, was found dead in his Santa Monica, CA, apartment on March 23, 1979. He was born in Somerville, MA, and made his Broadway debut in 1934. His film credits include "Winged Victory," "Joan of Arc," "The Big Night," "Thunder in the East," "Beyond a Reasonable Doubt," "Everything but the Truth," "Hemingway's Adventures of a Young Man," "Chamber of Horrors," "The Molly Maguires." He was divorced from actress Frances Reid.

LEE BOWMAN, 64, screen, stage, and TV actor, died of a heart attack on Dec. 25, 1979, in his home in Brentwood, CA. He appeared on Broadway before making his film debut in 1937, and subsequently made over 40 movies. His credits include "Three Men in White," "I Met Him in Paris," "Last Train from Madrid," "Having Wonderful Time," "Tarnished Angel," "Miracles for Sale," "Dancing Co-ed," "Fast and Furious," "The Great Victor Herbert," "Love Affair," "Another Thin Man," "Buck Privates," "Model Wife," "Married Bachelor," "Pacific Rendezvous," "Bataan," "Cover Girl," "Up in Mabel's Room," "The Impatient Years," "She Wouldn't Say Yes," "Smash-up," "A Woman Betrayed," and "Youngblood Hawke." He was the star of the TV series "Ellery Queen" in the 1960s. No reported survivors.

GEORGE BRENT, 75, Irish-born stage and screen actor, was found dead of natural causes in his Solana Beach, CA, home on May 26, 1979. His film career began in 1930 and he subsequently appeared in over 100 movies, including "Once a Sinner," "Charlie Chan Carries On," "Homicide Squad," "The Rich Are Always with Us," "Miss Pinkerton," "The Crash," "Luxury Liner," "42nd Street," "Lily Turner," "Baby Face," "Desirable," "Painted Veil," "Stranded," "The Goose and the Gander," "Special Agent," "In Person," "Golden Arrow," "Give Me Your Heart," "Submarine D-1," "Jezebel," "Wings of the Navy," "Dark Victory," "The Old Maid," "The Rains Came," "The Fighting 69th," "The Great Lie," "Twin Beds," "In This Our Life," "Spiral Staircase," "Tomorrow Is Forever," "Lover Come Back," "Temptation," "Illegal Entry," "Bride for Sale," and his last, in 1978, "Born Again." He was married five times, and is survived by a son and a daughter.

DAVID BUTLER, 84, San Francisco-born silent screen star who became the director of 65 movies, died of heart failure on June 14, 1979, in Santa Rosa, CA. As an actor he appeared in such films as "The Greatest Thing in Life," "The Girl Who Stayed Home," "Sky Pilot," "According to Hoyle," "Wise Kid," "Desire," "Narrow Street," "Code of the West," "Havoc," "Wages for Wives," "Seventh Heaven," "Village Blacksmith," "Hoodman Blind," "Blue Eagle," and "Salute." He began directing in 1927 and his credits include "High School Hero," "Movietone Follies of 1929," "Sunny Side Up," "High Society Blues," "Connecticut Yankee," "Handle with Care," "Have a Heart," four Shirley Temple films—"Bright Eyes," "The Little Colonel," "The Littlest Rebel," and "Captain January"—"Pigskin Parade," "Kentucky," "If I Had My Way," "Road to Morocco," "Thank Your Lucky Stars," "Shine on Harvest Moon," "San Antonio," "Two Guys from Milwaukee," "The Time, the Place and the Girl,"

EDGAR BUCHANAN, 76, Missouri-born character actor, died April 4, 1979, following brain surgery in Palm Desert, CA. Before becoming a film actor in 1940, he had been a successful dentist. He subsequently appeared in over 100 films, including "My Son Is Guilty," "Too Many Husbands," "Arizona," "Penny Serenade," "Texas," "Talk of the Town," "Buffalo Bill," "The Impatient Years," "Sea of Grass," "Framed," "The Swordsman," "Cheaper by the Dozen," "Shane," "Day of the Badman," "Cimarron," "Ride the High Country," "The Rounders," "Angel in My Pocket," and "Benji." On TV he was starred in "Judge Roy Bean," "Hopalong Cassidy," "Petticoat Junction," and "Cade's Country." His widow and their son survive.

"John Loves Mary," "Story of Seabiscuit," "Tea for Two," "Lullaby of Broadway," "Where's Charley?," "April in Paris," "Calamity Jane," and his last, in 1967, "C'mon Let's Live a Little." He also directed TV's "Bachelor Father," "Leave It to Beaver," and many segments of "Wagon Train," "Ironside," and "Felony Squad." He is survived by his widow and stepson.

CLAIRE CARLETON, 66, NYC-born film and stage actress, died of cancer Dec. 11, 1979, in her home in North Ridge, CA. Among her screen credits are "The Crooked Road," "Night of Adventure," "My Pal Wolf," "A Double Life," "Bad Men of Tombstone," "Red Light," "Born Yesterday," "Death of a Salesman," "Witness to Murder," "Buster Keaton Story," "Son of Dr. Jekyll," "Two of a Kind," "Unwed Mother," "Wabash Avenue," and "The Careless Years." No reported survivors.

PAOLO CARLINI, 53, popular Italian actor, died of a cerebral hemorrhage in Rome on Nov. 7, 1979. He had appeared in such films as "Baron Carlo Mazza," "Roman Holiday," "Cardinal Lambertini," "Bay of Naples," and "The Slave." No reported survivors.

JOHN CARROLL, 72, New Orleans-born Julian LaFaye, actor, died April 24, 1979, of complications from leukemia, in Hollywood, CA. His film career began in 1935 and he appeared in over 100 films. His credits include "Hi Gaucho!," "Murder on a Bridle Path," "We Who are about to Die," "Rose of the Rio Grande," "Only Angels Have Wings," "Susan and God," "Hired Wife," "Lady Be Good," "Rio Rita," "Flying Tigers," "Hit Parade," "I, Jane Doe," "The Farmer Takes a Wife," and several Zorro films. In addition to his wife of 35 years, he is survived by a daughter from a previous marriage. Burial was in Forest Lawn Park.

TED CASSIDY, 46, actor, died Jan 16, 1979, of complications following open-heart surgery. He had appeared in "Butch Cassidy and the Sundance Kid," "McKenna's Gold," "The Last Remake of Beau Geste," among others, but was probably best known for his servant Lurch in the TV series "The Addams Family," and as Bigfoot in "The Six Million Dollar Man." No reported survivors. Burial was in Forest Lawn Park.

JOAN CHANDLER, 55, film and stage actress, died May 11, 1979 in NYC. Her screen credits include "Humoresque," "The Street with No Name," and "Rope." A daughter survives.

LEWIS CHARLES, 63, character actor in films, theater, and TV, died of cancer Nov. 9, 1979, in Los Angeles, CA. His movie credits include "Panic in the Streets," "The Rose Tattoo," "Monkey on My Back," "Sweet Smell of Success," "Party Girl," "Al Capone," "Birdman of Alcatraz," "Who's Got the Action," "Soldier in the Rain," "A House Is Not a Home," "Our Man Flint," and "Topaz." On TV he appeared in the "Feather and Father Gang" series. Surviving are his widow and three stepdaughters.

DOLORES COSTELLO, 73, film star and stage actress, died March 1, 1979, of emphysema in Fallbrook, CA. She was the daughter of matinee idol Maurice Costello, and began her career on stage at 19. She made her film debut in 1923 in "Lawful Larceny," followed by such movies as "The Sea Hunt," "The Sea Beast," "Bride of the Storm," "The Little Irish Girl," "When a Man Loves," "Old San Francisco," "Tenderloin," "Glorious Betsy," "Noah's Ark," "Madonna of Avenue A," "Show of Shows," "Beloved Brat," "King of the Turf," "The Magnificent Ambersons," "This Is the Army." She was married and divorced from actor John Barrymore and Dr. John Vruwink. Two children survive, a daughter, and a son, actor John Blythe Barrymore.

EDITH CRAIG, 71, screen and stage actress, died March 2, 1979, after a long illness in Tenafly, NJ. She had appeared in over 40 films, including "Harmony Lane," "Behind the Headlines," "Smashing the Rackets," "Love on a Bet," "Condemned Woman," "Outcasts of Poker Flats," and "The Singing Marine." A sister survives.

| John Cromwell | Ann Dvorak | William Gargan | Corinne Griffith | Jack Haley | Jon Hall |

JOHN CROMWELL, 91, an actor and director in films and on the stage for over 70 years, died Sept. 26, 1979, of a pulmonary embolism in Santa Barbara, CA. Included among the over 40 pictures he directed are "Dance of Life," "The Texan," "Tom Sawyer," "Close Harmony," "Vice Squad," "The World and the Flesh," "The Silver Cord," "Spitfire," "Of Human Bondage," "The Fountain," "Little Lord Fauntleroy," "Prisoner of Zenda," "Made for Each Other," "Algiers," "Abe Lincoln in Illinois," "So Ends Our Night," "Since You Went Away," "The Enchanted Cottage," "Anna and the King of Siam," "Dead Reckoning," "Caged," "The Goddess," and his last, in 1961, "A Matter of Morals." His last acting appearances were in "Three Women" and "The Wedding" in 1978. Surviving are his fourth wife, actress Ruth Nelson, and a son, actor James Cromwell.

ANN DVORAK, 67, NYC-born Anna McKim, died Dec. 10, 1979, in Honolulu, HI. Her film career began at the age of 17 in "Scarface," followed by over 50 pictures, including "The Crowd Roars," "The Strange Love of Molly Louvain," "Three on a Match," "College Coach," "Housewife," "Love Is a Racket," "The Way to Love," "Massacre," "G Men," "Blind Alley," "Sweet Music," "Flame of the Barbary Coast," "Gangs of New York," "Street of Missing Women," "A Life of Her Own," "I Was an American Spy," and her last, in 1951, "The Secret of Convict Lake." She was the widow of actor Leslie Fenton.

GRACIE FIELDS, 81, (née Stansfield in Rochdale, Eng.), singer and comedienne, died from pneumonia Sept. 27, 1979, in her home on Capri, Italy. Her last public appearance was in February when she was made a Dame Commander by Queen Elizabeth II. She was the darling of the British music halls, stage, records, TV, and films. Her screen credits include "It's Love I'm After," "We're Going to Be Rich," "Smiling Along," "Shipyard Sally," "Stage Door Canteen," "Holy Matrimony," "Molly and Me," and "Paris Underground." Her third husband survives.

DICK FORAN, 69, one of the film's first singing cowboys, died Aug. 10, 1979, in Panorama City, CA. He first appeared in 1934's "Stand Up and Cheer" as Nick Foran, and subsequently was in over 200 films, including "Accent on Youth," "The Big Noise," "Shipmates Forever," "Dangerous," "The Petrified Forest," for which he received an Academy nomination, "Son of the Saddle," "Golden Arrow," "Love, Honor and Behave," "Cowboy from Brooklyn," "Four Daughters," "Boy Meets Girl," "Four Wives," "The Fighting 69th," "My Little Chickadee," "House of Seven Gables," "In the Navy," "Mob Town," "Keep 'Em Flying," "Butch Minds the Baby," "Fort Apache," "El Paso," "The Big Night," "Studs Lonigan," "Taggart," and his last, in 1967, "Brighty of the Grand Canyon." Surviving are his third wife and four sons.

TONY "TWO-TON" GALENTO, 69, NJ-born former heavyweight boxer and film actor, died of a heart attack July 22, 1979, in Livingston, NJ. He had several small parts in movies, including "On the Waterfront," "The Best Things in Life Are Free," "Wind Across the Everglades," and "Guys and Dolls." His widow and a son survive.

WILLIAM GARGAN, 73, Brooklyn-born actor on stage, film, and TV, died Feb. 17, 1979, of a heart attack aboard a plane in flight from NY to San Diego. His most memorable roles were as a tough detective. After a laryngectomy in 1960, he devoted most of his time to the American Cancer Society. Among his many film credits are "The Misleading Lady," "Rain," "The Animal Kingdom," "Night Flight," "Strictly Dynamite," "Traveling Saleslady," "Black Fury," "You Only Live Once," "Reported Missing," "The Crowd Roars," "Within the Law," "Broadway Serenade," "Three Sons," "Double Alibi," "They Knew What They Wanted," "Cheers for Miss Bishop," "Flying Cadets," "I Wake Up Screaming," "Destination Unknown," "Bells of St. Mary's," "Miracle in the Rain," and on TV, "Martin Kane, Private Eye." He leaves his widow and two sons.

JODY GILBERT, 63, singer-actress on screen, stage, and TV, died Feb. 3, 1979, in Los Angeles, CA, following an automobile accident. Among her over 150 films are "Ninotchka," "Seventeen," "Little Old New York," "Never Give a Sucker an Even Break," "Remember the Day," "Tuttles of Tahiti," "Blondie's Holiday," "Albuquerque," "Shaggy," "Are You With It?," "The Lovable Cheat," "Gene Autry and the Mounties," "Actors and Sin," "The Big Fisherman," and "Butch Cassidy and the Sundance Kid." Survivors include her mother, a brother, and a sister.

JOYCE GRENFELL, 69, British actress and monologist, died Nov. 30, 1979, in London. Her film credits include "Stage Fright," "Run for Your Money," "While the Sun Shines," "The Happiest Days of Your Life," "Laughter in Paradise," "Magic Box," "Pickwick Papers," "Genevieve," "Bells of St. Trinian's," "Blue Murder at St. Trinian's," "Happy Is the Bride," "The Pure Hell of St. Trinian's," "The Americanization of Emily," and "The Yellow Rolls-Royce." Her husband, mining executive Reginald Grenfell, survives.

CORINNE GRIFFITH, 79, beautiful "orchid of the screen," died July 13, 1979, in Santa Monica, CA. After winning first prize in a beauty contest, she was signed to a film contract. Her credits include "Yellow Girl," "Six Days," "Common Law," "Black Oxen," "Lilies of the Field," "Single Wives," "Love's Wilderness," "Declassée," "Marriage Whirl," "Classified," "Infatuation," "M'lle. Modiste," "Into Her Kingdom," "Syncopating Sue," "Lady in Ermine," "Three Hours," "Garden of Eden," "Outcast," "Divine Lady," "Saturday's Children," "Back Pay," and "Lily Christine," all released before 1935. She was married and divorced four times, but had no children. After she retired from the screen, she appeared in the theater, and became a millionaire real estate investor.

JACK HALEY, 79, Boston-born stage and screen actor, died of a heart attack June 6, 1979, in Los Angeles, CA. After Broadway success in musicals, he began his film career in 1930 with "Follow Through," followed by "Mr. Broadway," "Sitting Pretty," "Here Comes the Groom," "Girl Friend," "Redheads on Parade," "Poor Little Rich Girl," "Pigskin Parade," "Mr. Cinderella," "Pick a Star," "Wake Up and Live," "Rebecca of Sunnybrook Farm," "Alexander's Ragtime Band," "The Wizard of Oz" (his most memorable performance as the Tin Woodman), "Moon over Miami," "Beyond the Blue Horizon," "Higher and Higher," "Scared Stiff," "George White's Scandals," "People Are Funny," "Make Mine Laughs," and "Norwood" (a 1970 film directed by his son, Jack, Jr.). He is survived by his widow, his son, and a daughter.

JON HALL, 66, actor, née Charles Loeher, died of self-inflicted gunshot wounds Dec. 13, 1979, in his North Hollywood home. He had been undergoing treatment for cancer. After his film debut in 1935 in "Charlie Chan in Shanghai," he appeared in "Hurricane," "Sailor's Lady," "South of Pago Pago," "Kit Carson," "Aloma of the South Seas," "Tuttles of Tahiti," "Arabian Nights," "White Savage," "Ali Baba and the 40 Thieves," "Lady in the Dark," "Cobra Woman," "Sudan," "Michigan Kid," "Prince of Thieves," "On the Isle of Samoa," "Hurricane Island," "Last Train from Bombay," "White Goddess," "Pirate Ship," "Ramar" series, and "Beach Girls and the Monster." He was divorced from Frances Langford and Raquel Torres. Two sisters survive.

DARLA HOOD, 48, the dark-eyed, curly-haired female member of "Our Gang" comedy group, died June 13, 1979, in Canoga Park, CA. From 1935 to 1942 she appeared in 132 "Our Gang" comedy films, and subsequently in "The Bohemian Girl," "Born to Sing," "The Calypso Heat Wave," and "The Helen Morgan Story." She is survived by her husband, a son, and two daughters.

Arthur Hunnicutt	Jim Hutton	Claudia Jennings	Kurt Kasznar	Doris Kenyon	Ettore Manni

ARTHUR HUNNICUTT, 69, Arkansas-born film and stage character actor, died of cancer Sept. 26, 1979, in Woodland Hills, CA. His screen career began in 1942 with "Wildcat," and among his many other credits are "Fall In," "Johnny Come Lately," "Abroad with Two Yanks," "Lust for Gold," "Pinky," "Great Dan Patch," "Border Incident," "Broken Arrow," "Two Flags West," "Sugarfoot," "Red Badge of Courage," "Distant Drums," "The Big Sky," for which he received an Academy Awards nomination, "She Couldn't Say No," "The Cardinal," "Cat Ballou," "El Dorado," and "Harry and Tonto." Surviving is his widow.

JIM HUTTON, 45, screen and TV actor, died of cancer June 2, 1979, in Los Angeles, CA. Born in Binghamton, NY, he began his acting career in the army, and his first film in 1944 was "Destination Tokyo," followed by "Janie," "Hollywood Canteen," "Roughly Speaking," "Too Young to Know," "Janie Gets Married," "Time Out of Mind," "Love and Learn," "Wallflower," "The Younger Brothers," "And Baby Makes Three," "Man on the Eiffel Tower," "The Racket," "Casanova's Big Night," "Cinderfella," "The Secret Door," "The Vulture," "Green Berets," "Where the Boys Are," "Period of Adjustment," and "Sky Trap." On TV he was Ellery Queen during 1975–76. He was twice married and divorced, and leaves two daughters and a son.

JANE HYLTON, 53, British actress, died of a heart attack Feb. 28, 1979, in Glasgow, Scotland, where she was appearing in a play. Her film credits include "The Upturned Glass," "Dear Murderer," "My Brother's Keeper," "Daybreak," "Passport to Pimlico," "It Started in Paradise," "Frightened Bride," "The Weak and Wicked," "House of Mystery," and "Circus of Horrors." A daughter survives.

CLAUDIA JENNINGS, 29, née Mimi Chesterton, born near Chicago, died Oct. 3, 1979, in a head-on collision with a truck near Malibu, CA. She had appeared in such films as "Truck Stop Woman," "Unholy Rollers," "The Great Texas Dynamite Chase," and "Deathsport." She was also a Playmate of the Year. Her parents survive.

JAN KADAR, 61, the expatriate Czechoslovak director, died June 1, 1979, in Los Angeles, CA. He won an Academy Award in 1965 for his film "The Shop on Main Street." His other credits include "Death Is Called Engelchen," "The Defendant," "Katka," "Music from Mars," "The Angel Levine," "Adrift," and "Lies My Father Told Me." He came to the U.S. in 1968. He is survived by his wife.

ROBERT KARNES, 62, screen, TV, and stage actor, died of heart failure Dec. 4, 1979, in Sherman Oaks, CA. His career began as a radio announcer in his native Kentucky. Film credits include "Daisy Kenyon," "Captain from Castile," "Scudda-Hoo! Scudda-Hay!," "Road House," "Three Husbands," "From Here to Eternity," "Riders to the Stars," and "Gentleman's Agreement." His widow and a daughter survive.

KURT KASZNAR, 65, Vienna-born actor on stage, screen, and TV, died of cancer Aug. 6, 1979, in Santa Monica, CA. He appeared in over 20 films, including "The Light Touch," "Lovely to Look at," "The Happy Time," "Lili," "Sombrero," "Kiss Me Kate," "All the Brothers Were Valiant," "Valley of the Kings," "The Last Time I Saw Paris," "My Sister Eileen," "Anything Goes," "A Farewell to Arms," "The Journey," "Arms and the Man," "55 Days at Peking," "Casino Royale," "The Perils of Pauline," and "The Smugglers." He was divorced from his second wife, actress Leora Dana.

DORIS KENYON, 81, silent screen star, died Sept. 1, 1979, in her Beverly Hills, CA home. She made her film debut in 1917 in "A Girl's Folly," subsequently starring in such pictures as "Monsieur Beaucaire" with Valentino, "Conquest of Canaan," "The Traveling Salesman," "Born Rich," "Thief in Paradise," "Unguarded Hour," "Men of Steel," "Ladies at Play," "Blonde Saint," "Valley of the Giants," "Home Towners," "Beau Bandit,"

"Alexander Hamilton," "Road to Singapore," "Young America," "No Marriage Ties," "Voltaire," "Counsellor-at-Law," "Girls' School," and "Man in the Iron Mask." In 1964 she appeared in the TV series "The Tycoon." Her four marriages ended in divorce. Four grandchildren survive.

VICTOR KILIAN, 88, New Jersey-born character actor on stage, screen, and TV, was found beaten to death March 11, 1979, in his ransacked apartment in Hollywood, CA. He had appeared in over 70 films since 1929, including "The Wiser Sex," "Bad Boy," "Riffraff," "Ramona," "Seventh Heaven," "Tovarich," "Tom Sawyer," "Boy's Town," "St. Louis Blues," "Huckleberry Finn," "Only Angels Have Wings," "Young Tom Edison," "They Knew What They Wanted," "Tugboat Annie Sails Again," "Blood and Sand," "Reap the Wild Wind," "This Gun for Hire," "Ox-Bow Incident," "Belle of the Yukon," "Spellbound," "Gentleman's Agreement," "The Flame and the Arrow," and "Tall Target." He was best known as the Fernwood Flasher, the heroine's father on TV's "Mary Hartman, Mary Hartman." A son survives.

ETTORE MANNI, 52, Italian screen actor, accidentally shot himself to death July 27, 1979, in his Rome apartment. His credits include "White Slavery," "Women Alone," "She-Wolf," "Girlfriends," "Poor but Beautiful," "Revolt of the Gladiators," "Cleopatra's Legions," "Goliath," "Divine Nymph," "Defiance," and "Mademoiselle." He had almost completed his role in "City of Women." His daughter survives.

ZEPPO MARX, 78, youngest and last surviving member of the Marx Brothers comedy team, died Nov. 30, 1979, in Palm Springs, CA. He joined the brothers' vaudeville act when he was in high school, but left them in 1933 to become a theatrical agent. He appeared with them as romantic lead in their first five films: "The Cocoanuts," "Animal Crackers," "Monkey Business," "Horse Feathers," and "Duck Soup." He was married and divorced twice.

SHIRLEY MASON, 79, stage and silent film actress, died of cancer July 27, 1979, in Los Angeles, CA. Her credits include "The Seven Deadly Sins," "Come on In," "Treasure Island," "The Eleventh Hour," "The Talker," "What Fools Men," "Lord Jim," "Desert Gold," "Sweet Rosie O'Grady," "Let It Rain," "Vanity Fair," "So This Is Paris," and "Show of Shows." She retired when she married screenwriter Sidney Lanfield, who predeceased her. A sister, retired actress Viola Dana, survives.

PAUL MEURISSE, 66, French star of screen, stage, and cabaret, died of a heart attack Jan. 19, 1979, in Paris shortly after a stage performance. His film credits include "Bel Indifferent," "Back Streets of Paris," "Red Angel," "Diabolique," "Marie Octobre," "Picnic on the Grass," "Love and the Frenchwoman," and "The Truth." No reported survivors.

YVONNE MITCHELL, 53, British actress on screen, stage, and TV, died of cancer March 24, 1979, in London. In 1954 she was voted best actress of the year by the British Film Academy for her performance in "The Divided Heart," and in 1957 for "Woman in a Dressing Gown." Other film credits include "Queen of Spades," "Turn the Key Softly," "Blonde Sinner," "Escapade," "Sapphire," "Tiger Bay," "Conspiracy of Hearts," "Trials of Oscar Wilde," "Main Attraction," "Johnny Nobody." Her husband, film critic Derek Monsey, had died only a few weeks previously.

JACK MULHALL, 91, actor, died June 1, 1979, in Woodland Hills, CA. He played leading man to 101 stars, and was the first male actor to earn $1000 a week. Among the more than 65 films in which he appeared are "You Never Can Tell," "Within the Law," "Dulcy," "Friendly Enemies," "Mad Whirl," "We Moderns," "Sweet Daddies," "Subway Sadie," "Poor Nut," "Man Crazy," "Ladies' Night in a Turkish Bath," "Lady Be Good," "Butter and Egg Man," "Twin Beds," "Murder Will Out," "Road to Paradise," "Lover Come Back," "Sweet Adeline," "Big Broadcast of 1936," "Beloved Enemy," "100 Men and a Girl,"

| Shirley Mason | Zeppo Marx | Yvonne Mitchell | Jack Mulhall | Merle Oberon | Mary Pickford |

"First Love," "Son of Monte Cristo," "Cheers for Miss Bishop," "Sin Girl," "Kid Dynamite," "Deadline for Murder," "Around the World in 80 Days," and "Atomic Submarine." Surviving are his widow and a son.

BARBARA MULLEN, 64, Boston-born film and stage actress, died of a heart attack March 9, 1979, in London, where she had lived since 1934. She had appeared on the screen in such films as "Jeannie," "Thunder Rock," "A Place of One's Own," "Corridor of Mirrors," "You Can't Beat the Irish," "So Little Time," "Gentle Gunman," "It Takes a Thief." She is survived by her husband, producer John Taylor, and two daughters.

CLARENCE MUSE, 89, actor, producer, songwriter, screenwriter, and the first black to star in a film, died of a cerebral hemorrhage Oct. 13, 1979, in Perris, CA. He would have been 90 the next day. His career began in 1929 and included 219 films, among which were "Hearts in Dixie," "Rain or Shine," "Huckleberry Finn," "Lena Rivers," "Attorney for the Defense," "Winner Take All," "Massacre," "Count of Monte Cristo," "Broadway Bill," "So Red the Rose," "Show Boat," "Follow Your Heart," "Spirit of Youth," "Way Down South," "Tales of Manhattan," "Heaven Can Wait," "Watch on the Rhine," "Flesh and Fantasy," "Riding High," "Porgy and Bess," "Buck and the Preacher," "Broken Strings," "Car Wash," and "Black Stallion." Surviving are his widow, a son, and a daughter.

JUNE NASH, 68, child actress of the 1930s, died Oct. 8, 1979, in Hampton Bays, NY. Her credits include "Strange Cargo," "Dynamite," "Their Own Desire," and "Two Kinds of Women." No survivors.

AMADEO NAZZARI, 72, one of Italy's most popular actors, died Nov. 7, 1979, of cardiac arrest in Rome. He had appeared in over 150 films, including "Cavalry," "Pilot Luciano Serra," "The Bandit," "Brief Rapture," "Life of Donizetti," "Times Gone By," "Cabiria," "The Ten Commandments," "The Naked Maja," "The Best of Enemies," "The Little Nuns," and "Juliet of the Spirits." Surviving are his widow, and daughter, actress Evalina Nazzari.

BEN OAKLAND, 71, Brooklyn-born composer of more than 300 film scores and many popular songs, died of cancer Aug. 26, 1979, in Oakland, CA. His film credits include "My Little Chickadee," "The Awful Truth," "Funny Lady," "You Can't Take It with You," and "They Shoot Horses, Don't They?" He was nominated for Academy Awards for "I'll Take Romance," "Champagne Waltz," and "Gone With the Wind." No reported survivors.

MERLE OBERON, 68, Tasmania-born star of over 30 films, died Nov. 23, 1979, after having suffered a stroke in her Malibu, CA home. She was educated in India and moved to England in 1928. As Queenie Thompson she played bit parts in several films in London, where she was discovered by producer Sir Alexander Korda who married her in 1939 and changed her name. She divorced him in 1945, as she did two subsequent husbands. Her film credits include "The Private Life of Henry VIII," "Private Life of Don Juan," "Scarlet Pimpernel," "Folies Bergere," "Dark Angel," "These Three," "Beloved Enemy," "The Cowboy and the Lady," "Wuthering Heights," "The Lodger," "Forever and a Day," "Temptation," "Berlin Express," "Desirée," "A Song to Remember," "Hotel," and her last, in 1973, "Interval," which co-starred her fourth husband, Dutch actor Robert Wolders, who survives. Also surviving are two adopted children, Bruno Pagliai, Jr., and Francesca Bravo.

ERIN O'BRIEN-MOORE, 77, stage, screen, and TV actress, died May 3, 1979, in her native Los Angeles, CA. Her career was interrupted for several years while she recovered from burns received in a restaurant fire in 1939. Her film performances include "Dangerous Corner," "Little Men," "Seven Keys to Baldpate," "Two in the Dark," "Ring Around the Moon," "The Plough and the Stars," "Black Legion," "Life of Emile Zola," "Destination

Moon," "Phantom of the Rue Morgue," "Long Gray Line," "Peyton Place," "Girl on the Run," "John Paul Jones," and "How to Succeed in Business." She co-starred in the TV series "Ruggles." Her marriage to critic Mark Barron ended in divorce. No reported survivors.

SHIRLEY O'HARA, 68, NYC-born stage, screen, and TV actress, died of cancer May 5, 1979, in Hollywood, CA. Among her film credits are "A Gentleman of Paris," "The Wild Party," "Tarzan and the Amazons," "The Chase," "Miracle on 34th St.," "The Hostage," "Inherit the Wind," "Sweet Bird of Youth," "Fuzz," and "Rocky." A daughter survives.

JULIAN ORCHARD, 49, British comic actor, died June 21, 1979, in London after a short illness. His film credits include "Half a Sixpence," "Sherlock Holmes' Smarter Brother," "The Slipper and the Rose," "Carry on Doctor," "Hieronymus Merkin," and "Perfect Friday." A son survives.

GORDON PARKS, JR., 44, director and photographer, was killed Apr. 3, 1979, when his plane crashed on takeoff in Nairobi, Kenya. His credits include "Superfly," "Thomasine and Bushrod," "Three the Hard Way," and "Aaron Loves Angela." He is survived by his father, Gordon Parks, Sr., noted photographer, writer, and director, his mother, a sister, and a brother.

EMORY PARNELL, 86, character actor, died of a heart attack June 22, 1979, in Woodland Hills, CA. Among his many screen credits are "Call of the Yukon," "Doctor Rhythm," "Unholy Partners," "They All Kissed the Bride," "Arabian Nights," "Government Girl," "Address Unknown," "Miracle of Morgan's Creek," "The Falcon in Mexico," "Tall in the Saddle," "Abie's Irish Rose," "The Show-Off," "The Guilt of Janet Ames," "The Outlaw," "Wilson," "Mr. Blanding Builds His Dream House," "Words and Music," "Ma and Pa Kettle," "Call Me Madam," "Sweethearts on Parade," "You're Never Too Young," "Sabrina," and "The Hot Angel." On TV he was Hank Hawkins in "The Life of Riley" series for six years, and the owner of the Laramie Bar on "The Lawman" for four years. Surviving are his widow and a son.

MARY PICKFORD, 86, Toronto-born Gladys Smith, who became "America's Sweetheart" during the era of silent films, died of a massive stroke May 29, 1979, in Santa Monica, CA. After acting on stage, her film career began in 1909 and she quickly rose to stardom. She was the first movie star to have her name in marquee lights, the first to be paid in thousands of dollars per week, and the first to become an international star. Her first great success came in 1917 with "Poor Little Rich Girl," followed by such hits as "Little Princess," "M'liss," "Sparrows," "Daddy Long Legs," "Heart o' the Hills," "Pollyanna," "Little Lord Fauntleroy," "Tess of the Storm Country," "Little Annie Rooney," "Taming of the Shrew," "Kiki," and "My Best Girl." She received an Academy Award for her first sound picture, "Coquette," in 1929. She retired after she made "Secrets" in 1932, her 194th movie. In 1919 she was a co-founder of United Artists company with Douglas Fairbanks and Charles Chaplin. She married Mr. Fairbanks in 1920 after each received divorces, and lived in regal splendor at their home, "Pickfair." After their marriage ended, she married Buddy Rogers, actor and bandleader, who was 11 years her junior. They adopted two children, Ronald and Roxanne. They and Mr. Rogers survive. She was active in establishing the Academy of Motion Picture Arts and Sciences, and the Motion Picture Relief Fund.

JACK RAINE, 83, British-born actor, died May 30, 1979, in South Laguna, CA. He had moved to California after World War II. His film credits include "Suspense," "Night Birds," "Fires of Fate," "The Clairvoyant," "Mine Own Executioner," "My Brother's Keeper," "The Happy Time," "Above and Beyond," "Julius Caesar," "Dangerous When Wet," "Rhapsody," "Prince of Players," "The Power and the Prize," "Woman Obsessed," "My Fair Lady," and "Hello, Dolly!" He is survived by his wife.

| Richard Rodgers | Sydney Tafler | Mabel Taliaferro |

SALLY RAND, 75, Missouri-born Helen Gould Beck, dancer and actress, died of congestive heart failure Aug. 31, 1979, in Glendora, CA. Her sensational fan dance at the 1933 Chicago World's Fair launched a career that lasted for more than 30 years. Her film appearances were in "Man Bait," "Night of Love," "Getting Gertie's Garter," "His Dog," "A Girl in Every Port," "Hotel Variety," and "Bolero." She was married three times, and is survived by her adopted son.

NICHOLAS RAY, 67, Wisconsin-born director, died of lung cancer June 16, 1979, in NYC. After work in the NY theater, he went to Hollywood and directed such films as "Knock on Any Door," "They Live by Night," "In a Lonely Place," "Born to Be Bad," "Flying Leathernecks," "On Dangerous Ground," "Johnny Guitar," "Rebel without a Cause," "Bigger Than Life," "True Story of Jesse James," "Party Girl," "King of Kings," and "55 Days at Peking." He also acted in "Hair." He was married three times, and leaves two sons and two daughters.

JEAN RENOIR, 84, Paris-born director, died of a coronary occlusion Feb. 12, 1979, at his home in Beverly Hills, CA. Son of French painter Pierre-Auguste Renoir, he served as a cavalry officer in World War I, and afterward had a brief career as a ceramist before turning to films and becoming one of the world's most praised and respected directors. He directed 36 full-length films, wrote the scenarios for many, and acted in several. At least two of his films, "Grand Illusion" and "Rules of the Game," are ranked among the greatest of all movies. Other credits include "Night at the Crossroads," "Madame Bovary," "The Lower Depths," "The Human Beast," "This Land Is Mine," "The Southerner," "Diary of a Chambermaid," "Woman on the Beach," "Ways of Love," "The River," "The Golden Coach," "French Can-Can," "Picnic on the Grass," "Crime of Monsieur Lange," "Toni," and his last, in 1969, "Le Petit Theatre de Jean Renoir." He had been spending much of his confinement in writing. In 1975 he was given a special Academy Award but was unable to attend the ceremonies. He is survived by his second wife and a son. Although he became an American citizen, he was buried in France following a state funeral.

RICHARD RODGERS, 77, NYC-born and world-renowned composer, died after a long illness on Dec. 30, 1979, in his Manhattan home. In a career that spanned over 60 years, he composed 1500 songs (at least 85 regarded as standards), and 42 Broadway musicals, 19 of which were transferred to film. His most memorable collaborations were with Lorenz Hart and Oscar Hammerstein II. His film credits include "Dancing Lady," "Manhattan Melodrama," "Hollywood Party," "Mississippi," "Fools for Scandal," "Babes in Arms," "Too Many Girls," "I Married an Angel," "Stage Door Canteen," "Higher and Higher," "State Fair," "Victory at Sea," "Oklahoma!," "Carousel," "The King and I," "Pal Joey," "South Pacific," "Jumbo," and "The Sound of Music." He received an Academy Award for "It Might as Well Be Spring" from "State Fair." His widow and two daughters survive.

AARON ROSENBERG, 67, producer, died Sept. 1, 1979, after a long illness, in Torrance, CA. In 1934 he won All-American recognition on the USC football team, and the same year began his career in the film industry as an assistant director. As a producer, his credits include "Johnny Stool Pigeon," "Outside the Wall," "Winchester 73," "Air Cadet," "Iron Man," "Bend of the River," "The World in His Arms," "Thunder Bay," "Glenn Miller Story," "The Far Country," "The Shrike," "To Hell and Back," "Benny Goodman Story," "The Great Man," "Mutiny on the Bounty," "Shock Treatment," "Fate Is the Hunter," "Caprice," "The Detective," and "Lady in Cement." Surviving are his widow, a son, and three stepchildren.

VICTOR SAVILLE, 83, British director and producer, died May 8, 1979, in London. His many films include "Kitty," "Woman to Woman," "Good Companions," "I Was a Spy," "Friday the 13th," "Evergreen," "Iron Duke," "Dark Journey," "Storm in a Teacup," "Forever and a Day," "The Green Years," "Green Dolphin Street," "If Winter Comes," "Conspirator," "Kim," "The Citadel," "A Woman's Face," "The Chocolate Soldier," "Smilin' Through," "White Cargo," "Keeper of the Flame," "Above Suspicion," and "Loss of Innocence." No reported survivors.

GEORGE SEATON, 68, née Stenius in Indiana, versatile director, producer, screenwriter, and former actor, died July 28, 1979, after a long illness in his Beverly Hills, CA, home. He received Academy Awards for his screenplays of "Miracle on 34th Street" and "The Country Girl." His other credits include "A Day at the Races," "The Doctor Takes a Wife," "This Thing Called Love," "Charley's Aunt," "Moon over Miami," "Magnificent Dope," "Meanest Man in the World," "Coney Island," "Song of Bernadette," "Eve of St. Mark," "Junior Miss," "Chicken Every Sunday," "Little Boy Lost," "The Proud and Profane," "36 Hours," and "Airport." A son and daughter survive.

JEAN SEBERG, 40, Iowa-born actress, who had disappeared from her apartment, was found dead in her car in Paris on Sept. 8, 1979, apparently from an overdose of barbiturates. Her career began at 16 as Joan of Arc in "Saint Joan," and she subsequently appeared in "Bonjour Tristesse," "The Mouse That Roared," "Let No Man Write My Epitaph," "Breathless," "Time Out for Love," "In the French Style," "Lilith," "Backfire," "Moment to Moment," "A Fine Madness," "Birds in Peru," "Pendulum," "Paint Your Wagon," "Total Danger," "Airport," "Heat Wave," and "The Wild Duck." Her fourth husband survives.

PETE SMITH, 86, a former press agent, whose short comedies delighted movie audiences for over 20 years, jumped to his death Jan. 12, 1979, from the roof of a convalescent hospital in Santa Monica, CA. He had been in ill health for several years. In 1939 and 1941 he received Academy Awards, and a special "Oscar" in 1953. No reported survivors.

JACK SOO, 63, actor and former singer-dancer, born Goro Suzuki in California, died of cancer Jan. 11, 1979, in Los Angeles, CA. His films include "The Flower Drum Song," "Who's Been Sleeping in My Bed?," "The Oscar," "Thoroughly Modern Millie," and "The Green Berets." He was best known for his detective Nick Yemana on the TV series "Barney Miller." Surviving are his widow, a daughter, and two sons.

JOHN STUART, 81, British stage and film actor, died of natural causes, Oct. 18, 1979, in suburban London. His first film was "Her Son" in 1920, and his last in 1978, "Superman." Other credits include "Kitty," "Atlantic," "The Wandering Jew," "Bella Donna," "Flying Fortress," "Courageous Mr. Penn," "Madonna of the Seven Moons," "Young Winston," "Mary, Queen of Scots," "Hound of the Baskervilles," "Blood of the Vampire," "Village of the Damned," "Front Page Story," "Bottoms Up," and "Reach for the Sky." His widow and two sons survive.

SYDNEY TAFLER, 63, British character actor, died of cancer Nov. 8, 1979, in his London home. He had appeared in over 30 movies, including "No Room at the Inn," "Lavender Hill Mob," "The Assassin," "Cockleshell Heroes," "Too Many Crooks," "Make Mine Mink," "Alfie," "The Birthday Party," and "The Spy Who Loved Me." He is survived by his widow, actress Joy Shelton, and three children.

MABEL TALIAFERRO, 91, stage and silent screen star, died Jan. 24, 1979, in Honolulu, HI, where she had lived for several years. One of Broadway's first actresses to play in films, she appeared in 1911 in "Cinderella," and subsequently in "The Three of Us," "The Slacker," "Magdalene of the Hills," "The Snowbird," "Sentimental Tommy," and "My Love Came Back." No reported survivors.

DIMITRI TIOMKIN, 85, Russian-born composer, died Nov. 11, 1979, in his London home after having fractured his pelvis in a fall. He had 160 film scores to his credit, including "Lost Horizons," "Giant," "Guns of Navarone," "Friendly Persuasion," "Gunfight at the OK Corral," "The Sundowners," and his four Academy Award winners, "High Noon," "The Alamo," "The Old Man and the Sea," and "The High and the Mighty." His first wife, dancer-choreographer Albertina Rasch, died in 1967. His second wife survives.

VIVIAN VANCE, 66, Kansas-born stage, screen, and TV actress, died of cancer Aug. 17, 1979, in her home in Belvedere, CA. In films, she appeared in "The Secret Fury," "The Blue Veil," and "The Great Race." She appeared for 9 years as Ethel Mertz on the "I Love Lucy" TV series, and later with Lucille Ball again on "The Lucy Show" from 1962 to 1965. Surviving is her husband, publisher John Dodds.

CHARLES WAGENHEIM, 84, character actor, was beaten to death March 6, 1979, in his home in Hollywood, CA, probably by a burglar who was frightened away by the maid's arrival. His many film credits include "Two Girls on Broadway," "Meet Boston Blackie," "Sin Town," "Summer Storm," "Sergeant Mike," "Within These Walls," "House on 92nd Street," "Dark Corner," "Lady without a Passport," "House on Telegraph Hill," "Scudda Hoo! Scudda Hay!," "The Prodigal," "Tunnel of Love," "Toughest Gun in Tombstone," and "Beauty and the Beast." He was probably best known for his appearances in such TV series as "Gunsmoke," "All in the Family," and "Baretta." His widow survives.

JOHN WAYNE, 72, one of the world's most admired actors, died of cancer June 11, 1979, in Los Angeles, CA. Born Marion Michael Morrison in Iowa, he grew up in Glendale, CA, and began his film career as an extra in 1928. Director Raoul Walsh changed his name to John Wayne in 1930. He achieved stardom after "Stagecoach" in 1939. His last starring role was in "The Shootist" in 1976. He received an Academy Award for his performance in "True Grit," a 1969 film. He had appeared in over 200 films, including "The Long Voyage Home," "Seven Sinners," "Pittsburgh," "The Spoilers," "Reap the Wild Wind," "They Were Expendable," "Fort Apache," "Red River," "Three Godfathers," "She Wore a Yellow Ribbon," "The Quiet Man," "The Alamo," "Sands of Iwo Jima," "Flying Leathernecks," "Big Jim McLain," "Island in the Sky," "Hondo," "The High and the Mighty," "Sea Chase," "Jet Pilot," "Rio Bravo," "The Man Who Shot Liberty Valance," "Hatari," "The Longest Day," "How the West Was Won," "Greatest Story Ever Told," "El Dorado," "The Green Berets," and "Rooster Cogburn." He is survived by his third wife, and four daughters and three sons, including actor Patrick Wayne. Interment was in Pacific View Memorial Park.

RAY WHITELEY, 77, actor, singer, composer of western music, died Feb. 21, 1979, while on a fishing trip in Mexico. For his friend Gene Autry, he wrote the theme song "Back in the Saddle Again." His film career included roles in over 50 pictures, including "Hopalong Cassidy Returns," "Gun Law," "Painted Desert," "Renegade Ranger," "Racketeers of the Range," "West of the Alamo," and "Giant" (his last). Surviving are his widow and three daughters.

MICHAEL WILDING, 66, sophisticated British screen and stage actor, died July 8, 1979, after being injured in a fall in his home in Chichester, Eng. He had been in poor health for some time. His film credits include "Convoy," "Kipps," "In Which We Serve," "An Ideal Husband," "Piccadilly Incident," "Under Capricorn," "Stage Fright," "Maytime in Mayfair," "Torch Song," "The Egyptian," "The Glass Slipper," "World of Suzie Wong," "Breakout," "Best of Enemies," "The Law and the Lady," and "Waterloo." His fourth wife, actress Margaret Leighton, predeceased him by three years. Survivors include two sons by his second wife, Elizabeth Taylor.

DARRYL F. ZANUCK, 77, Nebraska-born flamboyant and controversial movie mogul, died Dec. 22, 1979, in Palm Springs, CA, following a heart attack that was aggravated by a stroke and pneumonia. He had risen from scriptwriter to be one of the foremost executive producers in film history, and was the only three-time winner of the coveted Thalberg Memorial Award. With the late Joseph Schenck, he was co-founder of 20th Century-Fox, but was forced out as chairman of the board in 1971. From 1956 to 1962 he was an independent producer, before returning to 20th as its president. During WW2 he served as supervisor for Signal Corps training films and the photographic record of the North Africa invasion. He was awarded the Legion of Merit. Three of his films received Academy Awards: "How Green Was My Valley," "Gentleman's Agreement," and "All about Eve." His other productions include "Les Miserables," "Message to Garcia," "Captain January," "Under Two Flags," "Pigskin Parade," "Seventh Heaven," "In Old Chicago," "Kidnapped," "Little Miss Broadway," "Alexander's Ragtime Band," "Alexander Graham Bell," "Young Mr. Lincoln," "Stanley and Livingston," "Grapes of Wrath," "Johnny Apollo," "Star Dust," "Lillian Russell," "Four Sons," "The Great Profile," "Tobacco Road," "A Yank in the R.A.F.," "Wilson," "Winged Victory," "The Razor's Edge," "Pinky," "Twelve O'Clock High," "Viva Zapata," "Snows of Kilimanjaro," "The Longest Day," "M*A*S*H," and "The Sound of Music." He is survived by his widow, former actress Virginia Fox, two daughters, and a son, producer Richard Zanuck. After cremation, his ashes were scattered on the Pacific Ocean.

Jean Seberg

John Wayne

Michael Wilding

INDEX

240

250